The Future of Journalism

The future of journalism is contested and uncertain reflecting developments in media technologies, shifting business strategies for online news, changing media organisational and
regulatory structures, the fragmentation of audiences and a growing public concern about
some aspects of tabloid journalism practices and reporting, as well as broader political,
sociological and cultural changes. These developments have combined to impoverish the
flow of existing revenues available to fund journalism, impact radically on traditional journalism professional practices, while simultaneously generating an increasingly frenzied
search for sustainable and equivalent funding – and from a wide range of sources - to nurture and deliver quality journalism in the future.

This book brings together journalists and distinguished academic specialists from around
the globe to present the findings from their research and to discuss the future of journalism,
the shifting quality of its products, its wide ranging sources of finance, as well as the economic and democratic consequences of the significant changes confronting journalism.

The Future of Journalism details the challenges facing the press in contemporary societies
and provides essential reading for everyone interested in the role of journalism in shaping
and sustaining literate, civil and democratic societies.

This book consists of special issues from *Journalism Studies* and *Journalism Practice*.

Bob Franklin is Professor of Journalism Studies at the Cardiff School of Journalism, Media
and Cultural Studies, UK where he is Director of the Journalism Studies Research Group. He
is Editor of the peer reviewed journals *Journalism Studies* and *Journalism Practice*. His
recent publications include *Journalism, Sources and Credibility: New Perspectives* (2011)
(with Matt Carlson), *Journalism Education, Training and Employment* (2011) (with Donica
Mensing), *The Future of Newspapers* (2009) and *Pulling Newspapers Apart; Analysing Print
Journalism* (2008).

The Future of Journalism

Edited by
Bob Franklin

Routledge
Taylor & Francis Group

LONDON AND NEW YORK

First published 2011
by Routledge
2 Park Square, Milton Park, Abingdon, Oxon, OX14 4RN

Simultaneously published in the USA and Canada
by Routledge
711 Third Avenue, New York, NY 10017

Routledge is an imprint of the Taylor & Francis Group, an informa business

This book is a reproduction of special issues from *Journalism Studies*, vol. 11, issue 4; and *Journalism Practice*, vol. 4, issue 3. The Publisher requests to those authors who may be citing this book to state, also, the bibliographical details of the special issue on which the book was based.

Trademark notice: Product or corporate names may be trademarks or registered trademarks, and are used only for identification and explanation without intent to infringe.

British Library Cataloguing in Publication Data
A catalogue record for this book is available from the British Library

ISBN13: 978-0-415-59869-9

Typeset in Helvetica
by Taylor & Francis Books

Disclaimer
The publisher would like to make readers aware that the chapters in this book are referred to as articles as they had been in the special issue. The publisher accepts responsibility for any inconsistencies that may have arisen in the course of preparing this volume for print.

Contents

CONTENTS

CONTENTS

Notes on Contributors

Laura Ahva is Research Fellow at the Journalism Research and Development Centre at the University of Tampere, Finland. She has published articles in *Journalism Studies* and *Javnost—The Public* on public journalism and professionalism. Currently she is working on the audience research project Towards Engaging Journalism. Her doctoral dissertation focuses on the development of public journalism in Finland.

Klaus-Dieter Altmeppen is Professor at the School of Journalism at the Catholic University Eichstaett-Ingolstadt, Germany. His research topics are journalism, media organisation, media economy, media management, and entertainment business.

Kevin G. Barnhurst (PhD, University of Amsterdam) is Professor of Communication at the University of Illinois at Chicago, where he teaches graduate theory, qualitative methods, and visual communication. For the International Communication Association, he was founding chair of Visual Communication and its newsletter editor. He has published widely on media form and design and has been Distinguished Fulbright Chair in Italy (2006), Fellow of the Shorenstein Center at Harvard University (2001), and Research Fellow at Columbia University (1991–1992), where he wrote *Seeing the Newspaper* (St. Martin's Press). This article is part of the Long News Project available online: http://www. uic.edu/_kgbcomm/longnews.

Paul Benedetti is a Lecturer in the Faculty of Information and Media Studies at the University of Western Ontario. He has more than 20 years experience as an investigative reporter, editor, columnist and magazine feature writer. His work has appeared in numerous publications including *Canadian Living*, *Hamilton Spectator* and *Globe* and *Mail* newspapers. He has extensive experience in the online world as a producer, writer and editor for the Southam New Media lab, AOL Canada and Canoe Travel. He is the co-author of the book *Spin Doctors: the chiropractic industry under investigation* (Dundurn Press, 2003) and the Deputy Editor and Interactive Editor for *J-Source*, The Canadian Journalism Project (www.j-source.ca), Canada's leading site on journalism.

Jay G. Blumler is an Emeritus Professor of Public Communication at the University of Leeds and Emeritus Professor of Journalism at the University of Maryland. His key books on political communication include *Television in Politics: its uses and influence* (with Denis McQuail, 1968), *The Crisis of Public Communication* (with Michael Gurevitch, 1995) and *The Internet and Democratic Citizenship: theory, practice and policy* (with Stephen Coleman, 2009). He is a Fellow and former President of the International Communication

Association, was founding co-Editor of the *European Journal of Communication* and, jointly with Michael Gurevitch, holds the Murray Edelman Distinguished Career Award.

Bonnie Brennen is the Nieman Professor of Journalism in the Diederich College of Communication at Marquette University. Her research focuses on journalism history, popular culture, and cultural studies of the relationship between media and society. She is the author of *For the Record: an oral history of Rochester*, New York newsworkers, and coeditor, with Hanno Hardt, of Picturing the Past: media, history & photography (1999) and *Newsworkers: toward a history of the rank and file*. She co-authored, with Hanno Hardt, *American Journalism History Reader* (Routledge, 2010. Her Second Life avatar is bonnie inkpen.

Carla Rodrigues Cardoso is a Lecturer at the School of Communication, Arts and Information Technologies (ECATI) at Universidade Lusófona (ULHT) and is also a freelance journalist. She has studied newsmagazines since 2000, and published two articles on the subject in 2009: "The Newsmagazine Cover as a Communication Dispositif", in the magazine OBS*, and "Patterns and Identities in Newsmagazine Covers" in the digital archives of the IV Annual Portuguese Association of Communication Sciences (SOPCOM) Congress. She is a member of ECREA and SOPCOM, and an investigator at CICANT and CIMJ.

Erika dela Cerna is a graduate student at the Diedrich College of Communication at Marquette University. She is under the communication studies and dispute resolution tracks. Her research interest includes interpersonal communication and alternative communities. Her avatar, Erika Urdaneta, can be occasionally found at Avatar Island and Info Island in Second Life.

Mihai Coman was born in Fagaras, Romania, in 1953. He was the first Dean of the School of Journalism and Mass Communication Studies within the University of Bucharest, being considered the founder of journalism and communication education in Romania. Until 1989 he had specialized in cultural anthropology studies on Romanian folklore. After 1989 he has elaborated the theoretical and analytical framework of the mass media anthropology. In 2003, as a synthesis of these investigations, he published with Presses Universitaires de Grenoble the book Pour une anthropologie des medias, and in 2005 he coedited (with Eric Rothenbuhler) the path-breaking reader *Media Anthropology* at Sage. He has also published numerous scientific studies in journals and collective volumes dedicated to the transformations in the mass media in post-communist countries and the books *Media in Romania (A Sourcebook)* (Vistas, Berlin, 2004), and *Mass Media and Journalism in Romania* (with Peter Gross) (Vistas, Berlin, 2006).

James R. Compton is an Associate Professor in the Faculty of Information and Media Studies at the University of Western Ontario. He is author of *The Integrated News Spectacle: a political economy of cultural performance* (Peter Lang, 2004) and co-editor of *Converging Media, Diverging Politics: a political economy of the news media in the United States and Canada* (Lexington, 2005). His work has appeared in *Journalism Studies*, *Journalism: Theory, Practice and Criticism*, *Canadian Journal of Communication*, and *UDC Communiqué*. He is a former reporter/editor with Canadian Press/Broadcast news.

Martin Conboy is Professor of Journalism Studies at the University of Sheffield. He is particularly interested in the confluence of language, national identity and cultural debate within both contemporary and historical journalism. His publications include *The Press* *and Popular Culture* (2002), *Journalism: a critical history* (2004), *Tabloid Britain: constructing a community through language* (2006) and *The Language of the News* (2007). He is also the co-editor of a series of books entitled Journalism Studies: key texts.

James Curran is Director of the Goldsmiths Leverhulme Media Research Centre, supported by a £1.25 million grant from the Leverhulme Trust. He has held a personal chair at Goldsmiths since 1989. He has also held endowed visiting chairs at Penn, Stanford, Stockholm and Oslo Universities. He is also one of seven senior researchers engaged in a five-nation media and public knowledge investigation, directed by Toril Aalberg, centred at the Norwegian University of Science and Technology. He has written or edited 18 books about the mass media, some in conjunction with others. His work is in four main areas: media political economy, media influence, media history and media theory. He was a member of the Annenberg Press Commission, USA and is currently the UK representative on the European Commission committee promoting research on broadcasting in Central and Eastern Europe.

Arnold S. de Beer is Professor Emeritus, University of Stellenbosch, South Africa. Arnie studied at RAU and Baylor (USA). He is a former journalist at *Die Transvaler* and *Die Burger*, was editor of *Potchefstroom News* and was, inter alia, editor of *Ensiklopedie van die Wêreld* (the first 10-volume encyclopedia in Afrikaans, published in Stellenbosch in the 1970s). He is the founding editor of *Ecquid Novi—South African Journal for Journalism Research* and an Editorial board member of *Journalism Studies, Global Media Journal, International Communication Bulletin* and *Communicatio, Communicare*.

David Domingo is Assistant Professor at the Department of Communication Studies at Universitat Rovira i Virgili (Tarragona, Catalonia). His research focuses on working routines and innovation processes in online newsrooms, including trends such as convergence and audience participation. He has co-edited *Making Online News: the ethnography of new media production* (2008).

Bob Franklin is Professor of Journalism Studies and Director of the Journalism Studies Research Group at Cardiff University, UK. He is the Editor of *Journalism Studies* and *Journalism Practice*. He also co-edits a new series of books published by Sage and titled *Journalism Studies: key texts*. His published work ranges widely across journalism studies and political communications and includes: *Journalists, Sources and Credibility: New Perspectives* (with Matt Carlson) (2011); *Journalism Education, Training and Employment* (with Donica Mensing) (2011); *The Future of Newspapers* (2009), *Key Concepts in Public Relations* (2009), *Pulling Newspapers Apart: analysing print journalism* (2008), *Local Journalism and Local Media: making the local news* (2006), *Television Policy: the MacTaggart lectures* (2005), *Key Concepts in Journalism Studies* (2005) and *Packaging Politics: political communication in Britain's media democracy* (2004).

Chris Frost is Professor and Head of Journalism at Liverpool John Moores University, Liverpool, UK. He is the author of *Journalism Ethics and Regulation* (Longman, 2007), *Reporting for Journalists* (Routledge, 2001) and *Designing for Newspapers and Magazines* (Routledge, 2003). He is also a member of the National Union of Journalists National Executive Committee, chair of the NUJ's Ethics Council and a former Chair of the Association for Journalism Education.

Heikki Heikkilä is Senior Research Fellow at the Journalism Research and Development Centre at University of Tampere, Finland. He has published articles in *Journalism*,

European Journal of Communication and *Communications*. Currently he is working on the audience research project Towards Engaging Journalism.

Ari Heinonen is currently Professor of Journalism (acting) at the Department of Journalism and Mass Communication of the University of Tampere, Finland. After working as a newspaper journalist, he has taught and researched journalism with special focus on the changing nature of professionalism, the interrelationship between journalism and new media, and journalistic ethics.

Alfred Hermida is an Assistant Professor at the Graduate School of Journalism at the University of British Columbia. He is an award-winning online news pioneer, having been a founding news editor of the BBC News website. During 16 years as a BBC TV, radio and online journalist, he covered regional, national and international news. His work has also appeared in *The Wall Street Journal*, *The Times of London* and *The Guardian*. His research interests include participatory journalism, emerging genres of digital journalism and new models of journalism education. His research has appeared in *Journalism Practice* and he comments on journalism trends at Reportr.net.

Michael Karlsson holds a Doctorate from Lunds University (2006) and is an Assistant Professor at the Department of Media and Communication at Karlstad University, Karlstad, Sweden. His research interests are primarily in online news and the digitalization of public opinion. His scholarly work has been accepted for publication in journals such as *Journalism Studies*, *Journalism: Theory, Practice and Critique* and *Observatorio*.

Risto Kunelius is Professor at the Department of Journalism and Mass Communication and Director of the International School of Social Sciences at University of Tampere, Finland. Recently he has co-edited the book *Transnational Media Events: the Mohammed cartoons and the imagined clash of cilivizations* (NORDICOM, 2008). He has published articles, for instance, in *Journalism Studies*, *Journalism* and *Javnost—The Public*.

Lisa Lynch is Assistant Professor of Journalism at Concordia University. Her research explores the intersection between culture, technology, and political change; including emerging media, the changing practices of journalism, the cultural reception of genetics, disaster narratives, visual culture, and human rights. From 2004 to 2006, she was the director, along with Elena Razlogova, of the Guantanamobile Project, a multimedia documentary about the US detention of prisoners at Guantanamo. Her work has appeared in publications ranging from *Literature and Medicine* and *New Literary History* to *Open Democracy* and the *Arab Studies Journal*. She is currently at work on a book about the document-leaking site Wikileaks and is exploring ways in which gaming might be incorporated into online journalism practice.

Donica Mensing, PhD, is an Associate Professor of Journalism at the Reynolds School of Journalism, University of Nevada, Reno. She teaches media ethics and online journalism and was director of the graduate program from 2006 to 2009. Her research focuses on online journalism, public journalism and journalism education and she blogs and writes regularly. She is a graduate of the University of California, Berkeley, George Washington University in Washington DC, and the University of Nevada, Reno.

François Nel has worked as a Journalist and Educator in the United States, South Africa and the United Kingdom, and is the founding director of the Journalism Leaders Programme at the University of Central Lancashire in Preston, UK.

Christoph Neuberger is Professor of Communication Science at the University of Münster, Germany. His main research interests include journalism theory, online journalism, online public sphere, and quality of media. He is co-editor of *Journalismus im Internet: Professionalisierung, Partizipation, Technisierung* [Journalism on the Internet: professionalization, participation, technization] (2009).

Christian Nuernbergk is a Research Associate at the Institute of Communication Science at the University of Münster, Germany. He is co-editor of *Journalismus im Internet: Professionalisierung, Partizipation, Technisierung* [Journalism on the Internet: professionalization, participation, technization] (2009).

Steve Paulussen is Senior Researcher at the IBBT research group for Media & ICT (MICT) in Ghent, Belgium. He is also a member of the Center for Journalism Studies (CJS) at the Department of Communication Sciences at Ghent University, where he teaches journalism studies. Further, he is a part-time lecturer in journalism theory at the Vrije Universiteit Brussel (VUB).

Bettina Peters is the Director of the Global Forum for Media Development (GFMD). Before joining GFMD in July 2007, Bettina worked as the director of programmes at the European Journalism Centre, where she was in charge of EJC's programme of media support and journalism training, in particular in the Middle East/ North Africa and in Eastern Europe. From 1990 until 2002 Bettina worked at the International Federation of Journalists, first as European coordinator and later as Deputy General Secretary. She was instrumental in setting up the IFJ's Project Division and was responsible for the IFJ's global programme on media development and capacity-building for journalists' organisations. In the course of her work, Bettina has supervised and managed media development projects in more than 80 countries. She holds a Masters degree in political science and journalism from the University of Hamburg and has edited a range of publications, including a global survey of women in journalism for the IFJ, the EJC handbook on Civic Journalism and the IFJ handbook on Human Rights Reporting in Africa. For the last five years, she has been a reviewer of the *Freedom House Press Freedom Index*. Most recently, she wrote the conclusions to *European Media Policy: The Brussels Perspective*, published in 2007.

Angela Phillips is responsible for undergraduate 'text' journalism and convenor of the MA Journalism at Goldsmiths, University of London where she teaches feature writing and journalism studies and is publisher of EastLondonLines.co.uk, an independent news website run by journalism students. She is interested in critical journalism research from a practitioner point of view. She worked with the Leverhulme-funded research group: "Spaces of the News", contributed to Natalie Fenton (Ed.), *New Media: Old News* (Sage, 2009) and was co-editor, with Elizabeth Eide and Risto Kunelius, of *Transnational Media Events: the Mohammed Cartoons and the imagined clash of civilizations* (NORDICOM, 2008). She is currently working on a further book based on the Leverhulme research.

Thorsten Quandt holds a Chair in Communication Studies at the University of Hohenheim, Germany. As a Professor of Interactive Media and Online Communication, he is focusing on new forms of media and innovations in public communication.

Zvi Reich combines rich journalistic experience as a former senior editor with extensive research activity in journalism and the sociology of the news. His book, *Sourcing the*

News, was recently published by the Hampton Press, and his papers have appeared in *Journalism Studies*, *Journalism*, and *Journalism & Mass Communication Quarterly*. Dr. Reich is a lecturer at the Department of Communication Studies, Ben-Gurion University of the Negev, Beersheva, Israel.

Anya Schiffrin is Acting Director of the International Media and Communications (IMC) program and an Adjunct Professor in the School of International and Public Affairs at Columbia University. She spent ten years working overseas as a journalist in Europe and Asia, writing for a number of different magazines and newspapers. She was bureau chief for Dow Jones Newswires in Amsterdam and Hanoi and wrote regularly for the *Wall Street Journal*. She was a former Knight-Bagehot academic fellow in business journalism at Columbia University Business School. Schiffrin is also the director of journalism training programs at the Initiative for Policy Dialogue, an international network of economists based at Columbia, and founder of journalismtraining.net.

Kim Christian Schrøder (http://www.ruc.dk/komm/Ansatte/vip/kimsc/) is Professor in Communication Studies at Roskilde University, Denmark. His books include *The Language of Advertising* (co-author, Blackwell, 1985), *Media Cultures: reappraising transnational media* (co-editor and contributor, Routledge, 1992), and *Researching Audiences* (coauthor, Arnold, 2003). His current research deals with news consumption in the media landscape of the digital age, and with methodological issues around the quantitative/ qualitative divide.

Jane B. Singer is an Associate Professor in the University of Iowa School of Journalism and Mass Communication, USA; from 2007 to 2009, she was the Johnston Press Chair in Digital Journalism at the University of Central Lancashire, UK. Her research explores digital journalism, including changing roles, perceptions, norms and practices. Before earning her PhD from the University of Missouri, she was the first news manager of Prodigy Interactive Services, as well as a newspaper reporter and editor.

Bent Steeg Larsen is Research Manager at *Politiken*, a leading Danish newspaper, part of the media company JP/Politikens Hus. He holds a PhD in media studies, based on a thesis (2000) about everyday use of different media types.

John Steel is a Lecturer in the Department of Journalism Studies at the University of Sheffield. His research interests include political thought and nineteenth-century newspapers, ideology and language in the media, press freedom and journalism education.

Rodney Tiffen is Professor, Government and International Relations in the University of Sydney, Australia. His teaching and research interests are in the mass media, Australian politics, comparative democratic politics, democratisation and Australian relations with Asia. His most recent book, co-authored with Ross Gittins, is *How Australia Compares* (Cambridge University Press, 2004).

Debra Reddin van Tuyll is Professor of Communications at Augusta State University. She is the author of *The Southern Press in the Civil War* and co-editor of *The Civil War and the Press*. Her third book, *Knights of the Quill: reassessing Confederate war correspondents and their Civil War reporting*, co-edited with two colleagues, will be published by Purdue University Press in 2010. Van Tuyll's doctorate is from the University of South Carolina. Her research interests focus on news culture and practices in the Civil War-era South. She is presently working on two projects, one that examines how nineteenth-century

Southern journalists thought about free speech issues, and the other examines communities of journalism in the mid-nineteenth century.

Marina Vujnovic is Assistant Professor at Monmouth University. Her primary fields of research are participatory journalism and new media studies, media history and gender, critical political economy and cultural studies. Her research interests focus on online journalism, international communication and global flow of information, journalism studies; explorations of the historical, political-economic and cultural impact on media; gender, ethnicity, and media. Vujnovic has a PhD from the University of Iowa.

Wendy Weinhold is a PhD candidate in the College of Mass Communication and Media Arts at Southern Illinois University Carbondale, USA. She is also Writing Coach for *The Daily Egyptian*.

Xin Xin is RCUK Research Fellow at the Communication and Media Research Institute, University of Westminster, UK. Her research interests include Chinese media and society, traditional and citizen journalism, international communication, China's 'Soft power' and public diplomacy.

Sally Young is Senior Lecturer in the School of Social and Political Sciences at The University of Melbourne. She specialises in political communication and elections and is the author of *The Persuaders: inside the hidden machine of political advertising* (Pluto Press, 2004), *From Banners to Broadcasts* (National Library of Australia, 2005) and editor of *Government Communication in Australia* (Cambridge University Press, 2007). She is currently completing a book on how the media reports Australian election campaigns, for Cambridge University Press.

FOREWORD
The two-legged crisis of journalism

Jay G. Blumler

A number of possibly transforming trends are sweeping the public communication systems of developed democracies these days-and will go on doing so for some time. Academic research into them is therefore enormously important, and it is encouraging that so many of them, particularly as they are affecting journalistic institutions, professions and practices, have already been so admirably (if necessarily partially at this stage) identified, described and analysed in this collection of essays. Let the good work continue and expand, I say, with increasing emphasis perhaps on: longitudinal analysis (tracking key trends over time); comparative, cross-societal analysis (but theoretically driven, not *ad hoc* or merely opportunistic); and relevance to specified normative concerns.

I come to this subject myself as a retired scholar of political communication. Of course politics and communication have always been closely linked. But today the publicising, even to some extent the conduct, of politics is heavily dependent on communication and must fight for its place in news media outlets more so than in the past, when it was at least partially sheltered by sacerdotal sentiments towards political institutions (whereas nowadays pragmatism is all!). Moreover, the place and portrayal of politics in communication systems is influenced by and vulnerable to changes in the latter's technological, financial and institutional infrastructures. This matters for the projection and reception of politics at present, not only because of what has been happening within those infrastructures but also because of the re-balancing of institutional powers outside them, which has gradually taken place over the course of the post-war period. In earlier times, political life was nourished by: strong political parties; social class identities and solidarities; family-based socialisation; and a relatively high "valuation of politics as such". But so much of all that has evaporated that at times we now seem to inhabit a veritable news-based polity.

But the journalism which services this polity is currently facing a crisis with two legs. One is a crisis of viability, principally though not exclusively financial, threatening the existence and resources of mainstream journalistic organisations. The other is a crisis of civic adequacy, impoverishing the contributions of journalism to citizenship and democracy. And although these two legs are interrelated (attached to the same body, to carry on the metaphor), it is highly important, particularly when thinking in policy terms, to understand that they are also distinct. That is, even if the viability leg was somehow to be mended, the civic one would not automatically be restored to acceptable health. To suppose otherwise is to indulge in wishful thinking.

Another way of looking at these two legs is to recognise that one is considerably shorter than the other (the metaphor is really getting out of hand now). Whereas the onset of the viability crisis has been relatively recent, the civic crisis has been building for quite some time. Cumulations of media research from the 1960s onward have demonstrated, over and over again, how adherence to conventional news values can: propagate ill-founded stereotypes (think unruly youth, or Muslims, or even, dare I say it, politicians); project distorted impressions of social reality (think the incidence of crime and violence);

generalise from exceptional specifics (think climate scientists' e-mails); and treat political ideas more as tokens in a political game than as ideas for consideration (think coverage of party conferences). Nor has the more recent emergence amidst all this of what Michael Gurevitch and I termed in 1995 "a chronic state of partial war" between politicians and journalists (see Blumler and Gurevitch, 1995) been at all helpful to the citizenship cause.

So how might the ongoing growth of the Internet relate to the civic leg of the crisis of journalism? It is still too early for a definitive pronouncement of course, which is why further monitoring research of the kind presented in these pages will be so essential. A provisional view, it seems to me however, is bound to be mixed yet quite troubled.

It is true that the emerging public communication system, in comparison with its predecessor, appears overall somewhat less "buttoned up", less controlled by convergent constraints perhaps, open to a few more centrifugal influences alongside the previously highly dominant centripetal ones. Thus, freedom of expression for individuals rather than just organisations has arguably increased; the near-stranglehold of networked television news over public discourse has eased somewhat; public authorities may sometimes find themselves being held to account through more channels; non-elite voices conveying people's experiences and opinions are heard more often in political reports; and opportunities to trial novel journalistic ventures (mainly small-scale though) have been created.

But although such developments are welcome and do reflect genuinely democratic impulses, they are not system-transforming, and for two main reasons they cannot on their own resolve journalism's crisis of civic adequacy.

First, there is precious little sign that mainstream journalists' coverage of public affairs is being reconstructed in a civic direction in response to the new media environment. There is no evidence, for example, that the news values by which they think about, report and solicit comments on current events are any different from what they used to be.

Second, several features of the new-style system can work powerfully against communication for citizenship, particularly since they apply across the board to new media and old media alike. One is the unprecedentedly enormous communication abundance that all-politicians, other opinion advocates, journalists, bloggers, etc.-must operate within. This has unleashed an intense competition for the attention of would-be message receivers, sometimes almost for its own sake, among all concerned. For journalists (but others too), this can privilege sensationalism over sobriety, events over context, the emotionally compelling over the informationally clarifying, and the negative over the positive. An increased premium on brevity also seems to inhere in this system. It is as if from the "shrinking soundbite" of television news we are gravitating toward the 140-character length of the tweet. Certainly one of the authors maintains below that the tweet is a model of more political communications to come. If so, they are unlikely to be able to do justice to the complexity and trade-offs inherent in real political issues. And then, finally, there is the encouragement and exhibition of mass populism, for which there is of course sometimes something to be said. Popular anger, frustration and resentment over how our economic and political elites have (mis)ruled their roosts in recent years are thoroughly understandable and justified-but they can't frame policy. As Aristotle once said, only the wearer knows where the shoe pinches-but he/she can't craft the shoe. Populism is an uneven force, sometimes on the side of justice but sometimes prone to impassioned irrationalism. With the system we now have, however, there is no way that the populist genie can be pushed back into its deferential bottle! (Nor should we try.) Yet it may run amok, for crowds are not necessarily wise. So the policy question is: how might the "parliament of the street" (to pick up a phrase used by one of the contributors to this collection) be converted into a somewhat more deliberative forum? And what contributions might journalists, if they worked in more viable and public-spirited organisations, be able to make to that process?

REFERENCE

BLUMLER, JAY G. and GUREVITCH, MICHAEL (1995) *The Crisis of Public Communication*, London: Routledge.

INTRODUCTION

Bob Franklin

2009 was a year of significant developments in the debate concerning the future of journalism. With hindsight, it was the year in which fiercely held conventional wisdoms and seemingly self-evident truths were rigorously interrogated, readily abandoned and promptly metamorphosed into yesterdays' news; it was also the year in which debate about the future of journalism became markedly less congenial.

Undoubtedly the most significant "truth" to be challenged was the long-held belief that journalists and news organisations must offer online content for free since the widespread availability of news on multiple sites means that exacting payments for access to one site will simply trigger readers to migrate to another where effectively the same news is available without charge; and all this at the click of a mouse. Rupert Murdoch's public pronouncement that News Corporation intended "to charge for all our websites" offered a radically different truth. His explanation for the change was that "quality journalism is not cheap and an industry that gives away its content is simply cannibalising its ability to produce good reporting" (Murdoch cited in McChesney and Nichols, 2010, p. 70). Expressing testament to this new conviction, Murdoch promptly closed his free *LondonPaper* which distributed 330,000 copies daily in the UK capital; another 60 jobs were lost (Brook, 2009).

Where Murdoch led, others quickly followed. In January 2010, the *New York Times* announced the introduction of a "metered" system which allocates readers a quota of free articles but applies charges when that quota is exceeded (Clark, 2010, p. 17). Sceptics expressed their doubts about the efficacy of this policy shift but offered at least a cautious two cheers of endorsement, wished Murdoch success and prayed that his simple Pauline conversion to placing journalism behind pay walls might resolve at a stroke the problem of how best to monetise online content and deliver resources to fund journalism.

Murdoch has adopted an increasingly abusive rhetoric to drive home his arguments and is now brusque in debate. When *Guardian* editor Alan Rusbridger suggested in his Hugh Cudlipp lecture that positioning pay walls around websites would lead the industry to "sleepwalk into oblivion" (Rusbridger, 2010), Murdoch's response was unequivocal; "that sounds like BS to me" (Murdoch cited in Greenslade, 2010).

Journalism and Change

These blunt exchanges undoubtedly articulate anxieties about the depth and significance of the changes which journalism confronts. Developments in media technologies, financial strategies, business models, organisational and regulatory struc-tures, the fragmentation of audiences and a growing public concern about some aspects of tabloid journalism practices and reporting, as well as broader political, sociological and cultural changes, have combined to impoverish the flow of existing revenues available to fund journalism. They also impact radically on traditional journalism practices, while simultaneously generating an increasingly frenzied search for sustainable and equivalent funding—and from a wide range of sources—to nurture and deliver journalism in the future.

In the global north, the future for journalism seems especially precarious for some sectors. The identified problems confronting the industry are routinely cited in both scholarly and professional analyses, while the well-rehearsed discussions of the causes of these difficulties has come to resemble a round up of the usual suspects (Franklin, 2009a; McChesney and Nichols, 2010; Project for Excellence in Journalism, 2009; Starr, 2009).

In print journalism, for example, journalists' jobs have followed the downward spiral of published titles, shrinking circulations, reduced pagination, the truncated range of editorial content and sections along with the volume of advertising revenues; and sometimes very rapidly and dramatically. Additionally, newspapers have been obliged to confront the challenge of substantially increased competition from news online, news updates distributed via mobile technology, news aggregators such as Google news and micro blogging sites like Twitter. The economic recession since 2007 has accelerated and exacerbated the consequences of such revenue shifts and trends for jobs, investment and the news product. A *New York Times* journalist queried wryly in a column about news room redundancies: "Clearly the sky is falling in. The question now is how many people will be left to cover it" (cited in Beam et al., 2009, p. 734).

Newspapers have responded to such digital and market challenges by supplementing print editions with an extensive online presence which distributes news as text, streams news in audio visual formats and offers podcasts for downloading. A key ingredient in this online presence has been print (and broadcast) journalism's expansive uses of readers' contributions to news via user-generated content (UGC) which includes posted comments, readers' blogs, but increasingly and more typically, readers' video clips and photographs submitted to newspapers and television stations. The BBC has established a "UGC hub" to "process" this innovative news source (Harrison, 2010), but research increasingly suggests that the development of a more participatory, "pro-am" model of news which reshapes the relationship between journalists and readers, prompting changes to news content and formats, has seemingly stalled, or at least faltered. Studies of UGC at the BBC (Williams et al., forthcoming), in the regional and local press in the United Kingdom (Singer, 2010) and in online newsrooms across Europe and the United States (Domingo et al., 2009) suggest that while readers' contribution to news has expanded considerably it has been "absorbed" into traditional journalism practices with journalists retaining their gatekeeping editorial roles. "Business as usual" offers a better description of the implications of UGC for news reporting than journalistic "revolution".

But new media technologies continue to create innovative opportunities for print journalists to tell stories in new and creative ways; and also to make money. Enthusiasm for the *Guardian* iphone App, for example, launched for use with mobile phones late in 2009, surprised even the editor with 70,000 sales in the first month (Rusbridger, 2010, p. 4). But the £25 million digital advertising revenues enjoyed by the *Guardian* in 2009 is promising but still modest and insufficient to sustain "the legacy print business" (Rusbridger, 2010, p. 6); the metaphor of bereavement is on the tip of every pundits pen. There remains a substantial shortfall between the recent digital revenue gains and the income lost by traditional newspaper sales of news to readers and readers to advertisers; closing this gap is a matter of some urgency. "The reality" as distinguished scholar Paul Starr notes, "is that resources for journalism are now disappearing from the old media faster than new media can develop them" (Starr, 2009, p. 28). For certain sectors of the local and regional press, especially the larger, city-based papers, the situation is acute as they confront and record alarming collapses of readership and plummeting advertising revenues (Franklin, 2006, pp. 4–7). Market sector is influential in shaping distinctive journalism destinies, with the decline of the Sunday titles, but especially Sunday tabloids, being markedly more evident than for the "quality", "broadsheet" or "compact" papers (Cole and Harcup, 2010, pp. 19–45; Franklin, 2008, pp. 5–10; Williams, 2010, pp. 221–42).

Broadcast journalism fares little better with commercial radio stations and the independent regional television stations in the United Kingdom suffering a dangerous collapse of advertising incomes, shifts in regulatory requirements and increasing challenges from Web-based alternatives which deliver news and information on demand, around the clock and in more audience-accessible formats (Starkey and Crisell, 2009, pp. 22–43). For radio, the transition to an online platform presents a paradox. On the one hand, the shift has been relatively easy with listeners readily downloading podcasts, listening to a vastly increased number of stations from around the globe on Internet-only radio, while tuning in via their computers more often than their radio. But on the other, such practices are so widespread that the "State of the News Media report 2009 claims they risk making "radio" redundant. "Radio" the report suggests, "is well on its way to becoming something altogether new—a medium called audio" (Project for Excellence in Journalism, 2009).

The BBC remains an influential, world-leading centre for journalism delivered on radio, television and online platforms, but it faces increasing opposition and sometimes stridently expressed demands from politicians, the public, but especially commercial rivals, to change the value and sources of its revenues (both licence fee and income from the market aspects of its operations), while reining in its editorial and programming outputs and reducing its currently over-dominant position in the UK broadcasting ecology. James Murdoch believes the BBC is engaged in nothing less sinister than a "land grab", describing "the scale and scope of its current activities and future ambitions" as "chilling". The expansion of the "state sponsored journalism" which Murdoch believes the BBC delivers, "is a threat to the plurality and independence of news provision which are so important for our democracy" (Murdoch, 2009, p. 16).

Amid all this curious mix of information, polemic and partisan babble, Murdoch raises an important issue: namely that the difficulties confronting journalism (whether local, regional or national) have significant consequences beyond journalism and the news media for the (local, regional or national) communities they serve, their economies and for peoples' prospects for accessing the kinds of political information, commentary and debate necessary to exercise democratic accountability within those communities (Fenton, 2010; Franklin, 2009b). Cuts in resources and journalism jobs means that certain foci for journalism coverage are no longer reported or can be reported only with journalists' over-reliance on corporate and public sector-sponsored press releases or agency copy, rather than journalists initiating their own inquiries (Davies, 2008). Any prospect of journalists fulfilling a fourth estate role by monitoring the activities of economically and politically powerful groups is considerably less likely when journalism is so poorly resourced. As Tom Rosenstiel notes, adopting the confused and tautologically expressive style of US politician Donald Rumsfeld, "More of American life will occur in the shadows. We won't know what we won't know" (cited in Starr, 2009, p. 28).

News journalism is increasingly focused on soft news, entertainment formats and celebrity news with a markedly reduced attention to foreign affairs—regrettably war reporting is the exception here. In the United States, newspapers are closing foreign bureaux and consequently "vast parts of the world are woefully under covered by the American press" (Hamilton and Lawrence, forthcoming). In the United Kingdom, the same neglect of foreign affairs is evident in broadcast journalism; and across a long period (Barnet and Seymour 1999; Franklin 1997; Starr, 2009).

Similarly, journalists have less time available for attention to national political events in Washington and Westminster or for Presidential and Parliamentary affairs, the reporting of local councils, devolved assemblies or state legislatures; again, spin and corporate-funded public relations step in to replace the missing journalists and fill the news hole (Franklin et al., 2010, pp. 202–13). Irreplaceable journalistic expertise and professional experience is being lost. PR specialists, bloggers and part-time citizen journalists offer the prospect of, at best, a second-class journalistic service for making the powerful accountable compared to the "significant body of full time paid journalists", working in "independent newsrooms" who receive "professional editing, fact checking and assis-tance" and "feel secure enough in their livelihoods to focus on their work" which is currently considered to be crucial to sustaining an effective working democracy (McChesney and Nichols, 2010, p. 81; Nichols and McChesney, 2010). There is, moreover, little prospect in the short to medium term that Web-based journalism will deliver sufficient funding to sustain an equivalent journalistic corps to fulfil these democratic functions of journalism (Compton and Benedetti[1]).

But much of the debate concerning the future of journalism has been conducted through the prism of American/European perspectives and experiences. The future looks radically different, of course, from the viewpoint of particular national settings, with their distinctive journalism cultures, divergent market sectors and particular media platforms. Similarly, diversely sourced funding revenues, generated by a host of distinctive business models and policy commitments ranging from public subsidies for journalism to funding via public service commitments, create complex and divergent prospects for journalism. From a global perspective, the future of journalism seems more complex, nuanced and layered.

In China, India, South America and parts of Africa, for example, journalism and journalism products are burgeoning and enjoying unprecedented growth in number of titles, readerships and advertising revenues both in print and online editions (Bhaskar, 2005, p. 19; Franklin, 2009a, pp. 2–3; World Association of Newspapers (WAN), 2009). By the end of 2008, global sales of paid daily newspapers achieved a new record of 540 millions or 1.9 billion readers; a year on year increase of 1.3 per cent. Sales in Africa grew by 6.9 per cent in 2008 but 38 per cent of countries reported circulation gains in 2008, rising to 58 per cent across the previous five years (WAN, 2009). Newspaper reach, moreover, remains extensive with many European countries reaching 70 per cent of the adult population: in Japan the equivalent figure is 91 per cent (WAN, 2009). In South Africa the new popular tabloids targeting black, urban and poor readerships enjoy expansive sales (Wasserman, 2009).

Given these multiple and diverse experiences of journalism's current status and prospects, soothsaying is rampant. Predictions oscillate wildly between despair at the demise of traditional (big media) journalism, on the one hand, and eulogies welcoming a new pluralistic, citizen or participatory journalism, on the other (Bruns, 2008). Diagnoses of the current malaise are similarly divergent. While many observers identify the Internet as by far the most significant single cause of the problems confronting journalism (Jarvis, 2007; Shirky, 2009), voices as divergent as US scholar Robert McChesney and distinguished UK journalist Peter Preston, suggest the antecedents for this crisis lie earlier in the history of the press. For Preston, "the net may be the deliverer of the coup de grace here, but it is not truly to blame for what's gone wrong over decades" (2009, p. 14). Instead it is necessary to consider longer-term changes in lifestyle and "human living patterns", the "inertia, fatalism and cost cutting" of the evening papers and the ability of the journalism industry to respond to problems with self-damaging solutions like cutting pagination, reducing news content, upping prices and thereby inviting readers to "pay more for less. A potty pitch nobody outside the closed world of newspaper introspection would give house room to"; and all this covered by "a slurry of self regarding pessimism" (Preston, 2009, p. 14).

McChesney and Nichols similarly acknowledge the significance of the Internet in the current crisis in journalism—indeed they claim it has been a "central factor in the collapse of commercial news media" (2010, p. 3). But more significant has been the corporate and monopoly ownership and control of the journalism industries which has persistently foregrounded the drive for profit at the cost of neglecting the democratic functions of journalism. News media's business strategy has prioritised high returns for shareholders above the investment of returns in greater levels of editorial resources to generate "good" (civic or democratic) journalism. The tension between the economic and democratic purposes of journalism means that news media have enjoyed business success but increasingly constitute an editorial and democratic failure (Franklin, 2006, p. xix; 2009b). As McChesney and Nichols understand it, the "deep seated and long term crisis" in journalism and news media has been "created by media owners who made the commercial and entertainment values of the market dramatically higher priorities than the civic and democratic values that are essential to good journalism and a good society" (McChesney and Nichols, 2010, p. 4).

Given this diagnosis, their prescription to cure these journalistic and democratic ills demurs markedly from the conventional wisdom which argues that what the Internet has broken, the Internet will mend—with a little help from the market—by delivering online news, blogs and citizen journalism to fill the void left by the collapse of traditional media and journalism. They reject the fables of "new media fabulists" and are unwilling to "simply relax and wait while entrepreneurs cobble together a new journalism system on the web" (McChesney and Nichols, 2010, p. 4). Their favoured policy prescription draws inspiration from founding fathers of the Republic such as Washington, Hamilton and Jefferson who established a system of postal and printing subsidies to guarantee press freedom (McChesney and Nichols, 2010).

Charging for Content Online: Digging Their Own Graves?

Since May 2009, attention has focused on Rupert Murdoch's announcement and rigorous defence of his intention to charge for online content in all News Corporation titles. Explaining the policy shift in his MacTaggart lecture in August 2009, James Murdoch was unequivocal. "It is essential for the future of independent digital journalism" he argued, "that a fair price can be charged for news to people who value it" (Murdoch, 2009, p. 16).

The dilemma confronting proprietors, editors and journalists working in print journalism in the context of online editions has been evident for some while. Setting aside premium news sites like the *Wall Street Journal*, news online is readily available for free which means print journalism is now increasingly denied the revenues which traditionally derived from copy sales. But charging for content will reduce traffic, advertising revenues and offer rival publishers—including bloggers and citizen journalists—opportunities to target their audiences. The dilemma seems intractable. "Either way", as Paul Starr observed, "by giving away their content or limiting access, they may be digging their own graves" (2009, p. 30). This "damned if they do and damned if they don't" perception has generated policy stasis, which Murdoch seems determined to resolve. *The Times* and *Sunday Times* began charging for online access in May 2010. The *New York Times* has also announced its commitment to publishing online "All The News That's Fit to Charge For" although Sulzberger acknowledges the shift constitutes "a bet" on "where we think the net is going" (Clark, 2009, p. 17). More parochially, in December 2009, UK-based local and regional publishers Johnson Press began a pilot scheme by charging for access to six online titles (*Independent*, 26 November 2009) including the *Northumberland Gazette* and the *Worksop Guardian*. There's a good deal of editorial quality and panache separating these local papers from the *Wall Street Journal* but the ambition is the same; how to monetise content sufficiently to fund quality journalism.

This policy shift to charging for online has been subject to critical interrogation by scholars and journalists alike. A number of arguments have been mustered against the proposal, not least the fact that it has been tried before and failed and that the circumstances which prompted failure in the 1990s currently seem even more adverse offering less propitious prospect of success (McChesney and Nichols, 2010, pp. 70–1; Williams and Franklin, 2007, pp. 45–9).

McChesney and Nichols, among others, offer five arguments against the use of pay walls. First, to be successful the policy would require all online news providers to adopt an untypically collectivist approach and support the strategy; even a single refusenik generates the killer question, Why pay for news when it is readily available for free? But even if such an exceptional degree of consensus could be achieved in the highly competitive markets which characterise the journalism industry, the strategy would create an unacceptable cartel, be unpopular with consumers who prefer the openness of the Web to the alternative of having news "locked in" behind pay walls and prompt a resurgence in hacking which would "make bootleggers during the prohibition era look like champions of the temperance movement" (McChesney and Nichols, 2010, pp. 71–3). But the "hackers" are now institutionalised, count their membership in tens of millions, pay to create their own para-journalism formats (Hermida) and routinely "twitter the news" to a global audience. The cliché of the modern media world that "most scoops have a life expectancy of about three minutes" seems not to have reached Rupert Murdoch's ears (Rusbridger, 2010).

Second, if Murdoch can create this coalition of commercial media securely ensconced behind pay walls, he must still confront the plethora of public service and public sector news and information providers which would continue to deliver news and information for free. Some of these providers, like the BBC, are influential global news operators which even the editor of the rival *Guardian* acknowledges to be "almost certainly the best news organisation in the world" (Rusbridger, 2010, p. 5). Moreover, governments, non-governmental organisations, think tanks, universities, interest groups and not-for-profit news organisations, whether "alternative" or "community based", all deliver news and information in ways which would breach the security of Murdoch's walls.

Awareness of such potential breaches perhaps informs James Murdoch's enthusiasm to denounce the free newspapers published by local authorities and distributed to local residents as "pocket-Pravdas" while the BBC's radio, television, but crucially Internet-based, news services are attacked for allegedly "dumping free, state sponsored news on the market place" which makes it "incredibly difficult for news to flourish on the internet" (Murdoch, 2009, p. 16). In a seemingly tactical response to such pressures in March 2010, the BBC's Director General announced plans to cut two BBC radio stations, reduce spending on sports rights and foreign programming, while significantly reducing the BBC website pages by half and cutting staffing and the £133.8 million budget for BBC Online by 25 per cent. This policy shift seems to continue the long-established BBC tradition that Director Generals get their capitulation in first. Columnist Jonathan Freedland suggested that "Mark Thompson feared that if he didn't jump from the second storey window, an incoming conservative government might push him off the roof" (2010, p. 29). Curiously and inconsistently, there is no plan to erect pay walls around the online operation of Murdoch's own television news outlet, SkyNews.

Third, pay walls are corrosive of the most creative and beneficial aspects of Web technology, the hyperlink which bloggers among others use to create connections between content and direct and encourage traffic to a range of news sites. Pay walls reduce journalists' ability to report news by using different media, which extend the form and content of stories beyond mere "text and still pictures". To quote Rusbridger,

> journalists have never before been able to tell stories so effectively, bouncing off each other, linking to each other (as the most generous and open minded do), linking out, citing sources, allowing response—harnessing the best qualities of text, print, data, sound, and visual media. If ever there was a route to building audience, trust and relevance it is by embracing all of the capabilities of this new world, not walling yourself away from them. (2010, p. 7)

In short pay walls threaten the way that journalism is now conducted in a multimedia environment along with the prospect for reaching substantial audiences. Hyperlinks, moreover, allow readers (in this sense at least, they constitute "produsers"), the prospect of following the unravelling news story in their own way by choosing which of a range of links to follow.

Fourth, moving to subscription or a payment for less routine access to news websites is likely to reduce income in the short term. Charging for content invariably reduces site traffic and, consequently, diminishes advertising revenues which remain crucial to funding journalism (Franklin, 2008, p. 25). Each new online reader moreover involves an opportunity cost of one less reader of the print edition; the problem of "cannibalisation" with disastrous consequences for advertising revenues since estimates suggest that "newspapers need between 20–100 readers online to make up for losing just one print reader" (*Economist, 2006*).

Finally, newspapers and their online editions are growing fast, expanding both readerships and advertising revenues. The UK *Guardian*, for example, has developed its overseas readership from 650 copies in 1956 to 37 million readers across print and online platforms in December 2009 making it the eighth most widely read newspaper globally and the second most widely read English-language paper after the *New York Times*.

The last three months of 2009 witnessed a 40 per cent year on year growth in readership with more Americans reading the paper than the *Los Angeles Times*. And readers are following quality editorial; the *Guardian*'s total marketing expenditure across the previous decade has been a mere $34,000 (Rusbridger, 2010, p. 11).

Other policy options and directions have been proposed to avoid journalists having to "dig their own graves". Most recently McChesney and Nichols (2010) and Downie and Schudson (2010) have outlined distinctive and complex systems of subsidy to provide funding for an effective and democratic journalism (see James Curran's plenary address). Press subsidies enjoy a long history in Europe (Picard and Grönlund, 2003). Since January 2009 the French Government, following an initiative by the Flemish Government (2004), offers young people a year's free subscription to a newspaper of their choice on their 18th birthday; in Belgium recipients of subsidised newspapers showed a marked preference for reading newspapers after two years (Raeymaeckers et al., 2009).

In the UK, the National Union of Journalists (NUJ) among other voices has argued that levies on major media corporations could be used to help finance the production of public service contents: an idea typically discussed in the context of broadcast journalism but appropriate also for local and regional papers (NUJ, 2009). Research conducted by the Institute for Public Policy Research (IPPR) signalled that a 1 per cent levy on Sky and Virgin would deliver £70 million annually, while the same levy on the top five mobile telephony companies would generate £208 million annually. The IPPR claims that such levies are popular with the public (IPPR, 2009, p. 4).

Another policy proposal, first touted in a column by Polly Toynbee (2009) but elaborated in more detail in Stephen Carter's *Digital Britain* Report (2009), argued for establishing not-for-profit, news consortia, involving community groups and civil society associations such as trades unions, universities, local business organisations, and politicians from local and regional assemblies, with a mission to make good the shortfalls in local and regional television news provision given the collapse of local news services on the ITV network. The idea has extended beyond this initial limited and utilitarian remit to provide a model for new and alternative forms of local media ownership, enhanced community engagement with news media, a mechanism to sustain locally relevant public service news organisations, as well as opportunities for new voices and increased diversity/plurality in the news environment (Franklin, 2009b; Witschge et al., 2009).

For the moment, charging for content is the favoured prescription for funding the future of journalism and pundits eagerly await the outcome of Murdoch's "experiment" with building pay walls. Some considerable part of the future of journalism seemingly hangs on the success of a business strategy which makes little financial, but even less journalistic, sense given that it represents only one of many business models and financial strategies to resource journalism. Moreover, the developments and changes evident in journalism and news media, along with their causes and consequences for the future of journalism, are hotly contested. But despite current problems, journalism continues to perform crucial functions which are not "bolt on" or optional extras but vital to societies' well-being. Journalism helps to shape, as well as reflect community identity, is central to the economic and cultural life of communities, and crucial to their democratic and civic processes.

Journalists have always been too creative and journalism too essential to communities' well-being to be cast in the role of grave digger. The problems confronting journalism are evidently substantial, but there are also more promising developments. The language of apocalypse can be seductive, while talk of reform, evolution and adaptation can seem more mundane. Journalism conducted via print and broadcast platforms has already agreed an editorial, if not yet satisfactory financial, accommodation with the Web. Journalism is now conducted across multiple platforms and beginning to offer unprecedented creative potential for journalists and exciting high-quality journalism products for consumers using an expansive variety of formats and ways of telling stories. There is no longer any need to place the qualifying adjective "multiplatform" ahead of journalism; it is now an embedded assumption in both journalism practice and public understanding. Journalism, moreover, is reaching wider (and more international) audiences than previously; and is continuing to make money! In the United States, for example, and despite recession, newspapers average profit margins for 2008 were 11.5 per cent, albeit down from 22.3 per cent in 2002 (Starr, 2009, p. 30). In the United Kingdom, the independent television network ITV turned a £2.7 billion loss for 2008 into a modest £25 million profit in 2009 (*Independent*, 3 March 2010). New recruits to journalism continue to enrol at university programmes and in record numbers; in the United Kingdom in 2009 applications for journalism programmes increased by 27 per cent; year on year the most substantial increase for any subject area (Franklin, 2009c, p. 730).

The future of journalism undoubtedly remains uncertain, nuanced and with highly variable prospects reflecting the dynamic and distinctive journalistic and national cultures, contexts and histories within which it is conducted. The conversation about that future has no evident closure and this informs the ambition to convene biennial conferences to bring together scholars from around the globe, to present the findings from their various researches, and fuel debate and discussion about the future of journalism. Thirty of the papers presented at the 2009 Conference at Cardiff are published in special issues of the journals *Journalism Studies* and *Journalism Practice* and in the Routledge collection *The Future of Journalism*. An additional 25 papers will be published in two edited collections in the "Journalism in Research" series published by Routledge, titled *Journalism, Education, Training and Employment* (edited by Bob Franklin and Donica Mensing, 2011) and *Journalism, Sources and Credibility: New Perspectives* (edited by Bob Franklin and Matt Carlson, 2011).

The Future of Journalism: The Conference

The Future of Journalism Conference hosted by the Cardiff School of Journalism, Media and Cultural Studies and sponsored by the publisher Routledge, Taylor & Francis, convened on 9 and 10 September 2009 to provide a forum for 200 scholars from more than 40 countries and five continents, to discuss recent developments in journalism and their implications for both journalism studies and journalism practice. The widespread concern about the future for journalism is exemplified by the results of a simple Google search which delivers 16,700,000 entries for the search term "The Future of Journalism". This global concern matches closely the purpose of these biennial conferences, launched in 2007 with a focus on the Future of Newspapers, to identify dominant and central issues of concern for scholars, practitioners and educators working in journalism studies. The response to the initial Call for Papers in 2009 produced more than 300 submissions with 120 research-based papers eventually accepted for presentation in 30 panel sessions across the two-day conference (a complete list of papers accepted for conference presentation is included in Appendix A at the end of this Introduction).

The Conference focused on five broad themes designed to address five key questions. First, in what ways is journalism changing and responding to developments in new media technologies, which facilitate new ways of reporting news including online journalism, citizen journalism and blogging? Second, how are these changes unravelling in distinctive national settings with their particular journalism cultures, audiences, media structures and histories? Third, how are changes in media technologies and journalism practice impacting on the revenue sources available to fund journalism and what business models are being developed to resource changing and newly emerging forms of journalism? Fourth, what are the implications of these developments for the education and training of journalists and their prospects for employment, as well as the changing nature of that employment? Finally, in what ways do these changes impact on day-to-day journalism practice, especially journalists' relationships with sources and the ethical decisions they confront?

These are big questions, important questions, which some scholars (Singer, 2006) have posed as existential questions which address fundamental concerns about who now is a journalist? And what is Journalism? What is it about what journalists do—and the ways that they do it—in the current information market, which marks them out as journalists and their products as journalism? And what distinguishes them (if anything) from the expansive army of bloggers and citizen journalists as well as a host of other communication professionals—not least their sources in public relations? The following five sections offer a brief introduction to the papers published here and presented at conference under these themed headings.

Online Journalism, New Technology and the Future of Journalism

The majority of papers submitted to the Conference focused explicitly on the implications of new media technologies for the future of journalism and/or explored those implications for journalism practice, media organisation and finance in particular national settings; the number of papers selected for eventual publication reflect that balance of scholarly interest and consequence for journalism.

Marina Vujnovic et al.'s 10-nation comparative study of online journalists and editors' perceptions concerning the economic impetus behind the expansion of online journalism concludes that participatory journalism is perceived primarily as a means "to increase competitiveness" although journalists and editors also acknowledge the absence of any "clear vision for why and how to adopt it, either for democratic or competitive purposes" (consult Appendix A for a full bibliographical reference). Christoph Neuberger and Christian Nuernbergk's research explores relationships between professional and participatory media via interviews with editors in 183 online newsrooms in Germany. Findings deliver little evidence that participatory media are replacing more traditional forms of journalism since the former tend to complement, more than compete or integrate with the latter.

Lisa Lynch examines the role of online sites such as Wikileaks which make resources available to expand the previously shrinking activity of investigative journalism, while Alfred Hermida analyses the implications of para-journalism forms such as Twitter, which "enable citizens to maintain a mental model of news and events around them": what he terms "ambient news".

Bonnie Brennen and Erika dela Cerna explore emergent forms of journalism in Second Life and, by assessing the impact of the online world on residents' off-line lives, the authors (and their Second Life avatars) raise important questions about freedom of expression. Kevin Barnhurst revisits his 2001 study which concluded that US newspaper electronic editions effectively reproduced the substance of print editions in order to sustain their relationships with readers. Barnhurst's current study reveals that by 2005, online editions were changing, especially in the form of news they present, while Martin Conboy and John Steel examine the changing definition of the "popular" by comparing the print and online editions of the *Sun* newspaper, anticipating that online editions would reflect a textual shift which Conboy and Steel describe as a "move from 'we' to 'me'".

Finally, Wendy Weinhold study uses the letters to the editor pages of three leading American journalism trade magazines between 1998 to 2008 to achieve an insider's perspective on media professionals' impressions about the future of journalism including debates about the shift to online publication.

The Future of Journalism; Global Perspectives

The papers presented under this theme illustrate the diverse ways in which journalism change has occurred in particular national settings. Carla Rodrigues Cardoso assesses the future of news magazines by analysing the covers and contents of six news magazines published in America (*Time* and *Newsweek*), France (*L'Express* and *Le Nouvel Observateur*) and Portugal (*Sábado* and *Visão*) across a 10-year interval, while Rodney Tiffen's content analysis focuses on six Australian newspapers (1956–2006) to identify radical changes in newspaper size, pagination, editorial content, advertising, visual presentation (photographs, cartoons, maps and graphs), the format and design of page one, as well as the changing segmentation and sections within newspapers.

Xin Xin assesses the political implications of the emergence of citizen journalism in China, by considering four case studies of citizen reporting to illustrate some of the complexities which emerge in a system where media remain largely under state regulation and control. Mihai Coman's analysis of how journalism has been "carved up" in post-Communist Romania reveals how, in this process, the initial ambitions for a free and independent press have been lost, while Arnold de Beer uses content analysis of television news reports during 2008 in three Western countries (the United Kingdom, the United States and Germany), two Arab-speaking countries (Qatar and United Arab Emirates) and an African country (South Africa) to explore the Afro-pessimism which typifies news reports of the so-called "dark continent".

Developing New Business Models

François Nel studied innovation in online business models at the 66 largest UK-based local and regional newspapers but found few pay walls, with advertising offering the most common source of online revenues. Companies essentially transferred traditional business strategies from the print context but revenue derived from these sources was insufficient to sustain current operations. Sally Young presented a comparative assessment of the current status and prospects for newspaper journalism in Australia, the United States, the United Kingdom, Canada and New Zealand, and provided an analysis of the particular strategies adopted by Australian newspaper businesses in order to offset decline and deliver funding to resource journalism. By contrast, Debra Reddin van Tuyll's "back-to-the-future" analysis argues that current business solutions to the problems of journalism reflect "a myopia that has infected American journalists for a century", and prescribes a cure for journalism's ills which involves a return to "earlier forms of journalism, in the partisan press that dominated American journalism through the nineteenth century".

Journalism Education, Training and Employment in a Changing Environment

Donica Mensing considers the need for fundamental changes to journalism education to match the substantial and structural changes to the journalism industry and journalists' daily professional practice. Illustrated by three case studies, her suggestion for a fundamental realignment of journalism education away from "an industry-centered to a community-centered model as one way to re-engage journalism education in a more productive role in the future of journalism", articulates nothing less than a battle cry for journalism educators. Writing from an African focus, Anya Schiffrin examines the role which foreign organisations (Thomson Reuters, BBC Trust) play in journalism education and training in Ghana, Nigeria and Uganda. Schiffrin argues that these programmes will have little effect since their beneficial consequences are overwhelmed by the combined adverse effects of lack of resources, government pressure on journalists and the declining quality of secondary education and professional journalism education.

Journalism Practice, Sources and Ethics

A number of presentations focused on the various ways that journalists' relationships with sources in the digital setting assume new meaning and give rise to issues concerning credibility and transparency. Angela Phillips uses interviews with journalists to explore the growth of what she terms "news cannibalism" (taking material from other news organisations, without attribution). She suggests that "Lifting" from cuttings is not new, but with the availability of electronic copy, journalists can "cannibalise" exclusive material such as significant quotes, within minutes of publication online; her data suggest the practice is widespread and growing. Phillips argues for new standards of transparency to protect professional reporting in the networked era and to improve ethical standards in journalism. Michael Karlsson also articulates concerns about transparency in online news and compares how leading mainstream online news media in the the United States, the United Kingdom and Sweden make use of "rituals of transparency" in news items.

For Chris Frost, privacy constitutes the key ethical restriction for journalists and proves contentious because it conflicts with the right to freedom of expression which informs journalists' claims to press freedom. He is concerned that definitions of privacy are being "tightened" by regulators (including the statutory broadcast regulators and the Press Complaints Commission (PCC)) in a number of recent adjudications. Since the PCC is self-regulatory, the press must either agree its rulings or reject them and risk making the Commission unworkable. Frost argues that recent PCC judgements are significant since they will have far more effect on the future of reporting in the prints and online than any of the much-criticised cases from the courts.

Plenary Speakers

The Conference opened with plenary addresses by two outstanding contributors to journalism studies and journalism practice. James Curran is among the most distinguished academics working in the field of journalism, media and communications scholarship. For 20 years, he has been Professor of Communications at Goldsmith's College, University of London, UK where he is Director of the Goldsmith's Media Research Programme. James has also held endowed visiting chairs at Penn, Stanford, Stockholm and Oslo Universities. He has been a member of the Annenberg Press Commission, USA and is currently the UK representative on the European Commission Committee promoting research on broadcasting in Central and Eastern Europe. He has written or edited 18 books including *Power Without Responsibility, Media and Cultural Theory, Mass Media and Society, Contesting Media Power: alternative media in a networked world* and *Media and Power*. In his plenary address James outlines four perspectives on the Future of Journalism, critiques them and concludes by offering a "compelling alternative" which he designates "public reformism" which "seeks to change the future through concerted action".

Bettina Peters is the Director of the Global Forum for Media Development (GFMD), a network of 500 media assistance organisations from around the globe. Before joining GFMD, Bettina worked as Director of Programmes at the European Journalism Centre (EJC) at Maastricht with responsibility for the Centre's programme of journalism training, especially in the Middle East/North Africa and Eastern Europe. From 1990 until 2002 Bettina worked at the International Federation of Journalists (IFJ) as European Coordinator and then Deputy General Secretary. She holds a Master's in Politics and Journalism from the University of Hamburg and has edited a range of publications including a global survey of women in journalism, the EJC Handbook on Civic Journalism and the Handbook on Human Rights Reporting in Africa. In a challenging plenary she spoke about the difficulties confronting journalism in the global south and stressed that the best route to secure a viable future for journalism does not necessarily involve following in the footsteps of the countries in the north.

ACKNOWLEDGEMENTS

I am very grateful to a number of people who helped with various aspects of organising the Future of Journalism 2009 Conference. This is my opportunity to thank them and I'm eager to take it. My editorial assistant Annie Rhys Jones worked incredibly hard and with great enthusiasm on all aspects of the planning and organisation of this conference. It is difficult to overstate her contribution and the conference would not have been so efficiently organised or half so much fun without her efforts. I owe her a real debt of gratitude. I need also to record thanks to Shelley Allen, Kath Burton and Greig Barclay at Routledge, colleagues at the Cardiff School of Journalism, Head of School Justin Lewis, but especially Deb Lloyd, James Clemas and Jon Adams and his technical colleagues for their support in making things work—but also thanks to Jonathan Cable, Ann Luce, Max Pettigrew and Reeta Toivanen who volunteered their time and services to assist in so many ways. Finally, I wish to thank all paper presenters, speakers and session chairs for their contributions, as well as the delegates who attended and contributed to discussion from the floor. We all learned, as well as contributed, a good deal to the two days of very exciting discussion and reflection. Mostly, I need to thank everyone who attended for helping to make the conference such an enjoyable and collegial occasion while offering such high-quality food for thought.

NOTE

1. When author names appear without a date this means they presented a paper at the Future of Journalism Conference and the full details of the paper and authors appears in Appendix A at the end of this Introduction.

REFERENCES

BARNET, STEVEN and SEYMOUR, EMILY (1999) *A Shrinking Iceberg Travelling South: a case study of drama and current affairs*, London: Campaign for Quality Television.

BEAM, RANDAL A., BROWNLEE, BONNIE J., WEAVER, DAVID H. and DI CACCIO, DAMON T. (2009) "Journalism and Public Service in Troubled Times", *Journalism Studies* 10(6), pp. 734–53.

BHASKAR, BABU (2005) "Flourishing Papers, Floundering Craft: the press and the law", in: Nahlinin Rajan (Ed.), *Practising Journalism*, New Delhi: Sage of India.

BROOK, STEPHEN (2009) "The London Paper Set to Close", 20 August, *Guardian*, http://www.guardian.co.uk/media/2009/aug/20/the-london-paper-close-plan, accessed 11 February 2010.

BRUNS, AXEL (2008) *Blogs, Wikipedia, Second Life and Beyond: from production to produsage*, New York: Peter Lang.

CARTER, STEPHEN (2009) *Digital Britain*; Final Report, http://www.gov.uk/images/publications/digitalbritain-finalreport-jun09.pdf

CLARK, ANDREW (2010) "All the News That's Fit to Pay For—New York Times to charge readers for online content", *Guardian*, 21 January, p. 17.

COLE, PETER and HARCUP, TONY (2010) *Newspaper Journalism*, London: Sage.

DAVIES, NICK (2008) *Flat Earth News*, London: Chatto and Windus.

DOMINGO, DAVID, QUANDT, THORSTEN, HEINONEN, ARI, PAULUSSEN, STEVE, SINGER, JANE B. and VUJNOVIC, MARINA (2009) "Participatory Journalism Practices in the Media and Beyond: an international comparative study of initiatives in online newspapers", in: Bob Franklin (Ed.), *The Future of Newspapers*, London: Routledge, pp. 203–18.

DOWNIE, LEONARD and SCHUDSON, MICHAEL (2010) "The Reconstruction of American Journalism", *Columbia Journalism Review*, http://www.cjr.org/reconstruction/the_reconstruction_of_american.php (accessed 24 February 2010).

ECONOMIST (2006) "Who Killed the Newspaper?", 24 August, http://www.economist.com/opinion/displaystory.cfm?story_id=7830218, accessed 26 February 2010.

FENTON, NATALIE (Ed.) (2010) *New Media, Old News: journalism and democracy in the digital age*, London: Sage.

FRANKLIN, BOB (1997) *Newszak and News Media*, London: Arnold.

FRANKLIN, BOB (Ed.) (2006) *Local Journalism and Local Media: making the local news*, London: Routledge.

FRANKLIN, BOB (Ed.) (2008) *Pulling Newspapers Apart: analysing print journalism*, London: Routledge.

FRANKLIN, BOB (Ed.) (2009a) *The Future of Newspapers*, London: Routledge.

FRANKLIN, BOB (2009b) "A Viable Future for Local and Regional Newspapers? Economic, organisational and democratic considerations", paper presented to the Campaign for Press and Broadcasting Freedom Conference Media for All? The Challenge of Convergence, 31 October, http://www.cpbf.org.uk/page2/page2.html, accessed 21 February 2010.

FRANKLIN, BOB (2009c) "Editorial: on *Journalism Studies*' tenth anniversary", *Journalism Studies* 10(6), pp. 729–33.

FRANKLIN, BOB, LEWIS, JUSTIN and WILLIAMS, ANDREW (2010) "Journalism, News Sources and Public Relations", in: Stuart Allan (Ed.), *The Routledge Companion to News and Journalism*, London: Routledge, pp. 202–12.

FREEDLAND, JONATHAN (2010) "The BBC Is Caving in to a Tory Media Policy Dictated by Rupert Murdoch", *Guardian*, 3 March, p. 29.

GREENSLADE, ROY (2010) "Rupert Murdoch: Rusbridger is talking bullshit", Greenslade Blog guardian.co.uk, http://www.guardian.co.uk/media/greenslade/2010/feb/03/rupert-murdoch-rusbridger-bs, accessed 12 February 2010.

HAMILTON, JOHN MAXWELL and LAWRENCE, REGINA (forthcoming) "Introduction", Special Issue on Foreign Correspondence, *Journalism Studies*.

HARRISON, JACKIE (2010) "UGC and Gatekeeping at the BBC", *Journalism Studies* 11(2), pp. 243–56.

INSTITUTE FOR PUBLIC POLICY RESEARCH (IPPR) (2009) *Mind the Funding Gap: the potential of industry levies for continued funding of public service broadcasting*, London: Institute for Public Policy Research, http://www.google.co.uk/search?hl=en&q=IPPR+Levies+on+Sky+and+Virgin+&btnG=Search&meta=&aq=o&oq, accessed 24 February 2010.

JARVIS, JEFF (2007) "Newspapers in 2020", essay for the World Association of Newspapers, *BuzzMachine* weblog, September, http://www.buzzmachine.com/newspapers-in-2020/, accessed 5 March 2010.

MCCHESNEY, ROBERT W. and NICHOLS, JOHN (2010) *The Death and Life of American Journalism: the media revolution that will begin the world again*, Philadelphia: Nation Books.

MURDOCH, JAMES (2009) "The Absence of Trust", The James MacTaggart Annual Lecture at the Guardian/Edinburgh International Television festival, 28 August, http://www.google.co.uk/search?hl=en&source=hp&q=james+murdoch+mactaggart+lecture+transcript&meta=&aq=0&oq=James+Murdoch+MacTaggart+Lecture, accessed 22 February 2010.

NATIONAL UNION OF JOURNALISTS (NUJ) (2009) "Review of the Local and Regional Media Merger Regime", NUJ Response to Office of Fair Trading (OFT), 31 March, http://www.google.co.uk/search?hl=en&source=hp&q=NUJ+%282009%29+Review+of+the+Local+and+Regional+Media+Merger+Regime+NUJ+Response+to+OFT+March+31st.&btnG=Google+Search&meta=&aq=f&oq=, accessed 24 February 2010.

NICHOLS, JOHN and MCCHESNEY, ROBERT W. (2010) "How to Save Journalism", *The Nation*, 7 January, http://www.thenation.com/doc/20100125/nichols_mcchesney.

PICARD, BOB and GRÖNLUND, MIKKO (2003) "Development and Effects of Finnish Press Subsidies", *Journalism Studies* 4(1), pp. 105–19.

PRESTON, PETER (2009) "The Curse of Introversion", in: Bob Franklin (Ed.), *The Future of Newspapers*, London: Routledge, pp. 13–21.

PROJECT FOR EXCELLENCE IN JOURNALISM (2009) "State of the News Media 2009", http://www.stateofthenewsmedia.org/2009/index.htm, accessed 16 February 2010.

RAEYMAEKERS, KARIN, HAUTTEKEETE, LAURENCE and HOEBEKE, TIM (2009) "Newspapers in Education in Flanders: a press policy to support the future readership market for newspapers", in: Bob Franklin (Ed.), *The Future of Newspapers*, London: Routledge, pp. 290–302.

RUSBRIDGER, ALAN (2010) "Does Journalism Exist?", The Annual Hugh Cudlipp Lecture, 25 January, http://www.guardian.co.uk/media/2010/jan/25/cudlipp-lecture-alan-rusbridger, accessed 26 January 2010.

SHIRKY, CLAY (2009) "Newspapers and Thinking the Unthinkable", http://www.shirky.com/weblog/2009/03/newspapers-and-thinking-the-unthinkable/, accessed 22 February 2010.

SINGER, JANE B. (2006) "The Socially Responsible Existentialist: a normative emphasis for journalists in a new media environment", *Journalism Studies* 7(1), pp. 2–18.

SINGER, JANE B. (2010) "Quality Control: perceived effect of user-generated content on newsroom norms, values and routines", *Journalism Practice* 4(2), pp. 127–42.

STARKEY, GUY and CRISELL, ANDREW (2009) *Radio Journalism*, London: Sage.

STARR, PAUL (2009) "The End of the Press: democracy loses its best friend", *The New Republic*, 4 March, pp. 28–35.

TOYNBEE, POLLY (2009) "This Is An Emergency: act now or local news will die", *Guardian*, 24 March, http://www.guardian.co.uk/commentisfree/2009/mar/24/regional-newspapers-lay-offs, accessed 24 February 2010.

WASSERMAN, HERMAN (2009) "Attack of the Killer Newspapers", in: Bob Franklin (Ed.), *The Future of Newspapers*, London: Routledge, pp. 157–68.

WILLIAMS, ANDREW and FRANKLIN, BOB (2007) *Turning Around the Tanker: implementing Trinity Mirror's online strategy*, Cardiff: Cardiff University.

WILLIAMS, ANDREW, WARDLE, CLAIRE and WAHL-JORGENSEN, KARIN (forthcoming) "'Have They Got News for Us?': audience revolution or business as usual at the BBC?", *Journalism Practice* DOI: 10.1080/17512781003670031.

WILLIAMS, KEVIN (2010) *Read All About It! A history of the British newspaper*, London: Routledge.

WITSCHGE, TAMARA, FENTON, NATALIE and FREEDMAN, DES (2009) *Carnegie UK Inquiry into Civil Society and the Media UK and Ireland: media ownership*, London: Carnegie UK.

WORLD ASSOCIATION OF NEWSPAPERS (WAN) (2009) "Newspaper Circulation Grows Despite Economic Downturn", http://www.wan-press.org/article18148.html, accessed 16 February 2010.

Appendix A

FUTURE OF JOURNALISM CONFERENCE

School of Journalism, Media and Cultural Studies (JOMEC), Cardiff University, 9 and 10 September 2009

Paper Titles and Authors

Stuart Allan *(Bournemouth University, UK)*
    Blogging Science: Re-assessing the future(s) of science journalism
Klaus-Dieter Altmeppen *(Catholic University Eichstaett, Germany)*
    The Gradual Disappearance of Foreign News in German Television: Is there a future for either global, international, world or foreign news?
Peter Anderson and Paul Egglestone *(University of Central Lancashire, UK)*
    The Development of Effective Quality Measures Relevant to The Future Practice of BBC News Journalism Online
Jocelyne Arquembourg *(Insitut Francais de Presse, France)*
    Media and the Construction of Events?
Chris Atton *(Napier University, UK)*
    Activist Media as Mainstream Source: What can journalists learn from Indymedia?
Piet Bakker and Mervi Pantti *(University of Amsterdam, The Netherlands)*
    Beyond News: User-generated content on Dutch media websites

Kevin G. Barnhurst *(University of Illinois, USA)*
The Form of Reports on U.S. Newspaper Internet sites: An update

Mine Gencel Bek *(Ankara University, Turkey)*
Turkish Journalists and Ethical Self-reflexivity Through On-line Training?

Peter Berglez *(Örebro University, Sweden)*
Global Journalism: An emerging news style and an outline for a training programme

Annika Bergström *(University of Gothenburg, Sweden)*
The Scope of User Generated Content

Valérie-Anne Bleyen and Leo Van Hove *(Vrije Universiteit Brussel, Belgium)*
Western European Newspaper Sites Reconsider Their Monetising Strategies: A case of herd behaviour?

Henrik Bødker *(Aarhus University, Denmark)*
Media Events as Bundles of Cultural Conflicts Within Inter-journalistic Dialogues

Jon Bramley *(Thomson Reuters)*
The Future of National and International News Agencies in a World of Citizen Journalism

Bonnie Brennen and Erika dela Cerna *(Marquette University, USA)*
Journalism in Second Life

Harry Browne *(Dublin Institute of Technology, Ireland)*
The Promise and Threat of Foundation-funded Journalism: In the future, when a journalist has an idea for a big story, will she talk to an editor—or write a grant application?

Axel Bruns *(Queensland University of Technology, Australia)*
Citizen Journalism and Everyday Life: A case study of Germany's *myHeimat.de*

Carla Rodrigues Cardoso *(Universidade Lusófona (ECATI)/Centro de Investigação Média e Jornalismo (CIMJ), Portugal)*
The Future of Newsmagazines

Matt Carlson *(Saint Louis University, USA)*
Wither Anonymity? Journalism and unnamed sources in a changing media environment

Tendai Chari *(University of Venda for Science and Technology, South Africa)*
The Future of the Printed Newspaper in the Context of the Internet in Africa: The case of Zimbabwe

John Cokley and Angela Ranke *(University of Queensland, Australia)*
The Long Tail Evident in Journalism Employment Opportunities, but Students Unaware

Mihai Coman *(University of Bucharest, Romania)*
Journalistic Elites in Post-communist Romania: From the heroes of the revolution to the media moguls

James R. Compton and Paul Benedetti *(University of Western Ontario, Canada)*
Labour, New Media and the Institutional Restructuring of Journalism

Martin Conboy and John Steel *(University of Sheffield, UK)*
From "We" to "Me" Via Wii! The future of popular tabloid journalism

Irene Costera Meijer *(University of Amsterdam, The Netherlands)*
Journalism and the Quality of Life: The citizen's agenda for local media—a case study

Simon Cottle *(Cardiff University, UK)*
Journalism and Crises in the Global Age

Jerry Crawford and Barbara B. Hines *(University of Kansas and President, AEJMC/Howard University, USA)*

Creating Partnerships to Strengthen the Future of Media: The evolution of ACEJMC accredited journalism programs at historically black colleges and universities

Arnold S. de Beer *(Stellenbosch University, South Africa and Sheffield University, UK)*

News In and From the "Dark Continent": Global journalism, media regimes and Afro-pessimism

Jeroen De Keyser, Karin Raeymaeckers and Steve Paulussen *(University of Ghent, Belgium)*

Are Citizens Becoming Sources? A look into Flemish journalists' professional contacts

Sallyanne Duncan *(University of Strathclyde, UK)*

Digital Doorstepping and the Death Knock: Ethical issues surrounding the use of social networking sites in reporting personal tragedy

Elisabeth Eide *(University of Oslo, Norway)*

Transnational Media Events and National Responses: Foreign reporters' blogs and post-modern journalism

Ivar John Erdal *(Volda University College, Norway)*

Structural Enablements and Constraints in Digital News Production Systems

Huub Evers *(Fontys Hogeschool Journalistiek, The Netherlands)*

News Ombudsmen as Quality Watchdogs

Carol Fletcher *(Hofstra University, USA)*

Online Education in Journalism: Why are we lagging behind?

Unni From *(University of Aarhus, Denmark)*

Cultural and Lifestyle Journalism in Online and Print Newspapers from a Reader/User Perspective

Chris Frost *(Liverpool John Moores University, UK)*

The Development of Privacy Adjudications by the UK Press Complaints Commission (PCC) and Their Effect on the Future of Journalism

Peter Gade *(University of Oklahoma, USA)*

The Organizational Integration of News Media: Restructuring to increase collaboration and competitiveness

José Alberto García Avilés and Alberto Nahum García Martínez *(Universidad Miguel Hernández de Elche and Universidad de Navarra, Spain)*

New Screens . . . New Languages? Spanish broadcast news content in the Web

Mike Gasher *(Concordia University, Canada)*

Producing the On-line News Audience: A textual analysis of three UK daily newspapers

Cherian George *(Nanyang Technological University, Singapore)*

The Re-emergence of Asian Journalism's Radical Roots

Will Gore and John Horgan *(Press Complaints Commission, UK and Press Ombudsman, Ireland)*

The UK Press Complaints Commission and the Irish Press Ombudsman

Maria Grafström and Karolina Windell *(Uppsala University, Sweden)*

Blogs and Business Journalists: News production in transformation

Robert E. Gutsche *(University of Iowa, USA)*

Missing the Scoop: The story behind the development of college student journalists through early media experience

Adrian Hadland *(Democracy and Governance Research Programme, Human Sciences Research Council, South Africa)*

The Enemy Without: How democratic states will shape the future of journalism

Mark Hanna and Karen Sanders *(University of Sheffield, UK and University of San Pablo, Spain)*
Should Editors Prefer Postgraduates? A comparison of British undergraduate and postgraduate journalism students

Tony Harcup *(University of Sheffield, UK)*
Back to the Future? "Citizen journalism" and the 1984–5 UK miners' strike

Heikki Heikkilä, Risto Kunelius and Laura Ahva *(University of Tampere, Finland)*
From Credibility to Relevance: Towards a sociology of journalism's "added value"

Alfred Hermida *(University of British Columbia, Canada)*
"Twittering" the News: The emergence of ambient journalism

Stig Hjarvard *(University of Copenhagen, Denmark)*
"News You Can Use"—When audience research comes to influence journalists' conception of the public

Joran Hok *(Sodertorn University, Sweden)*
Fragile Public Service in Danger: Perspectives for journalism in Afghanistan

Jan Fredrik Hovden *(Volda University College and University of Bergen, Norway)*
The Genesis and Anatomy of Journalistic Taste: An analysis of the structure of the Norwegian journalistic field

Fatima el Issawi *(Journalist, Asharq al Awsat Arab newspaper and Research Associate, Open University, UK)*
The Arab Émigré Media and the Hosting Environment: A difficult cohabitation?

Susan Jacobson *(Temple University, USA)*
Emerging Models of Multimedia Journalism: A content analysis of multimedia packages published on nytimes.com

Jan Jirák and Barbara Köpplová *(Charles University, Prague, Czech Republic)*
Journalists in the Post-transition Period: Czech journalists and their perceptions of their professional roles

Laura Juntunen *(University of Helsinki, Finland)*
Explaining the Need for Speed: Increasing competition and new ethical dilemmas in journalism

Michael Karlsson *(Karlstad University, Sweden)*
"Rituals of transparency": Evaluating online news outlets' use of transparency rituals in the US, UK and Sweden

Susan Keith *(Ruttgers University, USA)*
Sinking Subs and Collapsing Copy Desks? The future of front-line editing at newspapers and their Web sites

Nete Nørgaard Kristensen *(University of Copenhagen, Denmark)*
Uncritical Cultural Journalism—or cultural journalism in change?

Samantha Lay and Deirdre O'Neill *(University of Salford and Leeds Trinity and All Saints College, UK)*
Informing the Regions or News by Numbers? A comparative analysis of regional television news outputs, its audiences and producers in the North and South of England

Geoff Lealand *(University of Waikato, New Zealand)*
Will Media Studies Be the Salvation of Journalism?

Lisa Lynch *(Concordia University, Canada)*
Dangerous Pranks or Digital Sunshine? Wikileaks and the future of investigative reporting

David Machin and Sarah Niblock *(Cardiff University, UK and Brunel University, UK)*
The New Breed of Business Journalism for Niche Global News: The case of Bloomberg
Peter H. Martyn *(Carlton University, Ottawa, Canada)*
Mojos, Platypuses and News Work: Multimedia reporters in the eye of an economic and technological storm
Klaus Meier *(Dortmund University, Germany)*
Transparency in Journalism: Credibility and trustworthiness in the digital future
Noha Mellor *(Kingston University, UK)*
Arab Journalists Define Their Role
Donica Mensing *(University of Nevada, Reno, USA)*
Rethinking the Future of Journalism Education
Sonja Merljak Zdovc *(University of Ljubljana, Slovenia)*
Journalists as Activists in Newspapers
Marcus Messner and Asriel Eford *(Virginia Commonwealth University, USA)*
Twittering the News: How U.S. traditional media adopt microblogging for their news dissemination
Dimitra L. Milioni *(Cyprus University of Technology, Cyprus)*
Protest News in the Mainstream Press and Alternative Online Media in Greece
Seamogano Mosanako *(University of Botswana, Botswana)*
Journalism Challenges and Opportunities in Botswana in the 21st Century
François P. Nel *(University of Central Lancashire, UK)*
Where Else Is the Money? A study of innovation in online business models at newspapers in Britain's 66 cities
Christoph Neuberger and Christian Nuernbergk *(Wilhelms-Universität Münster, Germany)*
Competition, Complementarity or Integration? The relationship between professional and participatory media
An Nguyen *(University of Stirling, UK)*
Citizen Journalism in Vietnam: New technology, democracy and the still powerful role of the nation-state in a globalised news environment
Hillel Nossek *(College of Management, Israel)*
Global Terrorism as a Case Study of Global Journalism and Global News
Gunnar Nygren *(Södertörn University, Sweden)*
Passing Through Journalism? Journalists leaving the union or the profession—why and in what direction?
K. Mandy Oakham and Renee Barnes *(RMIT University, Australia)*
Britney Spears Ate My Crocodile: An analysis of online content Down Under
Henrik Örnebring *(University of Oxford, UK)*
Newswork Across Europe: Some preliminary research findings
Rune Ottosen and Arne H. Krumsvik *(Oslo University College and University of Oslo, Norway)*
Digitalisation and Editorial Change in Norwegian Media: Findings from a Norwegian research project
Julian Petley *(Brunel University, UK)*
Rules and Filters: Nick Davies and the Propaganda Model
Angela Phillips *(Goldsmiths College, UK)*
Transparency and the New Ethics of journalism

Thomas Poell *(University of Amsterdam, The Netherlands)*
Activist Media and the Mainstream Press in Daily Practice: Covering protests in The Netherlands (2004–2009)

Colin Porlezza *(Università della Svizzera italiana, Switzerland)*
"Bridges Over the Chinese Wall": The consequences of advertising pressure on the journalistic content of free newspapers

Manuel Puppis *(University of Zurich, Switzerland)*
Self-regulation by European Press Councils: Structures, procedures and the management of legitimacy

Elena Raviola *(Jönköping International Business School, Sweden)*
Web Meets the Paper: Just about technologies and organization of newswork?

Zvi Reich *(Ben Gurion University of the Negev, Israel)*
The Journalistic Shield and Its Fissures: Studying source credibility in the context of newswork

Omar Rosas *(University of Namur, Belgium)*
Online Journalism and Computer Ethics: Disclosing value-sensitive issues in computer-mediated journalistic practices

Stephan Russ-Mohl *(Università della Svizzera italiana, Switzerland)*
Creative Destruction? In search for new business models: How quality journalism might survive the decline of newspapers

Anya Schiffrin *(Columbia University, USA)*
Journalism Training in Sub-Saharan Africa

Kim Christian Schrøder and Bent Steeg Larsen *(Roskilde University, Denmark and Manager, Politiken newspaper, Denmark)*
The Shifting Cross-media News Landscape: Challenges for journalism practice

Carol Schwalbe and Bill Silcock *(Arizona State University, USA)*
Toward a Theory of Visual Gatekeeping

Lynette Sheridan Burns *(University of Western Sydney, Australia)*
Journalism in the Era of Convergence

Jane B. Singer *(University of Central Lancashire, UK and University of Iowa, USA)*
Separation Within a Shared Space: Perceived effects of user-generated content on newsroom norms, values and routines

Elanie Steyn *(University of Oklahoma, USA)*
Changed Business Models and Trends in the Post-apartheid South African Media—Efforts towards effective and efficient media transformation

T.F.J. (Derik) Steyn *(Cameron University, Oklahoma, USA)*
How Business Trends and Developments Affect Media Organizations' Management Models and Practices

Lucinda Strahan *(RMIT University, Australia)*
Sources of Arts Journalism: Who's writing the arts pages?

Leslie-Jean Thornton *(Arizona State University, USA)*
The Changing Role of Internships as Newsrooms Shrink and Evolve

Rodney Tiffen *(University of Sydney, Australia)*
Changes in Australian Newspapers—1956–2006, and beyond

Debra Reddin van Tuyll *(Augusta State University, USA)*
The Past Is Prologue, or: How 19th century journalism might just save 21st century newspapers

Maria Isabel Villa Montoya and Rosa Franquet i Calvet *(Unversitat Autònoma de Barcelona, Spain)*
Spanish Evolution of Online Photojournalism

Marina Vujnovic, Jane B. Singer, Steve Paulussen, Ari Heinonen, Zvi Reich, Thorsten Quandt, Alfred Hermida and David Domingo *(Monmouth University, USA; University of Central Lancashire, UK/University of Iowa, USA; Ghent University, Belgium; University of Tampere, Finland; Ben Gurion University of the Negev, Israel; Free University of Berlin, Germany; University of British Columbia, Canada and Universitat Rovira i Virgili, Spain)*
Exploring the Political-economic Factors of Participatory Journalism: A first look into self-reports by online journalists and editors in ten countries

Claire Wardle, Andrew Williams and Karin Wahl-Jorgensen *(Cardiff University, UK)*
"UGC" @ the BBC: Audience revolution or business as usual?

Herman Wasserman *(University of Sheffield, UK)*
The Meanings of Freedom: On practising journalism in post-apartheid South Africa

Wendy Weinhold *(Southern Illinois University Carbondale, USA)*
Letters from the Editors: American newspapers, the Internet, and the future of journalism

Martin Welker *(Macromedia University of Applied Science, Munich, Germany)*
Frequency and Type of Online Sources in Quality Media: Does the Internet really matter?

Debora Wenger, Lynn C. Owens, Michael Charbonneau and Kristine Trever *(University of Mississippi, USA and Peace College, USA)*
Help Wanted: An examination of new media skills required by top U.S. news companies

Charlotte Wien and Christian Elmelund-Præstekær *(University of Southern Denmark, Denmark)*
Developing a Model for the Dynamics and Structure of Intense Media Coverage of Single Issues

Marion C. Wrenn *(New York University, USA)*
Making the World Safe for Autonomy? The US initiative to reorient "foreign journalists" 1945–1970

Xin Xin *(University of Westminster, UK)*
Web 2.0, Grassroots Journalism and Social Justice in China

Sally Young *(University of Melbourne, Australia)*
The "Crisis" in Journalism: Is Australia immune?

THE FUTURE OF JOURNALISM

James Curran

The passage of time has a way of throwing custard pies at those who predict the future.[1] This is particularly true in the hype-ridden world of the media. In the 1940s, the Hutchins Commission, an august body of public intellectuals, predicted that the facsimile newspaper delivered by wireless would rejuvenate the American press (Hutchins Commission, 1947). In the 1970s, citizen's band radio was said authoritatively to be "taking the US by storm", and was poised to recreate a sense of community.[2] In 1982, Britain's Technology Minister, Kenneth Baker, informed the Commons that cable television "will have more far-reaching effects on our society than the Industrial Revolution 200 years ago" (1982, p. 230). In the 1990s, American industry experts like Tom Laster said that the CD-Rom was going to spell the end of the book in schools.[3] And in the mid-1990s through to the mid-2000s, it was predicted repeatedly that red button TV interactivism was leading to a fundamental shift of power from the TV director to the consumer in the home (Curran, 2010).

All these forecasts proved to be hopelessly wrong. So, heeding past mistakes, I will not attempt to read the runes. Instead, I will leave it to the better informed—farsighted media controllers, canny journalists, visionary academics and others gifted with foresight—to foretell the future of journalism. To start with, I will merely summarise in ideal-typical form what they have to say.

Continuity

The main line adopted by the leaders of the news industry echoes Gloria Gaynor's song: "I Will Survive" in which she sings:

At first I was afraid, I was petrified.
Kept on thinking I could never live without you by my side...

But "we will survive", declare industry leaders, without mass advertising. The future of journalism, they proclaim, has been stabilised through good judgement and leadership. They point out that so-called "dead wood" news media were quick to set up satellite websites in order to cling on to audiences in the new environment. Traditional media also took action to reduce costs through redundancies, improved productivity and the integration of online and offline news rooms. Further adjustments, industry leaders warn, will be needed. This will include negotiating a better deal with content aggregators, and persuading regulatory authorities to accept increased cross-media concentration as a way of reducing costs.[4] Above all, argue some media controllers, charges will need to be imposed on news websites. Whether this takes the form of a monthly subscription, day entry fee, micro-payment per article, metered fee fixed in relation to the duration of the website visit, an unobtrusive element in a subscription TV package, or a loss-leader strategy in which some content remains free but a charge is levied for entering the inner sanctum of premium content, is something that will be determined through research and experiment. But rest assured, say industry leaders: an effective conservation strategy is in place to secure strong journalism across a range of platforms. The more difficult the situation becomes, the more reassuring are their public pronouncements in Britain.[5] Journalism is not in crisis, they insist, but merely undergoing a process of well-managed transition. In brief, *the future of journalism is safe in their hands.*

Crisis

This view is now being questioned by a growing number of their employees. A study in the United States found in 2007 that "financial woes now overshadow all other concerns for journalists" (Pew Project for Excellence in Journalism, 2008a). The migration of advertising to the Web, compounded by the 2008–9 recession, has led to a rising number of newspaper closures, and also contractions in news operations, giving rise to increasing alarm.

Thus, between January 2008 and September 2009, 106 local newspapers (mostly freesheets) closed down in Britain,[6] while in America significant newspapers like the *Christian Science Monitor* and *Seattle Post* ceased print publication. The principal commercial television channel in Britain, ITV, is seeking to disengage from regional and local news reporting, while a growing number of local TV channels in the United States have stopped originating local news (Downie and Schudson, 2009).

The rise of the Internet has also led to the haemorrhaging of paid jobs in journalism. The Pew Research Center estimates that in 2008 "nearly one out of every five journalists working for newspapers in 2001 is now gone" in the United States (Pew Project for Excellence in Journalism, 2009a). In Britain, a major regional chain, Trinity Mirror, reduced its staff by 1200 in 2008–9 (Tryhorn, 2009); ITV cut around 1000 jobs during the same period; and Northcliffe Media set a target of shedding 1000 local press jobs in 2009 (McNally, 2009).

Closures and redundancies are undermining, it is argued, the quality of journalism. "Local and national democracy is suffering", warns Jeremy Dear, General Secretary of the [British] National of Journalists. "Councils, courts and public bodies are no longer being scrutinised" (Dear, 2009). This view is presented with ironic force in a Martin Rowson pastiche of the famous, Tenniel "Dropping the pilot" cartoon (about the sacking of Chancellor Otto von Bismarck).[7] In the Rowson version, the marine pilot stepping off the ship is the "Reporter" with the blindfolded figure of "Public Understanding", in front of him, stumbling into the sea. On the ship, an accountant is absorbed in a balance sheet, a bearded journalist gazes at Google on his computer, and a manic member of the public photographs with his mobile phone the departing "Reporter". In the sea, a forlorn "Citizen Journalist" clings to a life-buoy, with a shark circling nearby. The Rowson cartoon encapsulates a widespread view among journalists: *the current crisis of journalism is weakening public understanding, and poses a threat to democracy.*

Purgative

This view is challenged by radical millenarians, who regard the mounting financial problems of the press and the sacking of journalists as a cleansing purgative. The thought that the crisis of journalism could be terminal fills them with joy. As the radical American press historian, John Nerone, comments gleefully: "the biggest thing to lament about the death of the old order [of journalism] is that it is not there for us to piss on any more" (2009, p. 355).

In a similar vein, the radical environmentalist, George Monbiot (2009), refuses to shed even crocodile tears over newspaper closures. "For many years", he writes, "the local press has been one of Britain's most potent threats to democracy, championing the overdog, misrepresenting democratic choices, defending business, the police and local elites from those who seek to challenge them". There are, he suggests, a handful of decent local newspapers. But in general, "this lot just aren't worth saving" because they "do more harm than good".

Millenarians see the crisis of traditional journalism as an opportunity. It is supposedly creating openings for progressive initiatives that were effectively blocked when leading media conglomerates had a market stranglehold. In the hopeful words of John Nerone (2009, p. 355), "journalism will find its future when it finds its audience, and that audience will be many hued, sexually diverse, and composed mostly of workers". In short, this view can be summarised as: *things will get better because they are getting worse.*

Renaissance

The claim that journalism is mired in a deep crisis is challenged by a fourth interpretation, mostly advanced by liberal journalism educators, that proclaims the advent of a news media renaissance. Their case is built on three central arguments.

First, the Internet is said to be enriching the quality of old media journalism. Journalists now have instant access to a rich store of public and other information, and can incorporate more readily a range of different news sources. As a consequence, it is claimed, old news media are better able to verify stories, and to offer a wider range of views and insights.

Second, the Internet is bringing into being, it is argued, an efflorescence of Web-based journalism, which is compensating for the decline of traditional news media. In this view, the old order of monopoly journalism was a "desert of Macworld" (Johnson, 2009). This desert is now being reclaimed by a legion of bloggers, contributions from citizen journalists, and proliferating Web-based start-ups. This reclamation is now unstoppable, and will continue to expand. As Steven Berlin Johnson (2009) puts it, "there is going to be more content, not less; more information, more analysis, more precision, a wider range of niches covered".

Third, the two worlds of old and new journalism, it is predicted, will come together in a protean synergy. The crisis of the traditional *economic* model of journalism will give rise to a new *social* model based on a pro-am (that is, professional–amateur) partnership. This will take the form of "network journalism" in which members of the public draft, research or produce stories. In some cases, volunteer journalists will produce their own websites; in others, they will constitute a diverse feed chain, with professionals at the centre. The key to understanding the future, in this view, is to substitute the word *journalism* (with its association of vertical, gatekeeper institutions) with the phrase *journalistic activity*, based on open-ended, reciprocal, horizontal, collaborative, self-generating, extensive, and inclusive (the same buzz words keep being repeated) reporting and comment of a kind never experienced before.[8] Universities have allegedly a vital role to play in advancing this revolution. "Media studies", solemnly proclaims one academic, "must become a Networked Journalism thought leadership program" (Beckett, 2008, p. 170).

All these developments constitute allegedly a paradigm shift. Thus, Yochai Benkler ((2008), cited in McChesney and Nichols, 2010, p. 77) argues that we are shifting from a monopolistic "industrial model of journalism" to a pluralistic "networked model" based on profit and non-profit, individual and organised journalistic practices. Similarly, Guido Fawkes argues, in a more unguarded fashion, that "the days of media conglomerates determining the news in a top-down Fordist fashion are over ... Big media are going to be disintermediated because the technology has drastically reduced the cost of dissemination" (Fawkes, cited in Beckett, 2008, p. 108). In this last view, the cuts and closures taking place in traditional news media are merely the necessary price to be paid for shifting from a top-down to a bottom-up form of journalism.

This approach thus argues that the Internet is extending participation, connecting new voices to a general public, and reconstituting the organisation and practice of journalism. Its message is vastly reassuring: *the crisis is leading to the re-invention of journalism in a better form*.

What are we to make of this baffling difference of opinion? Millenarians declare that a journalism Armageddon is upon us; yet, media controllers say that there is no crisis. Anguished journalists warn that standards are plummeting; yet, liberal journalism educators proclaim the advent of a journalistic renaissance. Even this survey, geographically limited though it is, shows that there is no underlying agreement about the seriousness of the difficulties faced by old news media, still less a shared understanding about whether the future of journalism is rosy or bleak.

Perhaps, the best way to grope a way through these contradictions is to evaluate critically each position in turn.

Ostrich-like Denial

Media controllers are mistaken in thinking that they are in control of events, and that the future of journalism is safe in their hands. Their opening gambit of building *free* news websites attracted in some cases a substantial number of visitors, and led to some notable journalistic achievements. But these satellite websites failed to garner sufficient advertising to be financially self-sufficient. Indeed, American newspapers derive, on average, no more than 10 per cent of their total revenue from their loss-making websites (Pew Project for Excellence in Journalism, 2009a). The planned, selective moves towards charging for Web content in 2010/2011 are a response to this problem. Indeed, they are a tacit recognition that the initial free website strategy has failed in commercial terms. However, erecting paywalls offers no ready solution. It is likely to reduce greatly the number of visitors, and associated advertising, because people expect Web content to be free. In the case of national news websites, many users will be able to access free alternatives, and will do so rather than pay.

The managerial dilemma about whether to charge for online content is a response to a much bigger problem for traditional media. The Internet took off as a mass medium in the 2000s, in much the way that television had done in the 1950s. Thus, in Britain, home Internet access soared from 14 to 65 per cent of households between 1999 and 2008 (Curran and Seaton, 2010). Similar increases took place in other affluent countries during the same period.

How this affected audience demand for traditional news media is difficult to determine on the basis of current evidence. Demand for news in old media among the young in the United States seems to have declined (Patterson, 2007). However, audiences for television news remained resilient in some north European countries between 1997 and 2007 (Aalberg et al., 2010). There are also enormous divergences in newspaper circulation trends during this period, with most countries registering a decline but some a rise (Benson, 2010). However, what seems to have happened in most affluent western countries is that there was a *gradual*, and uneven, decrease of consumption of newspapers and television news coinciding with the popular rise of the Internet.

But in contrast to this modest decrease, there was a very pronounced redistribution of advertising. After a slow beginning, the Internet's share of total media advertising soared in western countries between 1999 and 2009, while that of television and the press fell precipitately.[9] Indeed, advertising expenditure on the Internet overtook that on television in Denmark in 2008, followed by Britain in January to June 2009 (Internet Advertising Bureau, 2009).

Old news media, in economically advanced countries, are thus confronted by a formidable, new rival for advertising. The Internet is cheap, and reaches a large audience. It is especially good at targeting consumers with a predisposition to buy (which is why "search advertising" has become the biggest category of Internet advertising in Britain, the United States and elsewhere). The Internet has already scooped a large proportion of press classified advertising. Thus, in Britain, between 2000 and 2008, the Internet's share of classified advertising expenditure soared from 2 to 45 per cent, while that of the local and regional press declined from 47 to 26 per cent, and that of national papers from 14 to 6 per cent (Office of Fair Trading, 2009). The Internet is now encroaching rapidly on television and popular newspaper display advertising, despite its reliance on crude banner ads.

It is difficult to predict media advertising trends because the 2008–9 crash makes it especially difficult to distinguish between structural and cyclical shifts of expenditure. The resumption of strong growth will revive advertising across all media. Even so, it is very likely that Internet advertising will continue to grow, in the medium term, at the expense of old media because home Internet access will continue to rise.

Indeed, what is especially ominous for the future of journalism is that some advertising has shifted not from traditional news media to their satellite news websites, but has leapfrogged instead to other parts of the Web which have nothing to do with journalism. In particular, local newspaper classified advertising has been partly redirected to advertising-only websites, like craigslist and net.lettings.co.uk. Advertising, in other words, is beginning to be decoupled from news production: the total subsidy for journalism, both online and offline, is declining.

In brief, the tide is flowing inexorably from an old media towards the Internet, with a force that media managements cannot control.

Millenarian Wish Fulfilment

However, old media are not faced by an apocalypse. This is wishful thinking by foes of established media organisations, hankering for the equivalent of divine retribution. The position of old news organisations is weakening: their audience share is less in the digital age than in the analogue era, and their advertising support is declining. However, traditional news media are not lame ducks. Survey research in Norway, Sweden, Britain and the United States confirms that television, not the Internet, is still the dominant source of news (Aalberg et al., 2010; Office of Communications, 2007; Pew Project for Excellence in Journalism, 2008b).[10]

Furthermore, leading news organisations have succeeded in colonising part of cyberspace. To understand what has happened it is useful to distinguish between general and news websites. In the general Nielsen Web ratings, old media organisations are generally absent from the top rankings. In Britain, for example, only one traditional media organisation (BBC) featured in the top 10 most visited websites in early 2009.[11] This reflected the ascendancy of search engines, social websites and shopping sites on the Web (and, more generally, the entertainment orientation of most Web-users). However, identification of the 10 most visited *news* websites in Britain reveals a very different picture. Two leading TV organisations (BBC News and Fox News), and five leading newspapers (*Guardian, Telegraph, Mail, Times* and *Sun*), accounted in 2008 for seven out of the 10 top UK news websites (with the remaining three being aggregators (UK MSN, Yahoo! News and Google News).[12] In the United States, the situation is broadly similar. Eight of the 10 *news* websites with the most unique visitors in 2008 were traditional news media (five leading TV organisations and three leading newspaper organisations): their top spot was shared only with Yahoo and AOL (Pew Project for Excellence in Journalism, 2009a).

Thus, the dominant news brands are still overwhelmingly dominant across technologies. What is not in immediate prospect is the reduction of established news media organisations to rubble on ground zero, creating a space in which progressive green shoots will rise up and take over. Dominant news organisations will decline, as audiences and advertisers decrease, leading to a falling off of investment and quality. But gradual degeneration is not the same as apocalyptic death and renewal—the millenarian fantasy.

A journalism Armageddon is not nigh: sandwich boards can be put away.

Renaissance Dreams

But if a Schumpeterian purge is not in prospect, perhaps a rebirth of journalism, as foretold by liberal journalism educators, is about to happen. This is so much to be desired that it would be good if it were true. But while there are some swallows on the horizon, these do not yet constitute a Spring.

The hope that the Internet is reinvigorating old media journalism may be realised in some places. But a recent study by the Goldsmiths Leverhulme Media Research Centre found that British journalists are under strong pressure to produce more, in less time, as a consequence of newsroom redundancies, the extension of news platforms, and the need to update stories in a 24-our news cycle. This is fostering "creative cannibalistion", the mutual lifting of stories from rivals' websites. It is also encouraging journalists to rely more on a restricted pool of tried-and-tested news sources as a way of generating increased output. And in general, it is giving rise to a more office-bound, routine, and scissors-and-paste form of journalism. While in principle the Internet should be encouraging greater editorial diversity and more extensive use of grassroots sources by leading news media, in practice it seems to be having the opposite effect in Britain (Fenton, 2010).

But at least a hopeful finger can be pointed to the way in which the Web has encouraged journalistic activity outside these news rooms. The growth of blogs has introduced new voices that hold mainstream media to account. Thus, in the much-cited Trent Lott saga, an indignant blogosphere shamed in 2002 leading American journalists into reassessing a news event—a speech given at a birthday party in which a leading politician, Senator Trent Lott, referred nostalgically to the racial-segregation politics of the past. Although this was largely ignored by the elite press corps at the time, growing protests from bloggers caused prominent news media to give belated coverage to Senator Lott's comments as well as to similar statements he had made previously. In the ensuing row, Lott was forced to stand down as the Senate majority leader. It marked the moment when bloggers became a journalistic and political force in the United States (Scott, 2004).

The Internet has also helped to facilitate new journalism at different levels. At an individual level, major international stories were broken or given additional impetus by bystanders who caught on camera the killing of Nada Soltan and Ian Tomlinson in demonstrations in Tehran and London, in 2009. At a local level, the *VoiceofSanDiego.org*, a website launched in 2005 and still operating in 2009 with 12 full-time staff, is said to have undertaken serious investigative journalism of the kind that *San Diego Tribune*, the established local paper, tends not to do (Pew Project for Excellence in Journalism, 2009c; Smillie, 2009). At a national level, the website, *Politico* (with a weekly print edition) demonstrates that Web journalists report as well as comment on the news. Among other things, it revealed in 2008 that vice-presidential candidate, Sarah Palin—viewed at the time as a typical ice-hockey mum—had spent $75,062 on just one shopping spree, and had a $150,000 wardrobe budget donated by the Republican National Committee (Cummings, 2008). And at an international level, the notable e-zine, *openDemocracy*, mediated a debate about the September 11 attacks, bringing different parts of the globe (including the Islamic Middle East) into dialogue with each other (Curran and Witschge, 2010).

But all these developments need to be put into perspective. The Web has not connected bloggers to a mass audience. In Britain 79 per cent of *Internet users* in 2008 had not read a blog during the last three months (Office of National Statistics, 2008). To judge from an American study, citizen news sites are relatively rare, and precarious (Pew Project for Excellence in Journalism, 2009c). While the Web has provided a low-cost springboard for some significant new publications, these are mostly niche publications with relatively small audiences. Thus, the much-cited *VoiceofSanDiego.org* attracted, in 2008, a modest audience of 70–80,000 unique visitors a month (Pew Project for Excellence in Journalism, 2009b). Even the handful of new website start-ups in the United States that have made a breakthrough, notably the *HuffingtonPost*, *Politico* and *Real Clean Politics*, each still obtained in 2008 less than one-seventh of the visits to popular news websites like those of MSNBC and CNN (Pew Project for Excellence in Journalism, 2009a).

There has been also a tendency to mythologise the role of the Web in "mainstreaming" minority journalism. A recent British study found that "no alternative news sites were returned in the first page of search results" for all five sample news issues on either Google or Yahoo (Redden and Witschge, 2010).[13] These aggregators in fact tended to privilege the best known news providers, reproducing their ascendancy. More generally, social network sites tend to respond to the news agendas set by dominant media (Redden and Witschge, 2010).

But perhaps the single most important point to underline is that new Web ventures are no more successful—indeed they are greatly less successful—in attracting advertising than established media. Bloggers in Britain are mostly hobbyists, dependent on their day job (Couldry, 2010). A 2009 Pew Research Center study found in relation to new, Web-based journalistic ventures in the United States that "despite enthusiasm and good work, few if any of these are profitable or even self-financing" (Pew Project for Excellence in Journalism, 2009a). Similarly, a 2009 *Columbia Journalism Review* study concluded that "it is unlikely that any but the smallest of these [Web-based] news organisations can be supported primarily by existing online revenue" (Downie and Schudson, 2009). The absence of a strong online revenue stream—whether in the form of donation, subscription and advertising—means that the future growth of independent Web-based journalism will be retarded, unless steps are taken to change this.

In brief, the Web cavalry riding to the rescue is too small and without sufficient firepower to offset the decline of traditional journalism.

Fog of Misunderstanding

Are, then, journalists' representatives right to argue that the growing crisis of journalism is undermining public understanding? The trouble with this argument is that journalism can sometimes foster public *misunderstanding*.

Commercial news organisations are under strong pressure, in a competitive news environment, to adopt three tried and tested ways of winning, and retaining, attention. These three methods are making audiences amused, angry or afraid, and can result in exaggeration or distortion. For example, a methodologically weak academic paper, based on 12 non-randomly selected children, published in 1998 suggesting there may be an association between the triple MMR vaccine and the onset of autism, became the launch pad for a long-running newspaper campaign, led by two leading British tabloid papers (*Sun* and *Daily Mail*). They warned that the triple vaccine was hazardous, even though this was refuted by extensive research conducted in four continents. Tabloid warnings caused the number of children receiving the triple vaccine to fall sharply between 1998 until 2004; and even though take-up of the MMR jab partly recovered subsequently, it was still in 2008–9 below the pre-scare level. The incidence of measles rose sharply, and was still increasing in 2009 due to reduced collective immunity. The tabloid campaign revived an avoidable disease (contributing to one death in 2005) (Boyce, 2007; Curran and Seaton, 2010; Triggle, 2010). However, it did sell a lot of newspapers.

Another cause of misinformation is that journalists have to work to short deadlines, and often write about subjects in which they are not expert. When authoritative news sources are agreed, yet mistaken, this can lead inadvertently to the propagation of error. Thus, the Bush administration's declaration in 2002–3 that Saddam Hussein had weapons of mass destruction was accepted by the leaders of the opposition Democratic Party, endorsed by the Pentagon, and supported by Iraqi exiles. It resulted in most American news media failing to scrutinise critically this spurious claim in the run-up to the 2003 Iraq War. A belief, once lodged in the public imagination, proved difficult to dislodge. More than one year after the invasion, in August 2004, 35 per cent of Americans thought that weapons of mass destruction had in fact been found in Iraq, even though official agencies had publicly admitted that this was not the case (Castells, 2009, p. 166).

The claim that the crisis of journalism poses a threat to public understanding thus overlooks occasions when journalists can contribute to a fog of misunderstanding. At some level, it is necessary therefore to go beyond just applauding journalistic activity in general as an aid to public enlightenment, and make some qualitative distinctions (at least at the level of analysis).

Public Reformism

Thus, all four prominent positions that have been considered—predicting the continuity, Armageddon, and renaissance of news media, and this last uncritical equation of journalism with enlightenment—all have defects. However, there is waiting in the wings a compelling alternative, which I will call public reformism.

Public reformism seeks to change the future through concerted action. In the past, this has led to the adoption of a variety of different ways of enhancing the democratic performance of the media. This has ranged from the American strategy of promoting a public interest culture among professional journalists, the public ownership and funding of leading broadcasting organisations in numerous democratic countries from Japan to Canada, legislation imposing public service objectives on commercial broadcasters (well entrenched in northern Europe), the Scandinavian policy of subsidising minority news-papers, through to experiments in community, mutual, worker and public trust media ownership (Curran, 2002, and forthcoming).

In this instance, the reformist approach is reluctant to allow advertisers' calculations of promotional efficiency to reconfigure the news system without any reference to the wider public good. In response to rising newspaper closures and journalist redundancies, it advocates public action to support independent news production.

The current crisis of journalism is especially acute in market-based news systems because its principal cause is a redistribution of a market subsidy. This has given rise to a flurry of reform proposals, best illustrated by two recent American reports. They come from different ideological homes, and in part advocate different things. The radical report (McChesney and Nichols, 2009) advocates a massive intervention costing some $35 billion, whereas the liberal report (Downie and Schudson, 2009) proposes a modest set of measures. Thus, the radical report proposes wide-ranging direct and indirect subsidies for news media, including paying half the capped salaries of journalists in post-corporate newspapers, a graduated postal subsidy, and financial support for high school journalism and rookie trainees. By contrast, the liberal report advocates a more voluntaristic approach, urging universities to play a more active role as centres of community media, charitable foundations to give more money to journalism, and for donations to journalism to be encouraged by expanding the legal definition of journalism ventures eligible for tax-deductible gifts.

But both reports also have some things in common. They stress that public media intervention is not un-American in terms of what has happened in the past; display innate fear and distrust of the American democratic state; and emphasise that public support for news media will not lead to political control. Both call for the enhanced funding and more local orientation of public radio and television (though whether this will have a profound impact may be questioned, given that the United States' emasculated public television (PBS) has less than 2 per cent share of viewing time). They also have at their core a funding proposal that, despite a big difference in the money involved, is not fundamentally dissimilar. The radical report proposes that every American adult gets an annual $200 voucher to donate to a news medium (or media) of her choice, providing that it passes a modest threshold of audience demand, takes the form of a non-profit or low-profit venture uncompromised by non-media interests, and makes its content freely available on the Web. The liberal alternative proposes a National Fund for Local News, which would provide grants for "advances in local news reporting and innovative ways to support it" in both commercial and not-for-profit media (Downie and Schudson, 2009, p. 27). Both reports also share common ground in that they seek to recycle money from the communications industries and their users to support journalism. The mechanisms for doing this, mooted in the two reports, are a levy on telecom users, a charge on TV and radio licences, a tax on broadcast spectrum or its sale, a surcharge on Internet service providers, a tax on consumer communication electronic durables or an advertising tax.

Journalism in countries where publicly funded broadcasters are strong has a less serious crisis than that in the United States, and calls for a different response. One battle, largely won in Europe, is to resist commercial media lobbies seeking to prevent public broadcasters from developing an online presence. The Web is a new terrain where public broadcasters can renew their public service mandate through journalistic innovation. To do this, they need to be adequately funded. This happened in the case of the BBC which developed a good website, attracting in early 2009 an average of 21 million unique visitors a week—vastly more than any other media organisation in Britain.[14] However, this public space needs to be defended from future encroachments. Commercial rivals are now clamouring for the BBC's budget to be cut on the grounds that the corporation is "too big": similarly, commercial media in Austria are arguing that the website of the public broadcaster should be restricted to programme-related content (as a way of limiting its attraction).[15]

The next step is to develop competition between public websites, and encourage differentiation between them. In Britain, this should take the form of using some of the proceeds of the 2012 digital switchover to fund an effective Channel 4 news website. It should be given the brief to foster pro-am partnerships and other forms of journalistic innovation; to cater for minorities; and to facilitate a journalistic dialogue between nations. Pew Research indicates that a number of large-scale pro-am experiments have been failures in the United States (Pew Project for Excellence in Journalism, 2009b). However, amateur participation is perhaps more easy to graft on to a European interpretive tradition of journalism than on the US professional, fact-oriented one. A large number of talented volunteers were mobilised in the Mass Observation surveys, when domestic anthropology was pioneered in Britain (Stanton, 2006). There is no reason to assume that this cannot be done again in relation to pioneer, popular online journalism. Without public support, global online journalism will also struggle and fail to fulfil the potential of Internet technology (Curran and Witschge, 2010).

The third initiative should focus on supporting green shoots of Web-based journalism. In Britain, this would perhaps best be organised as a Fund for Independent Journalism, financed by a broadband tax, which would provide grants for low-cost, Web-based journalistic initiatives that fill a demonstrable need and have a reasonable prospect of success. The grant-giving body would include all-party and civic society representation, ensuring a diversity of viewpoints and backgrounds. Without financial pump-priming, the potential of the Internet to sustain a rebirth of journalism will not be realised.

Different reformist proposals should be tailored to the needs of different media systems, and to what is possible within different political cultures. But whichever path is followed, one thing is perhaps worth reiterating. It is not enough to predict passively the future of journalism, and debate between contrasting Doomsday and Micawberish versions. Instead, we should seek actively to shape the future in order to have a better outcome.

NOTES

1. This is a modified and extended version of a plenary address given to the Future of Journalism Conference, Cardiff School of Journalism, in 2009.
2. See, for example, *US News and World Report*, 29 September 1975; *Washington Post*, 5 June 1978.
3. Reported in the *Boston Globe*, 7 November 1993.
4. For example, British media companies made this argument to the Office of Fair Trading (2009), only for it to be rejected.
5. See, for instance, Preston (2009), among many others.
6. Information supplied by the Newspaper Society.
7. One of a series of wonderful Rowson covers, it was commissioned by Routledge for the cover of Curran and Seaton (2010).
8. A substantial number of articles in "The Future of Journalism" special issue of *Journalism*, 10(3), 2009 veer towards the position, prompting me to label it the "liberal educator" approach.
9. See the reports of the Internet Advertising Bureau (United States) and (United Kingdom), IREP (France), and Interactive Advertising Bureau of Canada, among others.
10. The Pew figure for the United States is higher partly because respondents are able to cite more than one primary news source in its survey.
11. Nielsen NetRatings Website Ranking, January 2009. My thanks to David Cowling (BBC) for supplying this information.
12. "Reach and percentage growth for UK News websites" (table derived from Nielsen, September 2008), *BBC News Online: 2008's highlights*. My thanks again to David Cowling.
13. This matters because most Internet users in Europe and the United States do not go beyond the first page (Jansen and Spink, 2005, 2006).
14. See Note 11.
15. Information derived from Ina Zwerger at the Osterreichischer Rundfunk.

REFERENCES

ALBERG, TORIL, AELST, PETER VAN and CURRAN, JAMES (2010) "Media Systems and the Political Information Environment: a cross-national comparison", *International Journal of Press/ Politics* 15.

BAKER, KENNETH (1982) "Satellite and Cable Broadcasting Debate", *Parliamentary Debates*, 6th series, 22, London: Hansard.

BECKETT, CHARLIE (2008) *Supermedia*, Oxford: Blackwell.

BENSON, RODNEY (2010) "Future of the News: international considerations and future reflections", in: Natalie Fenton (Ed.), *New Media, Old News*, London: Sage.

BOYCE, TAMMY (2007) *Health, Risk and News*, New York: Lang.

CASTELLS, MANUEL (2009) *Communication Power*, Oxford: Oxford University Press.

COULDRY, NICK (2010) "New Online Sources and Writer-gatherers", in: Natalie Fenton (Ed.), *New Media, Old News*, London: Sage.

CUMMINGS, JEANNE (2008) "RNC Shells Out $150K for Palin Fashion", *Politico*, 21 October, http://www.politico.com/news/stories/1008/14805.html, accessed 19 December 2009.

CURRAN, JAMES (2002) *Media and Power*, London: Routledge.

CURRAN, JAMES (2010) "Technology Foretold", in: Natalie Fenton (Ed.), *New Media, Old News*, London: Sage.

CURRAN, JAMES (forthcoming) *Media and Democracy*, London: Routledge.

CURRAN, JAMES and SEATON, JEAN (2010) *Power Without Responsibility*, 7th edn, London: Routledge.

CURRAN, JAMES and WITSCHGE, TAMARA (2010) "Liberal Dreams and the Internet", in: Natalie Fenton (Ed.), *New Media, Old News*, London: Sage.

DEAR, JEREMY (2009) "The Media Are Failing Democracy. Politicians are failing the media", paper presented to the Media for All? The Challenge of Convergence Conference, Campaign for Press and Broadcasting Freedom, 31 October, http://www.cpbf.org.uk/index_conf.html, accessed 21 December 2009.

DOWNIE, LEONARD and SCHUDSON, MICHAEL (2010) "The Reconstruction of American Journalism", *Columbia Journalism Review*, http://www.cjr.org/reconstruction/the_reconstruction_of_american.php, accessed 10 January 2010.

FENTON, NATALIE (Ed.) (2010) *New Media, Old News*, London: Sage.

HUTCHINS COMMISSION (1947) *A Free and Responsible Press*, Chicago: University of Chicago Press.

INTERNET ADVERTISING BUREAU (2009) *Fact Sheet: online adspend—H1 2009*, London: Internet Advertising Bureau.

JANSEN, BERNARD and SPINK, AMANDA (2005) "An Analysis of Web Searching by European AlltheWeb.com users", *Information Processing Management* 41(2), pp. 361–91.

JANSEN, BERNARD and SPINK, AMANDA (2006) "How Are We Searching the World Wide Web? A comparison of nine search engine transaction logs", *Information Processing Management* 42(1), pp. 248–63.

JOHNSON, STEVEN BERLIN (2009) "Old Growth Media and the Future of News", http://www.stevenberlinjohnson.com/2009/03/the-following-is-a-speech-i-gave-yesterday-at-the-south-by-southwest-interactive-festival-in-austiniif-you-happened-to-being.html, accessed 4 February 2009.

MCCHESNEY, ROBERT and NICHOLS, JOHN (2010) *The Death and Life of American Journalism*, New York: Nation Books.

MCNALLY, PAUL (2009) "Northcliffe Takes Job Cut Target to 1,000 as Revenue Falls", *Press Gazette*, 23 March.

MONBIOT, GEORGE (2009) "I, Too, Mourn Good Local Newspapers. But this lot just aren''t worth saving", *Guardian*, 9 November, http://www.guardian.co.uk/commentisfree/2009/nov/09/local-newspapers-democracy, accessed 14 December 2009.

NERONE, JOHN (2009) "The Death and Rebirth of Working-class Journalism", *Journalism* 10(3), pp. 350–5.

OFFICE OF COMMUNICATIONS (OFCOM) (2007) *New News, Future News*, London: Ofcom.

OFFICE OF FAIR TRADING (2009) *Review of the Local and Regional Media Merger Regime*, http://www.oft.gov.uk/news/press/2009/71-09, accessed 23 December 2009.

OFFICE OF NATIONAL STATISTICS (2008) *Internet Access 2008: households and individuals*, London: Office of National Statistics.

PATTERSON, TOM (2007) "Young People and News", Joan Shorenstein Center on the Press, Politics and Public Policy Report, Harvard University.

PEW PROJECT FOR EXCELLENCE IN JOURNALISM (2008a) "Financial Woes Now Overshadow all Other Concerns for Journalists", Pew Charitable Trust Report, 17 March, http://www.pewtrusts.org/our_work_report_detail.aspx?id=36600, accessed 7 January 2009.

PEW PROJECT FOR EXCELLENCE IN JOURNALISM (2008b) "Internet Overtakes Newspapers as News Outlet", Pew Research Center, 23 December, http://people-press.org/report/479/internet-overtakes-newspapers-as-news-source, accessed 1 December 2009.

PEW PROJECT FOR EXCELLENCE IN JOURNALISM (2009a) *State of the News Media 2009*, Pew Research Center, 16 March, http://www.stateofthemedia.org/2009/narrative_overview_intro.php?cat=0&media=1, accessed 10 December 2009.

PEW PROJECT FOR EXCELLENCE IN JOURNALISM (2009b) *Special Report: new ventures*, Pew Research Center, http://www.stateofthemedia.org/2009/narrative_special_newventures.php?media=12&cat=2, accessed 21 December 2009.

PEW PROJECT FOR EXCELLENCE IN JOURNALISM (2009c) *Special Report: citizen-based media*, Pew Research Center, http://www.stateofthemedia.org/2009/narrative_special_citzenbasedmedia.php?media=12&cat=0, accessed 28 December 2009.

PRESTON, PETER (2009) "Reasons to Be Cheerful, Part 1: recession didn't stop the press", *Observer*, 27 December.

REDDEN, JOANNA and WITSCHGE, TAMARA (2010) "A New News Order? Online News Content Examined", in: Natalie Fenton (Ed.), *New Media, Old News*, London: Sage.

SCOTT, ESTHER (2004) "'Big Media' Meets the 'Bloggers': coverage of Trent Lott's remarks at Strom Thurmond's birthday party", Kennedy School of Government case program, Harvard University, www.ksgcase.harvard.edu, accessed 2004.

SMILLIE, DIRK (2009) "San Diego News Shoot-out", *Forbes.com*, 6 August 2009. http://www.forbes.com/2009/06/05/internet-advertising-newspapers-business-media-san-diego.html, accessed 21 December 2009.

STANTON, GARETH (2006) "Peckham Tales: Mass Observation and the modalities of community", in: James Curran and David Morley (Eds), *Media and Cultural Theory*, London: Routledge.

TRIGGLE, NICK (2010) "MMR Scare Doctor 'Acted Unethically', Panel Finds", *BBC Online News*, 20 January, http://news.bbc.co.uk/1/hi/health/8483865.stm, accessed 20 January 2010.

TRYHORN, CHRIS (2009) "Trinity Mirror Sheds 1,200 Jobs in 14 Months", *Guardian*, 26 February.

THE FUTURE OF JOURNALISM AND CHALLENGES FOR MEDIA DEVELOPMENT
Are we exporting a model that no longer works at home?

Bettina Peters

Large parts of media development work have focused on providing support to create privately owned, independent media in transition and developing countries. The accepted logic of many donor organisations has been that creating external pluralism, i.e. having many different private media companies operating in one country, is the best way to build democracy and to provide access and voice to citizens. Often the model of choice was the one that has dominated the media landscapes of the United States and Europe since the Second World War: privately owned media funded through advertising and sales revenues. But as advertising income dwindles for traditional media and as newspapers close at alarming rates, the question arises whether promoting this business model in the developing world is the right way forward. In developing a response to this question, this article explains how media assistance has developed, identifies the main characteristics of the current crisis in journalism in the developed world and indicates how some of the experience gained in media development can help to provide answers to the current crisis. Media development itself has come a long way in recent years and today adopts a more holistic approach that focuses not only on building private media but recognises the need for legal reform, civil society involvement, enhanced professional capacity, strengthened institutions that support media freedom and development of technical media infrastructure.

Media Development: A New Sector Emerges

In the last 20 years, media assistance has become a significant element in the field of development, helping countries to make democratic transitions, spur economic growth, conduct public health campaigns, and improve government accountability. Efforts to spread a free press have resulted in professional support for tens of thousands of journalists and the founding of hundreds of new media enterprises.

Until the 1990s, neither governments nor private foundations provided much support to building free and independent media. Communication for development dominated the field, which meant that donors (largely governments) supported communication and information campaigns undertaken as part of a general development programme—public health, anti-poverty or agriculture development, for instance. Primarily, media were identified as instruments of development. Building independent media was not the direct goal; instead, media were seen as conduits for information. This type of support still receives the largest amount of resources. Almost every development programme, whether to fight HIV/AIDS or to develop sustainable energy sources, includes a communication aspect.

But, following the Cold War, as international aid increasingly focused on democracy building and good governance, strengthening independent media was widely embraced as a key component in democratic development. Media assistance in the 1990s concentrated on the former Soviet Union and on Eastern Europe, particularly the Balkan states but later expanded to Asia, Africa and Latin America.

A recent study found that in 2008 about US$430 million were spent on media development programmes by the governments of the United States, Japan, United Kingdom, Germany, Sweden, Norway, the Netherlands, UNESCO and the European Commission and private foundations mostly based in the United States (Myers, 2009, p. 12). This is still less than the amount of funding governments put into so-called public diplomacy programmes (programmes aimed at improving foreign relations and the image of the country abroad) but, nevertheless, support has continuously increased in recent years. For instance, in 2006 the US government alone spent close to US$600 million on public diplomacy (US Government Accountability Office, 2006).

Media development today encompasses a wide range of work. Generally, it can be defined as actions in support of:

- A system of media regulation and administration that ensures freedom of expression, pluralism and diversity.
- Strengthening media capacity to inform people on issues that shape their lives.
- Plurality and diversity of media, transparent and equal market conditions and full transparency of ownership.
- Media as a platform for democratic discourse within a climate of respect for journalism that represents professional independence and diversity of views and interests in society.
- Professional capacity building and supporting institutions for advocacy and development of media freedom, independence, pluralism and diversity.
- Professional training and skills development and for the media sector as a whole to be both monitored and supported by professional associations and civil society organisations.
- Infrastructural capacity that is sufficient to support independent and pluralistic media so that the media sector is characterised by high or rising levels of public access and efficient use of technology to gather and distribute news and information (GFMD World Conference, 2008; IPDC General Council, 2008).

There are two normative assumptions at the heart of media development, both of which are agreed by the majority of those involved in this work:

1. That free, independent and pluralistic media as defined by the UNESCO Declarations of Windhoek, Santiago de Chile, Almaty, Sana'a and Sofia describe the type of media landscape that should be strengthened by media development.[1]
2. That programmes building free, independent, pluralistic media help ensure freedom of expression, foster democracy, and contribute to the area's economic and social development.

So the question in the sector is not so much about the aims of media development but rather, given scarce resources and the wide range of possible actions, what type of media development work should be supported? While no systematic overview detailing types of media development programmes exists, there is sufficient anecdotal evidence that training of journalists receives the most support followed by support to create new independent media companies (Center for Independent Media, 2008).

The Crisis in Journalism in the Developed World: The End of the Advertising Revenue Model

The bedrock of professional and independent journalism in Europe and the United States has been newspaper journalism. And as newspapers are disappearing at a rapid rate many observers are concerned that professional journalism aimed at providing citizens with accurate, timely and relevant information will disappear as well. Given the number of job losses in journalism this is not a spurious concern. An OECD study found that between 1997 and 2007 the number of persons employed in newspaper publishing has declined in most OECD countries by somewhere between 10 and 30 per cent (OECD, 2009a). Last year, in the United States alone 60,000 jobs were lost, mostly in newspaper publishing.

Some are saying that bloggers and citizen journalists will fill the gap left by the demise of newspapers and there are some positive developments on the Internet. For instance, http://inothernews.us/, a site run by volunteers (many of them former journalists), provides local news coverage in different US cities. Initiatives such as Global Voices (www.globalvoices.org) offer the user direct access to blogs and reporting from all over the world. Ethan Zuckerman describes how new media are helpful in providing an instant response to crises of various kinds. When the earthquake struck in Haiti, for example, it was local bloggers and citizens who provided news globally within a couple of hours; the foreign correspondents only arrived two days later (Zuckerman, 2010).

While the new Internet sites and blogs provide enormous breadth and width of information for those with the time and desire to seek it, they cannot replace one fundamental function of professional journalism that is vital to democracy: scrutiny of those in power. It takes time, effort, money and knowledge to monitor public affairs and to expose corruption in government and the private sector. Investigative journalism is not cheap although it is essential to holding those in power to account. Individual bloggers and small news sites do not fulfil this role. They may find a lead and publish a relevant piece of the jigsaw but they will not have the resources to investigate the whole story, check all the facts and bring the full story into the mainstream. An ever-more fragmented information space will leave room for those in power to go unchecked.

As Paul Starr (2009) explains, it is not just a speculative proposition that corruption is more likely to flourish when those in power have less reason to fear exposure. In a study published in 2003 in *The Journal of Law, Economics, and Organization*, Alicia Adsera, Carles Boix, and Mark Payne examined the relationship between corruption and "free circulation of daily newspapers per person" (a measure of both news circulation and freedom of the press). Controlling for economic development, type of legal system, and other factors, they find a very strong association: the lower the free circulation of newspapers in a country, the higher it stands on the corruption index (Starr, 2009, p. 31).

With traditional media in decline and less investment in journalism, it is not clear who will play the role of the watchdog in the future.

The traditional media business model in newspapers and broadcasting, which depended largely on advertising revenue, is no longer working and certainly cannot deliver the returns enjoyed by classis media enterprise over the past 60 years. Already before the current economic crisis, too many platforms competed for the advertising market: newspapers, magazines, broadcasters, cable and satellite TV stations and countless Internet sites. The Internet offered advertisers a new and for them better business model, in which they track their target audience and pay per ad clicked and viewed not by the simple exposure offered by traditional media. The Internet also created a culture of news free of charge. While the main news sites are still run by traditional media companies, most of them offer the content for free. Why then, many consumers ask, should we pay for a newspaper?

As Steve Kroll (2010) of the New America Foundation explains, the highly successful business model of newspapers and terrestrial broadcasters since the Second World War was in a way an accident of history. As consumption boomed and ever more companies wanted to advertise their products the newspapers and broadcasters were in the charmed position of controlling this market. Never before could money be made so easily in media. Now, traditional media no longer control the advertising market but have to compete with newer and more efficient conduits for advertising. Kroll (2010) predicts that the traditional advertising revenue model has come to an end.

But as John Nichols points out, the decline of commercial journalism predates the Web. Newsrooms began to give up on maintaining staffs sufficient to cover their communities—effectively reducing the number of reporters relative to the overall population—in the 1980s. Real cuts came in the 1990s and have accelerated since then. These trends went largely unnoticed because the dominant media companies continued to make enormous profits. By cutting reporting staff and focusing on less expensive journalism based on trivia, sensationalism and press releases, they were able for years to maintain boom-time profits (Nichols and McChesney, 2009).

It is not only the advertising revenue model that failed; also the market model has shown its weakness. It is only in the last 20 years that media companies have made huge profits. Most of the large media conglomerates were accustomed to profit margins of around 12%. The RTL Group, for instance, had a profit margin of 15.8% in 2006 with net results of some 560 million Euros.[2] It is unlikely that these levels of income will return and one must wonder how journalism is expected to survive without a new approach to media business.

Dealing with the Crisis: What We Can Learn from Media Development

While in the developed world the dominant view is that it is the market that defines the media landscape, in media development broader discussions about policies for shaping the media landscape are allowed. Anyone involved in this work knows that by supporting or carrying out a particular media assistance programme you intervene in the existing media market and landscape.

The crisis in journalism in the developed world has opened the door for debating many issues that before were often confined to discussions about media in countries of transition or under development: How to sustain professional journalism with few market opportunities? How to ensure independence? What type of media landscape should be constructed for media to play a role in building democratic societies? Who will pay?

At the same time, the media development sector has matured; it no longer only focuses on training media professionals and setting up new private media companies it now aims to provide support for comprehensive action that includes media law reform, strengthening supporting institutions such as independent media councils, journalists' and media employers' organisations, media non-governmental organisations (NGOs), promoting media literacy, building a media infrastructure that provides access and voice for all.

Some of the funding models currently discussed by those seeking answers to the market crisis of media in the developed world have been tested in media development. For instance, public and private funding has been provided for non-profit news services in many countries of the developing world. The model of the community radio, which exists throughout Africa, builds on a mix of professional journalists and volunteers who produce programmes together for their community. Most of the stations are non-profit organisations. Some of them receive external donor funding, some enjoy limited advertising income and also receive donations to pay for programming.

One useful model is that of the Media Development Loan Fund (MDLF; www.mdlf.org); a non-profit NGO established in the 1990s that gives low- or no-interest loans to independent private media companies in transition and developing countries. From 1996 to 2009 MDLF provided loans and grants of some US$95 million to 72 independent media companies in 24 countries. The Fund is not simply a bank with good conditions, it sets out to support quality journalism and transparent and independent media companies. Many of the loan recipients, such as radio KBR68H in Indonesia, are not only news providers but also support advocacy work and function as NGOs offering training and organising campaigns.

Media development programmes support networks of investigative journalists, for instance in the Arab World and in countries of the former Soviet Union. Donors recognise that the market in these regions does not provide for investigative journalism and public money is required to support these initiatives. We may see more of this type of mission-driven, non-profit journalism in the developed world as well. Most recently, the Foundation for Public Interest Journalism, a non-profit organisation based in Australia, has received a generous sum in donation to support its non-profit news project.[3] Similar initiatives exist in the United States. Increasingly, public funding for media—a heretical notion especially in US media circles—has come to the fore as a key answer to the crisis in journalism. If it is accepted that media play a key role in democratic society, it follows logically that this public good should receive public support. And even in the United States this argument is gaining ground.

A recent poll suggests that about 80 per cent of respondents in the survey believe that Public Broadcasting Service (PBS) is a worthwhile investment. Respondents said PBS is an "excellent use of tax dollars". The poll also shows that PBS is the most trusted source of news and information about public affairs among broadcast and cable sources. The results contrast with a previous poll, which suggested the partisan broadcaster, Fox News, was the "most trusted" news channel in the United States.[4]

In Europe, public service broadcasting has a long tradition and should be strengthened in the current crisis. But European governments also provide direct subsidies to private newspapers, mostly linked to policy aims such as preserving regional or other diversity. France, for instance, subsidised newspapers with 92 million Euros in 2008. Sweden provided 51 million Euros (OECD, 2009b). This shows that while the dominant debate of the 2000s focused on increasing consumer choice rather than public-interest journalism with an ever-increasing number of commercial news outlets, European governments provided direct funding to ensure diversity. Media development practitioners and donors learnt the lesson that the market is no guarantee for freedom. Many of the private media companies in the former Soviet Union that began as independent media with external donor funding morphed into commercial business ventures interested less in quality journalism than in profits and good relations with the authorities.

In the developing world there are many media owners who accept that publishing and broadcasting will pay the rent but will not make them rich. They struggle more with restrictive laws, intimidation and lack of infrastructure than with trying to meet the 15 per cent profit margin. We may see these types of owners returning to European and US media.

What these examples illustrate is that free, independent and pluralistic media, regardless of whether in the developed or the developing world, need comprehensive media policies and support.

The current crisis has shown that the developed world, as much as developing countries, needs media policies aimed at strengthening free, independent and pluralistic media. Policies should aim to create and strengthen a media system built on regulation and administration of law ensuring media freedom, a level playing field for media business, investment into journalism as a public good, adequate professional training, open access, commitment to giving voice to all groups in society and institutions that support free media.

Less trust in the market and support for a variety of models to fund journalism—advertising, sales, donations, paid services, public money, low-interests loans etc.—seems to be the way forward and Europe and the United States can learn from the experiences in building independent media in the developing world.

NOTES

1. See http://www.unesco.org/webworld/fed/temp/communication_democracy/windhoek. htm, accessed 15 February 2010.
2. See http://www.international-television.org/tv_market_data/european_media_companies_ revenues_results_margins_2007.html, accessed 30 August 2009.
3. See www.pbs.org/roperpoll2010/, accessed 28 February 2010.
4. See www.pbs.org/roperpoll2010/, accessed 28 February 2010.

REFERENCES

ADSERA, ALICIA, BOIX, CARLES and PAYNE, MARK (2003) "Are you Being Served? Political Accountability and Quality of Government", *The Journal of Law, Economics, and Organization* 19(2), pp. 445–90.

CENTER FOR INDEPENDENT MEDIA (2008) *Empowering Independent Media, Inaugural Report*, Washington, DC, December.

GFMD WORLD CONFERENCE (2008) *GFMD Constitution*, Athens, 10 December, www.gfmd.info.

IPDC GENERAL COUNCIL (2008) *Media Development Indicators: a framework for assessing media development*, CI-08/CONF.202/5, Paris, March.

KROLL, STEVE (2010) Presentation to the Future of American Journalism debate organised by the Open Society Institute, New York, January.

MYERS, MARY (2009) *Funding for Media Development by Major Donor Outside the United States*, Washington, DC: Center for International Media Assistance.

NICHOLS, JOHN and MCCHESNEY, ROBERT W. (2009) "How to Save Journalism", *The Nation*, 3 December.

OECD (2009a) *DSTI/ICCP/IE*, Paris, 4 December, p. 18.

OECD (2009b) *DSTI/ICCP/IE*, Paris, 14 December, p. 58.

STARR, PAUL (2009) "Goodbye to the Age of Newspapers", *New Republic*, 4 March, pp. 28–35.

US GOVERNMENT ACCOUNTABILITY OFFICE (2006) *US Public Diplomacy*, Washington, DC, 3 March.

ZUCKERMAN, ETHAN (2010) Presentation to the Future of American Journalism debate organised by the Open Society Institute, New York, January.

THE PAST IS PROLOGUE, OR
How nineteenth-century journalism might just save twenty-first-century newspapers

Debra Reddin van Tuyll

The death of the American newspaper has been predicted for years now, and reasons offered to explain its demise are legion, ranging from the simple (the economy) to the self-effacing (journalistic narcissism). Some suggest the biggest problem is the lack of a viable business model, and to some extent they have a point. Metropolitan dailies, "the elite press," are having particular difficulty finding readers willing to pay for their content. This does not mean, however, that American journalism is on its way to extinction. It is possible to preserve the newspaper industry by looking to earlier forms of journalism, in the partisan press that dominated American journalism through the nineteenth century. In fact, some newspapers have already taken unwitting steps in this direction, and this paper will point to other practices that could also contribute to the preservation of American newspapers.

Introduction

The American information market is exploding while the news market is imploding. Population growth no longer shields the news industry from the loss of audience. Nor is the loss limited to newspapers (Project for Excellence in Journalism, 2004). Suggested reasons for the crisis range from professional narcissism to commercialization (Aeikens, 2009, p. 3; McManus, 1994, p. 1; Perez-Pena, 2009, p. B7; Pincus, 2009, p. 54; Shirkey, 2009; Smith, 2009). Solutions include non-profit news organizations, on-line only editions and doing away with print and embracing an allegedly inevitable fully electronic world (Potts, 2009a; *The Economist,* 2009, p. 77; Yardley and Pérez-Peña, 2009, p. 1).

Each of these solutions is the product of a myopia that has infected American journalists for a century, namely the myth that the objective, commercial press is the highest form of journalism and anything else is inferior or trivial. Even Frederic Hudson, a firm proponent of the commercialized press in his 1873 history of American journalism, admitted that the nineteenth century's political press "had more enterprise, more reading matter, more advertisements, [and] more originality" than the commercialized press. However, the editorial independence of the commercial press outweighed all other considerations, in Hudson's opinion (1873, p. 142). Contemporary critics scorned Hudson's perspective as myopic (Thorn, 1980), but it has become the dominant perspective.

New media journalists are infected with a variant strain of this myopia: technological determinism. They predict a fully electronic future for news. Like the traditionalists, however, they still believe that journalism will remain objective, detached, daily, and New-York-City-centric (Nerone, 1989, p. 285). Adolph Ochs's *New York Times* was the progenitor of this form of journalism, which beat out competing models in 1897, history has argued, and has been the standard model ever since (Campbell, 2006, p. 103). Some are beginning to rethink this, thereby taking an important step to ensure the future health of the news industry (Meyer, 2008; Pincus, 2009, pp. 54–7), for the "*New York Times*" model of journalism was well-suited for the modernism of the twentieth century, but it is out of step with contemporary American society.

In the twentieth century, Progressivism taught Americans to believe in truth, objectivity, the perfectibility of humanity, and that a democratic republic should extend political power to all. Newspapers were expected to be conduits between public institutions and citizens. Neither that America nor that media mindset exist today. Pockets of old-time journalism remain, where community mindedness is balanced with the bottom line, but these tend to be smaller markets like Decatur, Alabama where Clint Shelton publishes the *Decatur Daily*.[1] Shelton, whose family has owned the paper for almost a century, has kept his newsroom staffed at its full complement of 20, even in this economy. He recognizes that this might be foolhardy—business has not been good—but he is trying to give his community what it needs: an informative newspaper (personal interview with author, May 20, 2009).

America today has much in common with its nineteenth-century self when politics were deeply partisan and citizens were divided by issues of race and region (Osthaus, 1994; Mills, 1978). In both times, conflicts have been fuelled by information explosions. Newspaper circulation in antebellum America was higher than anywhere else in the world. In 1850, New York dailies sold 153,000 copies to a population of 500,000, while London's 2.3 million people absorbed only 63,000 copies (Lehuu, 2000, p. 16). America then was in a "'twixt and 'tween" time when the country was poised on a threshold, just as it is now (Lehuu, 2000, pp. 7, 19). Social flux affects the press, and while media pundits have written extensively about a "revolution," they have not always realized that the industry's problems are an outgrowth of larger upheavals (Etheridge, 2009; Sennott, 2009, p. 25).

One of the key social changes that affects the press is the decline of mass society. Americans today celebrate their differences, and they prefer information tailored to particular tastes. Magazines felt this shift first. General-interest magazines like *Look*, *Life*, and *Saturday Evening Post*, lost their audiences in the 1970s and 1980s. A visitor to a grocery store today would be hard pressed to find a magazine for the whole family. She would, however, find at least two different magazines about how to live the refined life of a proper Southern lady.

News media are both products and producers of their culture, and as such, they must "fit" their society (An Independent Journalist, 1909, p. 321; Carey, 1989; Maurantonio, 2008, p. 160; McChesney, 2008, p. 197; Nerone, 1989, p. 98). The detached, neutral model no longer fits. Can the nineteenth-century experience show the way? In order to answer this question, we must turn to how journalism was practiced in olden days.

The Nineteenth-century Press

Two press forms emerged in the early nineteenth century. Commercialized news was the most innovative. It catered to base lower-class tastes and espoused egalitarianism. It dominated by century's end, due to the rise of a mass urban society. The more traditional partisan press catered to an elite audience with the background and interest to appreciate complex arguments and debates (Pasley, 2001).

Changing Journalism for a Changing Society

Nineteenth-century journalism operated in an environment of polarization, broad fascination with politics, and much fanaticism and acrimony. Citizens were far more engaged with public issues than today (Altschuler and Blumin, 2000, p. 3). Alexis de Tocqueville was amazed to everywhere find citizens either assembled in meetings or reading newspapers—a habit that astonished other Europeans too. Print culture reflected that, offering spirited content that produced a "carnival on the page ... a feast of becoming, change and renewal" (Lehuu, 2000, p. 4; Nerone, 1989, pp. 179–90). One British visitor estimated in 1840 that weekly circulation among 17 million Americans was greater than among the 233 million Europeans (Schudson, 2008, pp. 186–7). It could be true. In 1836, England had 11 dailies, while New York City alone had 15 (Chalaby, 1998, p. 12).

The variety of newspaper types was more extensive in the nineteenth century. Special-interest newspapers were common. These existed to filter news through specific perspectives (Hudson, 1873, p. 305) or even to promote a single issue or candidate. Newspapers were founded to promote abolition (in the North) or temperance, such as the Augusta, Georgia, *Washingtonian, or Total Abstinence Advocate*, even the repeal of property taxes. This often multitudinous cacophony of voices has definite similarities with present day.

However, between 1830 and the 1880s, "the press" was transformed into "journalism." This transition, in journalism historian Frank Luther Mott's Whiggish way of thinking, marked the triumph of news over opinion (Mott, 1962, pp. 167–80). The impetus for this transition has been attributed to technology, disgust with yellow journalism, commercialization, and even an evolution role of journalism (Thorn, 1980, p. 100). Whatever the cause, the result was a "depoliticization of the press" and a new definition of news (Altschuler and Blumin, 2000, p. 235; Chalaby, 1998, pp. 65, 89; McChesney, 2008, p. 195; Mott, 1962, p. 384). Reader tastes turned from the political, ideological, and intellectual, to sports, scandal and crime, society, and human interest (Summers, 1994, p. 61). The changed definition of news worked well for a century but now has led to problems for the industry (Chalaby, 1998, pp. 105, 106).

The Past is Prologue

Professional doctrine framed one of the nineteenth century's journalism forms as superior and uniquely acceptable. This was a costly error. Not only did it cut journalists off from a significant portion of their professional history, it forced them into a single, highly ritualized form of practice, and one of those rituals was blind acceptance of this "there's-only-one-way-to-do-journalism" mentality. Other forms of journalism can be just as vibrant as the commercialized version, especially today when journalists are dealing with many of the editorial and business issues that plagued the nineteenth-century press, too (Lauterer, 2008, p. 11).

Past Practices for Future Journalists

The professional practices most affected by societal changes are ones that underpin journalism: how news is defined and how news is gathered. Early on, news was whatever floated in the print shop door from travellers, foreign newspapers, or even visitors. Editors constructed newspapers from that information and their own commentaries. With the rise of the penny press in the 1830s, both the definition of news and the way news was gathered changed. The penny press needed information that had to be gathered, and so the job of reporter became institutionalized. As professionalization took hold in the early twentieth century, newspapers hired more qualified staff, and by the 1970s, a bachelor's degree had become a requirement for getting hired as a journalist.

Today, fewer news organizations can afford large staffs of highly qualified employees, and they have returned to certain nineteenth-century practices. Convergence, where media share staff-generated content, is one of those. At least 20 newspapers are cooperating with former rivals to share the work of their reporters, giving "full credit for items used, and no money changes hands" (*Augusta Chronicle*, 2009, p. 5A). Internet news aggregators do something similar by linking to a variety of news sites. This echoes the most common form of nineteenth-century news transmission: exchanges. Postal regulations adopted in 1792 allowed newspapers to mail a copy of each of its editions to others for free (Nerone, 1989, p. 32). The objective was to encourage the flow of information within the fledgling country. These news-sharing arrangements allowed newspapers to be more nimble, to cover more stories with smaller staffs, as did their nineteenth-century ancestors.

In the nineteenth century, even a nationally important newspaper could produce daily editions with one or two editors and a staff of printers (*Macon Telegraph and Confederate*, 1864; Van Tuyll, 2005, p. 77). Today's elite press employs journalists by the hundreds. The *Seattle Post-Intelligencer*'s conversion from print to Internet took the newsroom from 150 to 20 (Yardley and Pérez-Peña, 2009, p. 1), giving rise to questions about whether those 20 can produce the same comprehensive news as 150 did.

A nineteenth-century practice already adopted by some newspapers can help here, too: citizen journalism. In the eighteenth and nineteenth centuries, readers supplied a great deal of news: poetry, commentary, even speeches, and minutes of public meetings. Today, citizen journalists provide similar content, essentially as unpaid stringers. *The Economist* (2009, p. 78) has suggested that this practice could produce a viable new model of journalism, one where professionals produce commentary and receive news brought in by citizen journalists.

This passive journalism is one that modern readers may have trouble acclimating to, but it served generations of Americans well, and is certainly successful today. Talk radio, Web news aggregators, and many news programs offer partisan commentary, and they draw huge audiences. The *Huffington Post* has 4.5 million unique viewers monthly (comScore, 2008; *The Economist,* 2009, p. 77); Rush Limbaugh has become a very rich man with his daily doses of partisan ideology.

Partisan journalism is viewed as tainted, and it is true that its practitioners are influenced by its sponsors. However, commercial journalism has its own sponsors who have been known to exert control over news: advertisers. Further, its extremely competitive nature has produced excesses like the *New York Sun*'s notorious "Great Moon Hoax" (*New York Sun,* 1835, p. 1) or the *New York World*'s daring 1897 rescue of Evangelina Cisneros (Campbell, 2006, p. 6).

On the other hand, partisan or "sponsored," journalism sometimes offers substantial social and political value. The commercialized press is forced to cover politics as a form of entertainment in order to draw an audience, and this practice has contributed to the de-emphasis of political issues as substantive debates (Chalaby, 1998, pp. 107–8; Nerone, 2008, p. 143). Some have even argued that the cynical non-partisanhip of today's journalists "turns many off politics, as does its emphasis on strategy over substance" (Chalaby, 1998, p. 122).

Further, the requirement of non-partisanship means that journalists today define news in terms of timeliness and reader interest, rather than importance, values, or principles. Partisan journalism is not entirely dependent on the marketplace and that provides a different type of independence for journalists, one which allows them the freedom to serve reader desires as well as reader needs (Chalaby, 1998, p. 81).

Coverage issues are tied intimately to audience issues, and today's stratified audience is different from the mass audience the press served 100 years ago. Present day is marked by two-income households, or, too often, a single income from a single parent. The work day is long. Citizens do not have time to read newspapers before they head out in the morning, nor do they have the energy to read them when they get home in the evening. The worker who can sneak a peek at a website is likely the best informed person in the office.

Blogger Mark Potts (2009b) ruminated recently that perhaps newspapers are not as essential to citizens as journalists think. A noted defence economist recently commented to this author that, other than reading *The Economist* each week, his news consumption is hit-or-miss. He finds little necessity for dailies unless there is a major breaking story. "How often is there a 9/11?," he asked.

The current crisis is forcing the media to be creative about reaching audiences, and one of the healthiest changes being experimented with is one that could produce a press better suited to the news needs of people like this economist: reconstruction of the media market away from plain-song-one-size-fits-all journalism into a diversified marketplace that embraces a multiplicity of forms.

Commentary, localization, and contextualization will be important aspects of this new news world (Lauterer, 2008, p. 12; Meyer, 2008), and at least a few organizations are moving in this direction. A new on-line only international news site, the *Global-Post*, as well as the newly re-invented *Seattle Post-Intelligencer*, are both emphasizing commentary and contextualization of the facts they report (Sennott, 2009, p. 25; Yardley and Pérez-Peña, 2009, p. 1). Nineteenth-century editors understood that insightful, knowledgeable, fact-based commentary has economic value. Proof of this truth is offered by the jewel in Britain's publishing crown: *The Economist*.

Profits of this "dry and academic" newspaper rose 75 percent between 2003 and 2005 (Wray, 2008). Between 2001 and 2005, circulation grew from 760,000 to 1.3 million, complemented by 2.6 million unique visitors to its website each month (Garside, 2008; International Federation of the Periodical Press, 2005; The Economist, 2005). *The Economist* is not for everyone, however. Many readers want something more entertaining, dramatic, or dynamic, a type of news that may actually require more frequent consumption since events and issues within that sphere change more quickly than those in the political, social, and economic realms. Clearly, a diversified print culture is necessary to serve the information needs of these different audiences.

Newspapers are not the first communications medium forced to accommodate a shift in audience types. Theatre and magazines have seen their audiences shift tremendously over the years (Butsch, 2000, p. 250; Meyer 2008). Audiences today want information tailored to their interests—and this kind of specialization gives the Internet an incredible competitive advantage.

Business Model

News business practices changed radically a century ago. High-speed presses and burgeoning markets brought economies of scale that required fewer, bigger newspapers to meet the demands of a mass market. Many medium-sized competitors like the *New York Herald*, a paper with tremendous stature in the earlier nineteenth century, were forced to fold or merge with stronger journals, and even then, they did not all survive. The *Herald* collapsed in 1967 after publishing for more than 100 years (Chalaby, 1998, pp. 43–4).

The market for gargantuan newspapers no longer exists because mass society no longer exists. News organizations that reject the economies-of-scale model in favor of the specialized model of journalism will take a gigantic step toward that more nimble business model of the eighteenth and nineteenth centuries when newspapers were small and just about anyone who wanted to could start one (Chalaby, 1998, p. 43). Staffs were small and supplies were cheap: ink, paper, glue, oil, molasses, wood, potash, and press blankets (*Augusta Chronicle and Sentinel*, 1864, p. 2).

Technology

Technology is often blamed for the downfall of traditional news media, and some argue that it is time for newspapers and broadcasters to give way to the migration of news consumers to the Internet. The Internet, they argue, is vastly superior for democracy because of its openness and variety (Starr, 2008, pp. 40–1).

This does not address, however, the nature of the Internet audience. Statistics from the US Census Bureau show that the supposedly democratic web is actually fairly elite. Nearly a third of all Americans do not have Internet access at home, and nearly 40 percent do not use it, even if they do have home access (US Census Bureau, 2009). In Mississippi, only 53 percent have in-home access (Dawsey, 2009; US Census Bureau, 2009). Further, use is highly stratified. Only 19 percent of people who did not finish high school use the Internet, compared to 87 percent of those with college graduates. By contrast, 99 percent of households have television. Clearly, it is too soon to dismiss traditional news media as irrelevant and proclaim the Internet as the saviour of democracy (Pew Center for the People and the Press, 2008).

Funding Sources

In 1864, North Carolina Governor Zebulon B. Vance was running for re-election, and he desperately needed a newspaper to support his candidacy. His opponent was a powerful newspaper editor, and that redoubled Vance's need for a media voice. Vance was not wealthy enough to start a newspaper on his own, so he asked his supporters to fund the campaign newspaper that helped him win an election that changed the course of history (Van Tuyll, 2008).

Patronage today is being considered as a way of ensuring that high-quality news continues to be produced. Most proposals use the term "non-profit journalism," but the concept is the same: wealthy individuals or organizations pay the costs of information gathering and production (*The Economist, 2009*, p. 78). Patronage provided a stable funding source for 19th century newspapers, something they needed since readers then did not like paying for news any more than they do today. Then, as now, editors had to get creative.

A good number of newspapers went on the barter system, accepting produce or other farm products as payment (*Sandersville Central Georgian*, 1862; *Hillsborough* (North Carolina) *Recorder*, 25 January 1864). The Athens, Georgia *Southern Watchman* went the furthest, taking "any kind of country produce—corn, wheat, flour, rye, butter, hay, shucks, fodder, chicken, eggs—anything that can be eaten or worn, or that will answer for fuel" (1861, p. 2). An even earlier innovation was the single-copy sale, an invention of the penny press. Its readers would not have been able to pay for a year's subscription in advance, as was the practice then. But they could afford that one-cent daily, just as today's readers may not be able to afford, or willing to commit to, a full subscription to an Internet site. They might, however, be willing to make micro payments for particular content (*The Economist, 2009*, p. 78).

Conclusion

Journalists have always been a hysterical lot. In 1765, when the British crown imposed the Stamp Tax, American journalists claimed that print, and consequently liberty, was in its death throes (Lepore, 2009, p. 68). They draped their pages in heavy black borders, and one even fashioned that border into the shape of a tombstone with skull and cross bones (*Pennsylvania Journal and Weekly Advertiser*, 1765, p. 1). In 2009, technology, rather than taxes, is the culprit most often blamed for the death of print. Yet, journalism survived King George, and it has thrived through previous technology shifts.

Nevertheless, pundits claim that the Internet is killing newspapers; a recent poll of "media insiders" found that 65 percent believe the Internet has hurt journalism (Master, 2009; *The Economist, 2009*, p. 15). The truth is, journalism was in crisis long before the Internet and is in need of structural reform (McChesney, 2008, pp. 193, 202). That reform must recognize that there is more than one way to do journalism so that the press can return to the nineteenth century's vibrant print culture. The new reality is an old one: the market for news is volatile. News organizations have to be flexible. A return to smaller, independently owned, local and specifically targeted news products, with a limited number of important national and international journals, appears to be where the future lies.

Today's irony is that small papers have the resources to buy properties from the conglomerates. The *Decatur* (Alabama) *Daily*, for example, in April 2009 purchased its down-river neighbor, the *Florence Times Daily*, from the *New York Times*. Circulation is up at the Florence paper, and the Decatur paper is "doing fine," despite some revenue declines. In addition to maintaining the *Daily*'s staff, Shelton is building up the staff at the *Times Daily*. This is because he believes that "the newsroom is the heart and soul of the newspaper." His ultimate objective is to create newspapers that actually offer content to readers, unlike the copy of *USA Today* he picked up recently. "There was nothing in it," he said in a recent interview. "It was just like watching CNN" (personal interview with author, May 20, 2009).

The future of newspapers is in smaller staffs, more analysis, and more shared news, either through shared staffs or from other publications, print or electronic (*The Economist, 2009*, p. 77). Journalism's nineteenth-century ancestors lived in a similar place. They commented on the day's events and they borrowed stories from "piles of exchanges . . . limited only by the length of [their] arms" (*Anderson* (South Carolina) *Intelligencer*, 1860). This was one of an editor's most important jobs. One editor wrote, "Indeed, the mere writing part of editing a paper is but a small part of the work. The care is the time employed in selecting far more important matter and the fact of a good editor is better shown by his selections than by anything else" (*Alabama Beacon, 1860*).

Once, ideal journalism looked a lot like the *Decatur Daily*: a small-town family-owned, subscription-funded newspaper that had a clear division between advertising and news (An Independent Journalist, 1909, pp. 322, 327; Pincus, 2009, pp. 55–6; Smith, 2009). The profession lost sight of that vision for a century and a quarter, but more now see that news is at its best when it is tied tightly to its community through its owner's deep roots, and when readers recognize that news is a staple they should be willing to pay for (An Independent Journalist, 1909, pp. 329–30; Lacy, 2009).

NOTE

1. The author of this paper worked for the *Decatur Daily* from 1980 to 1982.

REFERENCES

AEIKENS, DAVE (2009) "Future of News Might Not be Rosy, But There's Always Reason to Hope", *Quill*, January/February, p. 3.

ALABAMA BEACON (1860) Untitled, 7 December, p. 2.

ALTSCHULER, GLEN C. and STUART, M. BLUMIN (2000) *Rude Republic: Americans and their politics in the nineteenth century*, Princeton, NJ: Princeton University Press.

AN INDEPENDENT JOURNALIST (1909) "Is An Honest and Sane Newspaper Press Possible", *American Journal of Sociology* 15, pp. 321–34.

ANDERSON (SOUTH CAROLINA) *INTELLIGENCER* (1860) "Marrying an Editor", 1 November.

AUGUSTA CHRONICLE AND SENTINEL (1864) "What It Costs to Print a Newspaper", 17 July, p. 2.

AUGUSTA CHRONICLE (2009) "Ex-rivals Cooperate: cuts force papers to share coverage", 5 January, p. 5A.

BUTSCH, RICHARD (2000) *The Making of American Audiences: from stage of television, 1750–1900*, Cambridge: Cambridge University Press.

CAMPBELL, W. JOSEPH (2006) *The Year That Defined American Journalism*, New York: Routledge.

CAREY, JAMES W. (1989) *Communication in Culture: essays on media and society*, Boston: Unwin Hyman.

CHALABY, JEAN K. (1998) *The Invention of Journalism*, Basingstoke: Macmillan Press.

COMSCORE (2008) "Huffington Post and Politico Lead Wave of Explosive Growth at Independent Political Blogs and News Sites This Election Season", 22 October, http://www.comscore.com/Press_Events/Press_Releases/2008/10/Huffington_Post_and_Politico_Lead_Political_Blogs, accessed 5 June 2009.

DAWSEY, JOSH (2009) "South Carolina Among Lowest in Internet Access", *Myrtle Beach* (SC) *Sun News*, 5 June, http://www.thesunnews.com/news/local/story/926937.html, accessed 5 June 2009.

ETHERIDGE, ERIC (2009) "Why Newspapers Can't Be Saved, but the News Can", *New York Times*, 16 March, http://opinionator.blogs.nytimes.com/2009/03/16/why-newspapers-cantbe-saved-but-the-news-can/, accessed 17 March.

GARSIDE, JULIETTE (2008) "Fight to Quality Bolsters Economist Circulation", *The Telegraph*, 20 June, www.telegraph.co.uk/finance/newsbysector/mediatechnologyandtelecoms/2791966/Flight-to-quality-bolsters-Economist-circulation.html, accessed 27 December 2008.

HILLSBOROUGH (NORTH CAROLINA) RECORDER (1864) Untitled, 25 January, p. 2.

HUDSON, FREDERIC (1873) *Journalism in the United States*, New York: Harper Brothers.

INTERNATIONAL FEDERATION OF THE PERIODICAL PRESS (2005) "How the Economist Made a Million", http://www.fipp.com/Default.aspx?PageIndex=2002&ItemId=12279, accessed 27 December 2008.

LACY, STEPHEN (2009) "The Future of Local Journalism", Hot Topics in Journalism and Mass Communication, http://aejmc.org/topics/2009/05/the-future-of-local-journalism/, accessed 23 May.

LAUTERER, JOCK (2008) "The Future of Newspapers", *Quill*, December, pp. 11–12.

LEHUU, ISABEL (2000) *Carnival on the Page: popular print media in antebellum America*, Chapel Hill: University of North Carolina Press.

LEPORE, JILL (2009) "The Day the Newspaper Died", *New Yorker*, 26 January, pp. 68–73.

MACON TELEGRAPH AND CONFEDERATE (1864) "Telegraph and Confederate Family", 17 December, p. 2.

MASTER, CYRA (2009) "Media Insiders Say Internet Hurts Journalism", *The Atlantic*, 10 April, http:theatlantic.com/doc/200904a/media insiders, accessed 10 April 2009.

MAURANTONIO, NICOLE (2008) "Journalism, Communication, and History", in: Barbie Zelizer (Ed.), *Explorations in Communication and History*, London: Routledge, pp. 159–61.

MCCHESNEY, ROBERT (2008) "The New Political Economy and the Rethinking of Journalism History", in: Barbie Zelizer (Ed.), *Explorations in Communication and History*, London: Routledge, pp. 190–210.

MCMANUS, JOHN H. (1994) *Market-driven Journalism: let the citizen beware?*, Thousand Oaks, CA: Sage.

MEYER, PHILIP (2008) "The Elite Newspaper of the Future", *American Journalism Review*, October/ November, http://www.ajr.org/article_printable.asp?id=4605, accessed 20 May 2009.

MOTT, FRANK LUTHER (1962) *American Journalism, a History: 1690–1960*, New York: MacMillan.

NERONE, JOHN C. (1989) *The Culture of the Press in the Early Republic: Cincinnati, 1793–1848*, New York: Garland Publishing.

NERONE, JOHN C. (2008) "Newsworld: technology and cultural form, 1837–1920", in: Barbie Zelizer (Ed.), *Explorations in Communication and History*, London: Routledge, pp. 136–56.

NEW YORK SUN (1835) "Great Astronomical Discoveries Lately Made", 25 August, http:// www.museumofhoaxes.com/moonhoax.html, accessed 5 June 2009.

OSTHAUS, CARL R. (1994) *Partisans of the Southern Press*, Lexington: University of Kentucky Press.

PASLEY, JEFFREY L. (2001) *"The Tyranny of Printers": newspaper politics in the early American republic*, Charlottesville: University of Virginia Press.

PENNSYLVANIA JOURNAL AND WEEKLY ADVERTISER (1765) Border, 31 October, p. 1.

PEREZ-PENA, RICHARD (2009) "Editors and Publishers in a Revolving Door", *New York Times*, 18 January, p. B7.

PEW CENTER FOR THE PEOPLE AND THE PRESS (2008) "December 2008 Political and Economic Survey Final Topline", http://people-press.org/reports/questionnaires/479.pdf, accessed 5 June 2009.

PINCUS, WALTER (2009) "Newspaper Narcissism: our pursuit of glory led us away from readers", *Columbia Journalism Review*, May/June, pp. 54–7.

POTTS, MARK (2009a) "Between Little Rock and a Hard Place", *Recovering Journalist*, http:// recoveringjournalist.typepad.com/recovering_journalist/2009/05/between-little-rock-and-a hard-place.html, accessed 19 May 2009.

POTTS, MARK (2009b) "Recovering from (the Rough First Draft of) History", *Recovering Journalist*, 12 May, http://recoveringjournalist.typepad.com/recovering_journalist/2009/05/learning-from-the-rough first-draft-of-history.html, accessed 19 May 2009.

PROJECT FOR EXCELLENCE IN JOURNALISM WITH RICK EDMONDS (2004) "The State of the News Media in 2004: newspapers—audience", http://www.stateofthemedia.org/2004/narrative_newspapers_audience.asp?cat=3&media=2, accessed 23 May 2009.

SANDERSVILLE CENTRAL GEORGIAN (1862) "Full Sheet", 8 January, p. 2.

SCHUDSON, MICHAEL (2008) "Public Spheres, Imagined Communities, and the Underdeveloped Historical Understanding of Journalism", in: Barbie Zelizer (Ed.), Explorations in Communication and History, London: Routledge, pp. 181–9.

SENNOTT, CHARLES M. (2009) "Roll the Dice: how one journalist gambled on the future of news", Columbia Journalism Review, March/April, pp. 23–5.

SHIRKEY, CLAY (2009) "Newspapers and Thinking the Unthinkable", http://www.shirky.com/weblog/2009/03/newspapers-and-thinking-the-unthinkable/, accessed 17 March 2009.

SMITH, JEFF (2009) "Recalling Our Heydey, When We Were Locally Owned", Tucson Citizen, 15 May, http://www.tucsoncitizen.com/ss/opinion/116653.php, accessed 19 May 2009.

SOUTHERN WATCHMAN (1861) "To Our Patrons", 16 October, p. 2.

STARR, PETER (2008) "Democratic Theory and the History of Communication", in: Barbie Zelizer (Ed.), Explorations in Communication and History, London: Routledge, pp. 35–45.

SUMMERS, MARK (1994) The Press Gang: newspapers and politics, 1865–1878, Chapel Hill: University of North Carolina Press.

THE ECONOMIST (2005) "Our History", http://www.economistgroup.com/what_we_do/our_history.html, accessed 27 December 2008.

THE ECONOMIST (2009) "Tossed by a Gale", 16 May, pp. 76–8.

THORN, WILLIAM J. (1980) "Hudson's History of Journalism Criticized by His Contemporaries", Journalism Quarterly 57(Spring), pp. 99–106.

THORNTON, J. MILLS (1978) Politics and Power in a Slave State, Alabama 1800–1860, Baton Rouge: Louisiana State University.

US CENSUS BUREAU (2009) "City and County QuickFacts (2006) for Seattle, Washington", http://quickfacts.census.gov/qfd/states/53/5363000.html, accessed 9 June 2009.

VAN TUYLL, DEBRA REDDIN (2005) "Essential Labor: confederate printers at home and at war", Journalism History, Summer, pp. 75–87.

VAN TUYLL, DEBRA REDDIN (2008) "Necessity and the Invention of a Newspaper: Governor Zebulon B. Vance's Conservative, 1864–65", Journalism History, Summer, pp. 87–97.

WRAY, RICHARD (2008) "Economist Magazine Chief Quits After 23 Years", Guardian, 10 April, http://www.guardian.co.uk/media/2008/apr/10/pressandpublishing1, accessed 9 June 2009.

YARDLEY, WILLIAM and PÉREZ-PEÑA, RICHARD (2009) "In Seattle, a Newspaper Loses Its Paper Routes", New York Times, 17 March, p. 1.

LABOUR, NEW MEDIA AND THE INSTITUTIONAL RESTRUCTURING OF JOURNALISM

James R. Compton and **Paul Benedetti**

Thousands of news workers were laid off in the United Kingdom and North America in 2008–2009. While daily newspapers were particularly affected, labour cuts also hit broadcasters and news magazines. Popular commentary has often attempted to explain the cuts as a result of Internet competition, aging audiences for news and a slumping global economy. Optimists suggest the rise of new media practices such as blogging and citizen journalism have, despite the contraction of newsrooms, expanded the range of information and opinion available to citizens. This paper is an attempt to clarify what is an unquestionably chaotic moment in journalism. Our focus is the labour of reporting—the quotidian work of gathering information of public interest and packaging it into a story. The paper uses Pierre Bourdieu's field theory to contextualize the use of new media technologies by amateur and professional journalists in an attempt to understand the power relations that inform the work of reporting. We argue that labour rationalization in combination with the use of new technologies, shrinking audiences, 24-hour news cycles, and intensified hyper-commercialization is fundamentally reorganizing the division of labour in newsrooms. Importantly, we argue there is little empirical evidence to suggest that unpaid citizen journalists will replace the lost labour of reporting—the work of collecting information, synthesizing it and presenting it for public consumption via storytelling.

Uncertain Times and Bold Predictions

After decades of calm—and profitable—smooth sailing, news media find themselves in a tumultuous and chaotic storm. Battered by the waves of declining circulation, rising costs, and crushing debt loads, newspapers across North America and the United Kingdom have slid into bankruptcy or sunk completely. Century-old newspapers such as Denver's *Rocky Mountain News* are gone, while *The Philadelphia Inquirer*, *Chicago Tribune* and the *Los Angeles Times* are in bankruptcy. American's flagship paper, the *New York Times*, teeters on the edge of insolvency. In early 2009 in the *Atlantic Monthly*, Michael Hirschorn posed a question that would have been unthinkable a year ago: "Can America's paper of record survive the death of newsprint? Can journalism?" A few months later, the situation, and the rhetoric, had become more extreme. *Globe and Mail* columnist John Ibbitson (2009) asked, "How does U.S. democracy survive without its newspapers?" In the meantime, a chorus of online pundits seemed to relish the decline of mainstream media, convinced that long, slow decline of the traditional news industry had reached an evolutionary turning point and that a shining, new online order was poised to replace it. The decades-long decline in audience for mainstream media; the concurrent rise of web-based bloggers and citizen journalism sites; the explosion in social media tools such as Facebook, Twitter and Flickr, and the recent and exacerbating worldwide economic collapse have all washed together to form a seemingly compelling though incoherent explanation for the inevitable replacement of traditional media and its paid armies of information gatherers—reporters and editors—by a robust, diffuse, distributed self-organized collective of citizens online. As one media columnist recently opined, "the changed media landscape favours the small, not the large. It favours the socially connected, not the financially inflated. It really favours the gift economy and the contribution of fans" (MacPhail, 2009).

This paper is an attempt to clarify what is an unquestionably chaotic moment in journalism. Our focus is the labour of reporting—the quotidian work of gathering information of public interest and packaging it into a story. Vincent Mosco frames the matter succinctly: "There is no future for journalism without journalists and the trends are not good" (2009, p. 350). How autonomous is the work of reporting likely to be in the wake of massive layoffs and corporate restructuring? Will the vaunted citizen journalist replace this lost labour? We agree with Chris Atton who argues that many academic studies of alternative media identify too strongly with their object of study; as a result some research suffers from an overly celebratory tone. "Such studies exemplify the kind of discourse found in critical media studies that emphasize media participation as a good in itself" (Atton, 2008, p. 217). It is true that online technologies such as weblogs lower barriers to entry, but this journalistic participation must be contextualized if we are to understand the power relations that inform the work of reporting.

Following Atton, we ask what is the context in which journalists, paid or unpaid, work? Are bloggers, so-called citizen journalists and other alternative media truly independent? How autonomous are they? And what kind of work are they likely to produce? Will it replace the labour formerly performed by salaried reporters? Does that even matter? To answer these questions we need to know something about the social, cultural and economic context in which paid and unpaid journalists work. We need to know something about the habitus of journalism practitioners and the social fields in which they labour (Atton, 2008; Bourdieu, 2005).

The Utility of Field Theory

What is required is a research strategy capable of accommodating both the micro-level practices of individual reporters (professional and amateur) and the macro-level institutional structures in which they invariably find themselves. That is to say, newsroom layoffs and the phenomenon of online communities of practice need to be situated within a broader cultural, political and economic context. How has the institution of journalism changed? What are the forces driving that change?

In what follows, we take up the challenge presented by a growing number of scholars (Atton, 2008; Benson, 1998, 2004, 2006; Benson and Erik Neveu, 2005; Couldry, 2003) who urge media researchers to engage with the research agenda of Pierre Bourdieu. In so doing we deploy Bourdieu's related concepts of habitus and social fields of interaction as principal tools of investigation.

Pierre Bourdieu's concept of the "habitus" provides a method of situating the practices of individual bloggers and paid newsroom employees within the broader culture and political economy of journalism. Bourdieu argues that individual and collective practices of everyday life are conditioned at the level of the habitus, by which he means the complex accumulation of experiences accrued through an individual's practical and historical engagement with social structures, such as the economy, class, race, family, gender, etc. Out of these experiences, people internalize the possibilities and constraints of social life (Bourdieu, 1990, pp. 53–54; 2005, p. 36). Habitus demands a dialectical approach to social agency. It is at the level of habitus that actors have a sense of how to act in any given social context or situation. Habitus is both structured by given social contexts and structuring in the sense that it helps to reproduce and incrementally change the social order by giving social actors a practical sense of how to act, i.e. a feel for the game.

The notion of habitus is, therefore, a serious challenge to the mythology of the rugged cyber individualist. Subjectivity is itself social, and must be understood relationally. As Bob Hanke argues in his Bourdieusian analysis of online *Indymedia*: "We must not only consider people's practices (including their shaping of technology), but also the microcosms within which people are positioned, the fields they react to, the capital they can draw upon, their conceptions of media and politics, and so on" (Hanke, 2005, p. 46). Social agents occupy positions within fields of social interaction that constitute the various spheres of social division in modern societies (e.g., fields of politics, economy, religion, and journalism).

Social fields, suggests Bourdieu, impose their own internal rules of organization. Those actors who enter a field are, therefore, obliged to play by its own autonomous rules of the game, or "nomos." In the journalistic field we observe forms of storytelling, and information gathering that structure the rules of the journalistic game. We may call these rules the "regime of objectivity" (Hackett and Zhao 1998). But this autonomy is itself relational, and must be understood as contingent upon the position of social agents *vis-à-vis* a field's "heteronomous" and "autonomous" poles. These poles are constitutive of the economic and political (heteronomous) power external to a field and the cultural (autonomous) power particular to a field.

Bourdieu argues that the journalistic field is losing its autonomy as economic (reliance on advertising, corporate ownership, etc.) and political constraints (public relations, political flak, etc.) impinge on journalistic cultural production (Benson, 1998, pp. 464–7). "To understand what is happening in the journalistic field," says Bourdieu, "one has to understand the degree of autonomy of the field and, within the field, the degree of autonomy of the publication that a journalist writes for" (Bourdieu, 2005, p. 43). In other words, one must understand the extent to which external social fields such as politics and economics overlap or extend into the journalistic field.

Field theory allows researchers to assess the impact of new entrants into a social field. According to Bourdieu, to be an agent within a field is to exert effects there which increase with the specific weight that one has (Bourdieu, 2005, p. 43). We can extend this analysis to the layoffs that have swept newsrooms throughout North America and Europe, keeping in mind that a complete mapping of the journalistic field is beyond the scope of this paper. In what follows, we examine the exogenous influences on the journalistic field related to the heteronomous pole of economic and political power. Secondly, we detail the principal effects of these changes on traditional newsrooms. And finally, we sketch out some of the responses to these morphological changes from entrepreneurs, non-profit organizations and the state. In each case we seek to map, in a provisional manner, the extent to which these responses are homologous with either the heteronomous pole of economic and political power or with the autonomous pole of cultural power specific to the journalistic field.

Heteronomous Economic Influences on the Journalistic Field

As Rodney Benson suggests, following David Harvey (1989), the most "significant shock to the news media ... is the broad transformation of capitalism toward a more intensely profit-driven, anti-union, anti-public sector model of 'flexible accumulation'" (Benson, 2006, p. 193). Benson argues the transition to Post-Fordist production "only further isolates the journalistic field from the everyday concerns of working-class and poor citizens" while weakening the hand of non-profit associations in relation to capital (2006, p. 193). These trends are longstanding, dating back more than 30 years. What Robert McChesney (2004) labels the "hyper-commercialism" of journalism has contributed to an overemphasis on short-term profits at the expense of public-service journalism; the increased production of spectacular media events and celebrity gossip is one outcome. Another outcome has been the intensified rationalization of productive resources, through aggressive corporate cross-media mergers and newsroom staff reductions. Demand for a more flexible labour force grew as formerly disparate newsrooms converged into multi-media workshops operating to fill the gaping maw of a 24-hour news hole (Compton, 2004).

The regime of flexible accumulation was supported by the state through neoliberal reforms that promoted financial deregulation and privatization. Combined with the widespread diffusion of information and communication technologies, capital flows gained an unprecedented mobility. More than ever before, corporations learned to discipline themselves or lose the support of stockholders. This particular dynamic gained strength within the media sector as news organizations became increasingly integrated into transnational capital during the 1980s and 1990s (Compton, 2009; Yong Jin, 2008).

News Institutions and the Wisdom of Crowds

The steady stream of newsroom layoffs has occurred alongside a parallel development in new media; weblogs and social networking sites such as Myspace, Facebook, and Twitter have attracted millions of producers and users. These "prosumers" are celebrated by libertarian and liberal writers who suggest their individual labours reveal a collective intelligence, or "wisdom of crowds" (Sunstein, 2006; Surowiecki, 2005).

Clay Shirky argues these new technologies have contributed to a seminal shift in people's ability to engage in collective dialogue. "The current change, in one sentence, is this: most of the barriers to group action have collapsed, and without those barriers, we are free to explore new ways of gathering together and getting things done" (2008, p. 22). This new media "ecosystem," argues Shirky, has weakened long-standing institutions, such as newspapers and news broadcasters. News media's publishing monopoly is gone; now, untrained amateurs can create their own content and publish their blogs without the "filter" of traditional news media.

Large-scale organizations, such as the BBC and the *New York Times*, employ a substantial workforce of reporters, editors, and producers, each of whom draws a salary. Shirky argues that the emerging new "ecosystem" makes such employment increasingly unnecessary. "We are used to a world where little things happen for love and big things happen for money. Love motivates people to bake a cake and money motivates people to make an encyclopedia. Now, though, we can do big things for love" (2008, p. 104).

Novel and emerging "communities of practice," argues Shirky, make possible new opportunities for amateur cooperation. So-called citizen journalists file frontline reports of train bombings in London and Madrid, or terror attacks in Mumbai using their cell phones. Or they can break the monopoly judgment of professional editors whose shared professional culture limits the range of stories considered to be newsworthy. Shirky cites the widely touted example of blog coverage of US Republican Senator Trent Lott and his public endorsement of the racist public record of GOP colleague Strom Thurmond (2008, pp. 61–6). In 2007 a witness used his hand-held video recorder to capture the police use of a taser gun on Polish immigrant Robert Dziekanski at the Vancouver International Airport. The dramatic video of his death following the taser blasts went viral after being posted online. The video evidence sparked public outrage and a full public inquiry that contradicted official police accounts. These examples point to how the global diffusion of hand-held audio-visual devices is expanding the range of "mediated visibility" and redrawing boundaries between public and private space (Thompson, 2004).

Popular blogger and instructor of interactive journalism at City University of New York Jeff Jarvis goes much further. He is convinced the perceived collapse of the traditional institutions of journalism, most notably newspapers, is not a problem; it is a welcome development in the emergence and evolution of Web-based, citizen-driven information sites. Jarvis envisions a world of abundant, accurate and timely information provided by an army of workers populating the Web with endless reportage, and in which professionals serve a reduced role as curators and aggregators of information (Jarvis, 2008). Canadian online columnist Wayne MacPhail (2009) agrees, writing:

> Traditional news organs are going to spend as much time curating that coverage as creating their own. And, when they do create their own, they'll be using the same cellphones and social networks as the rest of us. One or two big network eyes will be replaced by a network of small eyes bearing witness.

If Jarvis and MacPhail are correct, we have nothing to fear. Indeed, the exponential expansion of amateur cooperation should break free from the limits of traditional media, expanding the range and diversity of news coverage; citizen journalists will fill the void. But before we embrace this rosy vision of the future we need to critically examine the history of journalism as an institution. How exactly does this institution operate? What are its professional norms and conventions? What social interests are served? Finally, what if anything would be lost with its demise? Can amateur "communities of practice" adequately replace the diminished labour capacity of shrunken newsrooms? According to Clay Shirky (2009): "Nobody knows." We too have our doubts.

A Critical Sociology of News and New Media

Where do news reports come from? Romantic portrayals of rugged-individualists notwithstanding, news—the stories we read, watch and hear—have historically been a result of institutional norms of performance. Rules of conduct and organization regulate the work of journalism and make it predictable (Hackett and Gruneau, 2000; Tuchman, 1978). All news organizations must find a steady and reliable supply of raw news material; this is accomplished through the establishment of a "news net," otherwise known as the beat system, comprised of the courts, legislature, city hall, police, school boards, and corporate boards of directors, etc. The reliance on beats attached to particular bureau-cracies limits the kind of information journalists understand as news. The collection of news, therefore, is "bureaucratically organized" for reporters by representatives of various bureaucratic institutions (Fishman, 1980). A large body of critical scholarly research argues convincingly that the sourcing routines of reporters are based upon a hierarchy of credibility that reproduces a set of facts and values supportive of dominant social interests (Ericson et al., 1987; Glasgow University Media Group, 1976; Hall et al., 1978). That is to say, the "regime of objectivity" is itself ideological (Hackett and Zhao, 1998).

The institution of journalism also has its own political economy. Critical scholarship puts forward structural theories of media determination that suggest media production is constrained by market forces beyond the control of individual media organizations and their elite owners and managers (Baker, 2007; Herman and Chomsky, 1988; McChesney, 2004). This research counters neo-liberal claims that the market, when left unfettered by government regulation, can be a positive and democratic influence on media production. First, it ignores the increasing market dominance and corporate concentration of giant media conglomerates which can use their size and dominant position in the market to limit or freeze out competition. Secondly, it ignores the high capital cost of entry into the market place for new media outlets. Finally, the neo-liberal model ignores the critical funding role played by advertising in commercial media and the need to attract affluent audiences.

As we have seen, some critics of traditional mainstream newsrooms celebrate the autonomy amateur producers and citizen journalists have to break from institutional convention. Moreover, Shirky argues it is precisely the fact that barriers to entry have fallen that new amateur communities of practice can emerge. Axel Bruns (2008) touts, what he calls, the move from "gatekeeping" to the "gatecrashing" practiced by citizen journalists. Could it be true that the critique of critical media scholars no longer applies? We don't think so. There are a number of unexplored assumptions in Shirky's and Bruns's argument that require unpacking. First, it assumes the content lost by the weakening of traditional news organizations will be replaced by amateur producers; that in fact a sizable labour force of reporters would be available, capable and willing to replace the work formerly performed by salaried staff at metro dailies.

Critical scholars made clear that the work routines of reporters did not in any way mirror reality in an objective sense. News is socially constructed in a way that reproduces dominant social interests. The goal of the criticism was to change journalistic work routines in order to broaden the diversity of social interests found in news coverage; it was to create what Herbert Gans (2003) calls "multiperspectival news." We agree. But this critique was always predicated on its own assumption—that a large workforce would remain tasked with the job of reporting local, national, and international events. The state and its associated bureaucratic institutions (police, courts, councils, regulatory agencies and crown corporations) still exist and require constant scrutiny. The scale of newsroom layoffs and the concurrent expansion of a reserve army of freelance reporters or amateur bloggers have fundamentally altered the institutional context. This context requires mapping.

Axel Bruns (2008) explicitly argues that forms of citizen journalism, such as political bloggers and the online news organization *Ohmynews* in Korea, contribute to a Gansian multi-perspectival news production. At their best these online sites create space for deliberations that do not privilege expert opinion or the privileged view of the professional reporter. Citizen reporting is to be applauded if it provides a check on bureaucratically framed representations of reality and common sense—as was clearly the case in the Dziekanski taser incident. However, "it is nonetheless important to recognize the extent to which competing conceptions of citizen journalism revolve around crisis reporting" (Allan, 2009, p. 18), such as the Dziekanski incident and the posted cell-phone video of police crackdowns on Iranian street protests in June 2009. It is precisely in moments of crisis that the spot reporting of participant observers has been shown to alter the nomos of the field of journalism (Allan and Thorsen, 2009).

A model of journalism that is reliant on the serendipity of well-meaning, cell phone-equipped citizens is no substitute for the day-to-day grind of reporting and fact checking required to cover state institutions, such as the court system, or the financialization of the securities industry that contributed to meltdowns in the North American and UK housing markets. The fact that traditional news organizations failed to provide sufficient coverage of financial ponzi schemes or for that matter government war propaganda in the run up to the invasion of Iraq does not provide much comfort unless it can be demonstrated that citizen journalism can replace this unfulfilled labour. According to the data collected by the Project for Excellence in Journalism (2009) this has not occurred; independent online sites continue to rely on reports from traditional newsrooms.

Bruns speaks of an end to information scarcity and the ability of publics to find and access information on their own. He claims further that intuitional players and non-profit organizations increasingly speak directly to their constituencies, no longer relying on the mediation of news organizations (Bruns, 2008, p. 262).

Unfortunately, corporate, government and military bureaucracies remain largely opaque and determined to fight public scrutiny. Disclosure of information valuable to the public will continue to require long hours of labour—developing trusted and knowledge-able sources, studying documents and learning the complexities of such things as health care bureaucracies.

Bruns concedes that it is "too early" to know with certainty whether *Ohmynews* will be able to change the journalistic system for the better or whether it will "suffer subsumption into the day-to-day news cycle" (Bruns, 2008, p. 267). We can say with some certainty, however, that the flexible labour and production regimes of online news sites are largely homologous with dominant Post-Fordist regimes of flexible accumulation. Viewed dialectically, the eye-witness video clips posted to CNN's iReport.com supports the industry trend toward layoffs, repurposing content and the structuring of the 24-hour news wheel around dramatic breaking news events. In this sense, citizen journalism is integrated into the dominant logic of the heteronomous pole.

Late-capitalist social relations have not been superseded. The weakening of corporately-owned and advertiser-funded news organizations may be a welcome sign for those who wish to escape from under the corporate yoke, but it does not mean that capitalist commodity relations no longer structure everyday life, or for that matter the production of news.

Part of the problem with these optimistic views of a decentralized, largely volunteer army of online citizen journalists is that it is, to some extent, predicated on a misapprehension of the fundamental structures of the news industry. Shirky has contributed to the misunderstanding when he writes: "If you want to know why newspapers are in such trouble, the most salient fact is this: printing presses are tremendously expensive to set up and run" (Shirky, 2009).

Shirky mistakes the part for the whole. In fact, the most expensive part of running a news organization is the people, not the press, but Shirky's notion, widely disseminated and adopted by online pundits, skillfully avoids the issue of labour. The digital distribution of cultural artifacts has significantly reduced barriers to entry, but it does not address the issue of journalistic reporting. Unless they are in some way independently wealthy, as is the case with *Huffington Post* founder Arianna Huffington, amateur bloggers and salaried employees find themselves in a society that requires them to sell their labour power as a commodity to earn the money required to reproduce themselves and their families. Bloggers need to buy groceries, pay rent and raise their children too. Commenting on the creative intellectual labour of part-time academics, Marc Bousquet argues that "flex-timers generally pay for the chance to work" by shouldering the financial costs of professional development, "maintaining themselves in constant readiness for their right to work" (Bousquet, 2008, p. 63). What does this structural necessity mean for the work of reporting and editing? At the very least it calls into question Skirky's suggestion that communities of practice motivated by love can be relied upon to replace the lost labour of paid newsroom reporters.

Secondly, blogs, video and other user-generated content (UGC) are not products of unmediated agency. "The question of what drives users to contribute time and labour to an exploding number of UGC sites is crucial if we want to understand the volatile relationship between media companies and their worker–client base" (Dijck, 2009, p. 50). Citizen journalists and other so-called "prosumers" living in developed capitalist nations, such as the United Kingdom or United States, are members of a "society of consumers" which compels individuals to produce themselves as commodities as a precondition of participation in social life (Bauman, 2007). New media are not separated from this broader social context. They are a part of it.

José van Dijck argues that YouTube and Google have become "mediating platforms between the masses of aspiring amateurs" and corporate media (Dijck, 2008, p. 52). As a result YouTube has become "an Internet trader in the options market for fame" (2009, p. 53). If true, this development is extremely important for a journalistic field awash with under-employed labour seeking gainful employment.

Effects of Heteronomous Change on the Journalistic Field

The effects of field changes within traditional news organizations have been enormous, both on a macro and micro level. At the institutional level, previously autonomous news organizations have been forced by economic pressures to develop new content-sharing relationships with partner outlets in their organization or with competitors. In Canada, CanWest Global withdrew its chain of newspapers from the cooperative content-sharing arrangement of Canadian Press to form its own internal "wire service." Simultaneously, the chain developed a centralized content production centre in Winnipeg, creating uniform, packaged news pages to be repurposed by all of its member media outlets, introduced a national editorial policy and retired the title of "publisher" replacing it with "general managers" at each paper, reflecting the waning autonomy of the individual newspapers (Soderlund and Hildebrandt 2005).

At the newsroom level, the impact of structural changes greatly affects the fields in which individual journalists toil. In the United States, 23,000 newspaper jobs were lost between 2007 and 2009. Canadian and UK papers had suffered similar declines in staffing. The result is fewer reporters with heavier workloads, not solely in terms of coverage of news events, but in how those events are covered in the converging newsrooms. The remaining staffs are required to post to the Internet, collect audio and video clips, shoot digital photographs, post updates to blogs and most recently, update live to Twitter. In similar cost-cutting measures, some news organizations have outsourced their foreign coverage to a network of part-time correspondents (Adams and Ovide, 2009).

In perhaps the most extreme example of the labour displacement in newsrooms, the editor of a California-based news website, pasadenanow.com, engaged reporters in Mumbai, India to watch local town council meetings streamed live on the Web, leveraging low wages and the time difference to cut production time and costs (Associated Press, 2007).

New Beginnings and Old Problems

We are not apologists for the traditional newsroom nor for the business model that, for many decades supported it. Neither do we argue that mainstream news organizations are not responsible to some extent for their current struggles; they squandered a huge market advantage because of short-sightedness and greed; they failed to invest in research and development and to respond to changing demographics, tastes and emerging new technologies; and in a supreme display of hubris, they stood by complacently while upstart Internet-based initiatives ate into their once profitable classified advertising base. But, at the same time, we reject the growing mythology that simultaneous with this decline is the rise of the autonomous "citizen journalist," the unpaid, amateur enthusiast who, with an army of diffuse and self-organized others, will create autonomous opportunities for the pluralistic production of news that will replace the current, though declining, daily coverage of news provided by the mainstream media, specifically by village, town and city newspapers.

To be sure, a plethora of entrepreneurial alternatives have emerged out of the digital dust-up of the preceding few years, with some encouragingly homologous with the autonomous pole of cultural power specific to the journalistic field. Canada's *The Tyee* (www.tyee.ca) exemplifies a distinctly regional response to both the reduction of local coverage and its perceived homogenization by the corporate owners of the media chains that service those areas. Launched five years ago by journalist David Beers, the website is independent, supported by readers, investors, advertisers and funders. It is a lively mix of original reporting, investigative work, columns and opinion, all of which garnered it the Award for Excellence from the Canadian Journalism Foundation in 2009.

Similarly, voicesofsandiego.org is a recently-launched, non-profit, online news site supported by foundations, individuals and businesses. Their stated goal is, "To consistently deliver ground-breaking investigative journalism for the San Diego region. To increase civic participation by giving citizens the knowledge and in-depth analysis necessary to become advocates for good government and social progress" (http:voicesofsandiego.org). This site, and other similar start-ups such as Minnesota's Minnpost.com, are welcome initiatives in a depressed media landscape. Presumably, such organizations, not burdened with legacy buildings, high overhead and production and delivery costs, can operate with a higher level of efficiency and autonomy than traditional media outlets. But with a staff of 11, including six reporters and one photographer, voicesofsandiego.org is a Lilliputan-esque duplication of existing models employing displaced workers who are paid less and expected to do more. Though voicesofsandiego's stated intentions are laudable and their efforts a positive development in a troubled industry, the notion that a handful of reporters can adequately cover a city of more than one million people is fantastic.

At best, they can augment the coverage required to truly monitor the myriad institutions that constitute civil society. Similarly, sites such as *Huffington Post* in the United States or rabble.ca in Canada, are aggregative sites that provide opinion, but little, if any, original reporting. And more complicating, the very existence of these sites is, to some extent, predicated upon mainstream media which provides the news reports upon which the opinions are based, and, in some cases, pay for the commentary and opinion columns that are then repurposed and republished on these sites without fees. This, along with the unpaid work of contributors eager for exposure, constitutes, we would argue, an unsustainable model. The majority of blogs and citizen journalism sites produce little, if any, original reporting, relying for their content on the repurposing of reporting produced by legacy mainstream news organizations (Project for Excellence in Journalism 2009).

David Simon, a former *Baltimore Sun* reporter and creator of the television series *The Wire*, succinctly summarized the problem in a recent address to a US Senate Committee on Commerce when he said:

> High-end journalism is dying in America and unless a new economic model is achieved, it will not be reborn on the web or anywhere else ... You do not—in my city—run into bloggers or so-called citizen journalists at City Hall, or in the courthouse hallways or at the bars and union halls where police officers gather. You do not see them holding institutions accountable on a daily basis.[1]

Conclusion

Predicting the future of journalism is a dodgy proposition at the best of times, but particularly so during a moment of acute economic and social flux. Nonetheless, as we have seen, pundits have not shied away from suggesting journalism has entered a brave new age of citizen-produced democratic discourse. Old hierarchical journalistic institutions are said to be on their last legs, soon to be replaced by grassroots user-generated media.

The journalistic field is undergoing enormous change. Amateur content is increasingly part of the mix of traditional news media files, from CNN's iReports.com to aggregation sites such as nowpublic.com. But citizen participation is not an unambiguous social good; it must be contextualized.

The argument that citizen journalism creates autonomous opportunities for pluralistic production of news is a myth. We need to make a distinction between opinion and reporting. The former appears in abundance online; and if one looks hard enough a wide range of ideological views will be unearthed. This aspect of the emerging journalistic field supports those who argue the Internet has ended information scarcity. But it does not replace the daily work on the ground of reporting. What is lost is the daily drudgery of reporting; this unheralded labour is what makes possible a record of public life. The work of traditional newsrooms in this regard deserves to be challenged and questioned; it has always been partial and incomplete, but a model predicated on unpaid labour is not sustainable in our view. This point goes beyond the now stale debates pitting professional journalists against proverbial 'pajama-wearing' amateurs. The labour of reporting costs money; it takes time and the knowledge acquired through sustained effort. Piece-work reporting and participant-observer video captured during moments of crisis cannot replace the former institutional news net, flawed as it may have been. Corporate and state bureaucracies remain opaque behemoths that resist the light of public scrutiny.

NOTE

1.   Testimony of David Simon: Senate Committee on Commerce, Science and Transportation, Sub-Committee on Communications, Technology and the Internet, Hearing on the Future of Journalism, 6 May 2009.

REFERENCES

ADAMS, RUSSELL and OVIDE, SHIRA (2009) "Newspapers Move to Outsource Foreign Coverage", *Wall Street Journal*, 15 January, p. B4, http://online.wsj.com/article/SB123197973917183829. html?mod=todays_us_marketplace, accessed 18 June 2009.

ALLAN, STUART (2009) "Histories of Citizen Journalism", in: S. Allan and E. Thorsen (Eds), *Citizen Journalism: global perspectives*, New York: Peter Lang.

ALLAN, STUART and THORSEN, EINAR (2009) *Citizen Journalism: global perspectives*, New York: Peter Lang.

ASSOCIATED PRESS (2007) "Pasadena Local News Site Postpones Coverage by Reporters in India, *Editor & Publisher*, 14 May, http://www.editorandpublisher.com/eandp/news/article_display.jsp?vnu_content_id=1003584995, accessed 16 May 2009.

ATTON, CHRIS (2008) "Alternative Media Theory and Journalism Practice", in: Megan Boler (Ed.), *Digital Media and Democracy: tactics in hard times*, Cambridge, MA: MIT Press, pp. 213–27.

BAKER, C. EDWIN (2007) *Media Concentration and Democracy: why ownership matters*, New York: Cambridge University Press.

BAUMAN, ZYGMUNT (2007) *Consuming Life*, Cambridge: Polity.

BENSON, RODNEY (1998) "Field Theory in Comparative Context: a new paradigm for media studies", *Theory and Society* 28, pp. 463–98.

BENSON, RODNEY (2004) "Bringing the Sociology of Media Back In", *Political Communication* 21(3), pp. 275–92.

BENSON, RODNEY (2006) "News Media as a 'Journalistic Field': what Bourdieu adds to New Institutionalism, and vice versa", *Political Communication* 23(2), pp. 187–202.

BENSON, RODNEY and NEVEU, ERIC (2005) *Bourdieu and the Journalistic Field*, London: Polity Press.

BOURDIEU, PIERRE (1990) *The Logic of Practice*, Stanford, CA: Stanford University Press.

BOURDIEU, PIERRE (2005) "The Political Field, the Social Science Field, and the Journalistic Field", in: Rodney Benson and Erik Neveu (Eds), *Bourdieu and the Journalistic Field*, London: Polity Press, pp. 29–47.

BOUSQUET, MARC (2008) *How the University Works: higher education and the low-wage nation*, New York: New York University Press.

BRUNS, AXEL (2008) "Gatewatching, Gatecrashing: futures for tactical media", in: Megan Boler (Ed.), *Digital Media and Democracy: tactics in hard times*, Cambridge, MA: MIT Press, pp. 247–70.

COMPTON, JAMES (2004) *The Integrated News Spectacle: a political economy of cultural performance*, New York: Peter Lang.

COMPTON, JAMES (2009) "Newspapers, Labor and the Flux of Economic Uncertainty", in: Allan Stuart (Ed.), *The Routledge Companion to News and Journalism*, London: Routledge.

COULDRY, NICK (2003) "Media Meta-capital: extending the range of Bourdieu's Field Theory", *Theory and Society* 32, pp. 653–77.

DIJCK, JOSÉ VAN (2008) "Users Like You? Theorizing agency in user-generated content", *Media, Culture and Society* 31(1), pp. 41–58.

ERICSON, ROBERT V., BARANEK, PATRICIA M. and CHAN, JANET B.L. (1987) *Visualizing Deviance: a study of news organization*, Toronto: University of Toronto Press.

FISHMAN, MARK (1980) *Manufacturing the News*, Austin: University of Texas Press.

GANS, HERBERT (2003) *Democracy and the News*, Oxford and New York: Oxford University Press.

GLASGOW UNIVERSITY MEDIA GROUP (1976) *Bad News*, London: Routledge and Kegan Paul.

HACKETT, ROBERT and GRUNEAU, RICHARD (2000) *The Missing News: filters and blind spots in Canada's press*, Ottawa: Canadian Centre for Policy Alternatives; Aurora, Ontario: Garamond Press.

HACKETT, ROBERT and ZHAO, YUEZHI (1998) *Sustaining Democracy: journalism and the politics of objectivity*, Toronto: Garamond Press.

HALL, STUART, CRITCHER, CHARLES, JEFFERSON, TONY, CLARKE, JOHN and ROBERTS, BRIAN (1978) *Policing the Crisis: mugging, the state, and law and order*, London: Macmillan.

HANKE, BOB (2005) "For a Political Economy of Indymedia Practice", *The Canadian Journal of Communication* 30(1), pp. 41–64.

HARVEY, DAVID (1989) *The Condition of Postmodernity: an enquiry into the origins of cultural change*, Oxford: Blackwell.

HERMAN, EDWARD and CHOMSKY, NOAM (1988) *Manufacturing Consent: the political economy of mass media*, New York: Pantheon.

IBBITSON, JOHN (2009) "How Does U.S. Democracy Survive Without Its Newspapers?", *Globe and Mail*, 17 June, p. A17.

JARVIS, JEFF (2008) "Are Editors a Luxury That We Can Do Without?", *Guardian*, 18 August, http://www.guardian.co.uk/media/2008/aug/18/1, accessed 17 June 2009.

MACPHAIL, WAYNE (2009) "Twittering in Tehran and How Small Is the New Big", Rabble.ca, 15 June, http://www.rabble.ca/columnists/2009/06/twittering-tehran-and-how-small-new-big, accessed 20 June 2009.

MCCHESNEY, ROBERT W. (2004) *The Problem of the Media: U.S. communication politics in the 21st century*, New York: Monthly Review Press.

MOSCO, VINCENT (2009) "Future of Journalism", *Journalism* 10(3), pp. 350–52.

PROJECT FOR EXCELLENCE IN JOURNALISM (2009) "The State of the Media", March, http://www.stateofthemedia.org/2009/narrative_online_citizenmedia.php?media=5&cat=6, accessed 12 May 2009.

SHIRKY, CLAY (2008) *Here Comes Everybody: the power of organizing without organizations*, New York: Penguin Press.

SHIRKY, CLAY (2009) "Newspapers and Thinking the Unthinkable", shirky.com, 13 March, http://www.shirky.com/weblog/2009/03/newspapers-and-thinking-the-unthinkable/, accessed 14 March 2009.

SUNSTEIN, CASS R. (2006) *Infotopia: how many minds produce knowledge*, Oxford: Oxford University Press.

SUROWIECKI, JAMES (2005) *The Wisdom of Crowds*, New York: Anchor Books.

THOMPSON, JOHN B. (2004) "The New Visibility", *Theory, Culture and Society* 22(6), pp. 31–51.

TUCHMAN, GAYE (1978) *Making News: a study in the construction of reality*, New York: Free Press.

YONG JIN, DAL (2008) "Neoliberal Restructuring of the Global Communication System: mergers and acquisitions", *Media, Culture and Society* 30(3), pp. 357–73.

FROM "WE" TO "ME"
The changing construction of popular tabloid journalism

Martin Conboy and **John Steel**

In 1886, in "The Future of Journalism", W. T. Stead expressed the view that it was the "personal touch" in newspapers that would transcend the vapidity of a hypothesized "we". Nevertheless, it was to be the ability of newspapers, exploiting his own pioneering take on the New Journalism, to articulate a plausible version of a collective voice which was to dominate the journalism of the mass market of the twentieth century. A refinement of the language of this collective articulation of the interests and tastes of a mass readership comes in the popular tabloid newspapers of the period following the Second World War and reaches its most self-consciously vernacular expression in the Sun *from the 1980s onwards. However, when comparing the print version of the contemporary* Sun *with its online version, we might expect to witness a radical departure from traditional notions of the popular predicated on an appeal to a relatively homogenous collective readership and a move to a more atomized, self-assembling notion of the online reader. The "personalized" touch of this form of journalism is very different from that envisaged by Stead but by exploring the ways in which a theme which he considered central to journalism's mission (its address to an audience) is adapting to an online environment, we may be able to reconsider the changing definition and function of the "popular". In doing so, it may allow us to reflect upon the implications of a move from "we" to "me" in the articulation of audience in the online version of the* Sun.

Introduction

History teaches us that the future of journalism is not being discussed for the first time. It was reflected upon most explicitly by W. T. Stead as long ago as 1886. He had both cause and opportunity to ponder! The cause was the change being wrought within daily journalism by the confluence of voting reform, the subsequent growth of mass markets buoyed by the vast profits available from carefully directed display advertising and most significantly the popularizing influences on newspaper style and content emanating from democratic mobilizations in the United States (Schudson, 1978, p. 60). The opportunity for his deliberation was provided courtesy of his confinement in Holloway Prison for his part in the employment of a young girl, Lizzie Armstrong, in the sting which was to create the furore of investigative journalism exposing under-age prostitution in London's East End known as "The Maiden Tribune of Babylon" (Conboy, 2004; Örnebring, 2008). In "The Future of Journalism", he declaimed:

The future of journalism depends entirely upon the journalist . . . But everything depends on the individual—the person. Impersonal journalism is effete. To influence men you must be a man, not a muttering oracle. The democracy is under no awe of the mystic "We". Who is "We"? they ask; and they are right. For all power should be associated with responsibility, and a leader of the people, if a journalist, needs a neck capable of being stretched quite as much as if he is Prime Minister. For the proper development of a newspaper the personal element is indispensable. (Stead, 1886, p. 663)

Stead provided a euphoric vision of a journalism driven by ambitious individuals who could talk to and on behalf of a readership as a single constituency—a philanthropic view of journalism produced for the people or at least on their behalf; a platonic view with journalists as enlightened individuals reflecting the best interests of the people. Stead, despite his position as the instigator of much of the populist style of the New Journalism in Britain, was very much in the tradition of journalism as a form of education. In fact he stands at the threshold of the paradigm shift from the educational to the representational ideal of journalism (Hampton, 2004); one of the last in the line of educator-journalists before the arrival of a journalism whose main aim was not to educate a popular audience but to match their tastes. The individual address to the group which Stead articulates is radically altered by the eruption into the daily newspaper market of the *Daily Mail* in 1896 which shifts the discourse decisively towards an approximation of the tastes of the reading masses. Even its first sales slogan: "The penny paper for a halfpenny", hints at the newspaper's attempt to appeal to an audience who were upwardly aspirational in terms of a social composite. There may have been populist and commercial intent in the broadening out of this representational ideal but the intimacy of tone of the new mass journalism declared its personalized character strategically in order to mask the absence of any real bond with its readers beyond the rhetorical or the commercial (Salmon, 2000, p. 29). Furthermore, as readers were addressed in personal tones about matters which touched upon the everyday, they were increasingly marginalized from the politics which affected their daily lives (Hampton, 2001, p. 227) which meant that by the time of the *Mail*'s formative influence on the journalism of the twentieth century the "democratic component" of the Americanized import of the New Journalism (Wiener, 1996, p. 62) at the heart of Stead's vision for the future of journalism had well and truly been subordinated to a commercialized engagement with its audiences.

Such shifts of engagement with the audience of journalism are, however, nothing new and Smith has observed that these shifts have often had much to do with structural inadequacies within journalism's historical ambitions (Smith, 1979, p. 183). The current early twentieth-century reconfiguration of the relationship between product and producers, journalists and consumers seems to constitute another moment in this uneven progression where journalism is once again being forced to reconsider the "ideals and purposes" Smith suggests regularly come under pressure from technological, commercial and political demands. Yet the most significant aspect of this whole realignment is how to maintain a viable relationship with an audience for journalism.

Popular tabloid newspapers are of particular interest in any assessment of this configuration since the dominant trend within journalism in general, and particularly over the twentieth century, has been towards a popularization of its discourses. This was principally a commercial move by the mass dailies in the first instance but spread to other newspaper formats (LeMahieu, 1988) and eventually to other journalism media. From the *Daily Mail* onwards, the engagement of popular papers with their mass audiences became increasingly targeted to idealized versions of the reader profiles they were selling to advertisers. From 1931 the Audit Bureau of Circulation was providing regular and reliable circulation figures for the first time. This meant that knowing the audience mattered more than ever. However, this audience was increasingly constructed as a composite of an idealized individual acceptable to advertisers and recognizable to the audience themselves. By the eve of the Second World War the transformation of the popular newspaper market to a fully mass market, integrated with advertising, was complete (Bingham, 2004, p. 44) and key to this was the identification of the audience in composite form. Christiansen claimed that his "guiding principle" was whether his *Daily Express* at this time would be understood by people in the "backstreets of Derby" or by on "the Rhyl Promenade" in the 1930s (1961, p. 2). The rise of the individual voice in popular journalism first as the gossip columnist and then as the political columnist from Godfrey Winn to William Connor assisted in the carefully focused address to a particular reader-type in the relaunch of the *Daily Mirror* from 1934. Its subsequently increased profitability was rooted in the "successful projection of personality" of which Fairlie wrote in 1957 describing the "Old Codgers" section of the letters page (1957, p. 11).

Yet for all the success of mass circulation newspapers such as the *Daily Express* and the *Daily Mail* in attracting the broadest range of lower middle-class popular readers, it was the *Daily Mirror* which was to first define and then dominate the tabloid market with a language of specifically proletarian appeal (Bingham and Conboy, 2009). Engel has described its appeal from the point of its relaunch in the mid-1930s in the following terms:

> In the fuggy atmosphere of a bare-floored pre-war pub, the *Mirror* was the intelligent chap leaning on the counter of the bar: not lah-di-dah or anything—he liked a laugh, and he definitely had an eye for the girls—but talking a lot of common sense. (1996, p. 161)

It became a daily popular newspaper which articulated the views and aspirations of the working classes and perfected a vernacular style which transmitted that solidarity even if it was in an intensely commercialized form. A key element in this construction of a working-class voice was the use of letters such as "Viewpoint", "Live Letters" and "Star Letter", and later the replies of the "Old Codgers" to these letters as a barometer of readers' views. Also key to its development of a demotic printed language were the columns of Cassandra (William Connor) who provided an abrasive, populist political edge which railed against unemployment and appeasement and the complacency of the ruling classes in a language able to provoke debate and stir up passions.

The most significant, recent development in the history of British tabloid newspapers was the relaunch of the *Sun* in 1969. The *Sun* managed to articulate the resonance of Hunt's "permissive populism" (Hunt, 1998) of the 1970s and 1980s. Once the veneer of didacticism had been stripped away (Bingham, 2009), public discussion of the direct and vicarious pleasures of sexuality became commonplace within a language of vulgar celebration best epitomized by the descriptions of the Page 3 Girl: "Cor!"; "Wot a Scorcher!"; "Stunner!". Holland (1983) has provided a subtle reading of how the news agenda of the paper and its raucous appeal formed part of a linguistic endorsement of the power of pleasure in the lives of working-class readers, presenting itself as the champion of sexual liberation albeit of a particularly narrow, heterosexual, male-dominated variety. Thomas has summarized the epoch-defining pitch for a new, downmarket popular newspaper in Murdoch's conviction that that the *Daily Mirror* had become too highbrow for its readers by the 1960s and with former *Mirror* journalist Larry Lamb, he set out to produce an alternative that was explicitly based on an updated version of their rival's irreverent approach of previous decades (Thomas, 2005, p. 72). The *Sun* targeted younger readers, dropped the serious ambition of the *Mirror*, embraced the permissiveness of the age and provided a disrespectful, anti-establishment, entertainment-driven agenda. It reinforced its popular credentials by exploiting television advertising and an intensified interest in the off- and on-screen activities of the characters in soap operas on British television. Greenslade has linked this editorial content to its target readership thus: "It cultivated brashness, deliberately appealing to the earthier interests—and possibly, baser instincts—of a mass working-class audience" (2003, p. 337).

In addition, it was the ability of the *Sun* to transform the language of populist appeal away from the *Mirror*'s left-leaning progressive brand of politics to a new articulation of the sentiments and policies of the right which provided the *Sun* with its trump card, employing Walter Terry, former political editor of the right-wing *Daily Mail*, and Ronnie Spark to provide a demotic language to shape the editorial ambition for Murdoch/Lamb's shift to the right. In the 1970s and 1980s the Tories gained the support of the *Sun* (Negrine, 1994) which had become synchronized with the aspirations and identities of the classes which had been credited with the swing to Thatcher in the 1979 election. This represented an astute mapping of the newspaper's idiom on to the hegemonic shift to the ideological project of the Conservative Party in government. It soon perfected a style of vernacular address which highlighted the perceived interests of a newly empowered blue-collar reader.

Kelvin MacKenzie, the editor from 1981, encapsulated this new mood perfectly, articulating the idealized *Sun* reader variously from "White Van Man" to "*Sun* woman" but the reader remained identified as a composite of the newspaper's market identity and never so explicitly as in MacKenzie's vicious assessment of the typical reader he was writing for:

> He's the bloke you see in the pub—a right old fascist, wants to send the wogs back, buy his poxy council house, he's afraid of the unions, afraid of the Russians, hates the queers and weirdoes and drug dealers. (Chippendale and Horrie, 1992, p. 148)

The popularization of journalism has accelerated as technological convergence has been matched with a cultural convergence around what we could broadly call popular cultural values. This means that what happens in the popular tabloid press has implications for the broader journalism environment. The first trend towards an intensified form of popularization known as tabloidization is the literal transformation of broadsheets to tabloid format; from the *Daily Mail* in 1971 to the *Independent* in 2003. The second is the spread of the tabloid style and news values to the elite press. McLachlan and Golding (2000) chart that the growth in visuals in relation to text is one indicator of tabloidization, squeezing text out of the frame. Bromley observed this trend as it gathered momentum through the 1990s:

> At first, the "quality" press ignored the substantive issues of tabloid news; then decried them. These papers ... subsequently began reporting and commenting on the behaviour of the tabloid press, which led to the vicarious reporting of the issues themselves. Finally, the broadsheet papers, too, carried the same news items. (1998, p. 31)

The third trend has been the increasing incorporation of tabloid style and audience address into other forms of journalism (Conboy, 2006; Harrington, 2008). Journalism has always been as much about audience as about content. The matching of a particular style of news about the contemporary world to a particular audience able to pay enough to make a profit for the producers has been central to that balance between producer and consumer of journalism. What happens though when that balance is disturbed by fundamental social or technological shifts? Radio journalism had from its beginnings the intimacy of tone in what has been identified as its "sociability" (Scannell, 1996, p. 4) but certainly until the advent of television journalism it had, just like newspapers, articulated a view of the listener as a single audience but unlike newspapers it imagined them as a single organic national whole in empathy with the values of Reith's Presbyterian paternalism and the tones of Received Pronunciation. The popularization accelerated after the introduction of ITN in Britain in 1955 with its surge towards incorporation of entertainment values within televisual styles (Hartley, 1996).

Further technological changes would appear to have destabilized journalism's engagement with a composite notion of the audience. First, the introduction of the interactivity by web 1.0 gave a somewhat different shape to the editorial communication between audience and producers with more opportunity for quasi-live commentary, contribution and response but this was still more or less predicated on the mass as idealized individual. Next, web 2.0 appears, initially, to be destabilizing even that relatively recent model. The mass is being individuated and this is the future with which journalism is beginning to grapple as communities dissolve into aggregates of individuals and need to be addressed as such (see also Conboy and Steel, 2008; Deuze, 2004, 2006; Downes and McMillan, 2000).

The *Sun* first appeared online in 1999 with a site entitled CurrantBun.co.uk. In subsequent years the *Sun*'s online presence has undergone a number of transformations, the most recent being in 2008. The *Sun*'s current online presence could be described as a patchwork of its paper-based content: celebrity gossip, chat, sport, and news stories mixed with a number of interactive features and "converged" content (Deuze, 2008; Dupagne and Garrison, 2006; Quinn, 2005).

In terms of how the site is presented, the *Sun*'s tabloid newspaper identity is of course dominant, with bold headers and lots of pictures, usually of attractive young women in various states of undress (Sparks, 2000). Along the header bar are the "Home"; "MySun"; "Sun Lite" and "Suntalk—The Home of Free Speech" tabs. On the left-hand side of the home page we have a content selection area where users can access video (from "*Sun* exclusives", "celebs exposed" and "page three TV" to sport and links to BSkyB news video); news; sport; showbiz; women; health, all of which mirrors the paper version of the *Sun*. The video content resonates with the main frivolous subject matter of the paper version with titillating videos of "page three photo-shoots" and "viral babes" to viral videos of "extreme sheep herding" and "gorillas playing cricket". Across the site readers/ users are given the opportunity to comment on specific stories or share their views on the *Sun*'s many discussion boards. There is nothing here that is markedly different to other tabloid or even quality newspapers' online versions in that they are attempting to reflect the identity of the newspaper in an online form and promote a level of interactivity (see Chung, 2008; Hermida and Thurman, 2008).

The *Sun*'s online content provides a number of opportunities for people to contribute and "participate" in debate and discussion about the stories that interest them. A number of features of the website are significant with regard to interactivity. The most prominent is the link entitled "MYSun" which proclaims "Your News, Your Views, Your Life". This section of the website invites users to write and say what they think about any particular issue or comment on a *Sun* article. Within this section we see further links to particular forums from news, TV and reality forums, to football, lifestyle and even a forum entitled "pub banter". The discussions are moderated and as with many similar discussion boards readers are invited to report inappropriate content. Another feature under the "MYSun" tab is the Blogs section. Here users have the opportunity to write and update their own blogs. However, there is little evidence that there is much interaction by users though they do have an audience which is identified by the number of views column on the page. One of the more novel aspects of the *Sun*'s online site is the "SunTalk" section which advertises itself as "the home of free speech". Here we have *Sun* columnist Jon Gaunt or "Gaunty", chairing a daily talk radio show which can be accessed via the website. Listeners or readers can ring up and speak on air to Gaunty, or they can comment online on the discussion boards. The content is driven by the main news agenda of the day and the *Sun*'s editorial orientation. The talk show therefore gives the *Sun* the opportunity to articulate its editorial lines on whatever issues it deems relevant and also test the water in terms of the political and ideological orientations of their audience (Conboy, 2006). In contrast to the elite press—*The Times, Guardian* etc. it could be argued that in providing the interactive features that it does, the *Sun* online is providing what might be termed a space for an alternative non-elite public voice to issues of concern, a sort of tabloid version of an alternative public sphere (Örnebring and Jönsson, 2004) in which the everyday concerns of the *Sun*'s reading public can be voiced and aired. Or as Johansson has suggested, tabloids such as the *Mirror* and the *Sun* provide their readerships with the facilities to search for a sense of community, which as she says "helps explain the appeal of the sociability, collective identity and clarity as experienced through the *Sun* and the *Mirror*" (2008, p. 411).

However, the *Sun* also uses this space to reinforce its essentially authoritarian populist agenda (Billig, 1990) in which it seeks to both chime with and influence predominantly male, white, working-class culture. In a stark example of the delicate ideological line that the *Sun* walks (see Searle, 1989), we see "Gaunty" explicitly attempting to set out the boundaries of legitimate racialized discourse. In discussing the British National Party (BNP) and its recent limited success in the European elections, Gaunt attempts to draw a dividing line between the right-wing views of the *Sun* and the racism of the BNP. He proclaims:

> The only reason the BNP got voted into the European parliament is that mainstream politicians have been too afraid to tackle the subjects that really concern ordinary people. For the record, they are uncontrolled immigration, political correctness, law and order and benefit cheats ... You can be Right-wing, back the free market and want to quit Europe without being a racist. You can believe only people who have paid into our pot should be able to take out without donning a white hood.
>
> You can believe in capital punishment without becoming a member of a lynch mob. You can want to get rid of political correctness without calling people Pakis. You can want to protect British industry without hating Johnny Foreigner. You can believe people should fit in or ship out without denying their rights and culture. And you can wrap yourself in our flag and be proud of our history and successes. Unfortunately, if you expressed any of the above in recent years the fascists on the Left and in the BBC shut down the debate or tried to portray you as Little Englanders at best, and racists at worst. These deluded fools are to blame for Griffin and Darby—the Dumb and Dumber

of British politics—grabbing a foothold. But Griffin and his henchmen don't represent me and you shouldn't let them represent you. (Gaunt, 2009)

There are a number of things that are of interest here. The first, as noted is the attempt to draw a clear distinction between the values of the *Sun* and the BNP. Gaunt reaffirms his, and the *Sun*'s commitment to a set of right-wing values that it perceives chimes with their readership. Here, and elsewhere, when the *Sun* discusses the BNP it attempts to negotiate complex ideological terrain, some of which it arguably shares with the BNP—notions of British identity, pride in the nation, working-class identity, secure borders, Euro-scepticism, anti-Political Correctness etc. Gaunt is in a sense giving his readers permission to be "right wing" and articulate acceptable right-wing beliefs, without having to worry about being racist. Yet, of course, as Billig (1990) has demonstrated, the *Sun*'s dilemmatic ideological character enables it to offer "discursive variability" with which it can appeal to a spectrum of values and beliefs which are often internally incoherent. This then allows the *Sun* to "fence off" its rhetoric from that of the BNP while the *Sun*'s negotiation with the normative claims it makes regarding the BNP re-affirm the *Sun*'s commitment to a set of values which broadly chime with its perception of white working-class people. The *Sun* online continues, as one would expect, to attempt to negotiate this complex ideological terrain yet this is in the context of a set of individuated spaces that the *Sun* online constructs. The *Sun* then reverts to its familiar ideological role in attempting to offer normative popular rhetoric within an individuated yet paradoxically homogenized space.

What is also interesting in the quote from Gaunt is the way in which the *Sun* attributes the success of the BNP to the left in Britain, exemplified in the BBC and the "failures of mainstream politicians to tackle the subjects that concern ordinary people". It is obvious that the *Sun* should push this line given the perceived threat that the BNP poses to pick up traditional working-class conservative voters. Again we see the *Sun* conforming to Örnebring and Jönsson's notion of an alternative public sphere, offering a focus for peoples' frustration and anger at the political system in Britain, reflecting and shaping this view at the same time (Steel, 2009).

But in what sense does the *Sun* offer space for its readership to facilitate to the transition from "we" to "me"? Has the "me" been sidelined in preference for familiar ideological and professional values of the executives at News International and the journalists responsible for the *Sun* online, respectively? There has been significant research on the pressures of providing greater interactivity within mainstream media, on both institutions and individual journalists. For example, Domingo (2008) examines journalists' perceptions of interactivity in online news using ethnographic studies of four newsrooms in the United States. Domingo suggests that there is a strong culture in these newsrooms that adheres to traditional roles. Rather than seeing interactive features of online news sites as circumventing traditional power relations between the journalist and the public, journalists saw interactive features as a hindrance to their everyday routines (2008, p. 698).

Domingo argues interactivity is a myth that journalists have to deal with (often unsuccessfully) in their daily lives. Similarly, Paulussen et al. (2007), studying interactivity and user-generated content (UGC) in newspapers in Belgium, Finland, Germany and Spain, suggest that despite the "hype and high expectations", media in these countries have not delivered on audience participation. The authors suggests that notwithstanding the economic imperative which is driving newspapers to diversify and enhance their operations in relation to UGC, and external pressure from bloggers and users to move towards a more participatory type of journalism (cf. Singer, 2007), an internal commitment to traditional journalistic norms which favour a "top down" approach remains dominant. Moreover, as Singer (2005) suggests, even when journalists are involved in blogging and UGC they tend to adhere to traditional gate-keeping roles and seem reluctant to make the most of this purportedly democratizing medium (cf. Singer, 1997). O'Sullivan and Heinonen (2008) suggest that journalists by and large welcome the new challenges of the Internet and do not necessarily see these as a threat to their profession. However, so-called "citizen journalism" is rejected as not offering "real" journalism and potentially undermining the value of professional journalists. Moreover, their study confirms that journalism is reluctant to abandon its organizational and professional conventions even in the face of rapid technological change (O'Sullivan and Heinonen, 2008, p. 386). The authors question whether the profession can "maintain its status quo" or adapt to a more participatory model (2008, 386). Similarly, Domingo et al. looked at the way in which 16 online newspapers interpret online user participation mainly "as an opportunity for their readers to debate current events, while other stages of the news production process are closed to citizen involvement or controlled by professional journalists when participation is allowed" (2008, p. 326). The authors assessed their functionality in terms of how much power is relinquished by the journalist in terms of the development of a genuine participatory online news site. The view was that "the institutional media had largely kept the journalistic culture unchanged even when exploring participation opportunities for the audience" (Domingo et al., 2008, p. 335). The paper describes the various strategies that newspapers use but stresses their reluctance to "open up" to active participation as such "core journalistic culture remains largely unchanged" (2008, p. 339). Hermida and Thurman (2008) demonstrate a "massive increase in online opportunities across all but one of the 12 UK national newspapers" (2008, p. 353). They suggest that editors and executives fear being left behind and that the industry is "still working out whether and how to integrate user participation within existing norms and practices" (2008, p. 350), brand damage seemed to be an issue. Yet the authors also suggest that UGC can also help bond users to a newspaper brand. Also in line with other aforementioned research, the authors suggest that "news organisations tend to expand their operations to the Internet based on their existing journalistic culture, including the way they relate to the public" (Hermida and Thurman, 2008, p. 353).

In the context of this research it is relatively simple to understand why the *Sun* online clings to its traditional discourse and function, to step out from this mode would be truly revolutionary. The attempts at interactivity and encouraging reader participation, the *Sun* online, in the context of both a dominant brand and ideological orientation, highlights the difficulties faced by newspapers across the industry in attempting to negotiate the transition from "we" to "me".

In newspapers, as in commercial journalism generally, the business model which allowed mass audiences to be capitalized through advertising has crumbled. The fragmentation of mass audience into individuated and fractured spaces of consumption might well see the text as well as the advertising of newspapers follow this pattern of development from a mass to an individuated articulation of community and one driven more by the consumers than the producers of any overall audience design (Bell, 1991).

The popular paradox is that developments in contemporary online popular newspapers may lead us to ponder whether the future of journalism might in its fragmented, individuated construction of audience be better suited to answer the demands of the popular, namely to provide something more representative of the tastes and desires of the people than ever the aggregated audience, hypothesized as an idealized individual, was able to. There exists nevertheless a tension between the individuation that technology seems to promise and the culturally and politically normative aspects of tabloid journalism. As the popularity of tabloid journalism strengthens its influence on journalism in general, journalism's future will be to a large extent determined by its ability to resolve such tensions. Stead has been proved right in one aspect of the conclusions which emanated from his forced period of reflection on the future of journalism. The personal element remains indispensable. He is also right that the journalist remains the essential conduit in reshaping a personal connection to an audience as part of the generalized "We", albeit in very different times.

REFERENCES

BELL, ALLAN (1991) *Language in the News*, Oxford: Blackwell.

BILLIG, MICHAEL (1990) "Stacking the Cards of Ideology: the history of the Sun souvenir royal album", *Discourse & Society* 1(1), pp. 17–37.

BINGHAM, ADRIAN (2004) *Gender, Modernity and the Popular Press in Inter-War Britain*, Oxford: Oxford University Press.

BINGHAM, ADRIAN (2009) *Family Newspapers? Sex, private lives and the British popular press 1918–1978*, Oxford: Oxford University Press.

BINGHAM, ADRIAN and CONBOY, MARTIN (2009) "The Daily Mirror and the Creation of a Commercial Popular Language: a people's war: a people's paper?", *Journalism Studies* 10(5), pp. 639–54.

BROMLEY, MICHAEL (1998) "The 'tabloiding' of Britain: quality newspapers in the 1990s", in: Hugh Stephenson and Michael Bromley (Eds), *Sex, Lies and Democracy*, Harlow: Addison Wesley Longman, pp. 24–38.

CHIPPENDALE, PETER and HORRIE, CHRIS (1992) *Stick It Up Your Punter*, London: Mandarin.

CHRISTIANSEN, ARTHUR (1961) *Headlines All My Life*, London: Heineman.

CHUNG, DEBORAH S. (2008) "Interactive Features of Online Newspapers: identifying patterns and predicting use of engaged readers", *Journal of Computer-mediated Communication* 13(3), pp. 658–79.

CONBOY, MARTIN (2004) *Journalism: a critical history*, London: Sage.

CONBOY, MARTIN (2006) *Tabloid Tales: constructing a community through language*, Abingdon: Routledge.

CONBOY, MARTIN and STEEL, JOHN (2008) "The Future of Journalism: historical perspectives", *Journalism Studies* 9(5), pp. 650–61.

DEUZE, MARK (2004) "What Is Multimedia Journalism?", *Journalism Studies* 5(2), pp. 139–52.

DEUZE, MARK (2006) "Liquid Journalism", Working Paper, https://scholarworks.iu.edu/dspace/handle/2022/3202?mode=simple, accessed 22 June 2009.

DEUZE, MARK (2008) "The Professional Identity of Journalists in the Context of Convergence Culture", *Observatorio* (OBS*) 7, pp. 103–17.

DOMINGO, DAVID (2008) "Interactivity in the Daily Routines of Online Newsrooms: dealing with an uncomfortable myth", *Journal of Computer-mediated Communication* 13(3), pp. 680–704.

DOMINGO, DAVID, QUANDT, THORSTEN, HEINONEN, ARI, PAULUSSEN, STEVE, SINGER, JANE B. and VUJOVIC, MARINA (2008) "Participatory Journalism Practices in the Media and Beyond: an international comparative study of initiatives in online newspapers", *Journalism Practice* 2(3), pp. 326–42.

DOWNES, EDWARD J. and MCMILLAN, SALLY J. (2000) "Defining Interactivity: a qualitative identification of key dimensions", *New Media & Society* 2(2), pp. 157–79.

DUPAGNE, MICHAEL and GARRISON, BRUCE (2006) "The Meaning and Influence of Convergence: a qualitative case study of newsroom work at the Tampa News Centre", *Journalism Studies* 7(2), pp. 237–55.

ENGEL, MATTHEW (1996) *Tickle the Public: one hundred years of the popular press*, London: Gollancz.

FAIRLIE, HUGH (1957) "Brilliance Skin-deep", *Encounter* July, pp. 8–14.

GAUNT, JON (2009) "BNP Nick Griffin Wont Talk to Me? That's a badge of honour", *The Sun*, http://www.thesun.co.uk/sol/homepage/news/columnists/john_gaunt/2477555/Jon-Gaunt-BNP-Nick-Griffin-wont-talk-to-me-Thats-a-badge-of-honour.html, accessed 17 June 2009.

GREENSLADE, ROY (2003) *Press Gang: how newspapers make profits from propaganda*, Basingstoke: Macmillan.

HAMPTON, MARK (2001) "'Understanding Media': theories of the press in Britain, 1850–1914", *Media, Culture and Society* 23(2), pp. 213–31.

HAMPTON, MARK (2004) *Visions of the Press in Britain, 1850–1950*, Urbana: University of Illinois Press.

HARRINGTON, STEPHEN (2008) "Popular news in the 21st century: time for a new critical approach?", *Journalism: theory, practice and criticism* 9(3), pp. 266–84.

HARTLEY, JOHN (1996) *Popular Reality*, London: Arnold.

HERMIDA, ALFRED and THURMAN, NEIL (2008) "A Clash of Cultures", *Journalism Practice* 2(3), pp. 343–56.

HOLLAND, PATRICIA (1983) "The Page 3 Girl Speaks to Women Too", *Screen* 24(3), pp. 84–102.

HUNT, LEON (1998) *British Low Culture: from safari suits to sexploitation*, London: Routledge.

JOHANSSON, SOFIA (2008) "Gossip, Sport and Pretty Girls", *Journalism Practice* 2(3), pp. 402–13.

LEMAHIEU, DAN L. (1988) *A Culture for Democracy: mass communication and the cultivated mind in Britain between the wars*, Oxford: Clarendon Press.

MCLACHLAN, SHELLEY and GOLDING, PETER (2000) "Tabloidization in the British press: a quantitative investigation into changes in British newspapers, 1952–1997", in: Colin Sparks and John Tulloch (Eds), *Tabloid Tales: global debates over media standards*, Oxford: Rowman and Littlefield, pp. 75–90.

NEGRINE, RALPH (1994) *Politics and the Mass Media in Britain*, London: Routledge.

O'SULLIVAN, JOHN and HEINONEN, ARI (2008) "Old Values, New Media", *Journalism Practice* 2(3), pp. 357–71.

ÖRNEBRING, HENRIK (2008) "The Consumer as Producer—of What? User-generated tabloid content in the *Sun* (UK) and *Aftonbladet* (Sweden)", *Journalism Studies* 9(5), pp. 771–85.

ÖRNEBRING, HENRIK and JÖNSSON, ANNA M. (2004) "Tabloid Journalism and the Public Sphere: a historical perspective on tabloid journalism", *Journalism Studies* 5(3), pp. 283–95.

PAULUSSEN, STEVE, HEINONEN, ARI, DOMINGO, DAVID and QUANDT, THORSTEN (2007) "Doing It Together: citizen participation in the professional news making process", *Observatorio* (OBS*) 3, pp. 131–54.

QUINN, STEPHEN (2005) "Convergence's Fundamental Question", *Journalism Studies* 6(1), pp. 29–38.

SALMON, RICHARD (2000) "'A Simulacrum of Power': intimacy and abstraction in the rhetoric of the New Journalism", in: Brake Laurel, Bell Bill and Finkelstein David (Eds), *Nineteenth Century Media and the Construction of Identities*, Basingstoke: Palgrave.

SCANNELL, PADDY (1996) *Radio, Television and Modern Life: a phenomenological approach*, Oxford: Blackwell.

SCHUDSON, MICHAEL (1978) *Discovering the News: a social history of American newspapers*, New York: Basic Books.

SEARLE, CHRIS (1989) "Your Daily Dose: racism and the press in Thatcher's Britain", *Race and Class* 12, pp. 21–37.

SINGER, JANE B. (1997) "Still Guarding the Gate? The newspaper journalist's role in an on-line world", *Convergence* 3(1), pp. 72–88.

SINGER, JANE B. (2005) "The Political J-blogger: 'normalizing' a new media form to fit old norms and practices", *Journalism* 6(5), pp. 173–98.

SINGER, JANE B. (2007) "Contested Autonomy: professional and popular claims on journalistic norms", *Journalism Studies* 8(1), pp. 79–95.

SMITH, ANTHONY (1979) *The Newspaper: an international history*, London: Thames and Hudson.

SPARKS, COLIN (2000) "Introduction: the panic over tabloid news", in: Colin Sparks and John Tulloch (Eds), *Tabloid Tales: global debates over media standards*, Oxford: Rowman and Littlefield, pp. 1–40.

STEAD, WILLIAM T. (1886) "The Future of Journalism", *Contemporary Review* 50(November), pp. 663–79.

STEEL, JOHN (2009) "The Idea of Journalism", in: Bill Eadie (Ed.), *21st Century Communication: a reference handbook*, Thousand Oaks, CA: Sage.

THOMAS, JAMES (2005) *Popular Newspapers, the Labour Party and British Politics*, London: Routledge.

WIENER, JOEL (1996) "The Americanization of the British Press", in: M. Harris and T. O'Malley (Eds), *Studies in Newspaper and Periodical History: 1994 annual*, Westport, CT: Greenwood Press, pp. 61–74.

RETHINKING [AGAIN] THE FUTURE OF JOURNALISM EDUCATION

Donica Mensing

For many of the previous 100 years the role of a journalist was to find information, shape it into an accurate story and transmit it as quickly as possible to a mass audience via a mass medium. Today, information is no longer scarce, breaking news is no longer the province of professional journalists, mass media are declining in influence and news is easily personalized. Like many news organizations, journalism education programs are distinctly unprepared to respond to such deeply structural changes in the environment. Preliminary research indicates that the response to date has been primarily to expand technology training and reorient sequence and media emphasis tracks. The present study recommends a realignment of journalism education from an industry-centered model to a community-centered model as one way to re-engage journalism education in a more productive and vital role in the future of journalism. A community-centered focus could provide a way to conceptualize a reconstitution of journalism education to match that taking place in journalism beyond the university. Three examples from current journalism programs illustrate the implications of this analysis and provide an indication of future directions for realignment.

Introduction

The "future of journalism education" has been the subject of debate and contention for more than 100 years, making yet another essay on the subject a likely candidate for redundancy or irrelevance. Despite this history, however, the topic remains relevant and critical, never more so than in the current period of remarkable transition and upheaval. At a time when the established economic model for journalism is collapsing, news organizations are retrenching and the journalistic workforce is shrinking, the justification for journalism schools to continue graduating thousands of hopeful recruits is increasingly debated.

This upheaval creates an opportune time to rethink [again] the configuration of US journalism programs. For historical and institutional reasons, most journalism programs retain the structure, some more than others, of an industrial model of training. The mass production of journalism fashioned the practices we teach today and embody an understanding of communication as a process of transmission from producer to receiver. As Carey (2000) has noted, journalism education came to life in the "age of the reporter", when the role of a journalist was to find information, shape it into an accurate story and transmit it as quickly as possible to a mass audience via a mass medium. While journalism schools have diversified and now graduate a large percentage of students who never pursue reporting, the idealized perception of journalism education still centers on the reporter and the basic functions of information gathering, evaluation, production and distribution.

This model of journalism, taught in journalism schools and run as a business by news organizations, has remained unchanged for many decades. Adding multimedia, using new storytelling techniques and delivering the product over the Internet does not change the basic model. Students learn this model in courses organized by sequences that relate to modes of distribution, with the role of the reporter a central theme in early classes. Courses are frequently taught by practitioners using textbooks that have changed little in their basic outline since 1938 (Brennan, 2000). "Correct" ways to write, report, and produce stories form the basic curriculum. Students are often required to complete internships as part of their practical training. This configuration of curriculum, work experience and mentorship reinforces particular conceptions of what journalism is and how to practice it. While convergence and multimedia storytelling have introduced some significant changes, the essential flow of journalism education has changed little in response to the "epochal transformation" (Project for Excellence in Journalism, 2004) taking place within communications.

The purpose of this paper is to suggest that as journalism schools take up a rigorous examination of their own practices, they consider an alternative to the transmission-driven, industry-conceived model of journalism. Moving the focus of attention from the industry to the community could reconnect journalism with its democratic roots and take advantage of new forms of news creation, production, editing and distribution. Rather than conceptualizing an independent reporter as the "defining role in American journalism" (Borden, 2007), a community-oriented model of journalism would place the journalist as reporter, editor and facilitator within a community. This configuration would emphasize the needs of community first and make the journalist part of a network of relationships. It would re-emphasize journalism's natural connection with community, as described by de Tocqueville (1990 [1835]), Dewey (1927) and Carey (1989) and refocus attention on the role that journalism can play in the health of a community. Working with students in a laboratory of inquiry, researching how journalism matters and experimenting with ways to practice journalism in a rapidly reconfiguring environment could reinvigorate journalism programs and encourage more productive connections between the work of educators, scholars, and practitioners.

In the following pages I describe briefly the present alignment of journalism schools within universities and how the industry-centered model came to dominate journalism education. The assumptions embedded in this model make it difficult for journalism educators to respond fully to the present crisis/opportunities in journalism. By "journalism education" I am referring specifically to university programs that teach news and editorial courses and conduct research in journalism and communication. While many journalism programs include public relations and advertising, and the ideas in this paper are applicable to those professions as well, the focus in this paper is to think specifically about education for journalists. I will describe how a community-centered focus could provide a way to conceptualize a reconstitution of journalism education to match that taking place in journalism beyond the university. Finally, several examples from current journalism programs will illustrate the implications of this analysis and provide an indication of future directions for realignment.

The call to reinvent journalism education has been oft repeated. Dennis (1984), Medsger (1996), Reese (1999), Reese and Cohen (2000), Carey (2000), Adam (2001), MacDonald (2006), Deuze (2006) and many others have identified new ways to conceptualize journalism education. The realignment advocated in this paper follows most closely that articulated by James Carey and interpreted in an appreciation by Jay Rosen (2006) on Poynter.com:

> Carey suggests an alignment with democracy as the key to reforming journalism education. That is, the J-school can get into proper alignment with the society, the university, and the profession in only one-way: by thinking with and through "democracy." … There's an intellectual crisis in journalism, which creates an opening for those of us who do "journalism" in a university setting … following Jim Carey as he follows John Dewey, I can say we need to experiment with a new alignment between journalism education and the university; between the J-school and the society, especially the media; and between the teaching of journalism and practicing journalists.

Industry-centered Journalism Education

From its earliest conceptions, journalism education has been about training students to work for newspapers (Becker, 2003; Dickson, 2000; O'Dell, 1935). Over time schools have added training in broadcast, advertising and public relations, some have added design programs, management sequences and emphases on various types of reporting. Some schools offer education only at the undergraduate level, some at the graduate level and some in both. Throughout its history, however, a central theme of journalism education has been that of a professionally oriented program focused on educating students for jobs in the media industries (Becker, 2003; Dickson, 2000). This is apparent in the assessment required by accreditation standards, in the curriculum offered at many journalism schools, and in the division between journalism educators and journalism scholars (Zelizer, 2004).

Meanwhile, the news institutions that helped to shape this educational system are struggling. Demand for their products is falling. As in many other industries large industrial organizations find their markets taken over by more efficient, targeted start-ups. General interest journalism, written in a particular style and convention, does not resonate with readers who have more choices for information and entertainment. The Internet is a driving force in changing the way information is produced, consumed and paid for, affecting news companies in every way imaginable.

During times of disruption, maintaining practices that reinforce an unsatisfactory status quo is a disservice that reduces the credibility of the university. While many examples could be used, here are three industry-centered patterns of journalism education that do a dis-service to students in this environment:

1. A focus on creating professionals, despite trends towards de-professionalization and contested meanings of the term "professional."
2. A focus on teaching skills and techniques that reinforce one-way communication.
3. A focus on socializing students for a newsroom (that many will never enter), more than engaging in critical inquiry.

These tendencies artificially separate theory from practice, emphasize best practices more than new practices, and reduce the ability of students to be fully prepared for a rapidly changing environment. A fuller explanation of each point follows:

Educating Professionals

Journalism education was part of a US reform movement born in the Progressive Era that sought to improve journalistic standards by raising the educational level of newspaper employees (Gaunt, 1992; O'Dell, 1935; Sutton, 1945; Weinberg, 2008). By providing better training and expanding the education of printers, editors and reporters, newspaper publishers hoped to improve the content and operations of their papers (MacDonald, 2006). At the same time, this effort was seen as a way to make "a dent in the callousness and ignorance of practicing journalists" (Weinberg, 2008, p. 2). Despite significant scepticism from practicing journalists, interest in raising journalism from a trade to a learned profession gained momentum, highlighted most publicly by editor Joseph Pulitzer's gift of $2 million to Columbia University in 1903 for a professional School of Journalism (Boylan, 2003; O'Dell, 1935). Pulitzer stipulated that the curriculum of the school should "emphasize the professional significance of journalism" and exclude all courses related to advertising procedure, circulation and newspaper management (O'Dell, 1935, p. 65).

Debates about whether journalism meets the definition of a profession surface regularly. The argument was particularly sharp during the 1960s and 1970s, encouraged in part by the sociological study of journalism (Becker et al., 1987; Schudson and Anderson, 2009; Tumber and Prentoulis, 2005; Zelizer, 2004, p. 57). Calls for increased professionalism are often related to periods of concern about the commercial interests and profit motives of media organizations (MacDonald, 2006). Despite these concerns, major US journalism education initiatives, for example the 2005 Carnegie-Knight "vision for journalism education," an $11 million effort to reinvent journalism education, consistently assume professionalism is *the* goal of journalism education (Carnegie Corporation, 2005).

As a source of ethical motivation, professionalism is a noteworthy and useful orientation (Borden, 2007, p. 106). But the enterprise to professionalize journalism is problematic. The gulf between the idealized practice of journalism and the practices of journalism today are rarely addressed in depth in journalism classrooms. Educators stressing professionalism often focus on a narrow definition of what "counts" as journalism, widening the gulf between how journalism is imagined in the academy and how it is actually practiced and perceived "out there" (Zelizer, 2004, 2009). Placing the responsibility for reform on the behavior of individual journalists, as is assumed in programs such as that sponsored by Knight-Carnegie, ignores the organizational, structural and economic roots of the professional crisis and the profit orientation that often motivates calls for reform (MacDonald, 2006). Separating editorial and business functions as a matter of principle makes it difficult for journalists to respond to changing economic conditions within their own organizations as well as in the larger societal context.

Another concern regarding professionalization is the question of occupational power. As Carey describes it, the movement to professionalize places the public in the role of a dependent client, subject to the decisions of the professional journalist who controls information: "This knowledge is defined, identified, presented, based upon canons of professional expertise over which the audience exercises no real judgment or control" (1980, p. 6). Rather than teach our students an attitude of professional authority as an embedded ideology, it would be far better to help them to explore and test thoroughly the assumption of professionalism in ways that would help them remake what it means to be a journalist in this new environment.

Teaching Skills and Techniques

A second aspect of an industry model of journalism education is a focus on teaching skills suitable for entry-level jobs (Stephens, 2002). For as long as journalism education has existed, it has been under fire by both practitioners and academics for focusing too much on the teaching of skills and techniques (Dickson, 2000). Accreditation rules have encouraged a journalism curriculum that includes a small core of conceptual courses and an emphasis on reporting, editing, writing, and production courses (Accrediting Council on Education in Journalism and Mass Communications, 2004).

The challenge during a time of disruption is that what came before does not necessarily predict or lead to what comes next. The practices of today were created during a time when information was scarce and distribution was generally one way through channels that had monopolistic advantages that no longer exist. Students now need to develop a different set of skills to deal with information abundance, network distribution, intense competition and a communication process that is interactive, asynchronous and nearly free. Convergence of sequences and multimedia training are new skills often used in old ways; courses that emphasize standard news judgment, voice, style and production regardless of the medium used for distribution, still assume a particular model of journalism that may have limited applicability in a networked environment.

Socialization

The strong emphasis in journalism education on practical experience through internships and other hands-on training experiences means that students are early socialized to particular practices:

> The goal of journalism education, whether implicitly or explicitly stated, is socialization to the profession. In other words, the intent of the curriculum, including the internships and laboratory experiences and the areas of study outside journalism, is to produce an individual who can effectively and efficiently function in the occupations of journalism and mass communications. (Becker et al., 1987, p. 19)

Media professionals routinely recommend improvements to journalism education that involve hiring more professionals as teachers (Gaunt, 1999, p. 33; Medsger, 1996). These professionals not only deliver skills and mentoring, but also socialize students into the expectations, norms and traditions expected of them when they arrive at their first jobs. During periods of little change, this model works well. At times of rapid change, such a model of education can leave employees and employers less able to respond in creative or resourceful ways. Rather than reinforcing patterns of the past, journalism educators could work more deliberately to challenge students to understand how to improve their own work in this new environment, rather than imitate what has gone before. "Best practices" of the previous generation may not be effective guides to the future. Critical reflection about the practices students encounter during internships and on the job training could help them stay more flexible and responsive to future change, rather than resistant or indifferent.

The scope of change that journalism educators face as they contemplate the structure and practices of their university departments is no less significant than that faced by the industry:

our overall point is that journalism education has for the past half-century or more assumed a model of the educated journalist as a generalist—the liberally educated young man or woman able to "know what's news" and exercise news judgment, to tell stories, to be able to do some research, to provide some analysis. That is a model we think increasingly too narrow: we suspect that journalism as a craft is undergoing a transformation similar to that in the (other) intellectual professions—the simultaneous deprofessionalization or proletarianization of much of the work, and increasingly high standards of knowledge and expertise for the remainder. (Whitney and Wartella, 2000, p. 54)

In other words, continuation of the status quo within journalism schools is increasingly untenable. Developing new models more appropriate to the needs of this age, as opposed to that of the media industries of the past, is a compelling obligation for journalism educators and scholars.

Community-centered Focus

If we accept the premise that preparing students for industrial news production should no longer drive journalism education, we have to consider an alternative focus. Historically, journalism has been about community. Restoring that focus and developing a community-centered model of education would honor the obligations that journalists and educators have towards their communities. In the same way that the goal of engineering programs is not to prepare students for their first jobs at large engineering firms, but to build safe bridges and highways, the goals of journalism education should be about building functioning communication structures within communities. This is a more useful metaphor for organizing journalism education today for the following reasons.

First, as Dewey describes, "men live in a community in virtue of the things which they have in common; and communication is the way in which they come to possess things in common" (1916, p. 5). To the degree that people understand they have common aims and adjust their behavior in response to this knowledge, they form a community. Journalism is about identifying and making clear the common aims and stakes we all share within our various communities. However, journalism as practiced today often aims toward an imagined audience, or even a "phantom" public, to use Lippmann's (1927) term, not an identifiable group of people with common aims. Journalism that ignores a community dimension can end up being used as a tool to divide people by interests, rather than build relationships critical for functioning communities.

With the advent of the Internet, it is now much easier for people to find on their own others with whom they have things in common, and to form real as well as "virtual" communities, based on Dewey's definitions. These virtual communities are increasingly erupting into visible and "real" communities with power, from political power to cultural and economic power (Rheingold, 1993). If journalists cling to a vague sense of public, they will increasingly be out of touch with the ways that their imagined communities are actually functioning. A community-centered education would need to deepen student understanding of what constitutes community, from local to global, from place based to interest based, and the role that journalism can play within various types of community.

While journalism has long recognized a duty to community (Fallows, 1997; Kovach and Rosenstiel, 2001), this obligation has been complicated by the assumption that journalistic independence requires some separation from the people, institutions or communities covered by a journalist. While this perception is the focus of much discussion regarding objectivity, transparency and advocacy (Schudson and Anderson, 2009), in the context of this paper, I would argue that journalists would serve communities best by acknowledging their own participation as citizens and responsible partners in and with communities. Robert Manoff (2002) described it this way:

> Because the journalist is the handmaiden of the citizen, citizenship must be on the table as we consider the future of journalism and journalism education. To do so we must therefore begin by asking ourselves what kind of citizens we want to become, and what kind of citizens we hope our fellow Americans will become ... It is undoubtedly in some measure the doing of journalists that our political commons is in a state of disrepair ... It is in some measure journalists' responsibility—and that of those who aspire to educate them—to get the work of renovation under way.

Manoff puts responsibility for participating in the renovation of the public commons squarely on journalists and educators. Imagine how a faculty that took this responsibility seriously might respond. Instead of transmitting predetermined professional standards and practices to waiting students, the role of the faculty would be to understand the dynamics of community more thoroughly and to challenge themselves and their students to develop journalism and journalism scholarship aimed at renovation and renewal of public life.

To understand how this educational focus might be conceptualized, consider how the three trends described as part of the industry-centered model of education could be transformed in a community-centered model: (1) instead of emphasizing professionalization, explore with students how to work with a community to accomplish similar goals of accountability, responsibility and excellence without the dangers of paternalism (Borden, 2007; Schudson, 2008; Ward, 2009); (2) instead of teaching skills appropriate to one-way, reporter-centered education, develop skills appropriate for networked journalism (Beckett, 2008); and (3) instead of socialization, develop a culture of inquiry within journalism schools (Zelizer, 2004, 2009).

Alternatives to Professionalism

Professionalism can be divided in two ways: as a source of ethical motivation and as a source of power (Borden, 2007). Exploring with students the implications of professionalism in the context of community would deepen an awareness of the contradictions embedded in this concept. It could also encourage more creative thinking on the part of faculty and students about alternative forms of organization that would strengthen ties between journalists and citizens, rather than separate them. What are credible sources of ethical motivation? How can journalists better balance independence and accountability? How do different communities define ethical journalistic practices? How might citizens work to make ethical judgments more transparent in all the journalism produced within a community? For example, in response to a recent ethics controversy regarding a news council in Washington state, Ward argues that journalists must reject the "'we know better" attitude—the old journalistic attitude that the public are best kept at arm's length" (Ward, 2009, para. 21) and create new organizations that allow for direct public involvement in assessing journalistic quality. Community-centered education could explore ideas such as this more fully, experiment with alternatives, and share the results of research to add to the collective understanding of ethical journalism practices. These conversations and experiments could provide students with ideas and insights applicable in multiple contexts.

Networked Journalism Skills

Community-centered journalism education would recognize that producing journalism within a network is fundamentally different from industrial production and would help students develop skills that take advantage of these differences (Barabási, 2003; Beckett, 2008; Castells, 2000; Jarvis, 2006). Working with students to study information networks and to experiment with new types of information creation, distribution and organization would help re-form journalistic practices. At the same time, requiring students to collaborate in an ongoing manner with interested members of a community would deepen their understanding of how communities work and of what people need and want from journalism. It could develop their community facilitation and moderation skills. It could help students develop new forms for journalism beyond "the story." It could help them develop more effective practices for linking, sharing, sourcing and working in social media. Operating within a network expands journalism to a process as well as a product, changing the type of "output" we might require from our students as well as requiring new forms of assessment and evaluation.

The challenge for educators is how to provide these types of opportunities within a classroom setting in a limited time frame. Producing a story independently for an unspecified audience is far different from collaboration with known publics over time. Embedding students within communities is one way to structure the kind of learning they will need to be successful in the future. Charlie Beckett describes the User Generated Content Hub at the BBC as one example of networked journalism that has produced valuable public service projects (2008, p. 81). Studying this and similar experiments could help educators extract the kinds of lessons students need to learn to be successful in a networked environment.

Creating Communities of Inquiry Within Journalism Faculties

In an era of upheaval and transformation, schisms between professionals and scholars, between practice and theory, are counterproductive. Creating faculties that operate more as communities of inquiry than as autonomous, unrelated units could help educators, scholars and practitioners work together more productively, as Zelizer (2009) argues. Turning to the important work of nurturing the next phase of journalism, a focus on inquiry would improve and enrich practice, research and teaching. Rather than education through socialization or theory without application, an education of inquiry would encourage the self-reflective, critical evaluation and productive experimentation that seems particularly important at this stage in the development of journalism. It would be helpful for faculty to foster the same spirit of creativity among themselves that they want to see in their students and in the journalism industry as a whole. In this particular period, more collaboration between faculty on substantive projects may be required than was necessary in more settled times. Adjustments to personnel evaluation criteria will be important if community-centered work, collaboration and experimentation are going to have value and appeal in a university context.

Examples of Research and Development in Journalism Programs in the United States

The following three examples illustrate some of the possibilities of community-centered journalism education. Each of these projects required students to immerse themselves within a community to address specific problems. Faculty and students are working together to rethink journalistic practices by starting with community first and listening carefully to individual citizens.[1] None of them offers a perfect example, but each provides some illustration of how journalism education might be re-oriented.

Intersections: The South Los Angeles Reporting Project, William Celis and Willa Seidenberg, USC Annenberg School for Communication

This project is the result of a year-long collaboration between two faculty members and their classes with students in a local high school. The journalism students are learning about the South Los Angeles community by participating in a mentoring program, teaching high school students to produce audio slideshows, blogs and radio commentaries and, in return, learning much more about the community than they would in a more conventional "reporting" relationship. One of the faculty members wrote about the project for the *Online Journalism Review*:

> The South Los Angeles Reporting Project, www.intersectionssouthla.org, is a multimedia news site with multiple layers of community engagement, classroom instruction and different forms of news delivery. Willa Seidenberg, a colleague and director of the award-winning Annenberg Radio News, and [William Celis] have collaborated for the last year on this project, building community and school ties, constructing infrastructure, rethinking [their] classes and offering new courses designed to give students a deeper understanding of urban America and its institutions. It's all an effort to engage residents in telling their own stories and to train a new generation of journalists to see communities as a whole. (Celis, 2009)

News Mixer, Rich Gordon, Northwestern University

Professor Rich Gordon challenged six graduate students (including two Web developers) in his New Media Publishing Project class to develop a project that would engage young adults in the news through new forms of online conversation. The Knight Foundation funded the participation of the Web developers; the class cooperated with Gazette Communications in Cedar Rapids, Iowa. The students spent 12 weeks developing a live prototype of a site that used Facebook Connect to foster conversation around news articles on the Web. To do this, they researched ways that other news organizations have tried to build online conversations through existing commenting structures. They also conducted a series of surveys with 18–34-year-olds in Cedar Rapids. With the help of the Web developers in the class, they built a site called NewsMixer that combines Facebook Connect with open source software to allow readers to use their Facebook identities when commenting on newspaper stories (NewsMixer, 2008, p. 5).

While the project has not yet been implemented in Iowa, two other organizations have expressed interest in using the work of the students (Gordon, 2009).

Albany Today, Linjun Fan, UC Berkeley Graduate School of Journalism

Fan recently graduated from the master's program in journalism. She received an assignment during her first semester to start a community blog in nearby Albany, California, a community that had no local paper of its own. She ended up working on the project during her entire graduate career, creating a site that was "wildly successful" according to the dean of the journalism school (Henry, 2009). On the blog she invited community members to submit stories, statements from local school board candidates, and commentary on a variety of issues. Here is how she described her project in the last post she published on the site before moving back to China:

> I am very glad that I've served you well with meaningful news stories about the community in the past two years, and thankful for your trust and support of Albany Today. At the City Council meeting last week, Mayor Marge Atkinson presented me an award, each members of the Council said words of appreciation to my work, and the audience applauded heartily ... All the stories come from you. I just diligently collect them, and try to present them as accurately and fairly as I can. That's why sometimes I invited you to write or speak directly to the community, when I thought that was the best way to convey your ideas and stories ... Albany Today has published dozens of essays and commentaries from a variety of residents. (Fan, 2009)

Community members in Albany have pledged to keep *Albany Today* alive so it can continue to serve as a source of news and information for residents.

Conclusion

The recommendations in this paper are, most of all, a call for educators in the United States to expand their conceptions of what constitutes journalism and how to practice it. Conceiving of journalism as an act of community, a process as much as a product, will help educators and students respond to the deep changes catalyzed by the development of digital technologies. These changes offer new opportunities and challenges that universities are well positioned to help address, if faculty are willing to work through the difficult and exciting tasks of questioning assumptions, conducting careful research, redesigning curriculum, collaborating with colleagues and engaging with students in helping to develop new journalistic practices.

The next step in this research would be to collect examples of community-centered journalism being taught in journalism programs, identify key elements, and begin developing a more specific set of recommendations and expected outcomes. It would also involve researching the many experiments being conducted by news organizations to begin describing the contours of this next phase of journalism, analyzing successes and failures and thinking through the consequences of various alternatives.

Beckett's hope for networked journalism is that it "puts humanity back at the heart of news communications" (2008, p. 166). It may also bring life to journalism education, enabling educators to contribute to the construction of new journalistic practices that will enrich student learning, reinvigorate journalism and enhance public life.

ACKNOWLEDGEMENT

The author would like to thank Dr. David Ryfe, University of Nevada, Reno, for his helpful comments on earlier drafts of this essay.

NOTE

1. To continue documenting this kind of work, this list will also be available online for updates, comments and conversation on a blog titled "Networked Journalism Education" (http://www.networkedjournalismeducation.com).

REFERENCES

ACCREDITING COUNCIL ON EDUCATION IN JOURNALISM AND MASS COMMUNICATIONS (1994) *ACEJMC Mission Statement*, 6 May, http://www2.ku.edu/~acejmc/PROGRAM/mission.SHTML, accessed 9 August 2009.

ADAM, G. STUART (2001) "The Education of Journalists", *Journalism* 2(3), pp. 315–39.

BARABÁSI, ALBERT-LÁSZLO (2003) *Linked: how everything is connected to everything else*, New York: Plume.

BECKER, LEE B. (2003) "Introduction: developing a sociology of journalism education", in: R. Froehlich and C. Holtz-Bacha (Eds), *Journalism Education in Europe and North America: an international comparison*, Creskill, NJ: Hampton Press, pp. 11–17.

BECKER, LEE B., FRUIT, JEFFREY and CAUDILL, SUSAN (1987) *The Training and Hiring of Journalists*, Norwood, NJ: Ablex Publishing.

BECKETT, CHARLIE (2008) *SuperMedia: saving journalism so it can save the world*, Oxford: Wiley-Blackwell.

BORDEN, SANDRA (2007) *Journalism as Practice: MacIntyre, Virtue Ethics and the Press*, Burlington, VT: Ashgate Publishing.

BOYLAN, JAMES (2003) *Pulitzer's School: Columbia University's School of Journalism, 1903–2003*, New York: Columbia University Press.

BRENNAN, BONNIE (2000) "What the Hacks Say", *Journalism* 1(1), pp. 106–13.

CAREY, JAMES (1980) "The University Tradition in Journalism Education", *Carleton University Review* 2(6), pp. 3–7, quoted in: Steve Jones (2009) "A University, if You Can Keep It: James W. Carey and the university tradition", *Cultural Studies* 23(2), pp. 223–36.

CAREY, JAMES (1989) *Communication as Culture: essays on media and society*, New York: Routledge.

CAREY, JAMES (2000) "Some Personal Notes on US Journalism Education", *Journalism* 1(1), pp. 12–23.

CARNEGIE CORPORATION (2005) "A Vision for Journalism Education. The professional school for 21st century news leaders: a manifesto", Carnegie Corporation of New York, 26 May, http://www.carnegie.org/sub/program/initiative-manifesto.html, accessed 9 August 2009.

CASTELLS, MANUEL (2000) *The Rise of the Network Society*, Vol. 1, 2nd edn, Oxford: Blackwell Publishing.

CELIS, WILLIAM (2009) "South Los Angeles Community News Website Offers Lessons for All", *Online Journalism Review*, 29 April, http://www.ojr.org/ojr/people/BillCelis/200904/1707/, accessed 20 August 2009.

DE TOCQUEVILLE, ALEXIS (1990 [1835]) *Democracy in America*, Vol. 1, New York: Vintage Books.

DENNIS, EVERETT (1984) *Planning for Curricular Change: a report on the future of journalism and mass communication education*, Eugene: School of Journalism, University of Oregon.

DEUZE, MARK (2006) "Global Journalism Education: a conceptual approach", *Journalism Studies* 7(1), pp. 19–34.

DEWEY, JOHN (1916) *Democracy and Education: an introduction to the philosophy of education*, New York: Macmillan Co.

DEWEY, JOHN (1927) *The Public and Its Problems*, New York: Henry Holt.

DICKSON, THOMAS (2000) *Mass Media Education in Transition: preparing for the 21st century*, Mahwah, NJ: Lawrence Erlbaum.

FALLOWS, JAMES (1997) *Breaking the News: how the media undermine American democracy*, New York: Vintage Books.

FAN, LINJUN (2009) "You Can Make Albany Today Alive", *Albany Today*, 22 June, http://albanytoday.org/2009/06/22/you-can-make-albany-today-alive/, accessed 20 August 2009.

GAUNT, PHILIP (1992) *Making the Newsmakers: international handbook on journalism training*, Westport, CT: Greenwood Press.

GORDON, RICH (2009) "News Mixer Options: launch a site, use the code or be inspired", *MediaShift Idea Lab*, 2 February, http://www.pbs.org/idealab/2009/02/news-mixer-options-launch-a-site-use-the-code-or-be-inspired033.html, accessed 20 August 2009.

HENRY, NEIL (2009) "Open Forum: journalism students lead way", *SFGate.com*, 16 May, http://www.sfgate.com/cgi-bin/article.cgi?f=/c/a/2009/05/16/ED2V17KJC3.DTL&type=printable, accessed 20 August 2009.

JARVIS, JEFF (2006) "Networked Journalism", *Buzzmachine*, 5 July, http://www.buzzmachine.com/2006/07/05/networked-journalism/, accessed 10 August 2009.

KOVACH, BILL and ROSENSTIEL, TOM (2001) *The Elements of Journalism*, New York: Crown Publishers.

LIPPMANN, WALTER (1927) *The Phantom Public*, New York: Macmillan Co.

MACDONALD, ISABEL (2006) "Teaching Journalists to Save the Profession", *Journalism Studies* 7(5), pp. 745–64.

MANOFF, ROBERT (2002) "Democratic Journalism and the Republican Subject: or, the real American Dream and what journalism educators can do about it", *Zoned for Debate*, New York University, http://journalism.nyu.edu/pubzone/debate/forum.1.essay.manoff.html, accessed 20 July 2009.

MEDSGER, BETTY (1996) *Winds of Change: challenges confronting journalism education*, Arlington, VA: Freedom Forum.

NEWSMIXER (2008) "Final Report", Medill School of Journalism, Northwestern University, http://newmedia.medill.northwestern.edu/survey.aspx?id=110781, accessed 28 July 2009.

O'DELL, DEFOREST (1935) *The History of Journalism Education in the United States*, New York: Teachers College, Columbia University.

PROJECT FOR EXCELLENCE IN JOURNALISM (2004) "2004 Annual Report—overview", http://www.journalism.org/node/855, accessed 15 July 2009.

REESE, STEPHEN (1999) "The Progressive Potential of Journalism Education: recasting the academic versus professional debate", *The International Journal of Press/Politics* 4(4), pp. 70–94.

REESE, STEPHEN and COHEN, JEREMY (2000) "Educating for Journalism: the professionalism of scholarship", *Journalism Studies* 1(2), pp. 213–27.

RHEINGOLD, HOWARD (1993) *The Virtual Community: homesteading on the electronic frontier*, Reading, MA: Addison-Wesley.

ROSEN, JAY (2006) "Jay Rosen on James Carey: an appreciation", *PoynterOnline*, 23 May, http://www.poynter.org/content/content_view.asp?id=101810, accessed 7 August 2009.

SCHUDSON, MICHAEL (2008) *Why Democracies Need an Unlovable Press*, Malden, MA: Polity Press.

SCHUDSON, MICHAEL and ANDERSON, CHRIS (2009) "Objectivity, Professionalism, and Truth Seeking in Journalism", in: Karin Wahl-Jorgensen and Thomas Hanitzsch (Eds), *The Handbook of Journalism Studies*, New York: Routledge.

SKINNER, DAVID, GASHER, MIKE and COMPTON, JAMES (2001) "Putting Theory to Practice: a critical approach to journalism studies", *Journalism* 2(3), pp. 341–60.

STEPHENS, MITCHELL (2002) "A J-School Manifesto", *Department of Journalism: Zoned for Debate*, 6 September, http://journalism.nyu.edu/pubzone/debate/forum.1.essay.stephens.html, accessed 6 August 2009.

SUTTON, ALBERT (1945) *Education for Journalism in the United States from its Beginning to 1940*, Evanston, IL: Northwestern University.

TUMBER, HOWARD and PRENTOULIS, MARINA (2005) "Journalism and the Making of a Profession", in: Hugo de Burgh (Ed.), *Making Journalists*, London: Routledge, pp. 58–74.

WARD, STEPHEN (2009) "Let the Public Help Guide Journalism Ethics", *The Canadian Journalism Project*, 16 June, http://jsource.ca/english_new/detail.php?id=3964&PHPSESSID=469952d026680111dc5a126e25aa3c16, accessed 6 August 2009.

WEINBERG, STEVE (2008) *A Journalism of Humanity: a candid history of the world's first journalism school*, Columbia: University of Missouri Press.

WHITNEY, CHARLES and WARTELLA, ELLEN (2000) "On US Journalism Education", *Journalism* 1(1), pp. 52–55.

ZELIZER, BARBIE (2004) *Taking Journalism Seriously: news and the academy*, Thousand Oaks, CA: Sage.

ZELIZER, BARBIE (2009) "Introduction: why journalism's changing faces matter", in: Barbie Zelizer (Ed.), *The Changing Faces of Journalism: tabloidization, technology and truthiness*, New York: Routledge, pp. 1–10.

THE SHIFTING CROSS-MEDIA NEWS LANDSCAPE
Challenges for news producers

Kim Christian Schrøder and **Bent Steeg Larsen**

The article offers new insights for democracy and for news producers by mapping the use and users of today's cross-media news landscape, as the everyday consumption of news across the range of available news media and formats is shifting reflecting transformations of technology, culture and lifestyles. Theoretically the study is anchored in Habermas's notion of the public sphere, and its recent reconceptualizations in theories of "cultural citizenship", "civic agency" and "public connection". The project operationalizes these theories through the concept of users' perceived "worthwhileness" of news media, a user-anchored concept which incorporates the different functionalities of the situational cross-media use of news by citizen/consumers in everyday life. Empirically the article presents the findings of a large-scale survey that traces the imminent challenges facing players in the news market, as a consequence of accelerating divisions between "overview" and "depth" news media (across print, broadcasting and the Internet). The project is conducted in a partnership of university-based researchers and analysts from one of the major newspaper publishers in Denmark, and presents the first user-based analysis of the relative position of each individual news medium in the entire news media matrix.

Introduction

Over the years there has been an infinite number of studies into the democratic functions of the news media. The news media are rightly deemed to be crucial for the provision of democratic prerequisites, and the media research community has given a high priority to the exploration of the adequacy of the news media in bringing about these prerequisites.

Nevertheless, this vast body of research has been characterized by a number of significant omissions—or perhaps one should say rather that some aspects of the democratic process have been neglected, not completely ignored. One could label these omissions as having to do with the use and reception aspects of news media.

As an example, a recent excellent study (Curran et al., 2009) analyses the complex relationships between national media systems, news media content, the citizens' civic knowledge, and the state of democracy. These researchers find that there is "a connection between patterns of news coverage and levels of public knowledge" (2009, p. 14), so that "what the media report—or fail to report—affects what is known" (2009, p. 16). They demonstrate that there is a necessary causal connection between media system and citizenship, so that "the public service model makes television news more accessible on leading channels ... and therefore contributes to a more egalitarian pattern of citizenship" (2009, p. 22). Finally, they predict that since "a growing number of countries are converging towards the entertainment-centred model of American television, ... this trend seems set to foster an impoverished public life", i.e. an impoverished democracy.

It is not that the alleged connection between media system and democracy is not plausible. But the argument suffers from a missing link, which we need to investigate, if we want to understand how this connection comes about:

Media system (revenues, organization)
↓
News media: provision, amount and content of news
↓
Consumer-citizens' use and experience of news media
↓
The citizens' knowledge about society
↓
The citizens' democratic prerequisites

This missing link is what reception research has tried to provide over three decades, from the pioneering work of Morley (1980), Jensen (1986) and Lewis (1991) to the recent impressive studies of Couldry et al. (2007), Meijer (2007), Hill's work on factual television (2007), and Van Zoonen's analysis (2005) of the empowering political functions of popular media. The briefest possible way to define what we need to know more about is to paraphrase the catch-phrase of uses-and-gratifications research: "What do people do with the news?"—in the process that transforms it to "knowledge about society" and "democratic prerequisites"?

Our current research is trying to answer this question in what we see as two innovative ways. We adopt:

- an unequivocal user's perspective, which entails that for news users, news must be seen as a cross-media phenomenon. From a democratic perspective, It makes little sense to analyse the use of newspapers or TV news in isolation.
- an integrated quantitative/qualitative methodology, which builds added explanatory power through a research design that creatively merges qualitative and quantitative analysis.

Constellations and Typologies of Media Use

Towards the end of their impressive study *Media Consumption and Public Engagement*, Couldry et al. put forward, as one of their recommendations for future research, that one focus of future attention should be people's

> habits of media consumption ... *across particular media*, (because) *the particular constellation of media on which one individual draws* may be quite different than another's. It is at this level of habit—routine consumption practice embedded in a range of other routines, some social, some individual—that media come to make a difference, or not, as the case may be. (2007, pp. 190–1, emphasis added)

As its end goal, our research precisely aims to explore both "media consumption across particular media", and those "constellations of media on which one individual draws", and to explore at the level of the social formation of Danish society whether these constellations can be said to be somehow patterned, so that even though in principle there must be about four million such constellations of media in the adult population, nevertheless they fall into a finite number of types, which together constitute a typology.

The project is spurred by a general desire to explore the democratic condition in mediatized society, but also to discern the user-patterns which pose challenges to the news providers struggling to develop new content and new business models. It considers the variety of needs and functions filled by the available news media and genres, from the provision of vital democratic prerequisites, to the supply of lifestyle, celebrity and entertainment materials that serve as an input to the conversations of social networks.

"Doing Citizenship": The "Cultural Turn" Towards the Microdynamics of Democracy

Theoretically, the project can be aligned with recent thinking in some corners of cultural studies, where there is a growing awareness of the need to relocate the focus of political communication research towards "the microdynamics of democracy" (Dahlgren, 2006, p. 282; see also Jones, 2006; Schrøder and Phillips, 2007).

According to this theory, there is no gap between civic agency as a traditionally conceived political activity in the public sphere and the culture of the everyday: people in daily life may "self-create themselves into citizens" (Dahlgren, 2006, p. 272). In our project, similarly, the practices of daily life are seen as the site of identities and passions from which people can sometimes—*if the occasion arises*, so to speak—be "launched" into the public sphere, as the site of political practice in the classic democratic sense (Wahl-Jørgensen, 2006).

This is also the essence of Kevin Barnhurst's work on mediated citizenship. He is developing a new ideal of citizenship as a yardstick for evaluating ordinary people's political activity. Basically Barnhurst believes that the Habermassian ideal of citizenship is unproductive, because it "sets up an unreachable ideal that devalues how people enact citizenship in daily life" (Barnhurst, 2003, p. 134), and "requires levels of commitment to political activity that amount to more than full-time work" (2003, p. 137). Rather than denigrating people's actual political impulses in everyday life as unworthy of the label "politics", political communication research should perceive politics as something that "becomes intentional only in sporadic flashes" (2003, p. 133)—a view that echoes that of Wahl-Jørgensen (above).

Thus, when we explore people's use of the news media in this project, we do so without preconceptions that some media (for instance "broadsheet" newspapers) or news genres (for instance investigative TV documentary) are inherently of higher democratic quality than more popular forms of news. This agnosticism about the possible value for different people of the different news media is built into our theoretical notion of "worthwhileness".

Determinants of News Consumption: Perceived Worthwhileness

What are the factors that determine whether people use a particular news medium or not? We try to answer this question by adopting the heuristic concept of "*perceived worthwhileness*". The concept common-sensically denotes the individuals' subjective, implicit or explicit assessment of whether the medium in question is worth their while. An individual's answer to this question depends on a series of interrelated factors that enter into a personal "calculation" or routine that results in media use occurring or not, and, if it does, for a longer or shorter period of time, with a greater or lesser amount of attention.

The factors that collectively constitute a news medium's perceived worthwhileness include the subjectively experienced material, situational and functional circumstances that characterizes the medium's practice of use. So far, we see perceived worthwhileness as constituted by five factors: (1) time available; (2) the affordance of "public connection"; (3) price; (4) normative constraints; and (5) participatory affordances.

In the society of news media abundance one can only understand the worthwhileness of one particular news medium by considering the news users as effectively browsing the entire cross-media news landscape as a "news system", and each applying the criterion of worthwhileness across the news media that make up the system. As Finnemann argues for the media system as a whole,

> each medium has a set of distinct properties, while the specific role and use of any medium to some degree depends on the overall matrix of media available. You cannot analyse the role of any single medium independently of the overall matrix of media. (2008, p. 7)[1]

The commercial and social viability of any news medium depends primarily on two factors: its ability to win a share of citizens' available time and attention, and its ability to meet the needs of citizens for "public connection" in a wide sense. If people cannot fit a medium into their time schedule, it has no chance of being consumed, no matter whether it potentially fulfils their need for public connection. On the other hand, if people have available time at some point during the day, a medium can insert itself into that spatio-temporal context, and perhaps with time make itself indispensable in that context, if this medium carries a content which is perceived to be potentially crucial to one's public connection, possibly by replacing a less appealing medium.

"Public connection", a concept launched by Couldry et al. (2007), has to do with a medium's ability to satisfy through its content an individual's need to both equip himself for the role of citizen-member of the democratic order, and for the role of belonging as a community-member in the broadest possible sense. This includes being able to participate in social and cultural networks of all kinds in everyday life, being able to navigate adequately as a spouse, parent, neighbour, colleague, consumer and simply human being in late modern life, being able to communicate sensibly with significant others in one's close networks as well as with more distant others in relevant domestic, professional, commercial and institutional contexts.

In addition to the criteria of time and public connection, the worthwhileness of a given medium will also depend on a number of additional criteria, price obviously being one of them. For instance, the commuter who buys one of the established tabloids on a regular basis may decide to replace the tabloid with one of the free dailies. The decision to subscribe to a cable news channel will depend on its affordability in relation to household income and expenditure patterns.

A fourth factor is the normative pressures from significant others, a symbolic factor of potential stigmatization determining whether, for instance, you are willing to be seen reading a free daily on the commuter train. With media that are potentially prestigious among a given group, the normative pressure may work in the opposite direction and instigate adoption into one's media repertoire.

The factor called "participatory affordances" has to do with the participatory qualities afforded especially by Internet news services (Picone, 2007). Although one should not (yet) exaggerate the news users' active participation in news dissemination and production (Gentikow, 2008), it is probably the case that for some, especially younger news users, the various ways in which one can participate in and contribute to the news on Internet sites affect their assessment of the worthwhileness of such news sources.

It must be stressed that worthwhileness is a concept that has to do, not (as in uses-and-gratifications research) with rational individualized needs for specific media materials, but with socially produced, routinized meaning processes and discursive practices through which individuals make sense of their everyday lives, as inscribed into larger social practices and structures, through interaction with others in the mediatized society.

Finally, for someone to say that a particular news medium is worth his or her while should not be taken to mean only that the everyday use of this medium (say, a free daily) is "important" to them in an absolute sense, having to do with the lofty ideals of acquiring the prerequisites for being a citizen in the public sphere. While worthwhileness does include this sense of importance and indispensability, it is also intended to cover the sense in which a medium can be perceived as worthwhile in a particular spatio-temporal context, such as being available in a time-pocket of a daily 20-minute bus journey from home to work. The concept thus includes both media that are perceived as vitally important and media that come to be contextually relevant on a regular basis, i.e. as worthwhile by default.

Exploring Worthwhileness: Complementarities of Fieldwork

The project relies on two stages of fieldwork: the first, to be reported here, consists of a survey that maps the cross-media patterns of worthwhile news media of a representative sample of the Danish population. The second stage, currently ongoing, is an innovative design that integrates quantitative and qualitative methods in one hybrid research design. The method is derived from, but creatively transcends the method also known as Q-methodology (for methodological discussion, see Schrøder, 2004).

Our use of the survey method is traditional, but the cross-media lens we use is innovative: we asked the respondents about,

- *Worthwhileness of the news media available*, i.e. what news media they had used during the last week?[2] We inferred that the news media they had used were the ones they found worthwhile.
- We also asked about *Most worthwhile news medium*: among the worthwhile news media they had listed, we asked them to select the news medium that they considered most indispensable (i.e. most worthwhile).
- *Functionalities of worthwhileness:* Among the worthwhile news media they listed, we asked them about the patterning of these media according to two different functionalities: (1) which media they used to provide an *overview* over events of the day, and (2) which media they used to provide *"background information"* about the day's events. The same news medium could be selected for both functionalities.

What the survey analysis does is to provide interesting maps, from a high altitude, of the landscape of cross-media news consumption, as shaped by what we infer to be (i.e. what must logically be) people's perceptions of the worthwhileness of the various news media.

Mapping Cross-media Landscapes of News Worthwhileness

The survey was administered online to a representative sample of 1031 Danes over 18 years of age in November 2008. The findings presented here are national averages without demographic details. The results are significant at the 95 per cent level, except that the order of two media separated by less than 3–4 per cent in the tables could be the reverse.

Worthwhileness of News Media in the Past Week[3]

Unsurprisingly television news programmes are the most important news source in Denmark (88 per cent), closely followed by Internet news sites (78 per cent), and radio news (70 per cent) (Table 1).

While the top rank for Internet news may be seen as surprising, it is also surprising that Text-TV comes out in fourth place. National quality dailies are in seventh place (49 per cent). It is noteworthy that international news sources (TV and Internet) have been used by one-fifth of the respondents. Mobile news is used by 7 per cent.

Clearly many of these figures are not (just) interesting in themselves, but they will provide the starting point of a hopefully longitudinal study of the worthwhileness of news in years to come.

Most Worthwhile News Media (Indispensability)[4]

Television is clearly the news source which the largest number of people would not do without (37 per cent) (Table 2). Internet news is the second most indispensable (19 per cent), but far below TV. National dailies are in third place (14 per cent).

Functionalities of Worthwhileness: Overview Versus Depth Functions

Based on the assumption that all individuals see themselves as pursuing both overview and background news provisions at different times, we asked each respondent,

TABLE 1

Worthwhileness of news sources: Danish news users' ranking of 16 news media and news genres (for all categories, examples were provided for respondents)

	%
1. News programmes on main Danish TV channels	88
2. News on Danish Internet news sites	78
3. Radio news programmes	70
4. Text-TV news	60
5. Local free weekly newspapers	58
6. Current affairs programmes on Danish TV	53
7. National broadsheet newspapers	49
8. Free dailies	42
9. Local/regional dailies	36
10. Professional journals (e.g. trade unions)	31
11. Weekly and monthly magazines	30
12. Tabloids	27
13. News on international Internet news sites	21
14. News and current affairs on international TV	19
15. Radio current affairs	14
16. Mobile phone news	7
17. None of these	0

TABLE 2
Most worthwhile (most indispensable) news media

	%
News programmes on main Danish TV channels	37
News on Danish Internet news sites	19
National broadsheet newspapers	14
Radio news programmes	8
Text-TV news	5

based on the list of news media he or she had previously selected as worthwhile for him or her, which media they used for each purpose. They were free to mention the same news medium for both functions.[5]

When we ask people about the *single most important overview/depth news medium*, it turns out that for "overview" the Internet has become equal in importance to TV news (Table 3). Text-TV news is in third place, in front of radio and national newspapers.

For "depth", national newspapers are in first place (28 per cent), clearly surpassing TV (23 per cent). TV news receives a high ranking (second place) for both overview and depth, and is thus the most worthwhile all-round news medium—it is overall an important resource for civic agency and public connection.

We also asked people which other media they use for overview/depth information (Table 4):

- *All-round functionality*: the ranking on this question underscores the importance of TV news as *the* all-round news medium in Denmark, a clear no. 1 in both functionalities (55 per cent, 44 per cent). The Internet comes second, with a second place for overview, and a fourth place for depth.
- *For overview*, after TV and Internet, radio news is an important resource (40 per cent), but Text-TV news is a close runner-up to radio (36 per cent). National dailies are close to negligible for this function.
- *For depth*: the high ranking of TV has a female bias (41/47), while the high ranking of national dailies has a corresponding male bias (38/32). TV current affairs is in a clear third position (35 per cent).
- *Generalization about news functionalities*: TV news and to some extent Internet news bridge the two functionalities, while for other media there is a clear *functional differentiation*:
  - *Overview news media*: radio, Text-TV, free newspapers.
  - *Depth news media*: national dailies, TV current affairs, professional magazines.

TABLE 3
News functionalities: most important *single* overview and depth news medium

	Overview		Depth	
	Ranking	%	Ranking	%
News on Danish Internet news sites	1	28	4	9
News on main Danish TV channels	2	27	2	24
Text-TV news	3	15	–	–
Radio news programmes	4	13	–	–
National broadsheet newspapers	5	6	1	28
Free dailies	6	4	–	–
Current affairs programmes on Danish TV	–	–	3	14
Local/regional dailies	–	–	5	4

TABLE 4

News functionalities: most important *other* overview and depth news media

	Overview		Depth	
	Ranking	%	Ranking	%
News on main Danish TV channels	1	55	1	45
News on Danish Internet news sites	2	50	4	24
Radio news programmes	3	41	6	13
Text-TV news	4	36	–	–
National broadsheet newspapers	5	15	2	36
Free dailies	6	13	–	–
Current affairs programmes on Danish TV	–	–	3	35
Professional journals (e.g. trade unions)	–	–	5	13
Local/regional dailies	7	10	7	11
Radio current affairs	–	–	8	10
Local free weekly newspapers	8	9	9	7

Importance of Participatory Affordances of Internet News Sites

We asked respondents to rank the importance for regular news provision of Internet news sites on a scale from "very important" (0) to "not at all important" (100). The average ranking at 71 (of 100) confirms the central role of Internet news for contemporary Danes. Also confirmed is the response to previous questions about international Internet news sites: while such sites do form a not infrequent part of the news diet for many Danes, they are dispensable (32 of 100).

While Internet news sites offer a range of interactive opportunities, we found that it is still a minority (24 per cent) who report any kind of interactivity: 76 per cent said that in the last month they had not engaged in any interactive exchange (sent email to a journalist, participated in a debate, commented on a blog, etc.). It is consequently not surprising that the importance of such interactive functions is deemed to be low (33 of 100).

Worthwhileness: From Map to Typology

Through the survey we have mapped in a factual sense which media people say they find worthwhile. The next step of the fieldwork aims to explore why people find these news media worthwhile, and in a profound sense what constitutes worthwhileness for them.

The second stage of our fieldwork will thus investigate three dozen or so people's own sense-making accounts of the worthwhileness of the news media, in two different ways that are merged into one fieldwork design. First, by using the elicitation technique of "telling the story of *A Day in the Life with Media*", we will ask them in individual interviews to verbalize their routinized news media consumption in everyday life, thus providing a (qualitative) "thick description" of their perceived worthwhile news media.

Secondly, in the same sitting, we will ask informants to playfully sort a pile of cards with the titles of 20–25 news media and news genres on a continuum from most to least worthwhile. The individual constellation of news media worthwhileness which informants produce in this way will then be subjected to a (quantitative) generalizing factor analysis, whose output will be a typology of news media use.

At the end of the day, therefore, we will have obtained extensive new knowledge about people's lives with the news media. The maps described in this article provide the general picture of how citizen-consume.s in Denmark navigate in the cross-media news landscape. Such maps are a prerequisite of further research into the media/democracy nexus, since we need to know what news media people actually use on a daily basis, and how they assess the relative significance, for them, of the different components in the news matrix.

Tracking Changing News Media Preferences: The Value for News Producers

The survey also provides valuable information for news producers: it provides a snapshot of the 2008-distribution of competing news media platforms, and measures the extent to which these platforms are used and appreciated by the consumers. As a content provider of news it is crucial for a news company to be able to target and distribute its content to those platforms where news consumption is actually taking place, and where news consumers expect to find relevant news. The maps produced by the survey quantify the constellations of news consumption at the level of the news media marketplace and thereby plays into and gives proportions to the news producer's strategic focus.

The study usefully confirms many existing truths about news consumption (e.g. the diminishing role of national newspapers in the overall news landscape), and delivers a couple of genuine surprises. The very prominent role played by Text-TV news, both in absolute terms (see Table 1) and for the overview function (see Tables 3 and 4) was unexpected, but makes good sense when you take into account the situational affordances offered by this inconspicuous news medium—it can be switched on more easily than a home computer's news sites, and it is readily available to TV viewers as a default option during moments of non-attractive programming. Also the list of news stories provides for quick orientation, and, as a generic property, the individual news items are guaranteed to be succinct.

Secondly, the fact that Internet news is now equal in importance to TV news as the single most worthwhile overview news medium (see Table 3) was a cause of slight surprise, although the casting of Internet news as fast news, together with the well-known fact that news sites are the "visit generator" of the net should maybe have led us to anticipate this finding.

This first survey of its kind may serve as a "point zero" mapping, the first in a series of measurements undertaken with regular intervals, for instance annually, which document the shifts in people's use of different news platforms. Such tracking of changes in the population's news preferences will be an iterative monitoring of whether the news company's ventures in the different areas of the news market are responding to people's behaviour in terms of actual news demand.

In the present mapping, the distinction between overview and depth news media is particularly valuable, as it provides a new insight into the functionalities of the different news media and genres. Survey findings not reported in this article show that different demographic groups have different conceptions of the functionalities of some news media. For instance, the perceived significance of TV news as a depth medium increases with age, while the significance of Internet news media as a provider of depth and background is higher among the young adult groups. The more is known about these functional patterns, the better will news companies be able to strategically target their different news platforms accurately towards different population segments.

Studies of brand perceptions reveal that news consumers have very different perceptions of the strength and vitality of different players in the news market, irrespective of platforms. As a complement, the present study indicates that different news distribution channels are functioning under specific premises to do with the situation of use in everyday life, which thus associates a given news medium with a set of "situational affordances" that make it suitable for some kinds of news and not others. This is, for instance, the case with Internet news and daily newspapers, making it strategically important to diagnose the specific situational use value of different news channels, so as to be able to meet the conditions and expectations of the different user segments.

NOTES

1. The ambition of mapping people's consumption of cross-media is one that our project shares with the Institute of Advertising Practitioners' *Touchpoints* marketing tool. This tool analyses "how consumers spend their time" in everyday life, with a focus on cross-media use, and is intended as a multi-media planning tool for advertisers. For instance, Touchpoints "shows the best time and the right channels to hit office workers frequently" with advertising messages and how to "penetrate the cocoon of the car" (Beeftink, 2009). Touchpoints thus gathers information about the factual aspects of people's cross-media reachability and vulnerability to strategic media campaigns, trying to find their weak spots. The worthwhileness approach, by contrast, explores people's engagement with (news) media in order to find out how news media content plays into and enriches their lives, as they make sense of themselves performing the multiple roles required by the string of scenarios they move through on a daily basis.

2. The term "worthwhileness", being too technical and scientific, was not used in the questionnaire. We operationalized the term in various ways that will become clear from the reported findings (see the tables), so that we effectively got respondents to convey to us what media they found worthwhile, for different purposes, in everyday life.

3. The questionnaire presented a list of 16 news media and news genres and asked: "Which news media have you used (viewed, listened to, read) over the past week?"

4. The question was: "Which of the media you have mentioned is most indispensable to you?"

5. The question was: "Please choose one media type which is most important for you when you want an overview of what goes on in the community and in the country. And please choose one media type which is most important for you when you want a deeper insight into such events".

REFERENCES

BARNHURST, KEVIN (2003) "Subjective States: narratives of citizenship among young Europeans", *Multilingua* 22, pp. 133–68.

BEEFTINK, BELINDA (2009) "IPA Touchpoints—the first three years", presentation, Copenhagen, November.

COULDRY, NICK, LIVINGSTONE, SONIA and MARKHAM, TIM (2007) *Media Consumption and Public Engagement. Beyond the presumption of attention*, Basingstoke: Palgrave Macmillan.

CURRAN, JAMES, LUND, ANKER BRINK, IYENGAR, SHANTO and SALOVAARA-MORING, INKA (2009) "Media System, Public Knowledge and Democracy: a comparative study", *European Journal of Communication* 24(5), pp. 5–26.

DAHLGREN, PETER (2006) "Doing Citizenship: the cultural origins of civic agency in the public sphere", *European Journal of Cultural Studies* 9(3), pp. 267–86.

FINNEMANN, NIELS O. (2008) "The Internet and the Emergence of a New Matrix of Media", paper presented to the Association of Internet Researchers Conference, Copenhagen, October.

GENTIKOW, B. (2008) "Mediepublikumet i en brytningstid: revitaliseringer og transformasjoner", *Norsk medietidsskrift* 15(2), pp. 84–104.

HILL, ANNETTE (2007) *Restyling Factual TV. Audiences and news, documentary and reality genres*, London: Routledge.

JENSEN, KLAUS B. (1986) *Making Sense of the News*, Aarhus: Aarhus University Press.

JONES, JEFFREY P. (2006) "A Cultural Approach to the Study of Mediated Citizenship", *Social Semiotics* 16(2), pp. 365–83.

LEWIS, JUSTIN (1991) *The Ideological Octopus. An exploration of television and its audience*, New York: Routledge.

MEIJER, IRENE COSTERA (2007) "Checking, Snacking and Bodysnatching. How young people use the news and implications for public service media journalism", in: G.F. Lowe and J. Bardoel (Eds), *From Public Service Broadcasting to Public Service Media*, Gothenburg: Nordicom.

MORLEY, DAVID (1980) *The "Nationwide" Audience*, London: British Film Institute.

PICONE, I. (2007) "Conceptualising Online News Use", *Observatorio* 3, pp. 93–114.

SCHRØDER, KIM CHRISTIAN (2004) "Mapping European Identities: a quantitative approach to the qualitative study of national and supranational identities", in: Ib Bondebjerg and Peter Golding (Eds), *European Culture and the Media*, Bristol: Intellect Books, pp. 191–213.

SCHRØDER, KIM CHRISTIAN and PHILLIPS, LOUISE (2007) "Complexifying Media Power: a study of the interplay between media and audience discourses on politics", *Media, Culture & Society* 29(5), pp. 890–915.

VAN ZOONEN, LIESBET (2005) *Entertaining the Citizen: when politics and popular culture converge*, Lanham, MD: Rowman and Littlefield.

WAHL-JØRGENSEN, KARIN (2006) "Mediated Citizenship: an introduction", *Social Semiotics* 16(2), pp. 197–203.

RITUALS OF TRANSPARENCY
Evaluating online news outlets' uses of transparency rituals in the United States, United Kingdom and Sweden

Michael Karlsson

Transparency has been suggested as a new norm in journalism. However, few studies have investigated how the overarching notion of transparency is utilized in everyday news. The purpose of this study is to identify and compare how leading mainstream online news media in the United States, United Kingdom and Sweden make use of transparency techniques in news items. The results show that transparency has begun to affect online news but that current journalism practice is a long way from a fully fledged transparency norm.

Introduction

There is no doubt that journalism has moved online and that this movement has significance for journalism's core function—to gather, select and verify information in order to provide people with the information they need to be informed and self-governing.

In this context, the notion of journalistic objectivity has been central in the western hemisphere during the twentieth century. Although an abstract concept, it has been made operational by news professionals performing what Tuchman (1972) labels "rituals of objectivity". Through various "rituals of objectivity", journalism was supposed to be able to carry out its informative function and simultaneously win legitimacy. In an online environment, the traditional understandings of journalism have, however, been challenged and a rival and sometimes overlapping strategy for truth telling and the garnering of legitimacy has been proposed, namely transparency.

Similar to the notion of "journalistic objectivity", "transparency" is, however, an abstract phenomenon. To be useful as a concept and to have an impact upon actual news production, transparency needs to be translated into useful, everyday "rituals of transparency". Although the notion of transparency has received much attention, there is only a handful of empirical studies which have attempted to capture the use of transparency in everyday news production—especially in a comparative setting. Moreover, some research studies (Arant and Anderson, 2001; Cassidy, 2006; Singer, 2005) indicate that traditional routines remain strong in the online setting.

In this context, the purpose of this study is to explore and identify if and how leading United States, English and Swedish news media utilize what can be termed "rituals of transparency", that is working notions of transparency. In addition, the study compares the extent to which these rituals are already in use at three news sites in distinctive national settings.

Journalism's Authoritative Rituals

Routines are a way for media producers to reduce uncertainty and accomplish work (Lowrey and Latta, 2008). But routines also play a vital part in journalism's needs to distinguish itself from other sources of media work, since it builds legitimacy around the notion that journalism is the only form of media work with a commitment to the truth (Kovach and Rosenstiel, 2001; Zelizer, 2004). However, the truth cannot be told in the whole nor can it be ignored. If journalism is not to rely on the audience's blind faith that news is reported truth-fully, there seems to be a need for workable notions of truth that can be referred to if journalistic truth-telling is being questioned or criticized. Examples of such notions of truth-telling are what is referred to as rituals of objectivity (Shoemaker and Reese, 1996; Shoemaker and Vos, 2009; Tuchman, 1972) that serve the dual function of protecting journalists and news corporations from critique as well as building legitimacy. As time-constrained journalists do not have the time to contemplate whether they have established the whole truth of a story, objectivity routines, strategies and rituals serve as working notions of truth. Typically these rituals include relying on many sources, keeping the journalist's view out of the news story and relying on verifiable facts (Schudson, 2001; Shoemaker and Reese, 1996; Soloski, 1997). Subsequently, the information emerging from news media is required to have been subjected to certain standardized routines that transform mere *information* into *journalism*.

Another important dimension in the rituals of objectivity is that they need to be performed in front of the audience because, as Tuchman (1972, p. 661) argues, "the correct handling of a story, that is, the use of certain procedures discernible to the news consumer, protects journalists from the risks of their trade, including critics". The crucial word here is *discernible* as it suggests that these journalistic routines must be communicated to the outside world. Carey links ritualistic forms of communication (1992, p. 18) to terms such as *shared* (as discernible suggests) and more so to facilitate *participation* and *the possession of a common faith*. Thus for various routines to be working journalistic rituals they must be communicated to the audience but more importantly, understood and accepted as journalistic rituals by the audience in order for the audience to separate journalism from other forms of communication. Accordingly, in establishing these objectivity rituals as accepted ways of achieving legitimacy in journalistic truth-telling, standards are created by which journalism is evaluated and held accountable by the audience and peers. Failure to deliver according to these standards will, for instance, risk losing the trust of the audience (Tuchman, 1972) and be criticized by peers as was illustrated by the case of the infamous Jayson Blair at the *New York Times*.

Similar to rituals of objectivity, the rising journalistic norm of transparency faces the same challenges—namely how to translate the overarching notion of openness (Plaisance, 2007; Singer, 2007) into rituals that can be used in everyday journalistic work and be communicated to, understood and accepted as journalistic routines by the audience and peers. If this is achieved, transparency can serve the dual function (Allen,

2008) of serving as a system of accountability and a way of increasing legitimacy with citizens.

Identifying Rituals of Transparency

If there is one word to sum up what transparency stand for it is *openness* (Allen, 2008; Plaisance, 2007; Singer, 2007) and many scholars have pointed out that the new transparency norm could possibly have a significant impact on journalism (Deuze, 2003; Hayes et al., 2007; Kovach and Rosenstiel, 2001). Researchers have also provided illustrations that transparency standards are already in use and change the way news media operate (Allen, 2008; Plaisance, 2007).

In order to impact on journalism the general notion of openness that constitutes transparency has to be translated into specific techniques that can be used routinely by journalists and identified and understood by users, in much the same way that rituals of objectivity have been materialized in, for instance, the use of multiple sources. How, then, has previous research identified and described transparency in a more detailed manner?

Transparency has so far been understood in two sometimes connected strands. The first strand of transparency implies that news producers can explain and be open about the way news is selected and produced—a *disclosure transparency*. The second strand concerns users being invited to participate in different stages in the news production process—a *participatory transparency*. These two strands are often placed together but in reality they rely on different technological architectures as the first strand partly could have been implemented in a one-way medium while that is not the case with the second strand.

Disclosure Transparency

Disclosure transparency is concerned with whether news producers are being open about how news is being produced thus relating to making journalistic routines discernible (Tuchman, 1972) and communicating standards *to* but not necessarily *with* the audience. Disclosure transparency presupposes a common faith between the producers and consumers of news but does not facilitate explicit participation by news consumers.

Previous research has pointed out that explaining news selection, decisions and processes are transparency techniques (Kovach and Rosenstiel, 2001; Rupar, 2006; Singer, 2007) along with communicating the preferences and motifs of the media worker (Hayes et al., 2007). This was technically achievable but absent in the analogue media system as it was marked by a closed news culture (Bennet et al., 1985; Deuze, 2003).

Going into more detail, disclosure transparency has been claimed to be achievable by publishing links to original material and the sources that are used (Hayes et al., 2007; Lasica, 2004; Smolkin, 2006). Moreover transparency can also be made manifest by forthrightness concerning mistakes that have been made. When making an error, responsibility should be accepted by acknowledging the error and publishing the corrected information alongside the original information (Lasica, 2004).

Disclosure transparency is brought even more to the fore by the instant publishing model which has significant impacts on the content of online news because the content never truly finds a finite form and different, successive drafts are published. Quandt (2008) reports from a German context that online journalists edit news content on a regular basis. Kutz and Herring (2005) highlight that online news can be retracted or undergo major changes in the way it is presented. Tremayne et al. (2007) found that immediacy thrived and increased over time in online news.

Thus it can be argued that the high speed of online news publishing warrants disclosure transparency even more as the content frequently changes after the initial publishing. The arch portal of transparency is openness and in order to achieve disclosure transparency from an immediacy point of view, these changes could be stressed in different ways such as using detailed time stamps to highlight and explain changes that have occurred.

Participatory Transparency

While disclosure transparency places emphasis on communicating *to* the audience *participatory transparency* aims at getting the audience involved in the news production process in various ways. Previous research has associated various forms of interactivity that allows users to participate in the news process as transparency techniques (Bivens, 2008; Bruns, 2004; Deuze, 2005; Lowrey and Anderson, 2005; Robinson, 2007).

Connecting interactivity to transparency, Deuze (2005, p. 455) suggests that transparency can be viewed as: "the increasing ways in which people both inside and external to journalism are given a chance to monitor, check, criticize and even intervene in the journalistic process". Bruns (2004) goes into more detail and suggests that transparency requires that users can participate in every stage of news production, from newsgathering to reporting, publishing, analysis and discussion.

Other possibilities to achieve transparency could include (Friend and Singer, 2007; Platon and Deuze, 2003) a public discussion concerning the considerations taken into account when something is published. Furthermore, the continuous news cycle produces different drafts (as mentioned above) that not only can be addressed by the producers but can also be revised after inputs from users (Deuze, 2003).

To reiterate, it seems that any interactive feature that opens up possibilities for the user to either directly or indirectly produce or influence news contents or contexts can be considered as participatory transparency. Disclosure transparency, on the other hand, would include links to sources and original documents, openness on how information has been obtained, openness about and corrections of mistakes, and finally an effort to explain to the public how the dynamics of the 24/7 news cycle affects news content.

Method and Data Collection

Studying online content prompts many challenges (Deuze, 2008; McMillan, 2000; Shoemaker and Vos, 2009) and to date no standardized or commonly accepted methodology has been agreed to overcome the difficulties. This research employs explorative content analysis as methodology and studies the content of front-page news items ($N = 335$) on substantial, quality news sites in three countries across a sample news week (cluster sample). The United States is represented by the online version of *The New York Times*, the United Kingdom by *The Guardian* and finally Sweden by *Dagens*

Nyheter. The online versions of these major newspapers were chosen as the digital publishing form is a prerequisite for origins and procedures of transparency.

Much previous research on transparency has tended to be rather essayistic, anecdotal and/or focused at the news *site* level (Allen, 2008; Deuze, 2003, 2005; Hayes et al., 2007; Plaisance, 2007) thus illustrating or studying if there are different transparency techniques present at all in online journalism. This study investigates the extent to which transparency is present at the news *item* level. Different disclosure and participatory features presented at the news item level are thus viewed as workable notions of transparency. Additionally, individual news items are pointed out as a relevant entity to study (Shoemaker and Vos, 2009) since it is in the specific news content that the whole news production is manifest. Moreover, when objectivity rituals such as the use of many sources or keeping the journalists' personal view out of the news story are employed, they are used at the news item level. Thus rituals, objectivity or transparency can be argued to be most useful as truth-telling techniques when they address specific rather than general content. Put more clearly: a correction section somewhere at the news site will not be of much help if an erroneous news item itself remains unedited or is changed without this being highlighted. Furthermore, having a single news item that invites user participation cannot be considered as transparent as having every news item facilitating user participation. Thus news items offer a useful starting point when trying to establish whether or not and to what extent, news sites utilize different rituals of transparency.

The sample of news items was taken from the main news column on the front page collected at 5 pm local time during a full week in June 2009 using downloading software and/or screen grabs. The news items were scrutinized again two weeks later to investigate if any corrections had been published. An intrasubjective Holsti test on a 15 percent sample of the data was performed seven weeks after the original material was gathered and yielded satisfactory results (0.99).

Findings

The study returned 14 different features which can be considered workable notions of transparency given the previous literature review. The features and their impact on respective news site are presented in Table 1.

The first four features in Table 1 are related to disclosure transparency and the last 10 are connected to participatory transparency.

All sites have extensive use, as demonstrated in Table 1, of *detailed time stamps. The Guardian* is the most transparent news site and highlights both time of publication and (latest) update in almost nine out of 10 news items. Yet there is no way of knowing, given the methodology employed in this study, if all news items that have changes have their publishing time updated. However, it has been shown at least in a Swedish context (Karlsson, 2006) that news sites frequently fail to highlight that updating of the news item has occurred. *The New York Times* has its time stamp (for the greater part of this study) on the front page but not in the news item itself. Furthermore, it is unclear if the time stamp on the front page refers to the original time of publishing, updates or both—in Table 1 the time stamps on the front page have been treated as the original time of publication only.

While *The Guardian* acknowledges many updates to their news items they rarely *highlight and explain the changes* made, neither does *Dagens Nyheter. The New York Times*

TABLE 1

The different transparency features found and their proportionate impact on respective news sites (%)*

	Dagens Nyheter (N=189)	The Guardian (N=77)	The New York Times (N=69)
Detailed time stamps divided in:	97	99	91
Time of publication only	89	12	88
Time of publication and update	3	87	3
Time of update only	5	0	0
Highlight and explain changes (corrections)		3	7
External links	5	17	51
Original documents	1	1	13
E-mail	44	42	
Comment	46	22	29
Discuss	1		
Bloglinks	66		
Chat	2		
Poll	7		
Reader news	0.5 (1 item)		
Reader collaboration is wanted	2		1
Reader contribution is published	2		1
Report errors in news item	85	100	

*For instance, users are invited to post comments on the site at 44 percent of *Dagens Nyheter* news items, 22 percent at *The Guardian* and 29 percent at *The New York Times*.

publishes statements about changes (all changes are corrections) in almost one out of every 14 news items, thus indicating that news items are sometimes published too quickly. At the same time they utilize the elastic nature of digital media to change the jumbled news items while simultaneously declaring that these changes have been made as well as explaining why.

The last two disclosure features in Table 1 concern two forms of hyperlinks. The first is news items with *external links* that point the user to other websites such as sources or organizations that are mentioned in the text. This is a well-established practice in news items at *The New York Times* but the links rarely find their way into *Dagens Nyheter* while *The Guardian* is somewhere in between. The second form of hyperlink is labeled *original documents* and appears when the news site links to sources that contain specific facts derived from original sources that the news item has referenced. Again this appears to be an institutionalized way of doing news at *The New York Times* but not on the two European sites.

E-mail implies that the e-mail address of the journalist(s) that wrote the news story (*Dagens Nyheter*) or the editor responsible for the section (*The Guardian*) is available within the news item frame. This feature is not available to the NYTimes.com users while almost every other news item has this feature on the two sites.

All three news sites rather frequently offer users the ability to *comment* on the news item. In this way the news item is contextualized and framed by user communication. *Discussion* crops up twice on *Dagens Nyheter* and differs from comments insofar as the discussion takes place away from the page where the news item is published, and hence plays a lesser part in setting the frame for the news item.

One of the most frequent modes of user communication on *Dagens Nyheter*, occurring at 66 percent of the news items, is *bloglinks*. Bloglinks allow users to link their blogs to selected news items and a hyperlink to the blogger is then published in the vicinity of the news item referred to by the blog. The existence of "Bloglinks" is wholly dependent on referring back to the original article, thus enabling the site to judge and advertise the attention its news items are receiving from the outside world. In doing so the "bloglinks" support a symbiotic relationship between news sites and users where bloggers can achieve a bigger audience and the news sites can tap into the bloggers network. This feature is not present on the other two sites.

Other modes of user participation found in limited numbers on *Dagens Nyheter*, but missing on the others, are *poll* and *chat*. Both these features enjoy a rather limited degree of freedom compared to comment or bloglinks as they are heavily moderated (chat) or have predefined answer options (poll). Nevertheless, the features have the potential to allow the users to express themselves, at least to a certain degree.

Dagens Nyheter also stands out as the news outlet that most actively, along with *The New York Times*, although on a very small scale in both cases, invites and publishes users' contribution in, or as, news items. *Reader news*, found once in the study at *Dagens Nyheter*, signifies that the news item is presented as being wholly written by a user. *Reader collaboration is wanted* is when the news outlets advertize for user contributions to be supposedly published in a news item or as an illustration to a news item. *Reader contribution is published*, found at *Dagens Nyheter* and *The New York Times* in small numbers, is when the latent promise is fulfilled and user contribution is identifiably published as a part of the news item.

Report an error which is well established on both *The Guardian* and *Dagens Nyheter*, although absent on *The New York Times*, offers encouragement to users to be more involved in some aspects of news production. This implies that the news sites try to recruit users to do proofreading and fact checking but also trust the user with knowledge greater than the journalists' to refine the published version of a news item.

Taken together the findings presented in Table 1 illustrate that the news sites use many different features that can be, according to the previous literature review, considered rituals of transparency. Moreover, the results signal that *Dagens Nyheter* is the news site that employs participatory transparency but is rather opaque in how their news is being produced. Conversely, *The New York Times* appears to be concentrating on disclosure transparency and be straightforward about mistakes being made while keeping user involvement at arms length. *The Guardian*'s transparency rituals fall somewhere between the two.

An overview of the percentage of news items displaying any form of transparency is presented in Table 2.

TABLE 2
Percentage of news items on each site that have at least one transparency feature

	Dagens Nyheter	*The Guardian*	*The New York Times*
N	189	77	69
Percentage	99	100	100

Although the three news sites have implemented different rituals of transparency and their impact fluctuates, Table 2 illustrates that almost every news item in the study has at least one transparency technique.

All in all the results presented in Tables 1 and 2 indicate that the news sites have implemented some transparency rituals; some are used routinely others more scarcely. All three news sites utilize some kind of time stamp to indicate that online news stories are work in progress, thus acknowledging and informing the users of the liquid character of online news content.

The Swedish *Dagens Nyheter* has implemented user participation to a large degree while the audience does not have the same possibilities to participate at *The Guardian* and *The New York Times*. Bearing in mind that user participation at every stage, from news gathering to reporting, publishing, analysis and discussion, is viewed as transparency (Bruns, 2004; Deuze, 2005), *Dagens Nyheter* comes closest to allowing user involvement in all these stages apart from publishing.

The New York Times to a greater degree than the others, has embraced the possibility both to link to original documents and highlight and explain why the content of the news story has changed in the process, thereby fulfilling some news production disclosure transparency (Hayes et al., 2007; Lasica, 2004; Smolkin, 2006).

Overall these results show that transparency can be said to have made an impact in how news is presented at the news item level, supporting other research (Allen, 2008; Plaisance, 2007) reporting that transparency has had an effect. Another evident observation is that the transparency techniques implemented and their impact varies substantially between the news sites, suggesting that the execution of transparency is subject to the culture and policies of the respective news organizations and probably to various social factors in their respective countries.

However, the most noteworthy results from this study are that most news stories are produced the way news stories have traditionally been produced—without significant user participation in the vital parts of news production (reporting and editing), explanations of how or why they are being produced (Kovach and Rosenstiel, 2001; Rupar, 2006; Singer, 2007) or the personal preferences of the journalist (Hayes et al., 2007). Rather the news items appear on the news sites without any explicit rationale for their advent. If users are participating at all in the news production process, their involvement tends to be limited to various forms of commenting on already-published news items. Consequently, the online news portrayed in this study falls short of fully committing to the openness that is at the heart of transparency.

In view of journalism's need to rely on routines and rituals as shared and referable notions of truth-telling (Carey, 1992; Shoemaker and Reese, 1996; Tuchman, 1972), it seems reasonable to suggest that the online news covered in this study so far takes confidence from other more traditional rituals and routines than transparency as other research also signals (Arant and Anderson, 2001; Cassidy, 2006; Singer, 2005).

Conclusion

A somewhat divided conclusion can be drawn from this pilot study. On the one hand, it is clear that workable notions of the transparency norm are starting to impact on online news in different countries although the scale and the techniques introduced and implemented to date differ between news sites. On the other hand, it is also evident that this process is currently only slightly more than embryonic and that the transparency norm has yet to make the kind of impression forecast by many scholars. However, this process is in all probability slow and evolutionary as other research regarding concepts new to journalism (user-generated content and multimedia) has demonstrated.

As this is a pilot study focusing on one week's news items at three mainstream online news sites in western democracies, there are only limited possibilities to generalize the results. Further studies should embrace a larger sample, extended both in time and space, to establish the impact of transparency on a greater scale and with a higher degree of certainty. In addition, further research should also aim to investigate how users perceive and evaluate disclosure and participatory transparency as their involvement and judgment is crucial if the transparency norm is to have any lasting impact.

In spite of these limitations, the three news sites studied in this case study remain significant since they attract large audiences and are regarded as models when it comes to upholding and defining quality journalism in their respective countries. If the transparency norm is to have a significant overall impact in journalism, it most certainly has to have that impact on the biggest and most highly regarded news sites.

ACKNOWLEDGEMENT

The author would like to thank the Swedish Civil Contingencies Agency for the support that made this study possible.

REFERENCES

ALLEN, STUART D. (2008) "The Trouble with Transparency. The challenge of doing journalism ethics in a surveillance society", *Journalism Studies* 9(3), pp. 323–40.

ARANT, DAVID M. and ANDERSON, JANNA Q. (2001) "Newspaper Online Editors Supports Traditional Standards", *Newspaper Research Journal* 22(4), pp. 57–69.

BENNET, LANCE W., GRESSET, LYNNE A. and HALTOM, WILLIAM (1985) "Repairing the News: a case study of the news paradigm", *Journal of Communication* 35(2), pp. 50–68.

BIVENS, RENA K. (2008) "The Internet, Mobile Phones and Blogging. How new media are transforming traditional journalism", *Journalism Practice* 2(1), pp. 113–29.

BRUNS, AXEL (2004) "Reconfiguring Journalism: syndication, gatewatching and multiperspectival news", in: Gerard Goggin (Ed.), *Virtual Nation: the internet in Australia*, Sydney: UNSW Press, pp. 177–92.

CAREY, JAMES W. (1992) *Communication as Culture. Essays on media and society*, New York: Routledge.

CASSIDY, WILLILAM (2006) "Gatekeeping Similar for Online, Print Journalists", *Newspaper Research Journal* 27(2), pp. 6–23.

DEUZE, MARK (2003) "The Web and Its Journalism: considering the consequences of different type of news media online", *New Media & Society* 5(2), pp. 203–30.

DEUZE, MARK (2005) "What Is Journalism? Professional identity and ideology of journalists reconsidered", *Journalism* 6(4), pp. 442–64.

DEUZE, MARK (2008) "The Changing Context of News Work: liquid journalism and monitorial citizenship", *International Journal of Communication* 2, pp. 848–65.

FRIEND, CECILIA and SINGER, JANE B. (2007) *Online Journalism Ethics. Traditions and transitions*, Armonk, NY: M.E. Sharpe.

HAYES, ARHTUR S., SINGER, JANE B. and CEPPOS, JERRY (2007) "Shifting Roles, Enduring Values: the credible journalist in a digital age", *Journal of Mass Media Ethics* 22(4), pp. 262–79.

KARLSSON, MICHAEL (2006) "Nätjournalistik. En explorativ fallstudie av digitala mediers karaktärs-drag på fyra svenska nyhetssajter", dissertation, Lund Studies in Media and Communica-tion 9, Lund.

KOVACH, BILL and ROSENSTIEL, TOM (2001) *The Elements of Journalism. What news people should know and the public should expect*, New York: Crown Publishers.

KUTZ, DANIEL O. and HERRING, SUSAN C. (2005) "Micro-longitudinal Analysis of Web News Updates", paper presented at 38th International Conference on System Sciences, Hawaii.

LASICA, JOSEPH D. (2004) "Transparency Begets Trust in the Ever-expanding Blogosphere", *Online Journalism Review*, http://www.ojr.org/ojr/technology/1092267863.php, accessed 20 September 2007.

LOWREY, WILSON and ANDERSON, WILLIAM (2005) "The Journalist Behind the Curtain: participatory functions on the internet and their impact on perceptions of the work of journalism", *Journal of Computer-mediated Communication* 10(3), article 13.

LOWREY, WILSON and LATTA, JOHN (2008) "The Routines of Blogging", in: D. Domingo and C. Paterson (Eds), *Making Online News. The ethnography of new media production*, New York: Peter Lang, pp. 185–97.

MCMILLAN, SALLY J. (2000) "The Microscope and the Moving Target: the challenge of applying content analysis to the World Wide Web", *Journalism & Mass Communication Quarterly* 77(1), pp. 80–98.

PLAISANCE, PATRICK L. (2007) "Transparency: an assessment of the Kantian roots of a key element in media ethics practice", *Journal of Mass Media Ethics* 22(2), pp. 187–207.

PLATON, SARA and DEUZE, MARK (2003) "Indymedia Journalism, a Radical Way of Making, Selecting and Sharing News?", *Journalism* 4(3), pp. 336–55.

QUANDT, THORSTEN (2008) "Old and New Routines in German Online Newsrooms", in: David Domingo and Chris Paterson (Eds), *Making Online News. The ethnography of new media production*, New York: Peter Lang, pp. 77–97.

ROBINSON, SUE (2007) "'Someone's Gotta Be in Control Here': the institutionalization of online news and the creation of a shared journalistic authority", *Journalism Practice* 1(3), pp. 305–21.

RUPAR, VERICA (2006) "How Did You Find That Out? Transparency of the newsgathering process and the meaning of news", *Journalism Studies* 7(1), pp. 127–43.

SCHUDSON, MICHAEL (2001) "The Objectivity Norm in American Journalism", *Journalism Studies* 2(2), pp. 149–70.

SHOEMAKER, PAMELA and REESE, STEPHEN (1996) *Mediating the Message. Theories of influence on mass media content*, New York: Longman.

SHOEMAKER, PAMELA and VOS, TIMOTHY (2009) *Gatekeeping Theory*, New York: Routledge.

SINGER, JANE B. (2005) "The Political J-blogger. 'Normalizing' a new media form to fit old norms and practices", *Journalism* 6(2), pp. 173–98.

SINGER, JANE B. (2007) "Contested Autonomy. Professional and popular claims on journalistic norms", *Journalism Studies* 8(1), pp. 79–95.

SMOLKIN, RACHEL (2006) "Too Transparent?", *American Journalism Review*, April/May, http://www.ajr.org/Article.asp?id=4073, accessed 18 February 2010.

SOLOSKI, JOHN (1997) "News Reporting and Professionalism. Some constraints on the reporting of news", in: Dan Berkowitz (Ed.), *The Social Meaning of News. A text- reader*, Thousand Oaks, CA: Sage, pp. 138–54.

TREMAYNE, MARK, SCHMITZ WIESS, AMY and CALMON ALVES, ROSENTAL (2007) "From Product to Service: the diffusion of dynamic content in online newspapers", *Journalism & Mass Communication Quarterly* 84(4), pp. 825–39.

TUCHMAN, GAYE (1972) "Objectivity as Strategic Ritual: an examination of newsmen's notion of objectivity", *The American Journal of Sociology* 77(4), pp. 660–79.

ZELIZER, BARBIE (2004) "When Facts, Truth, and Reality are God-terms: on journalism's uneasy place in cultural studies", *Communication and Critical/Cultural Studies* 1(1), pp. 100–19.

JOURNALISM IN SECOND LIFE

Bonnie Brennen and **Erika dela Cerna**

Our research seeks to understand the emerging journalism practiced in Second Life—a computer-generated alternative reality. Framed by postmodernism, this study uses an ideological analysis to evaluate the three Second Life newspapers: the Alphaville Herald, *the* Metaverse Messenger *and the* Second Life Newspaper. *We suggest that journalism in Second Life focuses on community building and education, considers the influence of the on-line world to resident members' off-line lives and raises important questions about freedom of expression.*

As facts, truth, and reality continue to lose relevance in our postmodern world, media watchers are left to wonder if their absence signals the demise of traditional journalism. Our research suggests that important work is still being done in journalism, particularly using a variety of new media within distinct communities, which helps people to understand key issues and information about the political, economic, and cultural aspects of their lives.

This paper seeks to understand the emerging journalism practiced in Second Life (SL)—a computer-generated alternative reality. Its creator Linden Lab defines SL as a "free online virtual world imagined and created by its Residents" (SL, 2009a). Its users come from all over the world to construct virtual representations of themselves known as avatars that reside in SL and navigate and create the virtual environment as they participate in social, economic, recreational and educational activities with other avatars (Diehl and Prins, 2008, pp. 101–2). Residents use voice and text chat to communicate with each other (SL, 2009b), in this massive multi-player online role-playing game (MMORPG), and create new identities for their avatars. SL's open source coding allows residents the freedom to create objects and structures which are significant not only economically (residents may sell items to each other), but also socially as items may function as cultural signifiers.

SL distinguishes itself from other MMORPGs by granting its residents creativity, the ability to do or make whatever they want, and the right to own and control what they create (SL, 2009b). Ludlow and Wallace note that SL's Terms of Service "specifically grants residents ownership of the intellectual property rights in their creations" (2007, p. 76). According to York, unlike most MMORPGs, SL does not have player goals, because there are "no points ... no monsters to defeat, no 'levels' of gaming mastery to achieve and conclusions or 'endgame scenario' that ultimately finishes the 'game'" (2009, p. 4). Instead, SL is an open-ended environment where "players can tackle 'quests,' take on 'jobs,' form lasting relationships with other players and continue to develop their online characters for as long as they care to. There is no way to win or lose the game itself ... because the game itself never ends" (Ludlow and Wallace, 2007, p. 9).

SL's popularity spiked in 2006, with a growing resident population and as reportage of the virtual environment grew from digital newspapers and blogs to coverage in more mainstream, traditional media publications (Totilo, 2007). According to Guest (2007), when SL was launched in 2003, it had approximately 500 participants, which swelled to over 5.6 million users in 2007. This statistic refers to the number of individuals who have signed up throughout SL's history. Linden Lab reports significant usage growth during 2008 with "residents spending more than 400 million hours in Second Life" (Metaverse Messenger, 2009, p. 14) up from 246 million hours in 2007, an increase of more than 60 percent. More recently, as of June 13, 2009, 1,396,914 residents had logged in during the last 60 days; 557,224 had logged in during the last seven days (SL, 2009c).

Due to growing curiosity regarding SL, news powerhouses such as Reuters and CNN started SL bureaus, with Reuters establishing full time in-world avatar-reporters. Mainstream journalists reported on the many ways SL began to mimic real life (Totilo, 2007), often focusing on the novelty factor, which inevitably included themes of sex, violence or financial gain (Boellstorff, 2008; York, 2009).

This study explores print journalism as practiced by residents/reporters who actively participate in SL. Reporters in SL work in a three-dimensional Web environment, where truth and artifice are often blurred. Reporting on the activities and innovations of residents and the diverse cultures and subcultures in the virtual world, reporters reject mainstream journalism's obsession with reality and opt instead for in-world verification, rather than traditional fact checking.

In addition to magazines, blogs, news bureaus, podcasts and television stations, three newspapers, the *Alphaville Herald*, the *Metaverse Messenger* and the *Second Life Newspaper* are currently thriving in this virtual reality. All three newspapers are free and are available both in SL and through the Internet. Thus far there has been limited scholarly literature devoted specifically to journalism in SL (see Ludlow and Wallace, 2007; Totilo, 2008; York, 2009). The existing research primarily focuses on comparisons of coverage and content between traditional and in-world journalism. In contrast, this research seeks to understand the implications of practicing journalism in a virtual environment, where conventional reporting is redefined by the technological features of SL, and how the back and forth relationship between real life and SL inevitably influence and shape news content. Through an assessment of three SL newspapers, this research will address implications for the future practice of journalism.

We draw on postmodernism to frame our study of newspaper journalism in SL. Responding to the rise of a capitalist culture of consumption rather than production during the twentieth century, postmodernism is in Hardt's words "the passionate voice of disillusionment" (1998, p. 75) of contemporary citizens who continually compromise, concede and challenge the social and economic structures of commodity culture.

Strinati (2004) finds that theorists focus primarily on five fundamental societal changes inherent in the development of postmodernism: (1) the power of mass media to create our sense of reality and to construct all other social relations; (2) an emphasis on surface and style that dominates content, substance and meaning and celebrates its arbitrariness and constructedness; (3) the breakdown of distinctions between art and popular culture through the mixing of styles, forms and genres, which emphasize irony, parody, pastiche and playfulness and ignore relevant context or history; (4) the instability of time and space and the dismissal of linear narratives; and (5) the rejection of truth or absolute knowledge or any overarching theories or meta-narratives in favor of culturally diverse, ambiguous, and/or previously marginalized voices. These voices are thought to construct mini-narratives that are fragmented, temporary, contingent and situational and make "no claim to universality, truth, reason, or stability" (Klages, 2006, p. 169). Traditional frames of reference such as class or community are thought to disappear and a de-centered and fragmented individual subjectivity becomes the only authentic reality.

We find Baudrillard's (1994) concept of hyperrealism particularly relevant to the study of the virtual reality in SL. Arguing that postmodernism is a culture of the simulacrum in which the distinction between an original and a copy no longer exists, Baudrillard maintains that simulacra, as signifiers without signifieds, construct an inescapable and unavoidable sense of reality continually disseminated by media industries. Media-provided simulacra create models or codes, often lacking any connection to reality, which instruct consumers about what to believe, desire, buy, or even how to think. As simulacra become more "real" than any authentic experience, and as surface interests dominate authentic meaning, Baudrillard insists that we enter the realm of hyperreality. Within hyperreality differentiation between authentic experience and simulation implodes and distinctions between reality and fiction become less important as the real and the imaginary operate "along a roller-coaster continuum" (Storey, 2001, p. 152). Ultimately, within postmodern culture, there is no difference between "reality" and its representations and therefore virtual reality may be considered as real as any actual experience.

Cormack (1995) suggests that an analysis of cultural products is a useful way to study ideologically imbued representations because the culture of each society is made manifest through its material culture. From this perspective, the newspapers produced in SL exist as elements of material culture, which express a distinct view of reality that its readers are asked to share. While each ideological analysis should be framed within its specific historical context, Cormack includes five distinct categories of analysis important to consider: content, structure, absence, style and mode of address. Content includes assertions, opinions, judgments, descriptive language and the actions taken while the structure assesses the order of delivery, the use of binary oppositions, and the relationship between opening and closing elements. Finding absence crucial to a cultural product's ideological structure, Cormack explains that emphasizing elements that should be included but are missing as well as probing the literary style and the mode of address are also important considerations.

Specifically, this research project uses an ideological analysis to evaluate all images, graphics and text published in the February through May 2009 issues of the three newspapers in an attempt to understand the type of journalism practiced in SL. It also considers how the ideological position of postmodernism is made manifest in the newspapers.

As befitting its motto, "A real newspaper for a virtual world," the *Metaverse Messenger* (*MM*) is the most traditional of the three newspapers in SL. First published on August 9, 2005, the newspaper is formatted as a tabloid complete with banner headlines, bylines, striking images, classified and display advertising, and copy that jumps to inside pages. The newspaper includes articles from a variety of departments including: news, sports, fashion, comics, community events, editorial perspectives and a children's section. The *MM* embraces the ideology of journalism, striving for balance and neutrality particularly in its use of traditional journalistic sourcing. News stories regularly quote residents, software creators, Linden Lab spokespersons and website sources. The ability to actually reference events in SL makes it possible for both reporters and residents to verify information mentioned in news stories, resulting in articles that are accurate and highly relevant to SL residents. Retractions and corrections are published when the newspaper makes an error. The writing style used in news stories often combines inverted pyramid reporting with promotional rhetoric and/or an educational focus. Reporters on the *MM* hold themselves to traditional journalistic standards such as fact checking, accuracy, neutrality and detachment (Richard, 2009b, p. 21).

Debuting in June 2004, the *Alphaville Herald* (*AH*) was started by philosophy professor Peter Ludlow to understand the legal, economic and social considerations of the virtual world. Known for its acerbic and often sarcastic tone, *AH* articles read more like blog entries than newspaper stories. The newspaper makes no specific claims about balanced journalism—in fact their slogan is "always fairly unbalanced". This style, nevertheless, stays true to the newspaper's other mission as stated on its website: "to take a good, close, often snarky look at the online worlds that are becoming a more and more important part of everyone's offline lives."

Despite its tone, the newspaper provides readers with coverage on a wide range of issues, from users' rights and freedoms in SL and other MMORPGs, to the role-playing culture. The newspaper is written for highly involved and active residents and includes SL- and MMORPG-specific parlance, images and stylizing that makes it inherently more accessible to knowledgeable residents. For example, it covers news on "noobs" (new residents; *newb*ies) and "griefers" (players that harass other players; causing *grief*). The *AH* often uses spelling and emphasis similar to blogging—it is not unusual to read a headline like "Oh noooooooes! News delivery in video games", see emoticons peppered in articles, read terms like "lulz" (a variation of lol—laughing out loud) and observe words struck out as a tool of sarcasm.

The *AH*'s tone and stylizing is best illustrated by the newspaper's coverage of the Virtual Journalism Summit (McLuhan, 2009). While the article introduces journalists and their contributions to virtual journalism, the coverage and image slyly pokes fun of Helen Thomas, Bob Schieffer, and even the creator of SL, "whose reporting is so penetrating we can't even see it". The article also mocks Hamlet Au, the first journalist appointed by Linden Lab to cover news in SL: "Last but not least there is the crack journalism of uber-reporter Hamlet Au (nee Hamlet Linden) who was paid by Linden Lab to report on Second Life and retains an unspecified relationship with the Lab."

Founded in 2005 by SL resident, James T. Juno, the *Second Life Newspaper* (*SLN*) provides residents with an easy way to understand the SL grid. Unlike the *AH*'s critical coverage and *MM*'s aim to standardize journalism in SL, the *SLN* lacks a specific mission apart from reporting on happenings in SL in a blog format. Part of its content is reader submitted and the newspaper includes many interviews with residents and unconventional sections not found in other newspapers. Extra-Extra, for example, is a section for fictional stories, columns, and announcements and Red Light is a special section for sexual content.

Many of the *SLN*'s articles also function as press releases. The coverage is upbeat and complements artists, products and services it showcases, and it often includes contact information. Like the other SL newspapers, there is significant coverage on the activities of Linden Lab and considerable resident opinion. The newspaper's style, like the *AH*, is closer to blog entries than traditional newspaper articles. Like the *AH*, the writing style is not standardized, employing SL-specific and Internet parlance.

The creation and maintenance of community is a fundamental concern of the journalism practiced in SL. All three newspapers include frequent extended discussion of legal and technical issues and community concerns as well as provide detailed information to help residents navigate through SL. Residents are reminded to learn and follow Linden Lab's Terms of Service, which are considered the laws of the land, and to make informed decisions regarding their actions in SL. News stories provide background context considered necessary to fully understand larger issues associated with the news. For example, the lead article in the May 19, 2009 *MM* focuses on a new adult policy for SL content. While the article reports statements made by Ken Linden during a press conference on PR Island, it also informs readers that because Linden Lab is a privately owned company, that it can suppress objectionable or unacceptable content. Although this information is not addressed in the press conference, its inclusion in the news article provides necessary context that residents need in order to make informed decisions about SL.

Maintaining that traditional media are unaware of fundamental issues associated with SL as well as being uninformed regarding technical aspects of the grid, the *AH* regularly emphasizes community by critiquing traditional media coverage of SL. For example, an article on the closing of Sky News, by Leonminster (2009) comments that SL critics, or "virtual world Cassandras", will interpret the departure of the news bureau as evidence of SL's decline, rather than recognizing that "the economics of news reporting and delivery in Second Life is very different from real life, and spending lots of money to have virtual world analogs of real life newsrooms doesn't necessarily make any financial sense."

Similarly, Schumann's (2009b) *SLN* article "Second Life's media prejudice" discusses the sensationalist coverage of SL stories in traditional media while rarely covering the "actual productive uses of virtual worlds". Schumann emphasizes community sentiment asserting that SL is a place for residents to express themselves artistically, raise money for good causes, meet people they otherwise would not meet in real life, and serve as a refuge for people who "break their social isolation with virtual life".

Considerable space is allocated to community events, SL activities, and people with illnesses and disabilities. Listings for a variety of support groups including gatherings for the anxious, the depressed, victims of violent crime, those who want to lose weight, and those battling chronic illnesses are featured in the SL newspapers. Each issue of the *MM* features a resident of the week, several of whom are connected with nonprofit organizations that provide education and support for at-risk individuals. News stories go beyond reporting on the activities of charities to promoting fundraising strategies. For example, on June 1, 2009, SL residents were encouraged to wear purple clothing and decorate their residences and retail businesses purple to show support for the American Cancer Society's Relay for Life.

All of the newspapers showcase the concerns and needs of individuals with different abilities and residents are regularly informed about alternative cultures. For example, a front-page story in the March 17, 2009 *MM* focuses on communicating with the hearing impaired in virtual environments as well as the real world. In addition to providing excellent context about the deaf culture, the article includes detailed quotes from the speaker as well as reactions from residents who attended the lecture.

Technical issues are also addressed in depth. For example, Trefusis' (2009) *SLN* article about bots defines them as avatars controlled by machines, which functions as a simplified communication channel for widespread or regular communication. He finds that some bots, such as the copybot, can "steal a design, change permissions, sell the design/product in huge quantities without the original creator benefiting from his or her work". The article not only educates residents, but also urges readers to be responsible, as destructive actions directly affect the freedom of all SL community members. Similarly, the April 28, 2009 issue of the *MM* considers the issue of bots in the teen grid. Combining news reportage with editorial opinion, the article maintains that the use of copybots is contributing to the decline of the teen grid and urges residents to do something about the problem.

The blurring of the line between real life and virtual reality is a dominant theme addressed in SL newspapers. The formation of relationships, both romantic and platonic, is arguably one of its draws, as well as a topic that has captivated traditional media. One relationship covered extensively in the traditional press, which supports residents concern that mainstream press coverage of SL focuses on the "seedier side" rather than represents what occurs in SL authentically, involves a British couple who divorced in 2008 after the wife caught her husband's avatar having sex in SL with a virtual prostitute. The couple first met in an Internet chat room and became lovers in both the virtual and the real worlds. After the divorce, the woman began a relationship with a man she met in the World of Warcraft, a popular MMORPG, while the man has become engaged to another woman he met in SL (CNN.com/Europe, 2008).

For nearly four years, each issue of the *MM* has published the column "The Line" which considers the realm between the real and virtual worlds. Norinn Richard created the column, and writes most of the articles, but others also contribute to the discussion. For, *MM* publisher Katt Kongo, there is no line between real life and virtual reality: "Second Life is a huge part of my First Life and my First Life is a huge part of my Second Life" (2009, p. 6). Kongo, who augments her publishing duties by also attending college in SL, maintains that friendships she has formed in the virtual realm are as real as those established in real life.

In his column, Richard takes a balanced approach to interrogating the line: his language and tone acknowledges possible differences between virtual reality and real life and he sometimes struggles to make sense of his situation. Richard finds there are real-life ramifications for problems encountered in SL. His columns incorporate a variety of meta-statements, and he often wonders why he cannot leave SL issues and frustrations behind when he crosses the line into the real world. As Richard explains: "the problems are real to me. They may be about a virtual world, but they have real consequences" (2009d, p. 21). Richard discusses changing "comfort zone boundaries" along with changing cities, climates, and time zones during his recent job-related move. Detailing how friends from SL provided his family with accommodations and helped load and drive their moving truck, Richard, like Kongo, decides that "a friend in a virtual world is still a Real friend, with all the benefits and duties granting that title involves" (2009a, p. 21). One particularly intriguing experience addressed in the column discusses how both negative and positive emotions cross the line from SL to the real world. A guest contributor, detailing her own experiences with a love affair that ended badly, insists that SL is more than a game because not only "happiness, love, and joy cross the line, [but] fear, shame and anger do as well. Negative emotions are bitter things no matter where they come from" (Richard, 2009c, p. 6).

SLN reporter Schumann (2009a) chronicles the influences of virtual relationships on offline relationships, affirming Richard's sentiments that emotional affect caused by SL traverses the real life, cautioning that "we may only be avatars on computers, but the people that signed up are real". Philosophorum (2009) of the *AH*, on the other hand, tackles the issue of transgressions on self-identity when users become involved in relationships with avatars whose identities do not necessarily match who they are in real life: "There would be feelings of betrayal and hurt, but in the end, that person who you had cybersex with is as real as anything else on the Internet. Just because they might not match your gender expectations doesn't change you or your identity."

Because the construction of an avatar does not have to mirror a resident's actual age, ethnic background, physical features or sexual orientation in real life, the issue of gender bending has become an important topic addressed in all three SL newspapers. For example, the *MM*'s comic strip, Plywood, features a character, Gender Man, who is able to see the true gender of the players behind the avatars. The comic pokes fun at the commonness of gender bending in SL, as well as some residents' preoccupation regarding the relevance of real-life identity. Interestingly, articles also convey that the ability to reinvent an avatar's gender is one of the fundamental freedoms of SL residents. One article in the *AH* reports that a resident complained about losing money after planning a wedding with another resident who misrepresented his gender. The article, however, mocks the resident's formal request that Linden Lab should implement a gender verification system, commenting: "What are they going to do, take off their pants and send a picture to Linden Lab? Have a crotch inspector?" (Vielle, 2009b). Other coverage equates gender bending with revealing hidden desires and repressed identities, rather than an act of griefing. Writer (2009) suggests in the *SLN* that when users make an alternate avatar of the opposite sex, it still retains the real identity of the user. She finds that these avatars are probably an unconscious construction, which can be revealing of "who the hell we are".

Charges of censorship have been reported in all three newspapers following Linden Lab's announcement that it was creating a filtered search engine to augment a new SL continent for adult-rated content. The April 21, 2009 issue of the *MM* reports that Linden Lab's plans to create an adult-content continent met with widespread resistance from SL residents. Concerned that the decision would result in a major shift in SL culture, residents question how the community will function with restrictions. Some residents wonder how child avatars might fit into the plans while others suggest that Linden Lab's decision is based on attempts to stymie the use of SL in public schools and libraries.

While the *MM*'s coverage balances resident commentary, information gathered from Linden Lab with relevant context regarding legal issues associated with SL, the coverage in the *AH* and the *SLN* is more critical of the plans. Both newspapers primarily feature strong resident opinion against creating an adult-only continent. Rearwind's *SLN* (2009) article addresses the arbitrariness of the designation of adult, sexually explicit content, commenting that filtering would "affect the basic principles of freedom of expression and freedom of speech in a virtual world founded on the principle of 'Give the people a platform and let them create a metaverse'". Shuftan's (2009) *SLN* interview notes that censorship plans would change the behavior of SL residents, and suggests that behavior in the virtual world should be organic, and "not some artificial thing that comes about as a result of what users can and cannot do".

The *AH* goes beyond concerns of SL reporting on censorship and issues of freedom in other massively multi-player on-line games and even on social networking sites. For example, a May 13, 2009 article "Avatars and Humans Unite to Fight Facebook," critiques Facebook's terms of service, which currently do not allow avatars to have Facebook pages. The newspaper is also critical of certain Linden Lab policies and plans, especially those involving financial gain. Vielle (2009a) addresses residents' attitude that "Linden Lab is losing its focus, and grabbing for money more than the grassroots participation of the residents" by neglecting residents' needs and increasing charges for commodities, while seeking to make deals for corporations to extend their presence and/or involvement in SL.

Considering issues covered in the three newspapers, there seems to be a quasi-adversarial relationship between traditional and SL journalism. While SL residents and journalists have embraced the concept of hyperreality, traditional media largely emphasizes virtual and real worlds as mutually exclusive, especially by characterizing SL as a game. Nevertheless, our analysis yields evidence that there are intricate ties that bind real life to SL, influencing sense-making practices and the content of SL journalism. However SL, by itself, stands as a different plane of existence, which cultivates a separate culture and world-view, and ultimately an alternative reality—another feature equally apparent in our study.

The absence of critical commentary regarding the blurring of the line between virtual reality and real life can be seen as one way postmodernism is made manifest in the newspaper coverage. The virtual reality of SL belongs to Baudrillard's (1994) realm of hyperreality, in which the simulacra of the grid overwhelms any unmediated meaning becoming more real than any other reality and providing evidence that an authentic reality no longer exists. SL journalism rarely differentiates between fiction and reality, perhaps because distinctions between the two no longer seem relevant.

While the journalistic philosophies may differ, the three SL newspapers engage with their readers and are sensitive to audience members' backgrounds, interests, needs and desires. Each newspaper is interactive and uses a variety of journalistic strategies to educate and inform its readers. Occupying the border space between information and entertainment, journalism in SL raises important questions about freedom of expression in virtual worlds and focuses on community building and education as well as considering the influence of the on-line world to resident members' off-line lives. More than 100,000 regular readers have made the *MM* the most widely read newspaper in SL and in May 2009 *AH* staffers celebrated receiving the 50,000th reader comment. Clearly, journalism in SL is flourishing and traditional journalists might want to consider incorporating aspects of their user-friendly coverage.

REFERENCES

BAUDRILLARD, JEAN (1994) *Simulacra and Simulation*, Sheila Glasser (Trans.), Ann Arbor: University of Michigan Press.

BOELLSTORFF, TOM (2008) *Coming of Age in Second Life: an anthropologist explores the virtually human*, Princeton, NJ: Princeton University Press.

CNN.COM/EUROPE (2008) "Second Life Affair Ends in Divorce", 14 November, www.cnn.com/2008/WORLD/europe/11/14/secondlife.divorce/index.html/.

CORMACK, MIKE (1995) *Ideology*, Ann Arbor: University of Michigan Press.

DIEHL, WILLIAM and PRINS, ESTHER (2008) "Unintended Outcomes in Second Life: intercultural literacy and cultural identity in a virtual world", *Language and Intercultural Communication* 8(2), pp. 101–18.

GUEST, TIM (2007) *Second Lives: a journey through virtual worlds*, New York: Random House.

HARDT, HANNO (1998) *Interactions. Critical studies in communication, media and journalism*, Boulder, CO: Rowman & Littlefield.

KLAGES, MARY (2006) *Literary Theory: a guide for the perplexed*, New York: Continuum.

KONGO, KATT (2009) "The Line", *Metaverse Messenger*, 10 February, p. 6.

LEONMINSTER, SIGMUND (2009) "SHOCK! Sky News Closes Second Life News Bureau!!!", *Alphaville Herald*, 18 April.

LUDLOW, PETER and WALLACE, MAR (2007) *The Second Life Herald: the virtual tabloid that witnessed the dawn of the metaverse*, Cambridge, MA: MIT Press.

MCLUHAN, FIELD MARSHAL (2009) "Virtual Journalism Heavyweights Gather in Virtual Journalism Summit", *Alphaville Herald*, 6 April.

METAVERSE MESSENGER (2009) "Linden Lab Announces New Hires", 10 February, pp.14, 21.

PHILOSOPHORUM, LAPIS (2009) "But Does That Make Me Gay?", *Alphaville Herald*, 11 May.

REARWIND, FIREHORSE (2009) "The Changes to Second Life Announced", *Second Life Newspaper*, 9 May.

RICHARD, NORINN (2009a) "Moving", *Metaverse Messenger*, 17 February, pp. 6, 21.

RICHARD, NORINN (2009b) "You Write for a What?", *Metaverse Messenger*, 17 March, pp. 6, 21.

RICHARD, NORINN (2009c) "The Line", *Metaverse Messenger*, 21 April, pp. 6, 21.

RICHARD, NORINN (2009d) "No Fixin' This", *Metaverse Messenger*, 28 April, pp. 6, 21.

SCHUMANN, ALESIA (2009a) "This Is Just Life RL (1)", *Second Life Newspaper*, 12 January.

SCHUMANN, ALESIA (2009b) "Second Life's Media Prejudice", *Second Life Newspaper*, 23 February.

SECOND LIFE (2009a) "What Is Second Life?", http://secondlife.com/whatis/.

SECOND LIFE (2009b) "Frequently Asked Questions", http://secondlife.com/whatis/faq.php.

SECOND LIFE (2009c) "Economic Statistics (Raw Data Files), Logged in Users", 13 June, http://secondlife.com/statistics/economy-data.php.

SHUFTAN, BIXYL (2009) "Interview with Xantarius Cain", *Second Life Newspaper*, 13 May.

STOREY, JOHN (2001) *Cultural Theory and Popular Culture: an introduction*, 3rd edn, London: Prentice Hall.

STRINATI, DOMINIC (2004) *An Introduction to Theories of Popular Culture*, London: Routledge.

TOTILO, STEPHEN (2007) "Burning the Virtual Shoe Leather: does journalism in a computer world matter?", *Columbia Journalism Review* 46(2), pp. 38–44.

TREFUSIS, KIM (2009) "What's a Bot? A benefit or a menace?", *Second Life Newspaper*, 22 April.

VIELLE, TENSHI (2009a) "Op/Ed Catering to Corporations, Running Over Residents?", *Alphaville Herald*, 27 February.

VIELLE, TENSHI (2009b) "Is Your Second Life Woman a Real Life Man?", *Alphaville Herald*, 4 May.

WRITER, COVADONGA (2009) "SLOOP—in the name of hell/who are you/who are you?", *Second Life Newspaper*, 6 May.

YORK, CHANCE (2009) "Other Worlds, Other Media: an overview of Second Life journalism", paper presented at the annual AEJMC Midwinter Conference, Norman, OK.

THE FORM OF REPORTS ON US NEWSPAPER INTERNET SITES, AN UPDATE

Kevin G. Barnhurst

A previous study found that US newspaper electronic editions did not appear to reinvent themselves. In 2001, the Web versions reproduced the substance of print editions so as to relate similarly to readers. A replication of the study shows that by 2005 the online editions were changing, especially in the form of news. For readers, the laborious process involved in using the Internet editions in 2001 had changed, but many clicks and scrolls had shifted from mapping the content to managing reading. Multiple screens for each story exposed readers to more ads. Some interactive elements became standard, such as reader-produced comments and links to archives. But individualized hyperlinks to resources from other agencies or providers were rare, keeping traffic inside the site. The Internet versions were still visually meager compared to print, which has more typographical range and many more graphics and pictures. The study results suggest that print publishers have moved only tentatively into the new technology, continuing a long history as slow adopters of innovation and new techniques for informing the public. Their primary drive has been to serve the needs for revenue, not to provide for the comfort and information of citizens.

Introduction

US news organizations continue to struggle with transformations in the technology of delivering news, even though long predicted. Legendary editor William Allen White wrote in 1931 that "most of the machinery now employed" for news "will be junked by the end of this century" (*Quill*, 2007 Supplement, p. 25). Industry sources continually chastise journalists for resisting change. Neil Chase, editor of the continuous news desk at the *New York Times*, writes, "A decade after newspapers began to publish online, there is still trepidation about technology among reporters and editors" (*Nieman Reports*, Winter 2006, p. 64). Robert Kuttner, who has worked for the *Washington Post* and the *Boston Globe*, complains that "the mainstream press" has come "late to the party" of new technology (in *Columbia Journalism Review*, March/April 2007, p. 24). He also criticizes publishers, who, "in their haste both to cut newsroom costs and ramp up web operations, . . . are slashing newsroom staff and running the survivors ragged" (p. 26).

Although US news businesses still reap higher-than-average profits (*Nieman Reports*, Winter 2006, p. 63), fears persist about the end of journalism, as layoffs continue and some newspapers, in debt and unable to raise capital on Wall Street, close their doors. In June 2006, an *American Journalism Review* essay proclaimed, "quality journalism is in jeopardy" (p. 62). Christopher Lydon, a former *New York Times* reporter prominent in public radio, says, "The priesthood of gatekeepers is being disbanded" (in *Columbia Journalism Review*, March/April 2007, p. 24).

No known business model can sustain the US media system still in place, but trade publications hail the potential of Internet editions to reaffirm newswork in civic dialogue. Jan Gilmore, technology columnist at the *San Jose Mercury News*, says, "If contemporary American journalism is a lecture, what it is evolving into is something that incorporates a conversation and seminar" (*Nieman Reports*, Fall 2003, p. 79). And *Washington Post* executive editor Leonard Downie says that, online, "all the feedback improves the journalism" (in *Columbia Journalism Review*, March/April 2007, p. 27).

Industry discussions present important questions that previous research has not resolved: whether news organizations are still resisting technology, how Internet editions change news quality, and what kinds of public interactivity are emerging online. This study presents data showing how the form of news online has shifted, adapting to the Web and adjusting interactive options. But news quality has not necessarily improved from changes in the online options for public involvement at newspaper sites.

Literature

One theory of news form examines how Internet newspapers have expressed larger historical processes, news production systems, and ideas about politics and the public (Barnhurst and Nerone, 2001). Rather than a direct outcome of production technologies, the form of news in history expressed the definition of news and the practices to get a first account of events. Another perspective, the long news hypothesis (Barnhurst and Mutz, 1997), suggests an ongoing redefinition of news as a cultural product, after a century of news stories becoming longer, focusing on journalists and their interpretations of events.

Initial analyses of online journalism predicted that technologies would change the practice and form of news (Barnhurst, 2002). More Americans were getting news online, but visiting fewer sites, usually ones with brand recognition. Critics and scholars objected that the sites failed to adopt the capabilities of the Internet and held back content and scoops for the print editions. The Web was secondary to print, with identical text but less visual variety and fewer images.

Recent studies of online journalism continue to treat new technology as a force behind changing practices, but also predict a greater focus on the audience, resulting in expanded democracy. The high cost of print and distribution pushed the move online, although free access continued to make profit uncertain (Carlson, 2003). Surveys found that editors had begun to see the Internet as a faster and roomier venue for news (Singer, 2003) but that, relying more on email to reach sources, reporters still worried about message credibility and security (Garrison, 2004). Case studies found converging news operations changed the socialization of journalists (Singer, 2004), who tended to resist (Domingo, 2008). Email interviews also found practitioners hesitant about interactive features (Singer and González-Velez, 2003), and a survey found print journalists more committed to investigative reporting (Cassidy, 2005). The move online seemed to reinforce "current trends toward infotainment, news for the affluent, corporate and government publicity, and inexpensive, image-over-substance features" (Scott, 2005, p. 110). Further research should show whether news practice continues resisting change.

To test how news form affects audiences, scholars of information processing and cognition conducted experiments to test specific elements of online information. A comparison found that the *New York Times* in print exposed readers to a wider range of content than did the Internet edition, although in general anyone using either form regularly showed greater political awareness (Althaus and Tewksbury, 2007). Researchers attempted to discover what about the Web, such as site organization or hyperlinks, affected users' learning (Tremayne, 2008). Studies also examined how different story structures online might influence user interest and understanding (Yaros, 2006). Research in the Netherlands found no experimental differences in how readers use or recall news from print or the Web (d'Haenens et al., 2004), although surveys there suggest print broadens the less affluent, motivated, and interested readers more (de Waal and Schoenbach, 2008).

But most US research has not tracked changes in the quality of news, such as the structure and positioning of stories, as publishing moved online. One study found more wire stories but otherwise not much change in quality for sites in the process of converging the content of newspapers with other media (Huang et al., 2004). The growing uniformity in news design across media may push audiences to scan information (Cooke, 2005), and editors may be growing more open to user contributions (Singer, 2006).

Questions of how Web news quality and form influence audiences hinge on whether texts differ online, but the research is inconclusive. US editors say most Internet content comes from print editions (Singer, 2006), although at least CNN political reports have shifted away from *shovelware*, dumping content from the original outlet common among early news sites (Kautsky and Widholm, 2008). A study of Argentina found about half of stories had content overlap between print and online editions (Boczkowski and de Santos, 2007).

Although content studies support the criticism that newspaper sites incorporate few interactive features (e.g., Dimitrova et al., 2003), some interactive options, such as email addresses, increased by 2003 (Tremayne et al., 2007). Awards for news design also encouraged more photography in Web editions (Beyers, 2006). Research in Scandinavia found that not all stories appeared online, that print versions were more in-depth, with more visuals and staff-generated copy, and that only about half of Web stories linked to internal archives and almost none linked to outside sites (Engebretsen, 2006).

Despite its volume, research on Internet news editions is spotty. The functional experiments on users suggest that technical aspects such as the amount of clicking affect learning, but content studies rarely attend to those forms. Studies of interactive features do suggest some changes: email response links may be increasing. Research that includes aspects of site design points to a visual poverty relative to print but also sees improvements in the use of images. Replicating the 2001 study of the form of online newspaper sites provides consistent data to clarify the changing structure of news site pages, the qualities of design and interactivity, and the aspects of production such as staff versus wire authorship and ongoing coverage.

A Replication

The three cases span the range of US regions and markets. The *New York Times* is no longer "a local paper but a national one based in New York," according to its publisher (in *Columbia Journalism Review*, March/April 2007, p. 28). Despite recent declines, its Web edition has more distinct individual readers than any other US newspaper site (more that 20 million, according to Nielsen). The *Chicago Tribune* is a large regional newspaper with online dominance in the Midwest (more than four million). The daily *Portland Oregonian* serves communities around a mid-sized city on the Pacific coast. Its online edition is modest (under one million, according to Scarsborough Research). The three websites represent a range of online approaches: the stand-alone NYTimes.com, the city-based Web portal ChicagoTribune.com, and the affiliate of a larger portal, OregonLive.com/Oregonian.

The three span the national geography and circulation of the daily press at the mid-2000s, when online US news was no longer a novelty. This study follows research on the same outlets for a century (Barnhurst and Mutz, 1997) and replicates sampling and measures from 2001 (Barnhurst, 2002). A trained assistant drew a purposive sample of stories for three weeks in late June 2005, a period selected to avoid holidays during a slow news period, which can show routine as opposed to exceptional content.

Coders trained on stories from the 2001 sample to calibrate their work. Both studies employed the same main coder, who gathered both samples. For each topic, he scanned the pages following site navigation menus, then searched to find related stories without links. The census included all stories encountered up to 40 per topic for each site. Each story coding included site, date, and story topic and story production (staff or wire, first report or follow-up). Physical appearance included location on the site, links, and length in jumps and screens containing the story. Visuals include the display and text typography and a count of images with each story.

After the main coder completed 10 percent of stories, a second coder duplicated the procedure, with good reliability (averaging 0.89) that ranged (from 0.97 to 0.80) according to the difficulty of each step, from simple counts to subjective ratings. Another assistant then compared the online sample to the print edition, identifying identical, similar (with changes to headline or dateline), and dissimilar (such as a print brief of a full online story) stories, noting any that did not appear in print.

Finally, I examined the results for errors based on general knowledge of the news outlets and content categories and tested for sampling error (analysis of variance, F, with post hoc Scheffe tests). The results report not only statistical significance but also conceptual importance.

Results

In 2001, few stories (about one in eight) appeared on the main page, not unlike the selectivity of printed front pages, and two-thirds appeared on topical pages that echoed the sections of print (Barnhurst, 2002). By 2005, Web editions began abandoning the print model (see Table 1).

Home pages in 2005 used more capacity inherent online, signaling with headlines and some introductory blurbs almost half of stories. The *Oregonian* jumped from behind (with fewer than 10 percent of stories on the 2001 home page) to placing most stories there. ChicagoTribune.com also listed more content on its home page, up by more than

TABLE 1

Content structure: percentage of stories placed on the home, secondary, or tertiary section of three newspaper Internet sites for four topics, June 2005

Section	*Times*	*Tribune*	*Oregonian*	Politics	Jobs	Crime	Accidents	Total
Home page	19.4	37.5	86.2	50.8	36.7	53.3	50.0	47.7
Topical page	47.5	52.5	1.2	45.8	33.3	35.0	20.8	33.8
Other page	30.6	9.4	12.5	3.3	30.0	11.7	29.2	18.5
N	160	160	160	120	120	120	120	480

For site, Chi-square $=1.852$, df $=6$, $p<0.000$. For topics, Chi-square $=5.208$, df $=9$, $p<0.000$.

half, and NYTimes.com more than tripled its share, but remained the lowest site. The results confirm that editors acted on their belief in roomier websites (Singer, 2003).

Unlike 2001, when most content appeared on secondary pages, in 2005 the share dropped by more than half. NYTimes.com still placed almost half its content on the old-style topical pages. The other two sites arranged three-quarters of stories topically in 2001, but by 2005 the *Tribune* dropped almost by half, and the *Oregonian* had abandoned topical organization.

Stories on other pages remained about the same overall, but the sites differed. ChicagoTribune.com tripled the use to almost one in 10 stories. Third-tier pages required clicking links on topical pages, treating the stories as minor. Large changes in tertiary pages might suggest less ranking of newsworthiness, but the shifts were either small or involved few stories (for ChicagoTribune.com). NYTimes.com continued to expect the most digging from readers: three stories out of 10 appeared two or more pages away from home. The average pages a reader of the three sites had to traverse to reach a story (1.7) had dropped (below 2.0 in 2001).

The four topics all shifted to the home page. Each topic had triple the 2001 share, except for crime, which grew by a factor of six. Politics had the most main-page stories in 2001, followed by accidents, but in 2005 crime stories had the most. Employment coverage moved to tertiary pages, which became even with home and topical pages. Almost no politics stories appeared on third-tier Other pages, but almost half appeared on topics pages (see Table 1).

Overall, main pages contained much more content, topical pages declined, and so did tertiary pages, except at the *Times*, which continued to use topical pages like sections with links going deeper into the site. The changes in site organization may affect users' learning (Tremayne, 2008).

Movement Through

After navigating to a page, the reader still must move through the expanded listings, find a story, and then navigate the story's end. The sites overall squeezed more stories into fewer pages, but then stretched reading of individual stories across more pages (Table 2).

TABLE 2

Position and length: mean screen jumps to reach a story link and to scroll through a story text on three newspaper Internet sites for four topics, June 2005

	Link position	Story screens	Total screens
Overall	2.12	3.54	6.55
Site	*	***	***
A. *New York Times*	2.13	3.69[B]	7.26[B,C]
B. *Chicago Tribune*	2.26[C]	2.75[A,C]	5.83[A,C]
C. *Portland Oregonian*	1.97[B]	4.19[B]	6.56[A,B]
Topic	*	***	***
A. Politics	2.06	4.36[C,D]	6.97[D]
B. Employment	2.37[D]	3.76[D]	7.35[C,D]
C. Crime	2.11	3.38[A]	6.19[B]
D. Accidents	1.95[B]	2.68[A,B]	5.69[A,B]

One-way analysis of variance (df 2, 479) ***$p < 0.001$, *$p < 0.05$: Link: $F = 3.141$ (Site), 3.419 (Topic); Story: $F = 20.711$ (Site), 14.399 (Topic); Total: $F = 13.788$ (Site), 11.426 (Topic).
[A,B,C,D]*Post-hoc* Scheffe tests with significance level of at least 0.05.

The position of stories became about three-quarters closer in 2005, measured in screen jumps, but NYTimes.com shrank that distance the least. The average link for *Chicago Tribune* stories was still the furthest down the page (based on roughly six vertical inches of text on the typical browser window). The *Oregonian* required the least scrolling, although differences were slight, and the range among the sites dropped by half in 2005. The organizing pages of the sites had become more uniform in this dimension.

Once the reader reached the story, the sites imposed additional clicks down each page and onto continuation pages—more than three and a half screens' worth for the typical story. In 2001, the sites ranged less than a quarter screen (well within sampling error), but bigger differences emerged by 2005 (1.44 screens), ranging from the shortest, ChicagoTribune.com, to the longest, the *Oregonian*. The *Tribune* site (the shortest in 2001) now required even fewer clicks down pages and/or to other pages to finish reading a story. NYTimes.com required almost a third of a page more. But the *Oregonian* added almost a full page-click. The shift did not mean story text itself was getting longer at the *Oregonian*. On the contrary, all three sites ran shorter stories that year, and the *Oregonian* stories shrank the most (Barnhurst, 2009). Instead, Web form had adjusted, adding more screens and clicks, each one an opportunity to present such things as advertising as readers moved through a story.

The increase in story clicks meant that a reader had to go through even more total screens from home to the end of the average story, even though the sites shortened the distance of stories from the home page. In 2001, the *Oregonian* site required the shortest total scrolling, but in 2005 the *Tribune* site became shortest (by a margin of 1.43 screens because it had reduced both measures). At the other end of the range, the *Times* ran the longest both years (by about one-third of a screen). The overall total had grown somewhat, but the 2005 differences now went beyond sampling error. The three sites diverged substantially.

Links to employment stories appeared deepest on the page, supplanting crime, which the 2001 sites had buried. At the opposite end of the range (of 0.42), accidents played the closest to the top of pages, supplanting politics.

From 2001 to 2005, clicking through screens after reaching a story expanded most for politics (0.69 screen clicks), followed by jobs (0.36), and crime (0.34). Accidents, however, involved fewer screen clicks (-0.33). In 2005, the range (1.68 screens) was also more dramatic than in 2001 (0.54), but in both years political stories required the most clicking (and rose above sampling error), and accident stories required the least (with strong differences).

In 2005, the sites became more alike, positioning story links early, but expected more scrolling once readers arrived at a story, especially at the *Oregonian*. Even so, NYTimes.com differed enough to suggest another approach to its interactions with readers. The *Tribune* continued front-loading content, and the *Oregonian* split the difference, as in 2001. The data document different structures emerging for online sites, which influence the user experience (Yaros, 2006).

Design and Interaction

The visual design of each site did not range widely. Each used a limited typographic palette: serif headlines and text for NYTimes.com, sans serif for the others. Most stories still had no images (85.4 percent), despite increasing since 2001. The *Oregonian* went from none in 2001 to almost none in 2005 (seven images with five stories, or 3.1 percent). The *Times* again ran the most images, more than twice the 2001 number (66 with 42 stories, or 26.3 percent, ranging up to six for one story). The *Tribune* also ran twice the 2001 number (42 images in 23 stories, or 14.3 percent, ranging up to five with one story). The site differences were significant (Chi-square $= 4.29$, df $= 12$, $p < 0.001$).

Crime stories carried the fewest images (8.3 percent, with two stories having two images), and accident stories the most (19.2 percent, ranging up to five images). Politics (16.7 percent) and jobs (14.2 percent) each had more in 2005, with a greater range for politics (33 images for with 20 stories, one with six images) than for jobs (24 images with 17 stories, ranging only up to two).

Despite an increase in visuals, the numbers are still minor. In physical size, the images remained relatively small as well, but larger than in 2001, perhaps responding to emphasize photography (Beyers, 2006).

The sites expanded some interactive options, contrary to earlier criticisms (e.g., Dimitrova et al., 2003). In 2001, hyperlinks accompanied a minority of stories (75.8 percent had none), a condition that improved in 2005 (down to 30.0), although not for ChicagoTribune.com (81.2). Email addresses for the staff disappeared at the *Oregonian* (from 92.5 percent in 2001), replaced by links to reader discussions and other modes of feedback within the site (86.9 of links in 2005). The *Chicago Tribune* had some links to its own archived stories, available for purchase (8.1 percent), and a few of its own current stories, available for free (3.1 percent), but gave only two email links (1.2 percent). In 2001, almost half its links led to its own free, related reports. Only the *New York Times* site had at least one link with every story, most of them to paid archives (72.5 percent, up from 6.3 in 2001) or free *Times* content (18.8 percent, up from 12.5). Its chat or discussion links declined (to 1.9 percent from 18.8 in the previous study), but email links went from none in 2001 to a few in 2005 (2.5 percent).

The results for email links document a shift since research showed email addresses increasing in 2003 (Tremayne et al., 2007). Qualms of editors about email (Garrison, 2004) seem to reign in the 2005 data. Links to internal archives were lower in this study than in other research (Engebretsen, 2006), which also found almost no links to outside sites.

In this replication, any links to external sites or sources dropped dramatically—to only two in the 2005 sample, both in NYTimes.com (falling from 62.5 to 1.2 percent). ChicagoTribune.com had none (down from 11.8), as did the *Oregonian* (both years). The differences among sites were significant (Chi-square $= 7.01$, df $= 12$, $p < 0.001$).

Roughly the same share of stories had no link, paid archives links, and feedback/discussion links (30 percent or slightly less apiece), and the remainder linked to current stories. Politics and employment had somewhat more links to current stories (around 10 percent), but politics (35.8 percent) and crime (33.3 percent) had more feedback links; accidents (26.7 percent) and jobs (23.3 percent) had fewer. The differences paled compared to contrasts among the sites.

The sites used a narrow typographic palette but more images, sized smaller than in print. Interactively, the sites shifted from direct contact through email, especially at the *Oregonian*, and increased discussion boards and on-site feedback for readers, suggesting a change in mode, but not necessarily more openness to users (Singer, 2006). The strongest change was away from linking outside the newspapers' sites, even though linking grew, confirming a focus on the illusion, not substance, of interactivity (Scott, 2005).

Content Production

Finally, stories also emerge from a context, as products of staff or wire services and as first-day or follow-up reports. In 2005, the Internet editions shifted their focus to current events, providing fewer follow-ups, but the share of staff and wire stories remained stable overall (Table 3).

The proportions of staff and wire content remained constant from 2001 to 2005, contrary to previous research (Huang et al., 2004). But a large shift did occur away from follow-up stories, from more than a quarter of all reports in 2001 to just one 30-second in 2005. Wire-service follow-ups also declined by a third, from almost 10 percent in 2001 to a share similar to staff follow-ups in 2005.

The total shares stayed the same overall, but not for different sites. At the *Times* and *Tribune*, readers in 2001 found half of stories came from wire services, but by 2005 that share had dropped. The *Oregonian* went from none in 2001 to about a quarter of stories, but still well behind the others. All the sites increased staff-produced first reports, which doubled for ChicagoTribune.com, increased by half for NYTimes.com, and grew by a quarter at the *Oregonian* site. Even more dramatic, follow-ups dropped for staff and wire combined from about a quarter of *Times* stories in 2001 to a tenth in 2005 and from more than a third to a sixteenth of *Tribune* stories.

For topics, political reports were mostly staff-generated in both years, showing only a slight decline in 2005 (by just 1.6 percent), but follow-ups largely disappeared (from 35.8 percent in 2001). Staff members produced more accident stories in 2005 (up by 9.2 percent) but no follow-ups (from 18.3 percent in 2001). The overall percentage of staff writing remained the same for jobs and crime (64.1 percent), but follow-ups dropped: dramatically for jobs (from 28.3 percent in 2001) but not quite half for crime (from 18.3). Staff production continued to emphasize politics, but with less follow-through, and shifted toward accidents. Follow-ups evaporated, except for crime (politics had the most in 2001).

The universal 2001 focus was on *new* news, with two first-day reports to each follow-up, but that focus sharpened in 2005, with a ratio of almost 16:1. Where the *Times* and *Tribune* relied less on wire services, the *Oregonian* site restructured to include more wire stories.

A *post-hoc* comparison suggests that the online and print editions diverged in some ways (see Barnhurst, 2009, Table 6). The 2001 online articles usually matched what

TABLE 3

Content production: percentage of stories drawn from staff reports and from wire reports on three newspaper Internet sites for four topics, June 2005

	Times	Tribune	Oregonian	Politics	Jobs	Crime	Accidents	Total
Staff-produced								
First report	51.9	60.0	74.4	70.8	55.8	54.2	67.5	62.1
Follow-up	4.4	5.0	0.0	1.7	0.8	10.0	0.0	3.1
Wire-service								
First report	38.1	33.8	23.8	25.8	39.2	33.3	29.2	31.9
Follow-up	5.6	1.2	1.9	1.7	4.2	2.5	3.3	2.9
N	160	160	160	120	120	120	120	480

For sites, Chi-square $=2.589$, df $=6$, $p<0.000$. For topics, Chi-square $=3.391$, df $=9$, $p<0.000$.

appeared in print, but not in 2005 (cf. Boczkowski and de Santos, 2007). Only two-thirds of stories online and in print were mostly or entirely alike. A sixth of stories had greater changes, such as full online stories appearing only as a listing in print, and another sixth of online stories never saw print. Stories with differences tended to come from other news outlets, not from local staff. The sites ranged from the smallest reusing print stories most to the largest doing so least, but none merely dumped the print edition online (Kautsky and Widholm, 2008).

Political stories, the most important in professional news, appeared in about the same staff-produced version most of the time (and no staff-produced politics story appeared online only). Wires provided half of accident stories, but a quarter for crime and employment. Only one wire story had identical text in both editions, and three-fourths of all Web-only stories came from wire services. A combination of available resources and professional practices generated the differences observed in 2005 (Barnhurst, 2009). The main observations of this study would likely hold in a study of print editions.

Discussion

The organization of news in a medium proposes particular social and political structures, as well as expectations and roles that news producers assign to users of the medium (Barnhurst and Nerone, 2001). The form of the three Web editions assigned priority to news and conveyed their expectations of the reader by placing stories in the home page or a topical page, by positioning stories on pages, by requiring more or less clicking and scrolling to read entire stories, and by producing timely stories within the economic and visual resources available.

The sites placed stories on home pages with less selectivity, stepping back from mapping content, a characteristic of twentieth-century modern print news. Internet pages are more capacious, and the sites made readers sift through much more on the initial page, reverting to news structure not dominant since the nineteenth century.

For more than a century, newspaper topical organization revealed how news operators related with the public, especially their perception of audiences in the advertising market (Barnhurst and Nerone, 2001). Shifting content away from topical pages may suggest that journalists are providing a less hierarchical map of the social world, as well as that online markets for news are becoming less segmented or users more omnivorous.

Main pages became not only more extensive but also more full of accidents. Jobs stories got buried more, and content tilted toward crime, but politics became a topic more like any other. In topical placement, the sites subtly emphasized risk and deemphasized citizen participation and employment.

The same was the case when traversing to the end of a story. Employment was the most elaborate to get through, supplanting crime in previous research, and crime in 2005 involved the least effort, supplanting politics, which previously had the least. Topics, which had grown similar earlier, now diverged strongly. Politics and jobs differed most dramatically from crime and accidents. The civic and economic topics required more clicking and scrolling, and the topics involving danger required less. The pattern was consistent throughout the data. In follow-ups, civic reporting lost ground, replaced by more first reports of the spot variety, especially news of accidents but also continuing coverage of crimes.

The measures of navigation to the end of stories suggest how thorough news producers expected readers to be, what professional news values the industry applies to readers, and how conventional wisdom in the culture applies to the public. Spreading the story text across more screens allowed the sites to expose readers to more ads, making a key disadvantage for reading Web editions—all the clicks, jumps, and scrolling to finish a story—into a key to generating revenue.

The earlier study showed online newspapers failing to employ Web capabilities. By 2005, the sites had more links but a different selection, preferring those easily handled, such as feedback forms, or those readers generate, such as discussion boards, replacing the free-for-all of emails going directly to reporters.

Links to external sites dropped dramatically. The pattern of links sought to keep readers within the same site, either through their own discussions or through managed feedback. The emerging linking style may advance public discussion, but eliminating email addresses may reduce public access to reporters. Interactive facilities that aimed to draw income from users—paid content and more publicity—could backfire by driving users away. Likewise, the changes in interactivity could serve civic purposes better or make sites more commercial and journalists less accountable. The outcome does appear to confirm editors' hesitance about interactive features (Singer and González-Velez, 2003).

Measuring the context of practice reveals how journalists follow events and rely on wire services for materials beyond their own region or outposts. A greater emphasis on breaking events accompanied a loss: fewer stories followed up after a story first emerged. More stories were only electronic, appearing in print either as briefs or not at all. But much of online content that differed from print originated not in that newspaper but from external agencies. The bulk of locally produced news still reproduced substantially similar text in both venues.

Staff cuts at newspapers would dictate increased workloads or shorter, less elaborated stories, perhaps accounting for the dramatic shift away from second-day stories. But wire services also had fewer follow-ups, and so journalism practice may be focusing more on current reports.

Going on line did not initially change news; instead, outlets used the Web to hold onto local markets. How the sites claimed geographical expertise did not change in 2005 for users interested in Portland, Chicago, or New York City. And sites continued reflecting their economic resources. The *Tribune* continued front-loading content to give readers quick headlines and links to pursue their topical interests. The *Times* still rejected the quick rundown, expecting readers to have wide interests and read deeply. And the *Oregonian* split the difference. Interactively, the *Oregonian* became less accessible, substituting moderated forums for reporter email. The *Tribune* abandoned links generally, and the *Times* remained documentary and still mostly aloof.

The *Times* was an outlier in many ways. Other sites reduced topical sectioning online, but the *Times* followed modern practices of mapping news for dependent readers. NYTimes.com also continued using additional tiers to rank stories. Of the three sites, the *Times* remained the most resistant to change (Domingo, 2008).

Finally, the sites remained less rich visually than their print counterparts. Typography did not grow more elaborate, even though automated, expert type-style management for Web design emerged, compatible with consumer browsers. Images became more common, if not much larger, but, like other factors, focused more on accidents. Changing forms appear to respond to commercial forces, not journalism or public affairs.

Where earlier Internet editions promoted the print product, the 2005 sites had begun to reflect qualities of the new medium. They exploited the larger capacity of home pages compared to print front pages, but also interrupted reading to generate revenue, a tactic much easier to ignore in print. The initial evidence suggests US news changed as publishers and journalists saw their traditional product falling on hard times and focused on making Web editions into viable alternatives.

ACKNOWLEDGEMENTS

The author wishes to thank Matthew Barnhurst, Timothy D. Fox, and Ryan Henke for coding and research assistance on this study, presented at the Future of Journalism conference, Cardiff, UK, September 9, 2009.

REFERENCES

ALTHAUS, SCOTT L. and TEWKSBURY, DAVID (2007) "Agenda Setting and the 'New' News: patterns of issue importance among readers of the paper and online versions of the New York Times", *Communication Research* 29(2), pp. 180–207.

BARNHURST, KEVIN G. (2002) "News Geography & Monopoly: the form of reports on U.S. newspaper internet sites", *Journalism Studies* 3(4), pp. 477–89.

BARNHURST, KEVIN G. (2009) "The Internet and News: changes in content on newspaper websites", paper presented to the International Communication Association (ICA), Chicago, May.

BARNHURST, KEVIN G. and MUTZ, DIANA (1997) "American Journalism and the Decline in Event-centered Reporting", *Journal of Communication* 47(4), pp. 27–53.

BARNHURST, KEVIN G. and NERONE, JOHN (2001) *The Form of News, A History*, New York: Guilford.

BEYERS, HANS (2006) "What Constitutes a Good Online News Site? A comparative analysis of American and European awards", *Communications* 31, pp. 215–40.

BOCZKOWSKI, PABLO J. and DE SANTOS, MARTIN (2007) "When More Media Equals Less: patterns of content homogenization in Argentina's leading print and online newspapers", *Political Communication* 24, pp. 167–80.

CARLSON, DAVID (2003) "The History of Online Journalism", in: Kevin Kawamoto (Ed.), *Digital Journalism: emerging media and the changing horizons of journalism*, Lanham, MD: Rowman & Littlefield, pp. 31–56.

CASSIDY, WILLIAM P. (2005) "Variations on a Theme: the professional role conceptions of print and online newspaper journalists", *Journalism & Mass Communication Quarterly* 82(2), pp. 264–80.

COOKE, LYNNE (2005) "A Visual Convergence of Print, Television, and the Internet: charting 40 years of design change in news presentation", *New Media & Society* 7(1), pp. 22–46.

D'HAENENS, LEEN, JANKOWSKI, NICHOLAS and HEUVELMAN, ARD (2004) "News in Online and Print Newspapers: differences in reader consumption and recall", *New Media & Society* 6(3), pp. 363–82.

DE WAAL, ESTER and SCHOENBACH, KLAUS (2008) "Presentation Style and Beyond: how print newspapers and online news expand awareness of public affairs issues", *Mass Communication & Society* 11(2), pp. 161–76.

DIMITROVA, DANIELA V., CONNOLLY-AHERN, COLLEEN, WILLIAMS, ANDREW PAUL, KAID, LYNDA LEE and REID, AMANDA (2003) "Hyperlinking as Gatekeeping: online newspaper coverage of the execution of an American terrorist", *Journalism Studies* 4(3), pp. 401–14.

DOMINGO, DAVID (2008) "Interactivity in the Daily Routines of Online Newsrooms: dealing with an uncomfortable myth", *Journal of Computer-mediated Communication* 13, pp. 680–704.

ENGEBRETSEN, MARTIN (2006) "Shallow and Static or Deep and Dynamic? Studying the state of online journalism in Scandinavia", *Nordicom Review* 27(1), pp. 3–16.

GARRISON, BRUCE (2004) "Newspaper Journalists Use Email to Gather News", *Newspaper Research Journal* 25(2), pp. 58–69.

HUANG, EDGAR, RADEMAKERS, LISA, FAYEMIWO, MOSHOOD A. and DUNLAP, LILLIAN (2004) "Converged Journalism and Quality: a case study of the *Tampa Tribune*", *Convergence* 10(4), pp. 73–91.

KAUTSKY, ROBERT and WIDHOLM, ANDREAS (2008) "Online Methodology: analysing news flows of online journalism", *Westminster Papers in Communication and Culture* 5(2), pp. 81–97.

SCOTT, BEN (2005) "A Contemporary History of Digital Journalism", *Television & New Media* 6(1), pp. 89–126.

SINGER, JANE B. (2003) "Campaign Contributions: online newspaper coverage of election 2000," *Journalism & Mass Communication Quarterly* 80(1), pp. 39–56.

SINGER, JANE B. (2004) "More Than Ink-stained Wretches: the resocialization of print journalists in converged newsrooms", *Journalism & Mass Communication Quarterly* 81(4), pp. 838–56.

SINGER, JANE B. (2006) "Stepping Back from the Gate: online newspaper editors and the co-production of content in campaign 2004", *Journalism & Mass Communication Quarterly* 83(2), pp. 265–80.

SINGER, JANE B. and GONZÁLEZ-VELEZ, MIRERZA (2003) "Envisioning the Caucus Community: online newspaper editors conceptualize their political roles", *Political Communication* 20, pp. 433–52.

TREMAYNE, MARK (2008) "Manipulating Interactivity with Thematically Hyperlinked News Texts: a media learning experiment", *New Media & Society* 10(5), pp. 703–27.

TREMAYNE, MARK, WEISS, AMY SCHMITZ and ALVES, ROSENTAL CALMON (2007) "From Product to Service: the diffusion of dynamic content in online newspapers", *Journalism & Mass Communication Quarterly* 84(4), pp. 825–39.

YAROS, RONALD A. (2006) "Is It the Medium or the Message? Structuring complex news to enhance engagement and situational understanding by nonexperts", *Communication Research* 33(4), pp. 285–309.

THE GRADUAL DISAPPEARANCE OF FOREIGN NEWS ON GERMAN TELEVISION
Is there a future for global, international, world or foreign news?

Klaus-Dieter Altmeppen

Television news (especially foreign news) is under constant threat of being replaced by live sporting events or film award ceremonies, as hard news is increasingly substituted by soft news, infotainment, or popular journalism. These developments are indicators of structural forces acting to change the nature of television and journalism in Germany. However, the current media crisis has revealed that these forces are indicative of changing structures globally that are leading to a gradual disappearance of foreign news from TV channels. This paper aims to establish a theoretical setting that describes the structural characteristics of this disappearance of foreign news and its relevant mechanisms. Accordingly, this paper outlines a theoretical model for analysing the mechanisms of economisation (where economic factors rather than editorial standards drive news reporting), based on differentiation between the media organisation and newsrooms as the prominent organisational expression of journalism. The differentiation is based on the different functions and performances of media organisations and newsrooms. The (metaphorical) assumption is that journalism sells the news to media organisations, while they pay for the news (via resources), one reason for the disappearance of foreign news stems from the changing rules of the business of the media.

Introduction

Some academics dispute whether a global journalism still exists, because, in their definition, it is a news style rather than an identifiable phenomenon of the journalists' occupation worldwide. Thus, when news is global, the mode of journalism that reports the news item is also global. This idea is based on the perception of a larger amount of news coverage resulting from a greater amount of increasingly complex news material around the world.

A brief glance at the German media system shows a contradictory picture: most German media are locally oriented, and those media offerings covering international news have shown a decline in foreign news reporting. On television, for example, (foreign) news is under constant threat of being replaced by live sporting events or film award ceremonies; in addition, news is commonly replaced by soft news, infotainment, or popular journalism. These developments are indicators of structural forces acting to change the nature of television and journalism in Germany. However, as the current media crisis reveals, it can be assumed that these forces are indicative of globally changing structures that are leading to a gradual disappearance of foreign news from television.

This article aims to establish a theoretical setting that describes the structural characteristics of this disappearance of foreign news and its relevant mechanisms. Consequently, the basic structures that are typically required for broader foreign news coverage are defined as rules and resources. Today, rules and resources for foreign news reporting are altered primarily by the process of economisation, whereby decisions made in news offices are increasingly based on economic factors rather than editorial standards of news reporting.

This article provides a theoretical model for analysing the mechanisms of economisation, based on differentiation between the media organisation and newsroom as the prominent organisational expression of journalism. The differentiation is based on the different functions and performances of media organisations and newsrooms. The (metaphorical) assumption is that journalism sells the news to the media organisations, while the organisations pay for the news (via resources); one reason for the disappearance of foreign news arises from the changing rules of the business of the media. Based on these structural and long-term assumptions, it can be proposed that there exists no future possibility of an increasing component of foreign news, in particular for global news reporting.

Journalism, Media and Organisation

Organisation is an important feature in all societies. Political parties, tax offices, the Premier League, and ultimately all commercial companies, including media enterprises, are organisations. The reason for this ubiquity of organisations is that on every occasion that people work together to solve a specific problem or accomplish an aim, it is invariably necessary that they coordinate their efforts in a collaborative manner and motivate each other to achieve the desired goal. Hence, the primary function of an organisation is to coordinate the work and tasks of its members and to ensure their motivation.

All organisations are characterised by three specific features (Altmeppen, 2008). First, organisations have a long-term focus on achieving specific aims. The direction of these goals is of great importance to the entire organisation, as the goals formulated by management determine the nature of the work undertaken by the staff. The main goal of organisations, from an economic perspective, is "to make a profit" (Shoemaker and Reese, 1996, p. 145). The value of an organisation depends on its ability to pay wages to staff, to allocate facilities and equipment, and to satisfy the needs of the owners or stakeholders in general, and stockholders in particular.

Based on the nature of economic goals, the management gives a structure to the organisation. Thus, the second feature of organisations is that they inhabit an established and accepted order and structure. The method most commonly employed to describe the structure of an organisation is the organisational chart, which shows the various departments (e.g., Editor's office, Advertising, Circulation) and their roles (e.g., the executive editor heads other editors who in turn supervise reporters, photographers, etc.) (Shoemaker and Reese, 1996, p. 143).

The third feature of organisations is as follows: organisations coordinate their activities and available resources to ensure that they reach their goals of long-term survival. The more complex an organisation, the more complex is this feature. In complicated organisational structures, the task of coordination is of great importance, as this determines the number of business units and departments, and the nature of occupational roles. For example, new technologies present the organisation with changing demands that upset the existing structure in that they require new types of work flow. Declining revenues lead to a reduction in available resources and restructuring of organisational patterns. The management must answer these new challenges, which commonly means the establishment of new guidelines for coordination.

Since the organisation's answer to upcoming challenges is to re-structure itself, structure is the next most important term behind organisation itself. The primary structures of organisations are departments and roles. Every role encompasses the expectations for the individual hired in the role and the lines of authority. Moreover, the organisational approach claims to analyse not only the structure within certain departments of a media organisation: it also seeks to reveal the societal functions of organisations, a goal that is commonly built into the overarching objective of profit margins.

The institution responsible for decisions regarding goals is the management (Altmeppen, 2006). Hence, media management is another important term that must be considered when analysing media and journalism organisations. In the case that organisations must solve problems and achieve aims, the question arises as to who defines the problems and aims. This is the task of the media managers; e.g. of the entire organisation, this may be the owner, the sales manager, the advertising manager. In the newsroom, on the level of middle management, it is the editors, producers and coordinators who fill the organisational roles. At the top level, it is corporate and news executives, such as the editor-in-chief, who "make organisation policy, set budgets, make important personnel decisions, protect commercial and political interests of the firm" (Shoemaker and Reese, 1996, p. 151).

The field of media management deals with these questions of how the management establishes policy and the mode of governance of the organisation; it addresses questions of leadership and decision-makers in the organisation; and it studies the work of the media managers who organise, budget and work with people as well as being engaged in market analysis, product planning, promotion, production and distribution. Overall, the management determines the shape of the organisational structure via the question of who is managing the structure and in what way.

These structures affect the way in which news is produced because they influence the material reported by journalists, the news about which an editor writes, and the decision regarding what to publish. Organisational structures represent the constitutional conditions of producing news, because news

> does not merely come to be. It is produced by people, working in complex organisations embedded in a larger socio-cultural and historical context. Newswork is a social process, undertaken by occupants of roles, organised into social structures that serve to link individual occupational efforts in a way that allows the individual performers to function as members of a team that turns out a single, conjointly produced performance for the audience. (Gassaway, 1984, p. 16)

Organisational Analysis of Media and Journalism

Up to this point, several examples have been provided of what an organisation is, although without providing precise definitions of the terms "media" and "journalism"

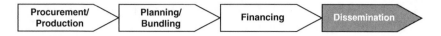

FIGURE 1

Value chain of media organisations

organisation. Furthermore, it has not been argued whether media organisations in total are different from newsrooms or whether significant distinctions can be made between the two. There are several reasons to believe that differences exist between media and journalism organisations.

Generally, media are placed on a level with journalism. Both scholars and the public fail to recognise any difference between the performance of media and journalism, especially regarding the public role. Certainly, reconciling the economic goals of media organisations with their public role is commonly seen as a cause for conflict between the owner and newsroom staff.

However, for most of the time the profit margin is the stronger argument. For this reason, the definition of a media organisation is largely dictated by the economic view. And there are several reasons to make a distinction between journalism and media. One such reason is the value chain process of media content. This process can be divided into at least four steps (Altmeppen, 2006) (see Figure 1): gathering and procuring information until finished copies are produced; planning and bundling the entire media setting, as there exists news content as well as advertising, promotion, and entertainment; the financing routines of the media business; and distributing the message. In the newsroom, the first step of gathering information comprises the work of reporters who investigate and check sources, and the work of writers who package the raw material. In the second step of production, the articles or broadcast reports are transformed into entire newspapers or broadcasts. The step of distribution entails transporting the message to the audience. The journalists only take part in the first step and part of the second, as these tasks are performed in the newsroom.

Most of the steps in the value chain (e.g., bundling news and advertisements to a newspaper or planning an entire broadcast programme, financing the media business, and, above all, the distribution of content) are what the media organisations yield. Their business is the dissemination of content, as they own the licences and the printing press, and the media organisations spare no effort in covering the Internet as a multi-level distribution channel. According to this view, media organisations are economic companies whose aims are firstly profit and secondly profit. The members of media companies deal with expenses and revenues, with cost–benefit calculations, and with marketing and promotion.

For their business of dissemination, media organisations require content, which they—and this is the thesis of the present article—procure from journalism. The newsroom as an organisation is the entity that enables groups of journalists to produce a newspaper, a magazine, a news website, or a radio or television programme. Journalism, which indicates an organisational perspective (and which is the focus of the present article), is only producing the news; journalism has neither the ability to organise the advertising business nor disseminate the news: that is the business of the media.

However, even news coverage is not the result of the work of individual journalists: it depends much more on specific organisational settings in the newsroom, the roles of various positions, the pre-settings determined by the goals of the journalistic organisation, and the influences of various technologies. Even if the individual level, with its analysis of role perception, for example, is of importance, the individual journalist is always embedded in organisational patterns that, as pre-arranged structures, influence journalists' work and behaviour in every newsroom.

Inside journalistic organisations, the journalists again have to meet the expectations of the entire organisation. This means that they have to yield certain benefits to the organisation. Consequently, that journalists are employees who receive salaries and who are provided with resources for their work which means that the organisation requests a specified amount of services in return, involving of course the completion of the tasks described in the employment contract. This structure is highlighted by the goals of the editorial office, which, in strong contradiction to the economic goals of media, is a societal one: to inform the society.

In the case that media and journalism are seen as one organisation, there is no doubt that the media pay for all the resources that journalism requires for news production. In the case that journalism and media are regarded as different organisations, it is obvious that the media (as economic institutions) are not required to provide anything. Thus, the relation between media and journalism depends on a barter trade: the media pay for the outputs of journalism; i.e., money for news.

The barter trade is the assignment of the management. Whereas writers, editors and reporters, as front-line employees, have no day-to-day contact with the owners of the media organisation, the middle- and top-level management do have such contact. The editor-in-chief and his representatives are integrated in the top-level management of the media organisation. They represent the needs of their newsroom department in the management's decision-making process. In negotiations that are commonly convoluted, they scramble over scarce resources with other managers from the advertising and distribution departments, and with the owners. Although the newsroom (and its staff) is a crucial department in media organisations, a reduction in available resources commonly leads to a reduced budget even for the newsroom. Reduced budgets and cost reductions usually have a direct effect on media content, as editorial decisions are changed when work must be performed by fewer staff or when less money or time is available for investigations. Budgets and costs, staff and money: these are the relevant components of structures. Thus, it is necessary to explore in detail the term structure.

Rules and Resources: The Components of Structures

In summary of the above, organisational structures influence the way news is produced by journalists and the way content is disseminated by media organisations. Structures as substantial conditions can be regarded as arrangements that both enable and restrict the processes of production and dissemination. However, the question is this: What are these structural arrangements? As the simplest definition, structures are elements that constitute an entity (e.g., a newsroom or a media organisation) and the manner in which the elements are linked. Structures, on the one hand, provide an order to the organisation and provide stability and constancy. This occurs while the members of the organisation (e.g., the journalists and media staff) are working under certain rules and while they need specific resources to perform their work. The routinised process of writing news, for example, takes place with regard to the rules of news selection. On the other hand, the journalist needs certain resources (e.g., news wires, technical support, and her/his own competence and experience) to perform the job.

But structures are neither as stable nor invariant as the above definition might suggest. Of course, management intends to establish long-term structures because they promise to minimise risk and uncertainty. However, as demonstrated by the current turbulence in the media industry, change, rather than stagnancy, is the challenge. Media markets are highly dynamic, and media organisations must steadily adjust their business to address competition, adapt to new technologies, and meet the changing needs of the audience. To alter the organisation's structure is therefore the proper and appropriate way. Hence, decisions about the amount of foreign news in television newsrooms, for example, are shaped by structural change, as outlined below.

Since change, even social change, is structural in nature, it seems necessary to precisely define this term. Given that in many organisational approaches to journalism and media, structures are described using the terms rules and resources, it might be appropriate in this context to refer to Giddens' structuration theory (1984), which describes structures as the interplay of rules and resources—a model that can explain the amendment of rules (e.g., the transition from departments to topic teams), the reasons for change (e.g., the requirements of cost-cutting) and how the allocation of resources is revised in the process of change. Rules in general are proceedings that enable actors to do the right things. Rules of signification represent interpretative schemes that, for example, give a precise meaning to the work of journalists (Giddens, 1984, p. 29). As far as journalists might pursue certain role conceptions, they find themselves in the core of journalism, as, in a societal perspective, the role of journalism is to keep the society informed, and from an organisational perspective the goals of journalism are represented in the various roles (e.g., editor, reporter, producer) and self-understandings (e.g., disseminator, critics and control). On the other hand, as far as the rules are set by market-driven journalism or a focus on reaching the widest possible audience, this refers to the goals of media organisations. Rules of signification explicate the reasons for what is done and provide the normative grounds. The goal of the media organisation (i.e., the profit orientation) is the most impressive kind of signification, and is commonly in conflict with the signification of journalism (i.e., the pubic role).

A further central rule is that of domination, which deals with various facilities that enable and constrain power. Hierarchy is such a facility, and the relationship between different organisations (e.g., the newsroom employees and the media management) expresses the rule of domination. Finally, the rules of legitimation constitute the normative basis of rules. These rules refer to ethical aspects; e.g., economic laws and accordingly those rules that allow the imposition of sanctions (Giddens, 1984, p. 29).

Resources, as the second term that constitutes structure in a broader sense, occur as two types: allocative resources that "refer to capabilities ... generating command over objects, goods or material phenomena" and authoritative resources that generate "command over persons or actors" (Giddens, 1984, p. 33).

This definition of structure, as given in the theory of structuration, has some advantages in explaining the disappearance of foreign news, as time, space and staff are crucial resources in journalism (Sigal, 1973, pp. 10–13). Unless the (not so) new demands balance business with journalism, structures become more important: "As profit margin pressures have persisted, newspaper executives have found themselves under pressure not only to improve editorial quality and offer niche products, but also to restructure their organisations for innovation" (Lewis, 1997, p. 103). The challenge, even for empirical research, is to find adequate criteria for measuring the structures and their change.

Structural change results from the variation, modification and rearrangement of rules and resources. If resources such as time (for investigating), space (for broadcasting) and staff (for producing) are the pivotal resources for foreign news, and if these resources are diminished step-by-step, then there is no bright future for foreign news (Hafez, 2002).

Organisational Differences and the Co-orientation of Media and Journalism

In the current crisis situation, journalism complains about the changed rules and altered resources of news reporting. The rules change in response to the impending competition provided by new distribution channels, the resources alter in the face of the new competition, and the worldwide financial crisis has pervaded the media system. And herein lies the fact: the crisis primarily concerns the media companies, not journalism. Journalism has no business model or cost–benefit calculations, but the media do, as their first goal is profit (and, as shown in the current crisis, their own viability) (see Figure 2).

If the perspective is geared towards journalism and media as organisations, and if their relationships are seen as a barter trade, journalism produces informative and newsworthy content that is offered and sold to the media organisations. The media, in turn, pay for the content that they require for their business of dissemination. "Sell" and "pay" are metaphors that describe the barter business between the two organisations that exist in co-orientation, knowing well that interdependence exists between journalists (who require resources for performing their work) and media (who require content for their business).

The co-orientation is somewhat like the equivalent to a (missed) trade contract that includes the rules for buying and selling outputs. The media do not pay money directly; instead, they allocate the resources required for the journalists' performance: salaries, facilities, technical support, etc. Consequently, the symptoms of the economic crisis strike first at the media companies; second, they strike the journalists because their operational capability depends on "payment" in the form of resources provided by the media. Again, this payment depends on the ongoing success of the business. The current situation is as follows: budgets are shrinking in response to declining advertising revenue, new competitors are entering the media market and demanding a share of advertising revenues, and the audience is switching to new content providers. In short, the traditional business and revenue models are collapsing and the media are facing enormous economic problems. Clearly, this situation also has significant implications for the production of foreign news.

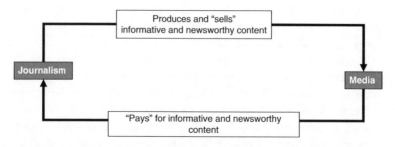

FIGURE 2

Relation between journalism and media from an organisational perspective

The Meaning of Structures for the Degree (Disappearance) of Foreign News

The cycle of paying resources (media) and producing programmes (journalism) still exists under the impact of the economisation of the media industry, as shown in Figure 2; however, the rules have changed. Stakeholders, especially stockholders, are seeking increased income return; target groups (or what media research holds for these) are to be served and satisfied by the programme; assumed markets are shared by increasing numbers of competitors; and prices for content are steadily increasing, at least for sports and blockbuster movies. All these processes have an impact on media organisations, especially the decisions made in the newsroom.

To date, the media, faced with the above challenges, have shown concordant reactions, even in times of crisis. Cost-cutting, outsourcing, reducing staff, and boosting the rate at which movies and series are repeated are proven strategies, all of which have at least one crucial effect: they alter the circumstances of the news production process (see Figure 3).

As far as budget cuts and staff losses are used as the first and sharpest instrument to keep costs under control, the editorial department faces great problems in ensuring the scope and depth of the news. While the number of newsworthy events and amount of information is ever-increasing, the reduced staff must cope with the selection, writing and editing of the news.

Whereas fewer staff are being asked to maintain an increased flow of news, the same employers are forced to meet new challenges in presentation forms such as popular journalism. Popular journalism is a form of differentiation on various levels:

- On the level of presentation, popular journalism uses modified presentation schemes; and
- on the level of selection, popular journalism uses modified criteria in selecting news; e.g., more soft news, concentrating on dramatisation, sensationalisation, fictionalisation, and personalisation.

These are forms of differentiation that are changing the working process of journalists who have had to integrate economic decisions into their newsroom routines.

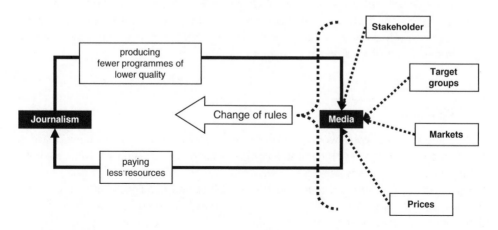

FIGURE 3
The changed rules for (foreign) news reporting

As an example, an economic consideration is to select sellable topics to attract a mass audience. These economic influences are the result of negotiation processes between media management and newsroom management. Since the media managers seek to achieve a positive balance, the newsroom staff seek to elude these dictates (Shoemaker and Reese, 1996, p. 146). Economic dictates force journalists to follow the prescribed line, since an imbalance exists between the editorial managers and media managers. Even in times of economisation, the bargaining power concerning resources for the newsroom lies on the side of the media.

Furthermore, these trends do not stand alone. A second process of differentiation of the routines of journalism reveals the further mechanisms of economisation. For example, some researchers in Germany point to forms of pseudo-journalism (Hohlfeld, 2002). This pseudo-journalism is in no way event-oriented; instead, it is loaded by media-intern event construction and orchestration. Such quasi-journalistic reporting is claiming to use journalistic routines for those topics that should be given credibility. However, this credibility is faked because the reporting is part of marketing and cross-promotion. Pseudo-journalism is an instrument of orchestration and self-marketing by the media, whereby events are calculated and arranged to ensure exclusivity, even for further reporting in other media.

The differentiation is bearing matters of broadcasting that reside at the periphery of what could be called television journalism. The criteria of recentness and relevance, usually most important in selecting news, are displaced or abolished and substituted by a focus on ratings and the assumed needs of the audience. Instead of news selection considering a critical, informing journalism, commercial aspects of selling news are the dominant factors. The use of cost and activity accounting acts to accelerate the disappearance of television journalism overall, and foreign news reporting in particular.

This disappearance results from decisions made in the background by media managers who are being challenged to legitimise their job in terms of improved ratings. Via co-orientation, they force their journalists into compliance on the following levels:

- The internal level of the news departments. This level is dominated by reductions in the number of staff working on foreign news (e.g., fewer correspondents), reduced time available for investigations, and a larger focus on target groups.
- The external level of ratings: the dominance of ratings as a measure of the success of a programme means that foreign news reporting is pushed aside. A popular sport (e.g., soccer) displaces the foreign news programme (from prime time to late in the evening) or results in it being dropped altogether.

Conclusion

In the so-called global world, foreign correspondents complain about the increasing trivialisation of foreign reporting. Journalism is accused of "treating foreign countries lightly" because it reports only crises, war, catastrophes, illness, crime and corruption (Breckl, 2006, p. 9). The news reporting is grouped around conflicts, politics and elites. Personalisation is of growing news value, exotic events become real, and ethnocentrism determines the investigation and gathering of news; consequently, the events are de-contextualised because of the decreasing space available for reporting (Breckl, 2006, pp. 54–62).

The future is bleak for global, international, world and foreign news. With the exception of events with the highest worldwide relevance (e.g., 9/11), there is declining space available for foreign news. While the entertainment market grows wider, the news market continues to narrow.

An important reason for these developments, but by no means the only reason, is the reliance of journalism on the success of media companies. As long as journalism is denied the resources of time, space, and staff that are so necessary for adequate reporting, foreign news will continue to disappear.

REFERENCES

ALTMEPPEN, KLAUS-DIETER (2006) *Journalismus und Medien als Organisationen. Leistungen, Strukturen und Management* [*Journalism and Media as Organizations. Performance, structures, and management*], Wiesbaden: Verlag für Sozialwissenschaften

ALTMEPPEN, KLAUS-DIETER (2008) "The Structure of News Production: the organizational approach to journalism research", in: Martin Löffelholz and David Weaver (Eds), *Global Journalism Research. Theories, methods, findings, future*, Malden, MA: Blackwell Publishing, pp. 52–64.

BRECKL, SYLVIA (2006) *Auslandsberichterstattung im Deutschen Fernsehen über die Dritte Welt am Beispiel von Weltspiegel und auslandsjournal* [*Foreign Reporting About the Third World in the German TV Using the Example of Weltspiegel and auslandsjournal*], Berlin: Frank & Thimme.

GASSAWAY, BOB M. (1984) "The Social Construction of Journalistic Reality", doctoral dissertation, University of Missouri.

GIDDENS, ANTHONY (1984) *The Constitution of Society. Outline of the theory of structuration*, Berkeley and Los Angeles: University of California Press.

HAFEZ, KAI (2002) *Die politische Dimension der Auslandsberichterstattung* [*The Political Dimension of Foreign Reporting*], Baden-Baden: Nomos.

HOHLFELD, RALF (2002) "Distinktionsversuche im Fernsehjournalismus. Das Verschwinden von Journalismus durch Inszenierung" ["Efforts of Distinction in TV Journalism. The disappearance of journalism through orchestration"], in: Achim Baum and Siegfried J. Schmidt (Eds), *Fakten und Fiktionen: Über den Umgang mit Medienwirklichkeiten* [*Facts and Fiction. About the handling with media realities*], Konstanz: UVK, pp. 101–13.

LEWIS, REGINA LOUISE (1997) "How Managerial Evolution Affects Newspaper Firms", *Newspaper Research Journal*, 18(1/2), pp. 103–25.

SHOEMAKER, PAMELA J. and REESE, STEPHEN D. (1996) *Mediating the Message. Theories of influences on mass media content*, 2nd edn, White Plains, NY: Longman.

SIGAL, LEON V. (1973) *Reporters and Officials. The organization and politics of newsmaking*, Lexington, MA: Heath.

THE FUTURE OF NEWSMAGAZINES

Carla Rodrigues Cardoso

More than 80 years ago, Time *magazine was launched in the United States, heralding the birth of a new journalistic genre. Since then, countless newsmagazines have appeared around the world. What are the elements that contribute towards the success of this journalistic genre today? And what are the perspectives for the future of newsmagazines? This study analyses 26 issues of six newsmagazines—*Time *(four copies),* Newsweek *(four),* L'Express *(five),* Le Nouvel Observateur *(five),* Sábado *(four) and* Visão *(four) during January 2009. The focus of the study is on the covers (cover lines, images, design) and the subjects that each magazine chooses for the front page. The objective is to cross-reference the data gathered using content analysis with the results of a previous study of newsmagazines in 1999. Comparing the reality of 10 years ago with newsmagazines today facilitates understanding of the differences between this genre and others, as well as the ways in which newsmagazines are adapting to the advances of digital journalism. It will also assist in understanding whether it is really possible to talk about a "newsmagazine genre", based on the differences and similarities found within the selected corpus.*

Introduction

This essay is part of an ongoing programme of research exploring the concept of the newsmagazine, or general contemporary information magazines, by examining six titles over the course of 2009. Four of these magazines have an international circulation, originating from America and France (*Time* and *Newsweek* in the first case, *L'Express* and *Le Nouvel Observateur* in the second). The remaining titles are two national Portuguese publications (*Sábado* and *Visão*). The research covers three different aspects of these magazines: (1) the crossover and universal nature of the concept of the newsmagazine; (2) the international newsmagazine; (3) the national newsmagazine.

With the help of content analysis, the January 2009 covers of the sample newsmagazines were compared with covers from a previous study across the first three months of 1999 (Cardoso, 2006). In this way, the aim is to clarify the evolution of newsmagazine cover stories and assess the identity traits that make each title unique despite belonging to the same press genre. The goal is to understand how today's newsmagazine is is put together, its importance in a media market increasingly influenced by digital media, and the main differences from the findings of the study a decade ago. This will enable us to envisage the future prospects for newsmagazines.

In 2006, the applicability of Michel Foucault's concept of "dispositif"[1] was validated for the magazine "cover" area, using a quantitative and qualitative methodology involving content and semiotic analyses. Foucault's concept is generically defined as a network that we can establish between elements. Gilles Deleuze emphasised that the dispositif "is, above all, a tangle, a multilinear set" composed of "lines of different nature" (1989, p. 185).

The magazine cover has lines of visibility (images); of enunciation (the title), of strength (the main headline and image); and of fracture (separation mechanisms for multiple subjects). It is an intermediate figure, which is part of the publication, but marks at the same time its opening, asserting itself as a window of contact with the outside. Each cover follows a specific strategy for storing the elements so as to give a consistent, overall reading of the dispositif.

As Hugues Peeters and Philippe Charlier are keen to suggest, many authors emphasise the hybrid nature of the dispositif concept—a trait applicable, for the reasons mentioned above, to the magazine cover. "The dispositif is a term that allows the researcher to designate a field composed of heterogeneous elements (for example, 'the said' and 'the unsaid'), and it is capable of treating this heterogeneity" (Charlier and Peeters, 1999, p. 15). The cover includes heterogeneous elements, of "the said" field (text) and of "the unsaid" type (graphic), organised in order to gain meaning.

Data gathered between January and March 1999 by analysing 48 issues of four different newsmagazine titles, identified certain facts concerning the understanding of the newsmagazine cover as a communication dispositif. The 2009 sample/corpus abandoned the Brazilian title *Veja*, a newsmagazine that proved to be substantially different from the others, but kept the titles *Newsweek*, *L'Express* and *Visão*. To enrich the analysis, the three magazines directly competing with each of those studied in 1999—namely *Time*, *Le Nouvel Observateur* and *Sábado*—were chosen for inclusion in the sample. These six titles embody a Western (European and American) journalism style, but are divided into two different areas: national (Portuguese titles) and international (all others).

In a pilot study, the findings from an analysis of the first two weeks of January 2009 revealed the initial data from the selected corpus (Cardoso, 2009). Based on this, various adjustments were made to the content analysis grid, most significantly in the areas of personalisation and subject matter. The first step was to include Gans' classification (1980, p. 8) of the figures portrayed in newsmagazines as "Known", "Unknown", "Animals, Objects and Abstractions". Concerning subject matter, Van Dijk's (2009, pp. 199–202) work was used in an attempt to identify ideologically controlled news structures on the newsmagazine covers and in the text inside—representing the subject that makes the cover.

Also in the area of subject matter, variables concerning news values were reformulated. Of the 10 variables of Traquina (2002, pp. 182–96) used in 1999, "Proximity" was kept, as well as "Time". All other criteria of newsworthiness gave rise to the classification by Harcup and O'Neill (2009, p. 168), excepting the "Newspaper Agenda", since it would be difficult to apply to such different publications in a reasonable way. The established synthesis thus analyses the existence of the following news values: "The Power Elite", "Celebrity", "Entertainment", "Surprise", "Bad News", "Good News", "Magnitude", "Relevance", "Follow-up", "Proximity" and "Ephemeris".

With respect to the content analysis grid, the categories and variables that proved to be the most significant in 1999 were retained. The grid used for the newsmagazines is divided into 64 categories and 338 fixed variables, plus seven categories with 45 variables applied according to the number of cover lines. The goal was to analyse the entire newsmagazine cover, the existence/absence of the cover lines in the magazine's summary and the main feature (defined as the cover's main theme) inside. The FileMaker Pro version 5.5 database (a number of later versions exist) and Microsoft Excel version 2007 spreadsheets were used.

Searching for Patterns

Over the course of January, data were gathered from 26 different magazines: eight American, 10 French and eight Portuguese. The first major difference is that the main titles of the magazines analysed in January 2009 are unanimously classified as expressive. Ten years ago, around 20 per cent (10 out of 48) were informative. If these data remain consistent over the 12 months, they signify that the newsmagazine cover dispositif has progressed, abandoning any focus on the raw, neutral, gimmick-free title. At least in January, all are far from the mere informative recording of facts, and all try to captivate readers and vie for their attention.

Some titles resort to dramatisation ("*Tragédia Sem Fim*" ["Unending Tragedy"], *Visão*, 15 January 2009), while others are built on the names of films and books ("*Tout Sur Obama*" ["Everything About Obama"], *Le Nouvel Observateur*, 15 January 2009; "*O Admirável Homem Novo*" ["Brave New Man"], *Visão*, 22 January 2009). Some also question, raise doubts or propose explanations ("*Will It Ever End? It Could—Here's How*", *Newsweek*, 12 January 2009; "*Le Destin d'Israel*" ["The Fate of Israel"], *L'Express*, 29 January 2009).

Moreover, only four of the 26 covers are not personalised. These data confirm one of the most consistent patterns in 1999, and denote a trend to intensify the human form on the faces of newsmagazines. Of the 22 personalised covers, 13 have a single human figure, a highly significant rise compared to the data from 1999, and a fact that holds true for all of the magazines analysed.

The "Number of Images Used" variable shows a gap between national and international newsmagazines, already demonstrated by the data from 10 years ago. Of the 26 covers analysed, more than half (14) use only one image to build their dispositif. However, these entail all of the four international titles analysed. None of the national newsmagazines dares to build its cover dispositif using just one image. In the case of *Sábado*, three of the four issues analysed use two images, while all of the editions of *Visão* use three or more images.

This result crosses over to those of two other variables, the "Number of Cover Lines" and the "Type of Cover" (Johnson and Prijatel, 2007,[2] pp. 284–6). Six of the 14 covers using only one image also present a single topic to the reader, unaccompanied by any secondary cover lines. For this reason, they are classified as "One Theme, One Image" covers, belonging exclusively to international titles, reinforcing their separation from national editions. With the exception of *Le Nouvel Observateur*, all the international newsmagazines' covers are built around a single cover line. The number of cover lines starts at two for *Le Nouvel Observateur*.

With regard to national magazines, *Sábado* has one cover with three cover lines, while the remaining copies have the same variable as all of the editions of *Visão*, with four or more cover lines. All the covers of *Sábado* and *Visão* are categorised as "Multi-Theme, Multi-Image", although the latter is unrivalled in exploiting the model. The 22 January edition of *Visão* is the most extreme case. In just one cover, the reader is offered eight different themes, including behaviour, international politics, economy, education, justice and entertainment, accompanied by five images.

So far as the subjects explored by each cover are concerned, two themes were common to all the publications: the inauguration of the American president and the conflict in the Gaza Strip accounted for 14 of the 26 covers. Barack Obama, in the month of inauguration and uncertainty concerning campaign promises, provides the basis for six international covers, four of them in the two American magazines, divided evenly. In the

Portuguese magazines, the American president did not go beyond the secondary cover lines.

Despite this similarity, American and French covers handle this topic differently. In the former, stories exalt, celebrate and idealise Barack Obama. The first issues of January are clear examples of this type of dispositif. *Time* elects Obama as "Person of the Year", and uses an original portrait by Shepard Fairey, author of the symbolic image of the "Hope" poster from the American President's campaign, evoking the ideology of Andy Warhol's mythical pop art creations.

In turn, the complex photographic illustration on the first cover of *Newsweek* aims to underscore the emergence of a new world elite in the political, economic, cultural and social realms. However, the dispositif created, where the only visible human figure is Barack Obama, in the centre, staring at the reader with crossed arms and a smile on his lips, elevates him to the uncontested leader of "The New Global Elite" named in the title in the header, above the magazine's logo.

The covers of the two French magazines handle the Barack Obama theme quite differently. The cover of *L'Express* from 15 January is the only one showing the American president accompanied by his wife, Michelle Obama. Positioned on the left side of the cover, the couple smile, looking towards the upper right-hand corner at something situated above them. The image reflects confidence, happiness and harmony, and is best suited to the title "The Obama Hope". *Le Nouvel Observateur* chooses a solitary, austere Obama with a grey sweatshirt and frowning brow, almost worried.

It is interesting to analyse the covers portraying Obama juxtaposed against the depictions of Bill Clinton at the start of 1999 in the aftermath of the Monica Lewinsky case. While 10 years ago the American president was portrayed in an aggressively negative manner by *Newsweek*, and only *L'Express* denounced the spotlight on the Clinton family as media persecution, the situation reversed itself in 2009. American titles glorify the president; French titles humanise him, while keeping their distance.

With the American President absent as a central theme, the two Portuguese magazines have a common national protagonist with one cover in each title. It is the Portuguese Prime Minister, José Sócrates, appearing under reports of the Freeport scandal (involving suspicions of political corruption). These two covers reveal a fact, seemingly pointing to a language of imagery that is common, transnational and timeless to the newsmagazine genre. Both dated 29 January, the two covers of *Sábado* and *Visão* bring two other *Newsweek* covers to mind, published 10 years before, featuring Bill Clinton. Specifically, the dispositif created by *Visão* recalls the petrified bust of the former American president engraved on the first cover of 1999. Moreover, the large outline of Sócrates on the cover of *Sábado* is very similar to that of Bill Clinton portrayed by *Newsweek* on 8 February 1999.

Personalisation and Photography on the Cover

Only Barack Obama and José Sócrates have their names featured in the main title of the January 2009 magazine covers. This occurs eight times: twice with Sócrates and six times with Obama. Together, the two political figures exhaust the "Known Figures" variable, although it was only possible to count seven covers, since the eighth cover (representing Obama) was classified as "combination" with the image of the American president being constituted by several "unknown figures".

Nevertheless, Gans' personalisation variable, Gans' "Unknown Figures" achieved the highest result in January 2009, with 12 covers. The Gaza Strip conflict helped to increase this outcome with seven covers directly related to this subject.

So far as gender of cover figures is concerned, 16 of the 26 (62 per cent) covers feature only men which represents a percentage increase compared to 1999 (22 male covers out of 48).

By contrast, there were three covers with solely female representation: two for *Le Nouvel Observateur* and one for *Sábado*; interestingly neither title was included in the 1999 analysis. Although the numbers between those covers which feature women and those which do not is considerable in the January sample, the six titles have the same number of female covers as the 48 covers in the 1999 sample.

The context in which the three female figures appear is also noteworthy: two are in a wartime setting, looking very fragile (one elderly, the other a child), and the third, apparently young, is wearing a chador (an Islamic garment that only shows the woman's eyes). The only female public figure appearing in January is Michelle Obama, the First Lady of the United States, although she is accompanied by her husband, a fact that makes this cover classifiable as "combination" in the gender variable.

Two further changes are evident. The first relates to the increase in "African Characteristics", accounting for five covers (in 1999, there was only one such cover across the three-month sample), and in the "Asian" variable, with six, the same number as 1999 in one-third of the sample period. The second change concerns a slight decrease in the cover variables of "Socio-economic Status", especially the variable "High Status" compared to 1999, although it still accounts for the most covers and is the only one found across all six titles; the increase in "Low Status" reflects the photographs of the theatre of war in the Gaza Strip, with four covers.

The results obtained in the area of personalisation are linked to those obtained reflecting the news structures' underlying ideologies. Of the variables analysed, half of the corpus (13 of the 26 covers), could be organised in the following manner: seven under "Nationalism"; three under "Racism" and three under "Sexism". Curiously, five of the seven covers that build their cover dispositif around a nationalist ideology belong to titles with international circulation, which raises the question of the degree to which newsmagazines designed to cross borders are able to disconnect themselves from the publication's country of origin and represent a global portrayal of world society, or, conversely, capitalise on this circulation to broaden ideological frontiers. Four of the newsmagazine issues under this variable are American (one from *Time* and three from *Newsweek*), with the fifth belonging to *L'Express*.

The second theme shared by all the titles, accounting for the most covers (eight), has all of the characteristics informing the maxim "bad news is good news", supporting the "Negativity" news value of Galtung and Ruge (1993 [1965]) and the "Death" of Traquina. Specifically, it involves the final period following the ceasefire of the war between Israel and the Palestinians. Only the Portuguese magazine *Sábado* avoids the theme as a cover story, although it appears as a secondary cover line.

As in 1999, the most commonly used type of image on magazine covers during January 2009 was photography (17 out of 26). Analysing the type of photography used most frequently, 10 covers choose "journalistic photos"—i.e. photographs taken by reporters who leave the newsroom and chase stories in the field. This result is linked to the Israeli–Palestinian conflict, which is represented on seven of the 10 covers that use "journalistic photos". These particular covers include five of the six images using "public spaces" (the street) as a backdrop, resulting in some of the more visually violent front pages of the January newsmagazines.

The Words of Newsmagazines

In the lexical component of the analysis, 112 words were identified in the titles that accompany the main theme of the 26 covers from January. Of these, 64 are classified as "full words" (Bardin, 2004, p. 78), i.e. words "with meaning": nouns, adjectives and verbs. Of these 64, only seven were repeated. Five are nouns: hope (appearing in the singular and plural), history, Israel, Obama and Sócrates. The remaining repetitions are adjectives: large and new.

Without the repetitions, 55 different words remain, reflecting a division already shown by the repeated terms. In this smaller group, nouns account for more than 60 per cent, with 34 occurrences. Adjectives and verbs have 11 and 10 occurrences, respectively. In an attempt to find a key to decipher the newsmagazine covers' language, the 34 nouns were grouped into five thematic units: "Countries and Protagonists", "Negative Words" (each with eight occurrences), "Neutral Words" (seven), "Mystery and Religion" (six) and "Positive Words" (four) (Table 1).

This organisation of the nouns found on the covers provides several clues to a better understanding of each of the titles. Only the "Countries and Protagonists" group is represented in all of the titles; the words in question refer to the three previously mentioned subjects of the inauguration of Barack Obama, the war in the Gaza Strip and José Sócrates' involvement in the Freeport scandal.

The seven "Neutral Words" are distributed among all of the titles except for *Newsweek*. The "Positive Words" group has only four different words; only *Visão* has none. The most pronounced gaps are found in the two remaining groups.

"Mystery and Religion" belongs entirely to French newsmagazines, although *L'Express* retains five of the six words, leaving only "God" to *Le Nouvel Observateur*. The biggest surprise occurs in the "Negative Words" group, which excludes the eight covers of the American magazines and the five covers of *L'Express*. Only the other half of the corpus, including the Portuguese titles and *Le Nouvel Observateur*, uses words such as "Persecution", "War", "Suspicions" and "Illnesses".

Although it is still early to move forward with the complex analytical category of news values, some data can be underscored. We attempted to identify the primary news value of each cover, since a number of associated news values exist in most cases. The result was a clear emphasis on the "Power Elite" variable (10 occurrences) with "Follow-up" (five) and "Relevance" (four) some way behind.

Beyond the Cover

Going beyond the covers of newsmagazines, one discovers the relationship between the presented cover lines (Johnson and Prijatel, 1999, p. 344) and the framework for the theme featured in the "Summary". Although each newsmagazine has its own variation on the name for this space, all titles have one, differing in length (one or two pages). It appears on the first pages (usually page 3) and summarises the contents in the magazine; it can be all textual or deploy a plethora of images. A closer examination of this structure was emphasised, since it offers a more detailed, broader presentation of the magazine's articles. Through this category, the more subtle differences between the six titles under analysis are gradually revealed.

In 17 of the 26 cases one or more cover lines are used as the main subject of the summary. In 10 cases, the newsmagazines opt to prolong the cover in the summary—the main theme that is already portrayed on the first page is developed and also presented as the most important one. The titles that use this strategy are all international: *Newsweek* (always), *L'Express* (three times) and *Time* (twice). The uniform approach of *Newsweek* forecasts the graphic revolution introduced on 25 May in the newsmagazine cover concept: a complete focus on a "one theme, one image" cover and the creation of a more aesthetic than informative first page.

Conversely, five newsmagazines use the summary to feature themes established as secondary cover lines. These include all of the issues of *Visão*, signifying the Portuguese

TABLE 1
Nouns found on 26 newsmagazine covers, gathered in thematic units (January 2009)

Thematic unit	Nouns
Countries and Protagonists	America
	Barack Obama
	China
	Gaza
	Israel
	José Sócrates
	Palestinians
	Portuguese women
Negative Words	Casinos
	Illnesses
	End
	Persecution
	Police
	Suspicions
	Tragedy
	War
Neutral Words	Food
	History
	Husbands
	Man
	News
	Science
	World
Mystery and Religion	Bible
	Destiny
	Future
	God
	Koran
	Mystery
Positive Words or Expressions	Elite
	Happiness
	Hope
	Person of the year

title's conscious focus on this model, and one edition of *L'Express*. *Sábado*, the other Portuguese newsmagazine, employs a different strategy from all of the other titles, by focusing on topics not appearing on the cover.

Finally, seven issues were classified under the "Not Applicable" variable. Two belong to *Time*, and are justified by the American title's balancing, with the same emphasis in the summary, the main cover theme and another that is not even showcased. In the case of *Le Nouvel Observateur*, the French magazine uses a condensed summary occupying a small space of less than a quarter page, completely typographic, featuring no theme at all. In this regard, the two French magazines could not be more different, since the summary of *L'Express* is spread over two pages with stylish chromatic interplay and several photographs.

Delving inside the magazine, we go to the main feature derived from what is presented on the cover. Different approaches are seen among international and national newsmagazines with regard to the length of articles, which are much longer in the former case.

In the international titles, a differentiation also begins to emerge in the number of pages allocated to each theme, according to the geographical proximity of subjects to the magazine's country of origin. For instance, in the case of the American magazines, at least in January 2009, cover themes relating to events in the United States or involving American people tend to be longer articles inside the magazine than the others.

Another category that proved to be significant was the section at the origin of the article on the cover. In most cases (14), magazines choose a particular name such as "Cover Story" (*Newsweek*); "*En Couverture*" ("On the Cover"; *L'Express*) or "*Destaque*" ("Featured"; *Sábado*). The remaining titles opt to include the article in its section. Nine cases fall under "International", two under "Society" and one under "National". This category should be studied further to more clearly determine which sections made the cover more often. This will entail a breakdown of the "Special" variable, which includes all of the previously mentioned sections with specific names for the cover story, into those sections providing their actual basis.

Conclusions

We cannot disassociate the study of newsmagazines from the history of each publication. We must also not forget that, in addition to media, these are companies belonging to transnational media groups who care about the economic and business returns of their products. For this reason, newsmagazines are both a historical journalism entity and a commercial product. The cover embodies this dual spirit and acts as a gateway between journalism and advertising.

The strategies laid out week after week are not random, nor are they created haphazardly. The digital revolution has shaken the press, and has led to the failure of media companies throughout the world. Newsmagazines are not immune to this, and have sought to adapt through proximity and reconciliation, together with attempts at differentiation, in an ongoing movement of attraction and repulsion.

A number of clues exist to weigh up the future of newsmagazines. Currently, the vast majority of national and international titles make reference to the corresponding website where information multiplies infinitely, empowered by the Internet. This rule applies to all of the selected newsmagazines in the study sample, except for *Sábado*, whether more discreetly (American titles) or more visibly (French magazines and *Visão*). So far as the connection to the digital world is concerned, the free electronic newsletters offered by magazines to everyone wishing to receive them, continue to multiply. Weekly publications in summary format (as in the case of *Time*) are the most common, although some magazines focus strongly on this medium, providing electronic newsletters twice a day (*Le Nouvel Observateur*) and thematic newsletters (international titles).

There are also internal revolutions. The most traditional entail the redesign of magazines, with *L'Express* and *Newsweek* offering new graphic projects in 2009, together with the subjects covered, with covers even using new media as a main theme. However, the most interesting facet might be the influence of the new media scene within the pages of newsmagazines. *Time*'s naming of the traditional "Letters from Readers" section as "Inbox" is a symbolic sign of the times. *Newsweek* and *Visão* go a step further by dedicating one of the first pages inside the magazine to an "electronic section". Entitled "Newsweek.com" and "Visão.pt", they act as a type of bridge between the paper and digital worlds, bringing the former to the latter with hints on what can be found at the respective websites and commentators' blog addresses, or vice versa, such as the results of an online poll.

A deeper knowledge of these clues will forge the path to discovering the future of newsmagazines, in their constant struggle to survive in times of economic crisis, where imagination is the only limit on the ability to reinvent.

ACKNOWLEDGEMENTS

Many thanks to the Media and Journalism Research Centre (CIMJ) which financed participation in the "Future of Journalism Conference 2009" at the School of Journalism, Cardiff University, UK. Thanks also to the Centre for Research in Applied Communication, Culture and New Technologies (CICANT) at Universidade Lusófona for its support in translating the paper and reviewing the final article for publication. To Patrícia Prijatel and Sammye Johnson, for their quick response, valuable bibliographical suggestions and advice and, finally, to David Sumner, for sharing the bibliography of his book *The Magazine Century: American Magazines Since 1900*, to be published in 2010.

NOTES

1. Foucault's concept of "dispositif" is sometimes translated into English as "device", although the more commonly accepted term appears to be "apparatus". Nevertheless, to preserve the identity and richness of the concept designed by the French philosopher in the mid-1970s, all references in the text mention "dispositif", following the recommendations of Kessler (2006).

2. The two editions of this book are included in the reference list because the concept of "cover line" as defined by the authors (short title, similar to the teaser in advertising) appears in a Glossary that is not in the second edition.

REFERENCES

BARDIN, LAURENCE (2004) *Análise de Conteúdo*, Lisbon: Edições 70.

CARDOSO, CARLA R. (2006) *As capas de newsmagazines como dispositivo de comunicação—Newsweek, Veja, L'Express e Visão—Janeiro a Março de 1999* (Dissertação de mestrado), Lisbon: FCSH-UNL.

CARDOSO, CARLA R. (2009) "Padrões e Identidades nas Capas de Newsmagazines: 1999/2009", *Actas Digitais IV Congresso SOPCOM—Sociedade dos Media: Comunicação, Política e História dos Media*, Lisbon: ECATI-ULHT, pp. 4331–43.

CHARLIER, PHILIPPE and PEETERS, HUGUES (1999) "Contributions à une Théorie du Dispositif", *Hermès—Cognition, Communication, Politique* (Le Dispostif—Entre Usage et Concept), Paris: CNRS Éditions, No. 25, pp. 15–23.

DELEUZE, GILLE (1989) "Qu'est qu'un dispositif?", *Rencontre Internationale: Michel Foucault Philosophe, Paris, 9, 10, 11 janvier 1988*, Paris: Seuil, pp. 185–95.

FOUCAULT, MICHEL (1994) *Dits et Écrits 1954–1988. Tome III: 1976–1979*, Paris: Gallimard.

GALTUNG, JOHAN and RUGE, MARI H. (1993 [1965]) "A Estrutura do Noticiário Estrangeiro—a apresentação das crises do Congo, Cuba e Chipre em quatro jornais estrangeiros", in: Nelson Traquina (Ed.), *Jornalismo: questões, teorias e «estórias»*, Lisbon: Vega, pp. 61–73.

GANS, HERBERT J. (1980) *Deciding What's News—a study of CBS Evening News, NBC Nightly News, Newsweek and Time*, New York: Vintage Books.

HARCUP, TONY and O'NEILL, DEIRDRE (2009) "News Values and Selectivity", in: Karin Wahl-Jorgensen and Thomas Hanitzsch (Eds), *The Handbook of Journalism Studies*, New York and London: Routledge, pp. 161–74.

JOHNSON, SAMMYE and PRIJATEL, PATRICIA (1999) *The Magazine from Cover to Cover—inside a dynamic industry*, Chicago: NTC.

JOHNSON, SAMMYE and PRIJATEL, PATRICIA (2007) *The Magazine from Cover to Cover*, New York and Oxford: Oxford University Press.

KESSLER, FRANK (2006) "Notes on *dispositif*", http://www.let.uu.nl/~Frank.Kessler/personal/notes%20on%20dispositif.PDF, accessed 2 February 2009.

TRAQUINA, NELSON (2002) *Jornalismo*, Lisbon: Quimera.

VAN DIJK, TEUN A. (2009) "News, Discourse, and Ideology", in: Karin Wahl-Jorgensen and Thomas Hanitzsch (Eds), *The Handbook of Journalism Studies*, New York and London: Routledge, pp. 191–204.

JOURNALISTIC ELITES IN POST-COMMUNIST ROMANIA
From heroes of the revolution to media moguls

Mihai Coman

In the 20 years since the fall of communism, the professional field of journalism has been increasingly carved up by press barons, on the one hand, and the majority of ordinary journalists, on the other. The euphoric attitude and the solidarity that marked the very beginnings of a free press slowly faded away. They were replaced by the fight to achieve and maintain control over the resources offered by mass media: economic status, political power and social prestige. In fact, one group has monopolized the economic resources, the access to centres of political decision-making and the channels of distribution of professionally legitimating discourse. This study examines the mechanisms used by a group of journalists to achieve economic and professional control. In other words, the study shows how star journalists became media moguls.

Introduction

During the period of communism, the communist party in Romania was the sole owner of the press. In order to gain total control over the mass media, the totalitarian party first obtained the "in amonte" power by nationalizing the means of mass communication. Thereafter, the state-party began to use its monopoly over press' materials and finances. Subsequently, the party controlled all the resources that were important for audiovisual programmes and the production of publications. This ownership guaranteed the "in aval" control, in other words the exercise of censorship (the control of media messages before their distribution). Another characteristic of the communist period was the centralization of resources distribution. A small group of people (the "apparatchiks") assumed control of different categories of resources and fixed distribution criteria according to its own interest. In this way, the paper quotas, established by the annual plan, limited newspaper and magazine production to the number decided by the Party. Consequently, the possibility of any alternative publication was denied. Following the same pattern, the number of radio and television frequencies and the number of broadcast programme hours were strictly limited. Furthermore, assuming control over the transportation, telecommunication and means of production (paper factories, typography, energy sources, radio and television studios) assured rapid broadcasting of their own mass media products and the elimination of any products considered "unacceptable".

After the fall of communism, when the euphoric period—related to the discovery of freedom of speech—passed, the economical realities of the press began slowly to emerge.

Different social actors, keenly interested in access to power, discovered that press power means the control of resources (legislative, production, information access) and of the "free speech" promoter's ideology. Achieving all this bestows a real sense of power. At the beginning of the democratic period, this control assumed forms associated with authoritarianism, which quickly gave way to more indirect forms based on hegemonic control. In this context, two convergent processes unravelled: (1) politicians tried to obtain favourable positions through buying media outlets and used them for promoting their political careers (a process known as press "berlusconization"); (2) mass media owners entered into collusive relations with different political groups in order to achieve economical advantages. This collusive system requires social actors with a clear identity (politicians constitute a category that quickly established itself, but media owners were less clearly defined with a far more heterogeneous field of recruitment). That is why this study outlines a new typology for media owners.

Owners as Owners

Post-communism brought the spontaneous privatization of the communist mass media and a rapid creation of new media enterprises. Control over almost all of the former communist print media—including the ownership of publication titles, facilities, equipment and staff—was quickly transferred from the state to private media companies. This included domestic or international business groups, professional journalist associations, individual investors, banks and other entities. New print media enterprises were also created. Small local and regional private radio stations sprouted throughout Romania in the immediate aftermath of communism's demise, operating illegally because the legal mechanisms for licensing them were not yet established. The state maintained its monopoly in the television field until the late 1990s when private, commercial television was, finally, given legal blessing (Coman, 2003; Gross, 1996).

The Law on Competition (1996) attempted to regulate commercial media and the tendencies toward monopolization, by creating the Council on Competitiveness which was given the remit of authorizing media mergers and acquisitions. Ownership of media outlets is, however, often secret. The pressure exerted by the Council on Competitiveness for full disclosure of ownership brought results; Sorin Ovidiu Vantu, for example, one of the most controversial businessmen in Romania, in February 2006, admitted to being the owner of Realitatea TV, a news TV station that he controlled behind several "front-men". Phantom companies or organizations in Cyprus or other countries are sometimes set up as media owners. Manuela Preoteasa (2004, p. 405) stated that "as a rule, Romanian legislation forbids anonymous ownership; every [media] company is obliged to register [the name of the owner] in the Trade Register Office and to communicate changes [in ownership]. In practice, few companies meet this obligation because there are no sanctions in force".

Foreign capital was slow to enter the Romanian media field, especially when compared to Hungary, the Czech Republic and Poland. When it finally arrived, it remained marginal at best, being most visible in the financial and economic press (Ringier), women's press (Burda, Hachette, Ringier, Axel Springer and Sanoma-Hearst), and the entertainment press (Gruner & Jahr, *Playboy* and *Hustler*).

During the period of the euphoric development of the post-communist press, financial independence did not seem to be an important topic for professional and public debate. Nobody considered such issues as financing sources, production costs, tax payment, unverifiable circulation, and an underdeveloped advertising market to be significant in comparison to the spectacular increase in the population's purchasing enthusiasm. After that initial momentum, when public interest in the press offer diminished, the economic problems became more visible and constituted major topics of public debate. Now, the issue of the freedom of the press becomes framed as the subject of the economic freedom of the press (or, from another point of view, the issue of political influence starts to be treated as the issue of political influence by economical control).

Advertising expenditures rose from $26.6 million in 1993 to $105.4 million in 1996, $287 million in 1999, $1,064 million in 2002, €1,499 million in 2004, to €4,460 million in 2007 (first decade estimates were in US dollars and only later in euros). Television has been the major beneficiary of these advertising expenditures and receives a much greater portion of advertising money than its counterparts in Western European countries. In 1999, television received 61 per cent of the aggregate advertising spend, compared to newspapers which received 23 per cent, radio 5 per cent, movie theatres 1 per cent, and outdoor advertising 10 per cent. These disparities continued to grow. In 2000, television received 73 per cent of total advertising expenditures, daily newspapers only 16 per cent, magazines 8 per cent and radio 3 per cent. From 2004 to the present day, television garnered 87 per cent of advertising expenditures, the print media 11 per cent while radio held steady at 3 per cent (Simion et al., 2007, pp. 21–7).

Across the period media moguls begin to emerge. The most important is Adrian Sârbu, who controls PubliMedia (journals, magazines, press agency), Pro Cinema and, with Central Media Enterprises, Media Pro International (with radio and TV divisions). Sorin Ovidiu Vântu recently created a media empire, which includes radio and TV stations, and a press agency, as well as with journals and magazines. At the same time, Dinu Patriciu (owner of rich Rompetrol group) is beginning to construct a similar trust, including daily newspapers and magazines. Dan Voiculescu, who controls television, radio stations and press publications through the Intact group, is involved in both economic and political life (he is the leader of the Conservative Party and a Member of Parliament). His media group has developed slowly since 1995 (unlike the rapid acquisitions made by Vântu and Dinu Patriciu). Officially, he is not involved in media activities any more, because he has handed over the management of the group to his daughter.

Essentially, the media landscape in Romania is controlled by what the journalist Iulian Comănescu calls the five "Bigs" (Ringier, Voiculescu, Sarbu, Vantu and Patriciu for the printed press; public radio and public television, Sarbu, SBS, Voiculescu and Vantu for audiovisual). Comparing the degree of concentration in 2006 with the situation in 2004, he writes: "The number of national newspapers whose owners are other than the five 'Bigs' decreased from 8 to 3. This situation is similar in other markets, such as TV niches or economic publications" (Comanescu, 2007, p. 21). Comanescu exaggerates the idea and extent of concentration, because he ignores the rich local media landscape. This evolution clearly shows not only that we are in the middle of a slow, but irreversible process of consolidation or "trustization", but also that the major actors on the stage of the press have acquired power and stability. Consequently, they do not depend on the political sector anymore, but negotiate their position from the same level as the political actors. However, such a position of power is not (so) damaging to the freedom of the press, because economic consolidation allows them to be less dependent on political interest (Coman, 2009).

Politicians as Media Owners

By the turn of the new millennium, and following a pattern evidenced in other Eastern European post-communist countries, an increasing number of local political and business leaders entered the press world, joining those who already owned or controlled national and local media. Dumitru Sechelariu, the former mayor of Bacau, who was also a local businessman, purchased the local 12,000-circulation daily *Desteptarea* and the local Radio Alpha and Alpha TV stations. Other examples abound: in the Oltenia region, the media group Media Sud-Est, led by Constantin Paunescu, owns the 30,000-circulation *Gazeta de Sud* and the station Radio Sud; in Brasov, the president of the County Council, ex-Democratic Party Senator Aristotel Cancescu, is the owner of the powerful radio and TV network Mix-FM (taken over by SBS Broadcasting Media in 2007); controversial business-man and Constanta Mayor, Radu Mazare, controls the daily *Telegraf* and Soti-TV; the mayor of the fifth Sector in Bucharest, Marin Vanghelie, purchased the daily *Monitorul de Bucuresti* in 2002. The mayor of Piatra Neamt, Gheorghe Stefan, is the owner of Radio Unu and Unu TV. Parliamentarians also control media enterprises. Victor Ponta, for example, controls Radio 21, Verestoy Attila, local print media in Harghita, and Gyorgy Frunda, Radio Gaga. In 2004, Liviu Luca, the leader of the syndicates from Petrom who owns Petrom Service, assumed ownership of the dailies *Ziua* and *Gardianul*, of Realitatea TV and Radio Total; in 2005, he sold his media holdings to the controversial businessman Sorin Ovidiu Vantu. The phenomenon of politicians owning media outlets raises a key question regarding the independence of the press: What are the prospects of an independent editorial policy when the press is controlled or influenced by individuals with political interests and aspirations? However, the political people who have invested in mass media were not able to receive representative positions (Ghinea and Fotiade, 2006, pp. 53–600; Preoteasa, 2004, pp. 34–51).

Journalists as Media Moguls

"The moguls", that is, the new owners of the new post-communist media, are only the tip of the iceberg. Behind them are the journalist-managers, courtiers who are reminiscent of the servitude of feudal times, who own shares in media enterprises. Their main objective is to retain their dominant position and to this end they are willing to accept or promote nefarious coalitions with economic pressure groups or with the political establishment. And so it is that, "In all Eastern/Central European countries, the dividing line between the business office and the editorial office frequently became blurred" (Hiebert, 1999, p. 117). These vassals of the owners also attempt to limit the access of other colleagues to decision-making processes by refusing to support any form of institutio-nalization of the mass media system and by promoting an ideology of "openness", which sustains the situation that there are no pre-conditions for entering journalism. Ultimately, in a take off from the "capitalism without capitalists—capitalists without capitalism" description of how capitalism was formed from the ruins of communism, we can say that these 10 years have led to a system in which the corps of journalists, and especially the leaders, control journalism without respecting the standards of the modern mass media. This has led journalists who do not practise journalism, to refuse to accept certain Western journalistic models and techniques, because these would undermine the control which this profession exercises over its own system (Coman, 2004; Gross, 2002).

Most successful broadcast and newspaper directors use their medium as personal platforms. On the eve of elections, directors and editors-in-chief of print media monopolize the political debates (see the cases of Ion Cristoiu, Octavian Paler, Cornel Nistorescu, Sorin Rosca Stanescu, Cristian Tudor Popescu, Horia Alexandrescu, Bogdan Chireac etc.). More specifically, they are on the front page of morning newspapers and then, as commentators and panellists, pontificate on the merits of political candidates on evening television shows. Some may appear on two or three shows on the same night. They assume the status of "specialists in everything", eclipsing *bona fide* political analysts such as political scientists, sociologists, diplomats, economists and others with a specialization in a field pertinent to an ongoing debate. They have made it their "official" right to express opinions on each and every issue, thus becoming the filter through which any political initiative, politician, party or societal group has to pass in order to be known and recognized. They have power but through this form of engagement with the political class they also give it a considerable amount of influence and, consequently, contribute to the lack of real media freedom and journalistic influence.

The battle for the control of the profession was the salient element in the post-communist media evolution; a large group that fought to enter and stay in the system and a small group that wished to create and legitimize instruments of control waged the battle, which continues to date. Both groups promote a missionary ideology and support the open, non-institutionalized character of the profession. One group exercises discretionary control over the system, and the other discovered that after 20 years of "transition" it was dispossessed of the instruments of control and also of any measure of auto-protection. The latter group failed to negotiate access to the system, salaries, working conditions, all aspects relating to daily journalism, ethical problems, and issues related to professional conscience. In addition, this group found itself dispossessed of its self-identifying discourse, which the other group articulated. Under these conditions the vast majority of journalists lost rights, control over the profession, and over the self-legitimating discourse, generating an acute crisis of identity (Coman, 1998, 2004).

These often slow and covert developments emerged during moments of conflict. A perfect example would be the so-called "three scandals" in 2004 and 2005 when the most important dailies in Romania experienced powerful internal conflicts which were highly mediatized. The conflicts were between the print media employers and journalist-managers on one side (Petre Mihai Bacanu at *Romania Liberă*, Cornel Nistorescu at *Evenimentul zilei*, Cristian Tudor Popescu at Adevărul), and media owners (foreigns or Romanians) on the other. In all three cases, in a veiled or direct manner, huge sums (measured against the usual income of the mass media) were extorted, benefiting the leaders of the newspapers. More important were the discreet ways used by these compradores-journalists to control important press companies (Sorin Rosca Stanescu at Alpha and Fulcrum or Mircea Toma at Academia Caţavencu).

Their managerial position allows them several opportunities:

1. The accumulation of capital, without the risks (that were placed upon employers, stockholders or the state's shoulders).
2. The construction of a "grey" market around those mass media products by creating their own companies with favourable contracts and draining an important amount of money from the publication funds.
3. The realisation of alliances with several economic and political circles.

4. The control of the event's public image construction—in this way every time the governors or employers attempt economic regulation of the media, the businessmen-journalists counter-attack with political commentaries in newspapers, TV or radio shows. In order to maintain legitimacy they role play "civil society" voices, expressions of the craft's indignation (hiding their own economical interests) and one of freedom's defenders that accuse politicians of obscure interests (again hiding their own agendas and commercial stake).

All three cases illustrate the huge amount of money that accrued to these newspapers' "historical" leaders or founders (as compared to a post-communist media journalist's usual income). More precisely: the wage incomes (fixed by them), the annual profits and dividends, the companies connected to the publication (and where these leaders were owners or main stakeholders) and the commissions received from the companies that had advertising contracts with them.

The three scandals were also about the limitation or even the loss of audiences. In other words, the editorial formula used by historical leaders (Bacanu, Nistorescu and Popescu) no longer impressed the public (at least not the new type of public born in Romania along with the explosion of "white-collar workers"). In the long term, different actors entered the market with suitable products for this type of audience, and made the old titles risk failure or the minimal accepted profitability. The foreign or autochthonous owners dealt with the perspective of losing the audiences and the advertising subsidising sources. This problem was unimportant for the manager-journalists as they supplemented their incomes using the "grey market" (commissions and profit from "tick companies"). This grey market was closed to the employers. In this way, the employers' group invested in loss while the newsroom leaders multiplied their incomes using Administration Council funds and control over the contracts with advertising firms; they were "capitalists without capitalism". This is not a new phenomenon, nor one specific to Romania (Coman, 2003; Sparks and Reading, 1998). Nevertheless, this phenomenon is hard to decode as in the name of the fight for "press freedom" the wolves dressed as lambs.

This professional group was only slightly interrogated (in a scientific or journalistic way). In order to identify the scale of their economic power, I will cite two investigations made by The Romanian Center for Investigation of Journalism (www.crji.org/arhivă/050906.html, 12 March 2006) and the magazine *Financial Week* (February 2008). Both of them cast light upon these new moguls' social status. The two documentaries devoted to "Romanian journalists' wealth" mix up some media owners' financial positions with no journalistic activities: television stars, talk-show hosts, managers, famous writers, independent analysts—all highly promoted by the media. If we focus on the journalistic group, formed by the manager-journalists (people involved in both the Editorial Board and Administration Council), we will find that:

1. Most of them own consulting firms with activities in political communication, mass media production and distribution, advertising; some even own firms in other domains (Sorin Rosca Stanescu has firms in agriculture, tourism, the wood industry, alcohol production and Mihai Tatulici's firms cover the food industry). This situation casts doubts upon some press campaigns started by these journalists' newspapers (without defending the public interest but promoting personal commercial interests). The most famous case is Bogdan Chireac's, which started a press campaign against a rival firm in order to get a state contract.

2. Concerning their belongings we have, on the one hand, those that display a Franciscan poverty (they either cheated the state, or created firms in their family members or colleagues names), and on the other, those that show off a seigniorial lux.

    A few examples:

*   Horia Alexandrescu has an enormous residence in Bucharest and one in Breaza, a very selective mountain resort, a class C Mercedes, Wrangler jeep and a VW Golf.
*   Cristian Tudor Popescu declares an apartment in Bucharest (worth 100,000 euros), a villa in Breaza (150,000 euros) and deposits of 450,000 euros (from selling his shares from Adevarul si Gandul dailies).
*   Bogdan Chireac owns an apartment in Bucharest (worth 300,000 euros), a residence in Mogosoaia (700,000 euros), a Toyota Rawa and 200,000 euros deposits.
*   Sorin Rosca Stanescu has an apartment in Bucharest, three holiday villas in different areas and land worth 2,000,000 euros.
*   Cornel Nistorescu owns three villas with land (1000 square metres each) in Bucharest, paintings worth 1,000,000 euros, owns 4,000,000 euros from selling his shares at *Evenimentul Zilei* daily and he drives a S80 Volvo and a BMW X5.
*   Dan Diaconescu has a house worth 1,000,000 euros, a 2,000,000 euros residence and a car collection that includes a Bentley Flying Spur, Rolls Royce, Infinity, Porsche, Alpha Romeo and Mercedes SLK.

All this is not to offer an apologia for poverty as honesty or to blame the acquisition of capital in a market-based media system! However, these journalists have significant fortunes judged not only by the standards of a less-developed country, but also in the context of a wealthy capitalist country. Moreover, these journalists did not invest money in launching a press business, but obtained money without risk, simply by taking advantage and manipulating their high-level position in the media system (they aggregated the status of manager, VIP, and opinion leader). The data confirm this covert, "underground" process that is described in my previous and other studies (Coman, 1998, 2003, 2004; Coman and Gross, 2006): a top media institution's management group used its power in order to obtain political and economical privileges. These journalists only very recently agreed to form an exclusive owner's group, because editorial control assured them influence over political life which in turn meant a source of economical privileges. By contrast, the media owners' position entailed risks and obligations. So to avoid them they exchanged their manager status and became members or leaders in Administration Councils, orienting the press institution's investments toward their own firms and received substantial commissions from the directly negotiated advertising contracts. By putting their "claws" over these resources, they bought stock and became the main stakeholders in other firms or in firms that had contracts with media enterprises; and they protected or promoted their own firms by media campaigns against competitors.

Often the hidden sources (from politician's thank-you-for-not-bothering-me money, to rewards for not investigating a manager or a company) that so-called star-journalists benefit from, are frequently the subject of media profession "folklore". Nevertheless, until 2006 no major journalism-related corruption case was brought to the public's attention or debated by the media. In 2006, however, six journalists from a local newspaper (*Gazeta de Cluj*) appeared in court charged with blackmailing some local businessmen. The media only presented the press releases of the six and the first few days of the event (charging the six, their reaction, the District Attorney's statement). Afterwards: total silence, the story has been forgotten.

While commenting upon the way this case was presented in the Romanian media, the authors of the report on media coverage of corruption remarked, not without some irony:

> Still, the journalistic guild did not look too surprised by the possibility that the accusations may be true. The event seems to have appeared against the background of some scepticism among the journalists: they knew that blackmail by the press was taking place in Romania. The real surprise seems to be that the Prosecutor's Office took a position in this case. (Ghinea and Fotiade, 2006, p. 38)

This third category of media moguls is atypical since it was formed by exploiting the system breaches, by reducing the economic risks and maximising the advantages they enjoyed as the "defenders of freedom of speech". Their history shows the effectiveness of a concept and a communist period-specific behaviour: "double talk". All these media moguls exploited the double talk resources: one aspect of this double talk was public, based on demagogical exaggeration of their role as defenders of freedom of expression; the other was underground, based on the cynical promotion of their personal interests.

REFERENCES

COMAN, MIHAI (1998) "Les Journalistes roumains et leur idéologie professionnelle", in: Ken Feigelson and Nicolas Pelissier (Eds), Télé-révolutions culturelles: Chine, Europe Centrale, Russie, Paris: L'Harmattan, pp. 183–200.

COMAN, MIHAI (2003) Mass Media in Romania Post-comunista, Iasi: Polirom.

COMAN, MIHAI (2004) "Media Bourgeoisie and Media Proletariat in Post-Communist Romania", Journalism Studies 5(1), pp. 45–58.

COMAN, MIHAI (2009) "Press Freedom and Media Pluralism in Romania: facts, myths and paradoxes", in: Andreea Czepeck, Melanie Helwig and Ewa Novak (Eds), Press Freedom and Press Pluralism in Europe: concepts and conditions, Bristol: Intellect, pp. 177–96.

COMAN, MIHAI and GROSS, PETER (2006) Media and Journalism in Romania, Berlin: Vistas.

COMANESCU, IULIAN (2007) Tendinţe despre reflectarea presei în presă III: concentrarea proprietăţii de media, Bucharest: CJI.

GHINEA, CRISTIAN and FOTIADE, NICOLETA (2006) Tendinţe în reflectarea presei în presă II: corupţia în presă, Bucharest: CJI.

GROSS, PETER (1996) Mass Media in Revolution and National Development: the Romanian laboratory, Ames: Iowa State University Press.

GROSS, PETER (2002) Entangled Evolutions: media and democratization in Eastern Europe, Washington, DC: Woodrow Wilson Center Press.

HIEBERT, RAY (1999) "Transition: from the end of the old regime to 1996", in: Jerome Aumente, Peter Gross, Ray Hiebert, Owen Johnson and Dean Mills (Eds), Eastern European Journalism: before, during, and after communism, Cresskill, NJ: Hampton pp. 79–122.

PREOTEASA, MANUELA (2004) "Romania", in: Brankica Petkovic (Ed.), Media Ownership and its Impact on Media Independence and Pluralism, Ljubljana: Peace Institute and Institute for Contemporary Social and Political Studies.

SIMION, CRISTINA, GHEORGHE, ANCA and COMANESCU, IULIAN (2007) *Cartea alba a presei: probleme economice ale presei*, Bucharest: AMP.

SPARKS, COLIN and READING, ANNA (1998) *Communism, Capitalism and the Mass Media*, London: Sage.

NEWS FROM AND IN THE "DARK CONTINENT"
Afro-pessimism, news flows, global journalism and media regimes

Arnold S. de Beer

The concepts news flow, global journalism/news and media regime are under theoretical construction. News media content is becoming increasingly deterritorialized, involving complex relations and flows across national borders and continents. Consequently, it becomes more difficult to categorize news in the traditional binary context as either national or international news as was the case with news flow studies since the mid-1990s. These changes are perhaps most evident in centres outside the global North, where rapid development of media infrastructures, coupled with political and social shifts as a result of widespread democratization since the mid-1990s, have brought about complex configurations of the local/global relationship in news. Global journalism/ news is suggested as an alternative concept and the notion of media regimes is introduced as a way to interrogate assumptions about global news flows as it relates to Africa. A content analysis of TV news channels in three world regions was conducted to facilitate the analysis.

Introduction

The concept global news is under theoretical construction, especially as it relates to news flow studies. News media content in a globalizing world is becoming increasingly deterritorialized, involving complex relations and flows across national borders and continents. Consequently, it also becomes more difficult to categorize news in the traditional binary fashion as either national or international/domestic and foreign news as was the tradition in news flow studies (Berglez, 2008, p. 845; 2009). Studies on the globalization of news flows (Archetti, 2007; Boyd-Barrett and Rantanen, 1998; Boyd-Barrett and Thussu, 1992; Rao, 2009) have shown that the concept "global news" could perhaps transcend the dichotomy between international (also foreign) and national (including local) news found in news flow research. If this is indeed the case, then these concepts are in need of more stringent definition. For instance, are the news reports of the global swine flu pandemic, or "blood diamonds" mined in Africa to pay for foreign armaments from European manufacturers, or the recession starting to bite in African countries as the West's "credit crunch" spreads, national or multi-national news? Are these stories bound to specific African countries, or are they rather part of global news, affecting not only specific countries in Africa, but the world at large (de Beer, 2009)?

News flow research itself is also under scrutiny and handicapped by a traditional binary view. As Chang (1998), Wu (2000) and others have shown, not all countries are created equal when it comes to news coverage—the core countries dominate the news flow (Chang et al., 2000), and news about the periphery is more often than not "negative" (Turan et al., 2009). It is especially Africa that suffers under the "bad news syndrome" of international/global media coverage (Golan, 2008; Hawke, 2004; Saidykhan, 2009; Saul, 2002).

Should one accept the notion that news could indeed be typified as global news and no longer only or mainly as international or foreign news (Thussu, 2007), then the inevitable follow-up question is: how should it be studied? The answer is not that evident. Global events post the Cold War era and post-9/11 also necessitate a re-examination of global news flows (Golan, 2008; Wu, 2000).

Formal and informal news institutions are pervasive agents of globalization, as well as democratization, and whilst strengthening the national state, it is paradoxically also facilitating the process of deconstructing the very notion of it in a globalization context (Curran, 2005; Lacher, 2006; McQuail and Siune, 2003). This change is not only occurring in established national democracies undergoing a transformation to new international and transnational structures, such as the European Union, but changing news institutions and processes, and 24-hour news channels (Cottle and Rai, 2008) amongst them, also affect developing nations in different stages of transition.

For instance, the fledgling African Union and the negative Western media images about the organization and its member states also form part of the changing global news process. Perhaps nowhere else is this so apparent than in Western news flow studies mapping out what has become known as the Afro-pessimism image of the so-called "dark continent" in Western media coverage. Present news flow studies do not adequately explain why such a portrayal seems to be persistent and regime analysis is proposed as a way to address this issue within the context of global journalism.

One way to implement such an analysis is to conduct a comparative content analysis (see Wu, 2000) on news flow about Africa, not only from a Western media point of view, but also from the Middle East and Africa as well in order to address the traditional North–South flow studies paradigm. Such an approach will also be in line with, for instance, Golan's (2008, p. 55) recommendation that in order to better explain the nature of news coverage of Africa, media outlets in other nations (such as Europe or the Middle East) could be examined.

Structure

This article consists of four parts:

- First, the problematic of international/global news is discussed as a way to describe news flows with regard to Africa.
- Secondly, the question is raised whether regime theory can contribute to our understanding of global news flows about Africa.
- Thirdly, a short overview is given of news flow studies as they relate to Africa and how they impinge on the construction of Afro-pessimism against the background of global news and media regimes.
- Finally, a content analysis in traditional news flow mode is presented regarding three groupings of countries (Western, Arab-speaking and African) and the question is asked whether this kind of research could be employed to better understand global news within a media regime framework as it relates to Africa.

Global Journalism

For some time now the definition of the global *vis-à-vis* international and transnational has been debated in especially the field of cultural studies (De Vereaux and Griffin, 2006). Even the terms transnational and national are controversial, as it assumes the nation-state as a basis of analysis. It is not a question of foreign news (i.e. media reporting about news elsewhere in the world) as such becoming more global in scope (e.g. Reese, 2001), but rather that local (domestic/national) news, also when reported by foreign journalists, are expanding into a new form of global journalism. The latter then becomes primarily the representation of (especially threatening and conflictual) complex relations in distinct domestic/national contexts on a global scale, involving issues of global space, powers and identities (Berglez, 2008, 2009).

In the case of Africa, media coverage of Aids is a prime example of news that transcends cultural and national borders, but so would news be about other issues that are usually being lumped together in the Afro-pessimism news flow "code book", such as famine, civil conflict and disputed elections (Golan, 2008). As the *New York Times* editorialized in 1994, in the eyes of much of the world, Africa south of the Sahara has become "a basket case: (e)very bit of bad news—civil wars, military coups, refugees, and displaced persons, drought and disease—has sadly reinforced a mood of fatalism or, still worse, callous unconcern" (Merrill, 1995, p. 2004).

If this is indeed the case, then the next question is whether such news can best be reported in traditional international news formats and styles adopted in Western media when covering mostly events, but also trends, "elsewhere in the world" (Hamilton and Jenner, 2004). Recently a number of studies addressed the need to come to a more comprehensive theoretical and empirical grasp of news and news flow processes (e.g. Cottle and Rai, 2008; Gunaratne, 2001; Hanitzsch, 2009; Paterson and Sreberny, 2004; Pfetsch and Esser, 2009).

At stake is not only the issue of theoretical analysis, but as Reese (2001, p. 173) argues, "(a)lthough it is not often explicitly stated, many media scholars would share the conviction that there should be an international standard of journalistic professionalism with basic shared values". For example, in the field of media ethics such efforts have been ongoing for some time (see Christians et al., 2008). In the field of Internet and other communication networks efforts have already been on the way for some time to find a regime that would address global needs and changes (see Braman, 2004, for the "emergent global information policy regime"), which opened the possibility of applying regime analysis to news.

Against the background of what Cottle and Rai (2008) term a "democratic lacuna" in news debates, regime theory is then suggested in this article as a possible way to study global news flows. In the present case about Africa, or as it was earlier described, the "dark continent".

Regime Theory

Given the role of the media in all stages of foreign and national policy formation (Naveh, 2002), it is rather surprising that regime analysis, a distinct theoretical approach in international studies (e.g. Rittberger, 1993), has not earlier been applied to news and especially news flow studies. This is even more notable when one considers that regime theory is closely related to management, and of the latter there have been ample studies in journalism, one of the prime examples being the way American media covered the US-led wars in the Middle East since the 1990s with clear indications of news management (Hall, 2000; Thussu, 2002; see also Tulloch, 1993).

Based on the well-known definition of Stephen D. Krasner (1982), regime theory refers to "principles, norms, rules, and decision making procedures around which actor expectations converge in a given issue area". More generally, regimes refer (Rittberger and Mayer 2002, pp. xii–xiii) to the "rules of the game agreed upon by actors and delimiting, for these actors, the range of legitimate or admissible behaviour in a specified context of activity". Regime analysis became important because it made possible the study of international management or governance outside the confinements of or in co-operation with governments. It succeeded, according to Rittberger and Mayer (2002), in tackling more successfully than other approaches, the puzzles of international co-operation and institution building in a virtual global world where no single government or organization is capable of making and enforcing international rules of conduct. As such, the application of regime theory can overcome the problem of news flow studies bound to the concept of nation-states and governments when involved in media management, such as the Middle East wars, or as in the case of this article, the media coverage of Africa. This is mostly so because regime theory offers the ability to surmount traditional theoretical confinements such as the restrictive definitions of national, transnational and international policies and news processes.

Presently there is a dearth of theoretical knowledge on whether regime theory, applied successfully in other fields of the social sciences, could also be applied to human communication and/or media processes such as news (however, see Braman, 2004 on an information regime; also the work done in the Centre for International Communication Research, Leeds University, UK). For the purpose of this article only one such distinctive publication could be found in the existing academic literature (especially with reference to a media regime in Africa), namely those of Shrivastava and Nathalie Hyde-Clarke (2004), whilst Meyer (2005) in his study on the utilization of regime theory offers a conceptual framework for examining information and technology and social change in organizations.

Meyer (2005, 2007) defines a regime (but adapted for the purpose of this article to news flows) as:

- a loosely organized social, political and technological network in which news processes and the news system are highly coupled;
- consisting of a set of implicit or explicit principles, norms, rules, and decision-making procedures around which the expectations of the news actors involved in the news process converge;
- the types of news communication are tightly coupled to the production system in which they are embedded;
- news institutions help to support and to regulate the news regime; and it is
- a system within which there are conflicts over control, over who enforces standards, over who bears the costs of change and who reaps the benefits of change.

The above description suggests that regime theory could be applied to the media in order to understand the multiple relationships involved in the news flow process. It is in this regard that Shrivastava and Hyde-Clarke (2004) offer perhaps the best application found thus far of regime theory to media studies, especially also because it is applied to a conflictual situation in Africa, namely the media in Zimbabwe.

In a globalized world it is becoming more difficult for world leaders "to create policies about transnational and/or technical matters in an interdependent world". On the other hand, "mass media networks, empowered by technological advances, defy those geographical boundaries, and affect the opinion of a much wider audience". Shrivastava and Hyde-Clarke (2004, p. 204) see a co-operation between democratic states since 1990 which was a "convergence around a common desire to manage the media to elicit and sustain public support". This was especially the case where news management practices attained the structure of media regimes when implemented in international conflict, and which occurred under the same conditions in consecutive crises. Thus far, this behaviour has been identified, for instance, during the Gulf War, and in the Kosovo crisis, as well as the war in Afghanistan (Shrivastava and Hyde-Clarke, 2004, p. 204). The authors argue that a particular form of media management was observable during these crises with identifiable principles, norms and rules, as well as decision-making procedures around which there was a convergence of common interest. As such a media regime emerged which could be repeated elsewhere—in their case in Zimbabwe.

Such a news regime would then be able to affect the creation, availability, dissemination, and use of information in a global media system. A news regime could also be operationalized through the planned production of news events, the creation of a manipulative relationship with journalists and media executives, demonizing the enemy, the selection of news coverage and events by way of techniques such as "generalizations, recalling past violations and suppressing and/or omitting information not conducive to the media regime" (Shrivastava and Hyde-Clarke, 2004, p. 207).

The relationship between Western governments and media houses, global interests and international conflicts and crises conveyed as news through media systems, indicate a pattern of behaviour which points to the emergence of a global media regime. In all these conflicts (and as discussed in this article, possibly also the negative media portrayal of Africa), news regimes are employed to maintain a certain perception and continuation of managed news images.

According to Shrivastava and Hyde-Clarke (2004), developments in information technology since 2000 have exacerbated the influence of the media, and the potential emergence of a news management regime among Western democracies during times of international and intrastate crisis is unwittingly providing a rationale and giving credence to similar policies in African states.

Shrivastava and Hyde-Clarke's (2004) article is aimed at the situation in Zimbabwe and a specific media regime geared towards state-enforced censorship (also see *Zimbabwe Independent*, 2009). This opened the way for regime theory to be applied to international news coverage and flows of news events in a global context (such as the wars in Iraq and Afghanistan). It is in this connection that the next section deals with news flows in and about Africa.

News Flow Studies and Afro-pessimism

Since the middle of the previous century a number of social science research methods have been developed to study news and news flows in local, national, international, transnational and more lately glocalized contexts and as contra-flows (see for instance Hanusch and Obijiofor, 2008; Rantanen, 2005; Thussu, 2007; Tumber, 1999). As a consequence, international news flow studies have become a dominant topic of international or global communication research of the last half century, ranging from gatekeeping, agenda-setting to news framing and other approaches. Much of this research was focused on the "operation of foreign news values; the unequal flows, and the emergent contra-flows of transnational news" (Cottle and Rai, 2008, p. 157).

However, in their analysis of journalism news flow studies, Hanusch and Obijiofor (2008) argue that the time is ripe to consider a more holistic approach, as many of the past and present news flow studies did not address deeper underlying issues, for instance the question whether traditional concepts such as core and peripheral nations are valid. Although there are "several unifying elements that underpin the way journalism is practiced in different parts of the worlds" (Hanusch and Obijiofor, 2008, p. 15), there is still no universal way to fully comprehend news flows on a theoretical level, or empirically predict how news is reported across cultures. This is in part due to the main body of international news research being conducted in the global North applying Northern theories and methods to the global South, which more often than not defy presumed "universal" research outcomes when compared to the reality of the Southern contexts.

Analysing news from a point of view of the global South, it is rather remarkable that most news studies about Africa appeared in the West, and then mostly in a negative light. This is especially the case with news flows studies. As was shown in De Beer and Schreiner (2009), very little research on news flow in and even about Africa is undertaken on the continent itself, be it with a focus on a few foreign news elements or more comprehensively. As such, African researchers effectively missed the first two decades of international news flow studies since the New World Information and Communication Order (NWICO) debate initiated the interest of researchers in the flow of foreign news between different countries—at the time mostly North–South flows (Hanusch and Obijiofor, 2008).

Since the mid-1990s and up to the 2000s only a very few African-based researchers focused on comparative news flow studies of African international news reporting on their own and other countries on the continent (Mogekwu, 2002). The exception being research undertaken during the 1990s and 2000s at the Institute for Communication Research, Potchefstroom University, as well as at the Institute for Media Analysis in South Africa, and Stellenbosch University (e.g. Annas, 1997; De Beer, 2000; De Beer and Schreiner, 2009; De Beer et al., 1996; Schreiner, 2003). Except to a certain degree for the latter study, all these South African studies confirmed the traditional unidirectional and unbalanced news flows model of Western news coverage of Africa (also see Archetti, 2007). Some of the earlier of these studies found their basis in the participation of the authors in the work of the international news flow project under the leadership of Robert Louis Stevenson and Annabelle Sreberny (see Eribo and Wu, 2008 for a discussion of the project).

A few news flow studies dealing specifically with African media also appeared from researchers from outside the continent. An early study was that of Ume-Nwagbo (1982), with Eribo (1999) analysing Nigerian media coverage of international news from 1979 to 1995. A number of studies since the 1970s dealt with international news reporting which would also include Africa or be directed at the way Africa is portrayed in media outside the continent (e.g. Wu, 2000).

From a research perspective, one would have expected that more African researchers would have come to the fore with the advent of the new millennium, not the least with news flow research bearing on the way the media portrayed news issues, newsmakers and news images in a post-colonial Africa finding its foothold in a globalizing world. The post-2000 lack of research, however, was still reminiscent of what transpired until the end of the previous century. This article is in part an effort to address this issue.

Media Coverage and Afro-pessimism

Since the 1980s, but more especially since the 1990s and into the new millennium, the continent's news image in the West has been in tatters. Efforts by the African Editors' Forum to "tell the African story" in order to counter-balance negative Western coverage, for example, has not yielded any viable results. Thabo Mbeki, a former South African president, was especially vocal on this topic, appealing to journalists and the media to avoid "negative type-casting of Africa" in international and national media coverage. He also directed his call to both governments and media to "act responsibly" regarding media freedom and media coverage of the continent (Saidykhan, 2009).

Calls for more "realistic" media coverage of Africa in the West, such as the one mentioned above by political leaders like Mbeki at the 60th World Newspaper Congress before some 1600 delegates from 109 countries, but also from within the academic research community (Hanusch and Obijiofor, 2008) regarding the lack of news flow studies to answer basic questions about media and circumstances in Africa, beg the question of how international or "news from foreign places" about Africa as a continent in the global south, could best be studied and researched, as it seems that both media coverage and news flow studies up to now have remained stuck in the view of Africa as the "hopeless continent" (Saul, 2002; *The Economist*, 2000).

It is a basic premise of this article that both media coverage and media flows research have come to subscribe, consciously or not, to a certain media or news regime depicting Africa in a predominantly negative fashion as a continent without hope at best, or as a basket case at worst (Chabal, 2008; Ramos et al., 2007; however also see Ibelema and Bosch, 2009, p. 293 for a possible change in this regime).

If Africa has made strides towards becoming more open and democratized, would it then be possible that new news flow studies on Africa would perhaps portray the continent in a less dismal light than was the case in the latter part of the previous century? For instance, De Beer and Schreiner (2009) found in their recent study of print and television news flow a relative change in the traditional north–south paradigm when media in the global south (such as South Africa) report on the activities of a non-Western country (such as China) in Africa. Would the same result follow if a news flow analysis of Western and non-Western coverage of Africa is conducted and would this inform the way global journalism and news regimes could be used to better understand news? (e.g. see Turan et al., 2009).

Content Analysis and Research Questions

As an initial step regarding the above, a comparative content analysis was conducted of African television news coverage in three Western countries (the United Kingdom, the United States and Germany), two Arab-speaking countries (Qatar and the United Arab Emirates (UAE)) and an African country (South Africa) in 2008 to investigate the following two research questions:

1. Is Africa underreported in Western media, as well as in Arab and African media?
2. Is the tone of the reporting on Africa predominantly negative in Western media, as well as in Arab and African media?

Data Collection

Traditional content analysis was undertaken (Berelson, 1952, p. 18; Stempel and Westley, 1981; Tan, 1982, pp. 51–3). All TV news reports were coded, but excluding the re-broadcast of "highlights" after advertising breaks. The time frame for the analysis is from 1 January to 31 December 2008. The analysis was executed by trained analysts and data capturers of the Media Tenor Institute for Media Analysis in Zürich, Switzerland, and Pretoria, South Africa (www.mediatenor.com).

- *Coding*: Regions and news topics were selected from an extensive drop-down list as well as a purpose-developed code book. Instructions were given to the coders to select only the single most important topic prevailing amongst the others, determined by time slots (five-second units of each TV news channel report).
- *Tone of news:* The overall ratings (positive/neutral/negative) when derived from the combination of context (when the content is embedded in positive or negative context) and explicit ratings (when the journalist uses or cites words of clearly positive or negative judgement).
- *Inter-coder agreement*: The intercoder percentage agreement ranged between 85 and 90 per cent (news coverage and tendency of news tone).
- *Television news channels*: The following TV news channels were analysed: US TV: *NBC Nightly News*; *ABC World News Tonight*; *CBS Evening News*; UK TV: *Six o'Clock News* (BBC 1); *Ten o'Clock News* (BBC 1); *ITN Early Evening News*; *News at Ten* (ITV); *Newsnight* (BBC 2). Middle East TV: Al Arabiya; Al Jazeera. South Africa: *SABC Afrikaans News, SABC English News, SABC Zulu/Xhosa News*, and e.tv-news.

Findings

The findings offered both what one could have expected in terms of Western coverage of Africa, but also some rather interesting, if not new results on Arab and African coverage of the continent.

News Coverage of World Regions

In the Western TV news media (Figure 1) Asia (25.5 per cent), the Middle East (22.0 per cent) and North America (21.4 per cent) did get more than 20 per cent of the coverage, but Africa (10.8 per cent) received substantially more coverage than South America (1.9 per cent).

On the other hand, in the Arab media (Figure 2), Africa (28.1 per cent) received almost as much coverage as Europe (28.8 per cent), but more than North America (16.1 per cent) and Asia (12.7 per cent). South America, again, received only 1.8 per cent.

In the African media (Figure 3), Africa (21.3 per cent) received slightly less than Europe (24.7 per cent), and more than North America (13.5 per cent) and Asia (12.4 per cent). Again, South America (1.7 per cent) received very little coverage.

In terms of Golan's (2008, p. 41) rhetorical question "Where in the World is Africa?", the analysis shows that Africa is not that absent from the Western news media, and far more visible than South America. In terms of Berglez's (2008) argument that international news is global in nature, and Shrivastava and Hyde-Clarke's (2004) argument that international news can functionally be studied within regime analysis, it is suggested that,

Region	n	%
1.Asia	3816	25.5%
2.Middle East	3290	22.0%
3.North America	3202	21.4%
4.Africa	1613	10.8%
5.Europe	621	4.2%
6.Central America	397	2.7%
7.South America	288	1.9%
8.Oceania	220	1.5%
Total	14957	100%

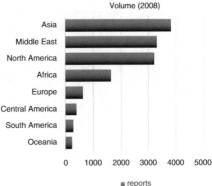

N = 14 957 Time frame: 1 January to 31 December 2008. Main evening news.

FIGURE 1
World regions in UK, US and German TV news (2008)

based on the analysis conducted for this article, a viable comparative analysis would be to ask the question why Africa (10.8 per cent) receives more than double the coverage offered to Central and South America combined (4.6 per cent) in the Western media. While the same question could also be asked in terms of Arab and African coverage, the reasons might differ, which might again be an indication of global journalism and regime dynamics at work.

Tone of News Reports

The analysis (Figures 4–6) found support for the general perception of bad news in the West (Figure 4) about Africa, but it is noticeable that this is also the case in Arab and African TV news. Though Africa received, as expected, the most negative tone of news (54.1 per cent) in the Western media (Figure 4), the percentage for Central America was even slightly higher (55.4 per cent). Of the world regions, Africa (7.2 per cent), along with

Region	n	%
1.Europe	1595	28.8%
2.Africa	1556	28.1%
3.North America	889	16.1%
4.Asia	701	12.7%
5.South America	99	1.8%
6.Oceania	65	1.2%
7.Central America	27	0.5%
Total	5535	100%

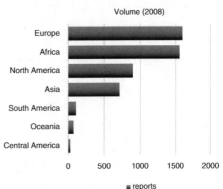

N = 14 957 Time frame: 1 January to 31 December 2008. Main evening news.

FIGURE 2
World regions in Qatar and UAE TV news (2008)

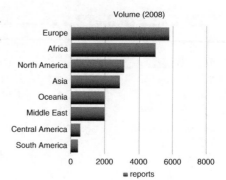

African TV	No. of reports	%
Europe	5733	24.7%
Africa	4942	21.3%
North America	3134	13.5%
Asia	2879	12.4%
Oceania	1977	8.5%
Middle East	1970	8.5%
Central America	546	2.4%
South America	401	1.7%
Other	1627	7.0%
N= 23209		100.0%

FIGURE 3

World regions in South African TV news (2008)

Continent	%Negative	%Neutral	%Positive
Asia	41.3%	43.4%	15.3%
Middle East	42.0%	50.2%	7.8%
North America	31.3%	50.7%	18.1%
Africa	54.1%	38.7%	7.2%
Europe	37.5%	41.2%	21.3%
Central America	55.4%	40.1%	4.5%
South America	28.5%	45.1%	26.4%
Oceania	21.4%	48.2%	30.5%

N=14 957 reports.   Period: 1 January 2008 – 31 December 2008

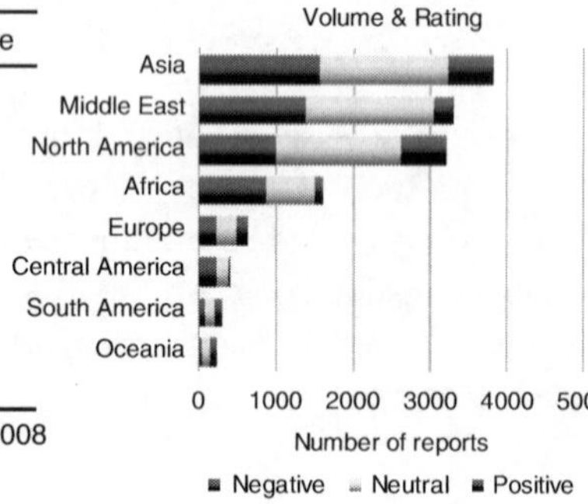

FIGURE 4

World regions: tone of news on UK, US and German TV (2008)

Central America (4.5 per cent) and the Middle East (7.8 per cent) and Asia (15.3 per cent), received less positive coverage than Oceania (30.5 per cent), South America (26.4 per cent) and Europe (21.3 per cent).

Both in terms of global news flow and regime theory, this situation offers cause for further investigation. For instance, while analysis showed that Africa received more

Continent	%Negative	%Neutral	%Positive
Europe	14.4%	55.9%	29.7%
Africa	27.4%	57.5%	15.2%
North America	18.2%	53.2%	28.6%
Asia	25.5%	60.9%	13.6%
South America	6.1%	60.6%	33.3%
Oceania	6.2%	33.8%	60.0%
Central America	14.8%	63.0%	22.2%

N=5 535 reports.   Period: 1 January 2008 – 31 December 2008

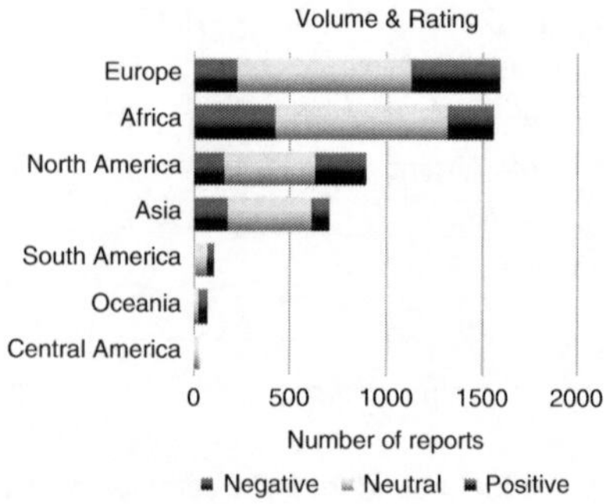

FIGURE 5

World regions: tone of news on Qatar and UAE TV (2008)

Continent	%Negative	%Neutral	%Positive
Europe	20.2%	49.4%	30.4%
Africa	43.0%	45.4%	11.5%
North America	24.4%	44.6%	31.0%
Asia	33.3%	39.3%	27.4%
Oceania	14.6%	53.1%	32.3%
Middle East	53.4%	37.7%	8.9%
Central America	30.6%	53.1%	16.3%
South America	34.7%	39.4%	25.9%

N=23 209 reports.   Period: 1 January 2008 – 31 December 2008

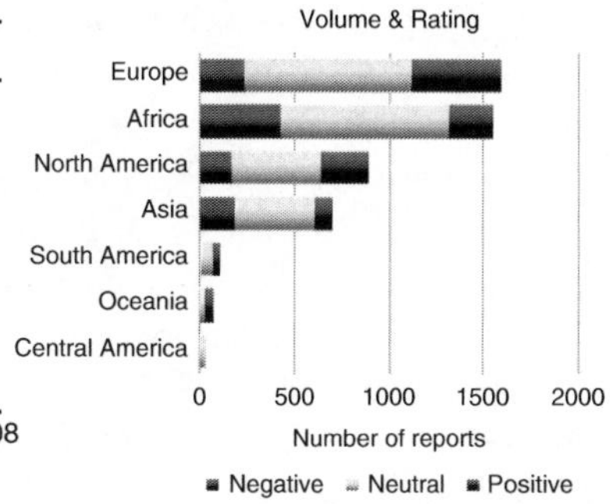

FIGURE 6

World regions: tone of news in African TV news (2008)

negative news in all three world regions under study (Figure 4: 45.1 per cent in the West; Figure 5: 27.4 per cent in the Arab countries; Figure 6: 43.0 per cent in the African news (except for the Middle East being higher with 53.4 per cent)), a further analysis might try to ascertain why the African continent received such negative ratings (27.4 per cent) in the Arab countries and (43.0 per cent) in Africa if negative news about the continent is apparently a Western phenomenon. This might be more to do with globalization and global news, as well as media regimes (both state and media) than initially meets the eye.

Conclusion

In what is effectively a qualitative analysis, the data not surprisingly showed trends well documented in other news flow studies, but also the prospect of considering new possibilities for further news flow research within the context of global journalism, media regime analysis and news regimes as they relate to Africa.

ACKNOWLEDGEMENTS

The author wishes to thank Irina Hristova and Chris van Coppenhagen of the Media Tenor Institute for Media Analysis (South Africa) for the data extraction, tabulation and graphic representation for the project reported on in this article, as well as Wadim Schreiner, managing director of MTSA, for the use of the data. The author acknowledges the financial support received from the South African National Research Foundation's 'Incentive Fund for Rated Researchers' for research pertaining to this article. Opinions expressed and conclusions drawn are those of the author.

REFERENCES

ANNAS, ROLF (1997) "News Flow Out of Africa: are western media striving for excellence in communication standards?", *Ecquid Novi* 18(2), pp. 196–207.

ARCHETTI, C. (2004) "Are the Media Globalizing Political Discourse? The war on terrorism case study", *The International Journal of the Humanities* 2, pp. 1301–8.

ARCHETTI, C. (2007) "A Multidisciplinary Understanding of News: comparing elite press framing of 9/11 in the US, Italy, France and Pakistan", *Journal of International Communication* 13(1), pp. 86–118.

BERELSON, BERNARD (1952) *Content Analysis in Communication Research*, New York: The Free Press.

BERGLEZ, PETER (2008) "What Is Global Journalism?", *Journalism Studies* 9(6), pp. 845–58.

BERGLEZ, PETER (2009) "Global Journalism: An emerging news style and an outline for a training programme", paper presented at the Future of Journalism Conference, Cardiff, September.

BOYD-BARRETT, OLIVER and RANTANEN, TERHI (Eds) (1998) *The Globalization of News*, London: Sage.

BOYD-BARRETT, OLIVER and THUSSU, DAYA K. (1992) *Contra-flows in Global News: international and regional news exchange mechanisms*, London: John Libbey.

BRAMAN, SANDRA (2004) "The Emergent Global Information Policy Regime", in: Sandra Braman (Ed.), *The Emergent Global Information Policy Regime*, Basingstoke: Palgrave Macmillan, pp. 12–37.

CHABAL, PATRICK (2008) "On Reason and Afro-Pessimism", *Africa* 78(4), pp. 603–10.

CHANG, TSAN-KUO (1998) "All Countries Not Created Equal to Be News", *Communication Research* 25(5), pp. 528–63.

CHANG, TSAN-KUO, LAU, T. Y. and HAO, XIAOMING (2000) "From the United States with News and More: international flow, TV coverage and world system", *Gazette* 62(6), pp. 505–22.

CHRISTIANS, CLIFFORD G., RAO, SHAKUNTALA, WARD, STEPHEN J. A. and WASSERMAN, HERMAN (2008) "Toward a Global Media Ethics: theoretical perspectives", *Ecquid Novi: African Journalism Studies* 29(2), pp. 135–72.

COTTLE, SIMON and RAI, MUGDHA (2008) "Global 24/7 News Providers: emissaries of global dominance or global public sphere?", *Global Media and Communication* 4, pp. 157–81.

CURRAN, JAMES (2005) *Media and Power*, London: Routledge.

DE BEER, ARNOLD S. (2000) "New Mirror in a New South Africa? International news flow and news selection at the Afrikaans Daily, Beeld", in: Abbas Malek and Anandam P. Kavoori (Eds) *The Global Dynamics of News: studies in international news coverage and news agendas*, Stamford, CT: Ablex Publishing Corporation.

DE BEER, ARNOLD S. (Ed.) (2009) *Global Journalism: topical issues and media systems*, 5th edn, Boston: Pearson.

DE BEER, ARNOLD S., SERFONTEIN, LYNETTE and NAUDÉ, ANNELIE (1996) "The New South Africa and International News Flow: is it new or is it much of the same story", *Communicare* 15(2), pp. 12–24.

DE BEER, ARNOLD S. and SCHREINER, WADIM N. (2009) "Of 'Ominous Dragons' and 'Flying Geese': South African media coverage of China in Africa", paper presented at the Annual Convention of the Association for Journalism and Mass Communication Education, Boston, August.

DE VEREAUX, CONSTANCE and GRIFFIN, MARTIN (2006) "International, Global, Transnational: just a matter of words?", http://www.eurozine.com, accessed 13 January 2006.

ERIBO, FESTUS (1999) "Global News Flow in Africa: Nigerian media coverage of international news, 1979–1995", *The Western Journal of Black Studies* 23(3), pp. 154–63.

ERIBO, FESTUS and WU, H. DENIS (2008) "Introduction to the Special Issue on Global News Flows: a tribute to Robert L. Stevenson", *Journal of Mass Communication* 1(1/2), pp. 7–8.

GOLAN, GUY J. (2008) "Where in the World Is Africa?: predicting coverage of Africa by US television networks, *International Communication Gazette* 70(1), pp. 41–57.

GUNARATNE, SHELTON A. (2001) "Prospects and Limitations of World Systems Theory for Media Analysis: the case of the Middle East and North Africa", *Gazette* 63(2/3), pp. 121–48.

HALL, JIM (2000) "The First Web War: 'bad things happen in unimportant places'", *Journalism Studies* 1(3), pp. 387–404.

HAMILTON, JOHN M. and JENNER, ERIC (2004) "Redefining Foreign Correspondence", *Journalism* 5(3), pp. 301–21.

HANITZSCH, THOMAS (2009) "Comparing Media Systems Reconsidered: recent development and directions for future research", *Journal of Global Mass Communication* 2(1), pp. 4–13.

HANUSCH, FOLKER and OBIJIOFOR, LEVI (2008) "Toward a More Holistic Analysis of International News Flows", *Journal of Global Mass Communication* 1(1/2), pp. 9–21.

HAWKE, BEVERLY, G. (2004) *Africa's Media Image*, Santa Barbara, CA: Praeger.

IBELEMA, MINBABERE and BOSCH, TANJA (2009) "News from and in the 'Dark Continent'", in: De Beer, Arnold S. (Ed.), *Global Journalism: Topical issues and media*, Boston: Pearson, pp. 293–336.

KRASNER, STEPHEN D. (1982) "Structural Causes and Regime Consequences: regimes as intervening variables", *International Organization* 36(2). Reprinted in Stephen D. Krasner (Ed.) (1983), *International Regimes*, Ithaca, NY: Cornell University Press, pp. 1–21.

LACHER, HANNES (2006) *Beyond Globalization: capitalism, territoriality and the international relations of modernity*, London: Routledge.

MCQUAIL, DENIS and SIUNE, KAREN (Eds) (2003) *Media Policy: convergence, concentration and commerce*, London: Sage.

MERRILL, JOHN (1995) *Global Journalism: topical issues and media systems*, 3rd edn, Boston: Pearson.

MEYER, ERIC T. (2005) "Communication Regimes: a conceptual framework for examining IT and social change in organizations", *Proceedings of the American Society for Information Science and Technology* 42(1), http://eprints.rclis.org/5232, accessed 14 March 2010.

MEYER, ERIC T. (2007) "Socio-technical Perspectives on Digital Photography: scientific digital photography use by marine mammal researchers", MA dissertation, University of California, Santa Barbara.

MOGEKWU, MATT (2002) "African Union: xenophobia as poor intercultural communication: research section", *Electronic Publishing* 26(1), pp. 5–20.

NAVEH, CHANAN (2002) "The Role of the Media in Foreign Policy Decision-making: a theoretical framework", *Conflict and Communication Online* 1(2), pp. 1–14.

PATERSON, CHRIS and SREBERNY, ANNABELLE (Eds) (2004) *International News in the 21st Century*, Eastleigh: John Libbey.

PFETSCH, BARBARA and ESSER, FRANK (2009) "Conceptual Challenges to the Paradigms of Comparative Media Systems in a Globalized World", *Journal of Global Mass Communication* 2(1), pp. 14–31.

RAMOS, HOWARD, RON, JAMES and THOMS, OSKAR N. T. (2007) "Shaping the Northern Media's Human Rights Coverage, 1986–2000, *Journal of Peace Research* 44(4), pp. 385–406.

RANTANEN, TERHI (2005) *The Media and Globalization*, London: Sage.

RAO, SHAKUNTALA (2009) "Glocalization of Indian Journalism", *Journalism Studies* 10(4), pp. 474–88.

REESE, STEPHEN (2001) "Understanding the Global Journalist: a hierarchy-of-influences approach, *Journalism Studies* 2(2), pp. 173–87.

RITTBERGER, VOLKER (Ed.) (1993) *Regime Theory and International Relations*, Oxford: Clarendon Press.

RITTBERGER, VOLKER and MAYER, PETER (Eds) (2002) *Regime Theory and International Relations*, Oxford: Oxford University Press.

SAIDYKHAN, MUSA (2009) "Avoid Negative Type-casting Africa", *Afrol-New*, http://www.afrol.com/articles/25622, accessed 17 August 2009.

SAUL, JOHN S. (2002) "Taming the Transition: the real Afro-pessimism", *Politikon* 29, pp. 101–12.

SCHREINER, WADIM N. (2003) "Bad News from Africa on Africa", paper presented at the 11th biennial conference of the Council of Communication and Education in Africa, Cairo, September.

SHRIVASTAVA, MEENAL and HYDE-CLARKE, NATHALIE (2004) "International Media Regime and News Management: implications for African states", *Politikon* 31(2), pp. 201–18.

STEMPEL, GUIDO H. III and WESTLEY, BRUCE H. (Eds) (1981) *Research Methods in Mass Communication*, Englewood Cliffs, NJ: Prentice-Hall.

TAN, ALEXIS, S. (1982) *Mass Communication Theories and Research*, Columbus, OH: Grid.

THE ECONOMIST (2000) "Hopeless Africa", 11 May, p. 1, http://www.economist.com/opinion/displaystory.cfm?story_id=E1_PPPQNJ, accessed 14 March 2009.

THUSSU, DAYA K. (2002) "Managing the Media in an Era of Round-the-Clock News: notes from India's first tele-war", *Journalism Studies* 3(2), pp. 203–12.

THUSSU, DAYA K. (Ed.) (2007) *Media on the Move: global flow and contra-flow*, London: Routledge.

TULLOCH, JOHN (1993) "Policing the Public Sphere—the British machinery of news management", *Media, Culture and Society* 15, pp. 363–84.

TUMBER, HOWARD (Ed.) (1999) *News: a reader*, Oxford: Oxford University Press.

TURAN, AYKUT HAMIT, COLAKOGLU, SELCUK and COLAKOGLU, BENGU EMINE (2009) "Perceptional Differences of International News: western media influence on non-western media", *China Media Research* 5(2), pp. 55–63.

UME-NWAGBO, EBELE N. (1982) "Foreign News Flow in Africa: a content analytical study on a regional basis", *International Communication Gazette* 29(1/2), pp. 41–56.

WU, H. DENIS (2000) "The Systemic Determinants of International News Coverage: a comparison of 38 countries", *Journal of Communication* 50(2), pp. 110–30.

ZIMBABWE INDEPENDENT (2009) "Zimbabwe: country needs a new media regime", 11 June.

THE JOURNALISM "CRISIS"
Is Australia immune or just ahead of its time?

Sally Young

Australia is facing many of the same trends in journalism that are occurring in other countries with mature media industries including declining numbers of journalists, fragmenting audiences, a loss of advertising revenue for media organisations and other challenges to their traditional business models including shifting patterns of news consumption, new competitors for old media and new technologies that demand more time from audiences. However, Australia is also in a unique position. It has a small population and unusually concentrated media ownership; recent newspaper circulation declines have not been as large as in the United States or United Kingdom; and Australia's major media organisations have "colonised the Web" to a larger degree than in many other countries. This has led to suggestions that Australian journalism will be immune from many of the most damaging international trends. Yet other evidence suggests Australia is already in the midst of an economic and professional crisis in newspaper journalism and that this is even more advanced than in other countries such as the United States and United Kingdom. This paper tests these competing propositions.

Introduction

Newspapers are major employers of journalists and traditionally the largest injectors of new stories into the news cycle. While countries such as China and India have been recording record growth in newspaper circulation, in many other countries (including the United States and the United Kingdom) newspapers are ailing (World Association of Newspapers (WAN), 2008a). Emily Bell of the *Guardian* argued in 2008 that: "We are on the brink of two years' carnage for Western media ... [of] systematic collapse, not just a cyclical downturn" (Media Entertainment and Arts Alliance (MEAA), 2008, p. 4). *The Financial Times* (10 December 2008) quoted a report from Deloitte that "The newspaper and magazine industry could be 'decimated' in 2009". Even before the global financial crisis, Philip Meyer (2004) famously predicted that newspapers would run out of readers in 2043 and *The Economist* (2006) claimed that "half the world's newspapers [were] likely to close in the foreseeable future". There is currently a debate underway in Australia about whether Australia's small population and concentrated media ownership regime makes it particularly vulnerable to the decline of newspapers versus a perception that such factors will protect it from the more damaging trends. This paper tests the evidence by providing a comparative assessment of the position of newspaper journalism in Australia and four other mature industrial, English-speaking democracies—the United States, United Kingdom, Canada and New Zealand. It also considers what strategies Australian newspaper businesses are pursuing to try to protect themselves from decline.

Australia as a Case-study

Of all the factors that make Australia a unique case-study of newspaper industry viability and the future of journalism, media ownership is the most significant. Twenty years ago it was observed that the Australian newspaper industry had "the most concentrated pattern of ownership of any Western country" (Windschuttle, 1988, p. 86). Since then, ownership has consolidated even further and Australia seems to retain this dubious honour among established democracies. There are only three major newspaper owners in Australia—News Ltd (the Australian subsidiary of Rupert Murdoch's News Corporation), Fairfax Media and APN News. These three companies now own every Australian newspaper except one metropolitan (*West Australian*) and two regional dailies (Australian Press Council (APC), 2008, pp. 1–3). Two of the companies—News Ltd and Fairfax—control more than 90 per cent of newspaper circulation (Tiffen, 2010, p. 85). However, the past two years have not been good ones for Australian newspaper owners. Media company stocks plummeted even before the general stock market collapse and fell further than many other stocks. Newspaper circulations continued to decline (APC, 2008). Fairfax cut 550 jobs and News Ltd/News Corporation signalled future job losses. Remaining journalists complained of increased workloads, lack of resources, and training (MEAA, 2008). How does this downturn compare to other similar countries? Has ownership concentration protected Australian journalism or made it more vulnerable?

Assessing the Evidence

Taken at face value, Australia's newspaper industry does seem comparatively well-off. It did not face the imminent closure of titles that threatened the newspaper industries in the United States and United Kingdom in 2009 and Australia's newspaper companies continue to insist that they are in a more fortunate position than in other countries. APN News, for example, has argued that Australian newspapers are less dependent on classifieds and have a high subscription base (*West Australian*, 2009). Writing in a Fairfax newspaper, former editor Max Suich argued that "The Australian newspaper industry is not remotely like the US industry ... In Australia ... oligopoly protects the major companies. They have colonised the web ... Circulation of Australian newspapers has held up remarkably well compared with the US" (Suich, 2008, p. 13). The APC also argued that circulation in Australia, "when compared to the US and the UK, for example, is reasonably stable" (2008, pp. 2–7).

These claims require some context. The first thing to note is that the accuracy of circulation figures in Australia is heavily debated (e.g. Simons, 2008). Even the APC admits circulation figures are "rubbery" (2008, pp. 1–2). The Audit Bureau of Circulation has changed its methodology several times in recent years which has made comparability over time difficult. Recent changes seem to give a more generous account of readership and circulation but there have also been suggestions that newspapers artificially inflate their sales figures through a variety of tactics (Simons, 2009; *Vexnews*, 2009).

Bearing this in mind, it is true that Australia's circulation declines do not appear to be as sharp as in the United States or United Kingdom. Between 2006 and 2008, total reported circulation of metropolitan dailies in Australia declined by "only 0.7 per cent" (APC, 2008, pp. 2–8).[1] By contrast, in 2007, the circulation of US dailies fell 3.03 per cent while paid circulation in the United Kingdom dropped 3.46 per cent (WAN, 2008b). However, if we consider longitudinal trends a different picture emerges. In 1986–7, media law changes in Australia led to a frenzy of buying and selling of media assets including a number of mergers and closures. Between 1987 and 1992, all of Australia's afternoon newspapers closed, these were newspapers with a circulation of 1.22 million (Tiffen, 2010, p. 82). With the closure of so many titles, as Tiffen and Gittins show, Australian "newspaper penetration almost halved ... [between 1980 and 2007]" (2009, p. 181). Therefore, if Australian newspaper circulation in the past two years looks comparatively strong, this is only because it was starting from such a weak position. As Table 1 shows, Australia actually has the lowest paid circulation per capita of comparable countries.

Australia also has fewer newspaper titles (Table 2). Aside from Sydney and Melbourne, all other Australian cities have only one metropolitan daily newspaper. There are only 3.1 newspaper titles per 100 of population, placing Australia second last behind the United Kingdom in a five-country comparison.

However, if we move away from paid circulation to look instead at reach, a contrary picture emerges (Table 3). According to the reported data, Australian newspapers reach more adults than in all other comparable countries except Canada. Audience reach figures are heavily contested in Australia. As circulation has declined, readership has gone up which seems improbable. There have been claims that free copies of paid newspapers are being distributed to boost the figures. One right-wing blogger recently alleged that Fairfax was "giving away more free samples than Sunsilk [shampoo]" (*Vexnews*, 2009). While circulation is usually accepted as the far more reliable indicator, even if we do accept the comparative position of Australia on Table 3, it is noticeable that readership in Australia is declining at a much faster rate than in comparable countries. If circulation and readership declines represent some worrying trends so too do shifts in the economic basis of Australian newspapers.

Of all of the economic factors impacting upon newspapers, one of the most serious is the decline of classified advertising (Beecher, 2005; Meyer, 2004). Websites have taken a large share of such ads and even when newspapers do control a portion of online classifieds (e.g. Fairfax's Domain website for housing ads), they cannot charge advertisers the same amounts as they did for print ads when there were few competitors. In most analyses the loss of classified advertising is particularly detrimental to the long-term viability of newspapers. On this criterion, Australian newspapers appear to be especially vulnerable as they earn "almost two thirds of their revenue from advertising" (Tiffen and Gittins, 2009, p. 181). As Tiffen and Gittins point out, Australia's newspapers are "unusually dependent on classified advertising" (2009, p. 181) (Table 4). It is the "quality" broadsheet press that has been particularly reliant upon classifieds, and in December 2008 classified

TABLE 1

Paid circulation of daily newspapers per 1000 population, 1980 and 2007

	1980	2007
United Kingdom	417	308
New Zealand	334	216
United States	270	213
Canada	221	173
Australia	323	166

Source: Tiffen and Gittins (2009, p. 180).

TABLE 2
Number of paid newspaper titles per 1000 population, 2007

	2007
New Zealand	7.0
United States	6.0
Canada	3.7
Australia	3.1
United Kingdom	2.1

Source: Tiffen and Gittins (2009, p. 180).

advertising in the two most read broadsheets—the *Sydney Morning Herald* and *The Age*—dropped by 38 per cent (Tabakoff, 2009a).

The "Good" and "Bad" News for Australian Newspaper Companies

On other criteria, the evidence is less discouraging and more mixed. In the larger economic context, Australia weathered the fallout from the global financial crisis better than other industrial economies. The Australian Government claimed external evidence showed Australia had become, during that period, "the strongest performing advanced economy in the world" (Swan, 2009). Other external agencies confirmed Australia's relatively strong economic position (Glyn, 2009). Industry buyers also argued that the Australian advertising industry was in much better shape than, for example, in the United States (*Business Spectator*, 2009). All three Australian newspaper companies retain significant assets and income. Even the smallest of the three made over A$140 million in profit in 2007–8 (see Table 7). However, all anticipated difficult times ahead. News Corporation reported a sharp fall in operating profit in 2008 and estimated a further fall in 2008–9 profits. Murdoch signalled "leaner operations" in Australia including redundancies (Tabakoff, 2009a). APN News trimmed its earnings forecast for 2009 (Australian Association Press, 2009). Fairfax is rated particularly poorly by financial analysts. It has taken on large debts in recent years, making it particularly vulnerable in difficult economic circumstances. In 2008, Fairfax's shares dropped 68 per cent to a 15-year low (Maiden, 2008; Mayne, 2008).

However, in a weak retail and declining classifieds market, there is one specific economic advantage that Australian newspapers have over their counterparts in other countries. This advantage comes with an important caveat though: what is good

TABLE 3
Newspaper reach (as % of adults), 2007

	2005	2007	Change
Canada	77	75	−2%
Australia	61	54	−7%
New Zealand	50	49	−1%
United States	52	48	−4%
United Kingdom	32	34	+2%

Source: WAN (2008a).

TABLE 4
Contribution of classified advertising, 2007

	Classified advertising as % of advertising revenue
Australia	58
Canada	35
United States	31
United Kingdom	22

Note: No data on New Zealand were available.
Source: Tiffen and Gittins (2009, p. 180).

for Australian newspapers' economic viability is not necessarily good for Australian democracy.

Government Advertising as a Revenue Stream

A startling economic advantage that Australian newspapers enjoy is exemplified in Table 5 showing the top newspaper advertisers in Australia. In 2006, half of the top 10 newspaper advertisers were governments (four state governments and the Commonwealth government). As Table 6—which shows the top newspaper advertisers in the United Kingdom and United States in the same year—reveals, this level of press dependence on government advertising is unprecedented. In economic terms, the Australian newspaper companies have a unique stream of income but in democratic terms, the implications are worrying and especially in times of fiscal crisis and declining retail advertising when Australian newspapers will be even more reliant on government patronage.

Expanding Overseas and Moving Away from Newspapers as a Core Business

Another key advantage that Australian newspaper owners have had is a sympathetic ear from governments which have made media ownership law changes that have benefited the major players at a time when those players argued that ownership

TABLE 5
Top newspaper advertisers in Australia, 2006

	Advertiser	Expenditure (thousands of Australian dollars)
1	Coles	79,001
2	Woolworths	55,887
3	Commonwealth Government	54,079
4	Harvey Holdings Ltd	51,317
5	Victorian Government	35,128
6	New South Wales Government	29,426
7	Telstra	24,668
8	Queensland Government	24,461
9	Western Australian Government	20,204
10	Toyota	20,122

Source: WAN (2008a).

TABLE 6
Top newspaper advertisers in the United States and United Kingdom, 2006

United States Advertiser	Expenditure (thousands of US dollars)	United Kingdom Advertiser	Expenditure (thousands of British pounds)
Macy's	715,300	Dell Computer Corp	30,700
Verizon Communications	687,800	DFS Furniture	29,600
News Corp	553,000	Currys Group	22,300
Sprint Nextel	495,700	BT	22,200
AT&T	483,500	Tesco	20,800
General Motors	406,000	Argos	19,700
Ford	364,500	PC World	19,100
Valassis Communications	340,700	Sainsbury's	19,100
Time Warner	297,100	COI Communications	18,600
Toyota	282,400	British Sky Broadcasting	17,200

Source: WAN (2008a).

concentration was necessary in Australia due to economies of scale (Hilmer, 2002). The last major deregulation of media laws occurred in 2006 when the Coalition government amended media ownership laws to water-down restrictions on cross-media and foreign ownership. Previously, newspaper owners were prevented from owning either radio or TV assets in the same market. When these laws were relaxed, it prompted another buying up of assets. Murdoch bought a 7.5 per cent share in Fairfax, his long-time competitor. News Ltd also bought Federal Publishing Company's (FPC) newspaper, magazine and online assets (APC, 2008, pp. 3–4; *Sydney Morning Herald*, 2007). Fairfax merged with Rural Press (which reduced the number of major newspaper owners by one) in a A$9 billion deal and Fairfax also entered into a complex deal with two other media groups (Macquarie Media Group/Southern Cross) which netted it several radio stations. This was widely viewed as a pre-emptive move to enlarge Fairfax to avoid it being bought out by any other large player but it was an expensive strategy that contributed to Fairfax's A$2.3 billion debt. Even before the law changes, Fairfax had been buying up other newspaper assets, including in New Zealand (Table 7).

Overall, Fairfax is imitating two of the key strategies of its competitor, News Ltd— which grew from an Australian newspaper company into one of the world's major media companies. It has (1) expanded overseas and (2) developed into a multi-media company. As a multinational conglomerate, News Corporation has a wide, global reach and business interests across many different platforms. This has meant that its recent earnings have been driven more by film, DVD sales and pay TV which subsidise the newspaper arms of the business. For example, its Fox News channel yielded a 27 per cent rise in operating profit in 2008 (Tabakoff, 2009a). While News Ltd has books, films, television, cable television and information services, Fairfax has focused on radio, websites, agricultural magazines and music. APN News has focused on outdoor advertising. Therefore, although Australian newspapers are reliant on classified advertising as a high percentage of their advertising revenue, they also have other income sources. This is deliberate and Fairfax, for one, is banking on this strategy to save it. According to Fairfax Media, "Taken together, our

TABLE 7

Key business strategies of major newspaper companies in Australia and New Zealand, post-2000

	Fairfax	News Ltd/News Corp	APN News & Media
2007–8 revenue	A$2,934,007,000	US$32,996,000,000	A$1,226,400,000
2007–8 net profit (after tax)	A$387,490,000	A$5,790,000,000	A$140,100,000
Newspapers (Australia only)	*The Age* *The Australian Financial Review* *The Canberra Times* *The Sun-Herald* *The Sydney Morning Herald* *The Sunday Age* Plus over 45 regional/ community newspapers.	More than 110 national, capital city and suburban newspapers including: *The Advertiser* *The Australian* *The Courier-Mail* *Daily Telegraph* *Gold Coast Bulletin* *Herald Sun* *The Mercury* *NT News*	14 regional newspapers, more than 75 community publications.
Cost-cutting measures	As at 2009, Fairfax had a $2.3 billion net debt. 550 staff retrenched in 2008. Sold *Southern Star* in 2009 to reduce debt levels.	Using other profitable arms of the business to prop up declining newspaper profits. There have been staff cuts in 2008–9. News Ltd is also pursuing a strategy of centralisation to reduce costs.	In 2007, moved to outsource sub-editing functions for many of its NZ newspapers resulting in job losses. In 2008, APN indicated that it had shed 200 jobs as part of a cost-cutting programme.
New media—online newspapers, online classifieds and non-news websites	Started brisbanetimes.com.au and WAtoday.com.au to compete in the one-newspaper towns of Brisbane and Perth. Other websites include: *Australia* www.autoguide.com.au	2006: bought MySpace Other websites include: *Australia* Careerone.com.au Carsguide.com.au FoxSports.com.au	*Australia* Websites include: bargainfinda.com.au carfinda.com.au finda.com.au propertyfinda.com.au search4jobs.com.au

TABLE 7 (*Continued*)

Fairfax	News Ltd/News Corp	APN News & Media
www.businessquickfind.com.au	News.com.au	
www.buyersguide.com.au	www.nrl.com	
Countrycars.com.au	Taste.com.au	
Cuisine.com.au		
Domain.com.au (housing)	*Other*	
Drive.com.au	www.AmericanIdol.com	
Essentialbaby.com.au	www.askmen.com	
www.feedstuffs.com	Cricinfo.com	
www.holidaysaway.net	Fox.com	
Investmart.com.au	FoxSports.com	
www.jobsguide.com.au	hulu.com	
Leaguehq.com.au	www.ign.com	
www.lifeislocal.com.au	kSolo.myspace.com (online kar-	
Moneymanager.com.au	aoke)	
Mycareer.com.au	www.Milkround.com (graduate	
Mysmallbusiness.com.au	jobs)	
www.plantorder.com	www.RottenTomatoes.com	
www.propertyguide.com.au	www.Scout.com	
Realfooty.com.au	www.scrum.com	
Rsvp.com.au (dating ads)	www.SpringWidgets.com	
Rugbyheaven.com.au	www.WhatIfSports.com	
Stayz.com.au		
www.tackntogs.com		
Thebigchair.com.au		
TheVine.com.au		
Tradingroom.com.au		
www.yourguide.com.au		
New Zealand (NZ)		
www.trademe.co.nz		
www.stuff.co.nz		

TABLE 7 (Continued)

	Fairfax	News Ltd/News Corp	APN News & Media
Other businesses	Magazines and agricultural publications	Magazines and publications	Magazines and agricultural publications
		Other businesses (Australia and NZ)	*Australia and NZ*
	Satellite Music Australia	FOX Sports Australia	APN Outdoor Advertising
		Fox Studios Australia	
	Radio stations (Australia)	FOXTEL	*Radio (Australia)*
	2UE Sydney	Fuel TV Australia	APN's Radio division is the Australian
	3AW Melbourne	Harper Collins Australia	Radio Network (ARN).
	4BC Brisbane	Newsphotos	12 metropolitan stations:
	6PR Perth	Newspix	*Radio (NZ)*
	Magic 1278 Melbourne	Newstext	More than 120 stations
	4BH Brisbane	DVD Unlimited Online	
	96fm Perth	Distribution	
	(plus regional stations)		
		Plus:	
		Books	
		Television	
		Cable television	
		Film	
Free commuter newspapers	Started *Melbourne Express* in 2001—closed it down six months later.	*MX* began the day after *Melbourne Express* in February 2001. Is still going and launched in Sydney in 2005 and Brisbane in 2007.	

Note: This table does not include all acquisitions/sales—especially for News Ltd—it focuses on key areas of impact on Australian newspapers. APN News & Media revenue relates to year 2008 as the full annual report for 2007–8 was not available on the website at the time of writing.

Sources: APN (2008, 2009); Fairfax Media (2009); News Corporation (2009); *Adelaide Now* (2008).

growth in these key [non-newspaper] areas ... [now] generate 80% of the company's earnings" (2008, p. 3).

As Table 7 emphasises, Australian newspaper companies are diversifying and have interests in a wide range of new and old media. Their new media sites range from online classifieds selling cars and houses and advertising jobs as well as dating, social networking, sport and online karaoke. At Fairfax, this is called a "strategic reorientation of the company" (Fairfax Media, 2008, p. 3). It is one that media observers in Australia are watching keenly. As the only non-Murdoch source of broadsheet news, Fairfax is considered to be especially significant in Australia but its business strategies in recent years have also changed the company considerably. Critics have argued that Rural Press's commercial and "slash-and-burn ethos" have heavily influenced Fairfax's approach since the two merged (Green, 2008).

Table 7 shows some of the major business strategies the three companies have employed over the past decade. Aside from mergers and acquisitions, cost-cutting—including what the companies coldly describe as "head-count" savings (i.e. redundancies)—and developing websites have all been key strategies.

Journalism Practice and Journalism Content

Internationally, some newspaper companies have experimented with a range of journalism-practice models including "citizen journalism" and "crowd sourcing" but the Australian companies have been reluctant to experiment or innovate in this area, perhaps a reflection of the lack of competition they have traditionally faced. Their main response has been to cut staff and, journalists allege, to neglect training and development (MEAA, 2008). This has led to concerns that Australian media companies are performing a "suicide spiral" where "cost-cutting follows declining advertising revenues, leading to a poorer product which alienates readers, compounding circulation woes" (APC, 2008, pp. 2–5).

In terms of content, changes are noticeable. Tiffen (2009, p. 386) has observed that Fairfax "was the most punctilious in observing the separation of ... editorial matter and commercial considerations. But financial stress and management upheavals have eroded such traditions". In 2007, Fairfax journalists accused the company of "prostitution" over an advertising-driven front-page wraparound supplement on an edition of the *Sydney Morning Herald* (*Australian*, 26 October 2007, p. 3). Fairfax recently directed its advertising and editorial departments to work together to make "customised *editorial* products ... for special clients ... that are charged at a premium" such as "DriveLife, a motoring lifestyle section targeted at women ... tourism and back to school magazines" (WAN, 2009, italics added).

The advertisements on Fairfax's online newspapers have become more prominent and more difficult to ignore. They sometimes open up over the main headlines or follow the visitor's mouse around the screen. There are sometimes noticeable links with editorial content. In 2009, an ad for Apple notebooks opened over the top of *The Age*'s main news headlines and, beneath this, once the visitor closed the ad, a main news headline was: "Apple Opens New Melbourne Store". When the visitor clicked on this link a very promotional news story opened headed: "Thriving Apple Opens Melbourne Store". Sounding more like a PR release than a news story, the article gushed that: "Not even the recession seems able to dampen the iPod. Apple is still investing in its now-huge global retail empire ... Apple has 252 stores around the world ... [attracting] more than 3 million visitors a week" (Barker, 2009).

Colonising the Web

The new media push is indicative of the Australian newspaper companies trying to transplant their history of media and advertising dominance online. That they have been more successful in this than their overseas counterparts who face greater competition (for example, in the United States from Craig's List and Monster.com) is a bragging point for the Australian companies. According to Fairfax, "We have far stronger online positions than our peers overseas, yielding ... a greater share of online classified and display revenues" (Fairfax, 2008, p. 3). The APC claims that online newspaper website visitors have "doubled" in the last two years (APC, 2008, pp. 2–14) and among websites defined as specific "news" websites, the two major newspaper owners figure prominently although they also face competition from public broadcaster the ABC and from Google News and NineMSN (a joint venture between an Australian TV channel and Microsoft) (APC, 2008; Roy Morgan Research, 2006). One of the perks of cross-media ownership has been that the companies can heavily cross-promote their websites, including in editorial content of their newspapers. For example, when News Ltd's jobs classified website CareerOne was launched in 2000 and revamped in 2003, News Ltd newspapers ran promotional pieces in the "news" sections of its papers (*Media Watch*, 2003).

Aside from online newspapers and online classifieds, the companies have also bought websites that include online dating, sport, music, holidays and social networking sites such as MySpace. In many cases, they have been able to use these as advertising vehicles. For example, MySpace tailors advertising based on user's profiles.

The Online Product

Media organisations across the world are trying to work out how to make the Internet pay for all of the things that print traditionally did. A range of online models have been tried including annual subscription fees and "upselling" (where the site provides a basic service for free but then charges for added features such as ad-free sites or special news alerts, for a news archive or a crossword). With its niche and lucrative audience, Fairfax's *Australian Financial Review* is already subscription-based. In 2009, Murdoch signalled his company was going to begin charging for online content in a more widespread manner. At the time of writing there was only speculation about how this would be done but Chris Mitchell, editor-in-chief of News Ltd's only Australian broadsheet *The Australian*, confirmed that: "We will look to charge [for online content] in the next 12 to 18 months" (Tabakoff, 2009b). This suggests that both of Australia's national newspapers could be subscription-based.

This issue, coupled with the ongoing digital divide, raises concerns about access to information as the most successful online news sites are increasingly those addressed at "the concerns of the elite" (Sparks, 2003). Table 8 shows how the online audiences for both broadsheets and tabloids in Australia are younger than for the printed versions of the newspapers but they are also significantly more likely to be male, university educated, with high incomes and in professional or managerial work.

TABLE 8

Comparison of the audiences for four online Australian newspapers and their printed editions (%)

	National population	Broadsheets Sydney Morning Herald Printed	Online	The Age Printed	Online	Tabloids Daily Telegraph Printed	Online	Herald Sun Printed	Online
Men	49	56	62	52	64	56	64	52	61
Women	51	44	38	48	36	44	36	48	39
Have university education	41	73	76	75	77	34	58	37	59
Personal income under A$15k	33	21	20	23	20	29	21	31	23
Personal income A$50k+	26	45	51	41	49	27	52	27	41
Personal income A$70k+	14	29	32	22	29	12	31	12	20
Professional/manager	18	35	43	33	45	17	37	16	34
White-collar worker	19	22	23	28	25	20	23	21	30
14–17	7	3	3	4	2	4	3	4	4
18–24	12	10	15	10	15	11	12	11	15
25–34	17	16	26	16	29	16	27	14	24
35–49 years	27	27	30	27	31	27	33	27	33
Over 50 years	38	45	26	49	23	43	25	45	24

Note: Figures are rounded.

Source: Data supplied to the author by Roy Morgan Research (Single Source Australia, July 2007 to June 2008).

Compounding the potential impact of News Ltd's move to charging is that, after Murdoch's announcement, Fairfax responded that it would also be "open" to charging for online news and even to forging some sort of agreement with its rival News Ltd (Zappone, 2009). Given the concentration of ownership in Australia and the role that newspapers (whether printed or online) have played, any such agreement would have a major impact on Australian journalism and, more broadly, on the Australian public sphere.

Conclusion

What has occurred in the US newspaper industry is severe and, as Andrew Edgecliffe-Johnson (2009) points out, is the result not only of declining advertising and the rise of digital media but also because "an often monopolistic grip over local classified advertising had sustained an array of titles". For an Australian audience, this is all very familiar. As Max Suich (2008, p. 13) notes: "The rationalisation the US industry is going through, occurred here [in Australia] 20 years ago". It is the evening dailies in the United States that have been losing the most circulation—five times more than declines for morning newspapers (WAN, 2008b). Australia has no evening or afternoon newspapers to lose. In comparative terms with the United States, United Kingdom, Canada and New Zealand, Australian newspaper circulation is already lower, reliance on dwindling classified advertising is higher, circulation has declined more rapidly than other comparable countries and recent figures show that newspaper reach, although higher, is declining faster. Buying new assets, diversifying into non-newspaper businesses and shedding staff have been key strategies in Australia. Oligopoly, a lack of diversity and government patronage for established players (in terms of both advertising and public policy), have helped the established Australian media owners to a degree that is remarkable, but in a chaotic and rapidly changing news environment, they may still be vulnerable and not least because of their own complacency and short-term economic goals. Conversely, cartel behaviour, online colonisation and greater commercialisation may save them as businesses but dent their effectiveness as journalism organisations. One of the key issues for the future therefore is not merely whether the Australian newspapers will survive but whether their business strategies may see them lose what made them unique and valued in the first place.

ACKNOWLEDGEMENTS

This research was supported by the Australian Research Council's Discovery funding scheme (project DP0663208) and the University of Melbourne Arts Faculty's Research Grant Scheme. The author wishes to thank Rodney Tiffen for providing access to resources and his forthcoming work, Stephanie Younane for her able research assistance and Michael Gawenda for his feedback. The usual disclaimer applies—any errors or omissions that remain are my responsibility.

NOTE

1. There is some confusion on this point. The WAN report (2008a) states that "Year-on-year data of September 2007 show an overall circulation decline of just over one percent". But a table in the report (Table 3.b) indicates a decline in total paid-for dailies between 2006

and 2007 of −5.35 per cent (more than for the United States (−3.03 per cent) and the United Kingdom (3.46 per cent)). The report also states that "new circulation laws apply [in Australia] since 2007; figures cannot be accurately compared with previous years data" [*sic*].

REFERENCES

ADELAIDE NOW (2008) "News Corp Posts $5.8bn Profit", 6 August, http://www.news.com.au/adelaidenow/story/0,,24136344-5005962,00.html.

APN (2008) *Annual Report 2007*, Sydney: APN.

APN (2009) *2008 Full Year Result*, Sydney: APN.

AUSTRALIAN ASSOCIATION PRESS (2009) "APN Forecasts Flat Profit for 2009", 7 November.

AUSTRALIAN PRESS COUNCIL (APC) (2008) *State of the News Print Media in Australia: 2008 Report*, Sydney: APC.

BARKER, GARRY (2009) "Thriving Apple Opens Melbourne Store", *The Age*, 19 May (posted 1:34 pm).

BEECHER, ERIC (2005) "The Decline of the Quality Press?", in: Robert Manne (Ed.), *Do Not Disturb: is the media failing Australia?*, Melbourne: Black Inc, pp. 7–27.

BUSINESS SPECTATOR (2009) "Interview: media held to account", 11 March, www.businessspectator.com.au.

EDGECLIFFE-JOHNSON, ANDREW (2009) "When Newspapers Fold", *Financial Times*, 16 March, http://www.ft.com/cms/s/0/d00f013a-1261-11deb816-0000779fd2ac.html?nclick_check=1.

FAIRFAX MEDIA (2008) *Annual Report*, Sydney: Fairfax Media, http://www.fxj.com.au/announcements/sep08/FXJ_Annual_Report_FINAL_v3.pdf.

FAIRFAX MEDIA (2009) *Annual Report*, Sydney: Fairfax Media.

GLYN, JAMES (2009) "Australian Financial System Weathers Crisis Better Than Others, Says RBA", *The Australian*, 19 August.

GREEN, JONATHAN (2008) "Jaspan Dumped as *Age* Editor", *Crikey*, 27 August, http://www.crikey.com.au/2008/08/27/jaspan-dumped-as-age-editor/.

HILMER, FRED (2002) "Why the Cross-media Laws Should Go—for all our sakes", *The Age*, 5 June, p. 15.

MAIDEN, MALCOLM (2008) "Crunch Time for Fairfax as It Faces Its Debt, Cutting Dividends", *The Age*, 6 December.

MAYNE, STEPHEN (2008) "Can the Murdoch and Fairfax Families Support Their Debt Laden Public Empires?", *Crikey*, 16 October.

MEDIA ENTERTAINMENT AND ARTS ALLIANCE (MEAA) (2008) *Life in the Clickstream: the future of journalism*, Redfern, NSW: MEAA.

MEDIA WATCH (2003) ABC Television, broadcast 11 August, http://www.abc.net.au/mediawatch/transcripts/s921911.htm.

MEYER, PHILLIP (2004) *The Vanishing Newspaper*, Columbia: University of Missouri Press.

NEWS CORPORATION (2009) *Annual Report*, www.newscorp.com/report2008/AR2008.pdf.

ROY MORGAN RESEARCH (2006) "Old Media Dominates Online", 1 March, http://www.roymorgan.com/news/press-releases/2006/464/.

SIMONS, MARGARET (2008) "Readership v Circulation: curious newspaper mathematics", *Crikey*, 14 March.

SIMONS, MARGARET (2009) "A Bumper Boost: crunching the Fairfax circulation figures", *Crikey*, 16 February.

SPARKS, COLIN (2003) "The Contribution of Online Newspapers", *Trends in Communication* 11(2), pp. 111–26.

SUICH, MAX (2008) "Facts Spoil a Good Story", *The Age*, 15 December.

SWAN, WAYNE (2009) "Press Release: mid-year economic and fiscal outlook 2009–10", 2 November, http://www.treasurer.gov.au/DisplayDocs.aspx?doc=pressreleases/2009/113.htm&pageID=003&min=wms&Year=&DocType=0.

SYDNEY MORNING HERALD (2007) "News Ltd Buys FPC's Magazines, Newspapers", 2 April.

TABAKOFF, NICK (2009a) "Fairfax Dive Undermines Raising Chances", *The Australian*, 21 February.

TABAKOFF, NICK (2009b) "Readers Not Averse to Paying for Online Content", *The Australian*, 11 May.

THE ECONOMIST (2006) "More Media, Less News", 26 August.

TIFFEN, RODNEY (2009) "Australian Journalism", *Journalism* 10(3), pp. 384–6.

TIFFEN, RODNEY (2010) "The Press", in: Stuart Cunningham and Graeme Turner (Eds), *The Media and Communications in Australia*, Crows Nest, NSW: Allen and Unwin, pp. 81–95.

TIFFEN, RODNEY and GITTINS, ROSS (2009) *How Australia Compares*, 2nd edn, Melbourne: Cambridge University Press.

VEXNEWS (2009) "They Can't Give It Away", *Vexnews Online*, http://www.vexnews.com/news/2777/they-cant-give-it-away-the-ages-genuine-sales-in-freefall-despite-giving-away-more-free-samples-than-sunsilk/, accessed 6 March 2009.

WEST AUSTRALIAN (2009) "Embattled APN Eyes Return to the Black", 25 February.

WINDSCHUTTLE, KEITH (1988) *The Media*, Ringwood, Victoria: Penguin.

WORLD ASSOCIATION OF NEWSPAPERS (WAN) (2008a) *World Press Trends* [database], Goteburg: WAN.

WORLD ASSOCIATION OF NEWSPAPERS (WAN) (2008b) "World Press Trends: newspapers are a growth business", Media release, Goteburg, 2 June.

WORLD ASSOCIATION OF NEWSPAPERS (WAN) (2009) "Strategies for Newspaper Success from Australia", Paris, 3 March.

ZAPPONE, CHRIS (2009) "Fairfax Media Ready to Discuss Charging for Online News: CEO McCarthy", *Business Day* (Fairfax Digital), 24 August, http://www.businessday.com.au/business/fairfax-ready-to-discuss-charging-for-online-news-ceo-mccarthy-20090824-evh4.html.

FROM CREDIBILITY TO RELEVANCE
Towards a sociology of journalism's "added value"

Heikki Heikkilä, Risto Kunelius, and **Laura Ahva**

Uncertainty about the future of journalism and what may be expected from the news media have generated special interest in how news organisations connect with the audience. In this paper three analytical approaches are described: institutional connection, market connection and public connection. While the two former approaches are more familiar to the media industry, it is argued that the latter seems theoretically and empirically more useful. Future studies on journalism's public connection should consider the fact that the relevance of journalism for its readers is embedded in the social fabric of their everyday lives. This approach needs to be informed by the key sociological concepts of networks, habits and interests. At the end of the paper a short outline of an audience research project recently launched in Finland is introduced.

Introduction

If journalism as an economic activity and the news business are to survive, we must find ways to alter practice and the skills to create new economic value. Journalism must innovate and create new means of gathering, processing, and distributing information so it provides content and services that readers, listeners, and viewers cannot receive elsewhere. And these must provide sufficient value so audiences and users are willing to pay a reasonable price. (Picard, 2009)

In his recent speech at the Reuters Institute for the Study of Journalism, Robert Picard (2009) poignantly captured the tone in which business realities are currently interpreted in news organisations. In his story, journalists are no longer in charge of the transmission of information. Thus, their importance does not automatically follow from the social position they used to have and journalists need to find ways to prove convincingly that they perform a valuable task.

Picard's lecture indicates how the earlier separate economic and professional discourses about journalism are being converged. In newsrooms, this convergence lends support from the realisation that journalists are urged to prove that their stories, separately and in total, have "added value". Added value has become a key point for strategic decisions about forms and contents of journalistic output and human and technical resources allocated for journalistic work.

This strategic language of added value is incorporated into general ideas and imaginaries about technology, culture and democracy. In this paper our interest lies in how current concerns about the future of journalism and the quest for its added value are mobilising varying ideas about audiences. Our general argument is that journalism research needs to develop ways of understanding the value of journalism which help journalists to see the added value of their work more clearly. Our discussion paves the way to describing briefly a two-and-a-half-year research project "Towards Engaging Journalism" that aims constructively and critically to contribute to discussions about the future of journalism (in Finland).

Three Modes of (Dis)connection

From its mediating position between the system-world and the life-world, journalism is expected to help in connecting these two realms together. In the face of a dramatic downturn of circulations that swept across newspapers in Finland in the 1990s,[1] the general idea of a disconnection in this relationship was widely shared. Analytically speaking, this disconnection is perceived, made sense of and acted upon, through three lines of thought. These perspectives refer to a particular set of problems and while seeking ways to solve them, they draw inspiration from different theories and ways of analysing the audience. Our framework here is purely analytical. In their process of sense-making, news organisations may very well tap into more than one approach.

The first disconnection (see Table 1) is perceived at the institutional level, wherein a healthy relationship of journalism and readership is defined in the vocabulary of political science and representative democracy. With regard to *institutional connection* it is assumed that journalism has a social duty to provide truthful and relevant information to audiences constituted of informed citizens. The audience, in turn, is expected to use public information for keeping themselves updated in public affairs, forming their opinions and participating politically with the means available (voting, involvement in political parties, associations etc.). Low turnouts in elections, decreasing interest in public affairs, and

TABLE 1

Three modes of connections between journalism and audience

	Institutional connection	Market connection	Public connection
Journalism–audience relationship	Provision of information to facilitate opinion formation and political participation.	Serving audiences with a rich variety of information goods. Appropriating media use to individual tastes and preferences.	Helping audiences to transform into publics in issues they find salient.
The disconnection	Low voter turnouts decreasing trust in public institutions.	Fragmentation of audiences.	Social networks separated from political and news discourse.
Audience research	Asking audiences to give their collective report on how the news media maintain their social role.	Mapping individuals' values and consumer preferences to understand how identities and cultures emerge from individual choices.	Understanding how people orient to public affairs, or withdraw from them.
Impact on journalism	Collective legitimation of the social role of journalism. Competition between credible "news brands".	Focus on everyday life, tailor-made sections, expression of emotions.	New means for listening to and reporting on citizens' deliberations.

evidently growing mistrust of public institutions registered in surveys, however, suggest that there are serious problems with the institutional connection.

In surveys measuring public trust the relationship between journalism and audience is often taken formally and collectively. The motivation for understanding this relationship is restricted to social roles of institutions and citizens, respectively. The relationship is also regarded structurally hierarchical, as people understood against the role of audience are given only two options: they can either say they believe in news and trust in journalism, or that they do not. Their response gains weight as aggregation insofar as it is able to signal clearly, whether or not journalism as an institution enjoys credibility and legitimacy.

Given these restraints, it is not surprising that the institutional legitimacy of journalism appears to be good, or mediocre at least. Thus, surveys in their own right do not give clear answers to what added value means for journalism. What it seems to have brought into journalism, however, is that credibility has begun to be seen as an asset in competition between "news brands". For instance, in its newest annual report YLE, the public broadcasting company of Finland, rather complacently announces that:

> YLE News reaches Finns and they also trust the news. From one year to the next, YLE News is the Finnish news source that they consider the most trustworthy (grade 4.8/5). (YLE, 2009, p. 8)

The second connection is drawn in the market. Habitually, the *market connection* is measured by circulations, ratings and how these figures break into varying target groups. This information has for long instructed media organisations to provide information goods for varying uses: "not everything to anyone, but rather something to everyone".

Due to the abundance of information on goods and services, audiences are seen to be fragmenting, reflecting distinctive tastes, lifestyles and interests. When faced with this enigmatic environment, news organisations—with the help of audience research—aim at moving beyond the collective and the formal framework, to examine audiences against the fluid context of consumer cultures. It is in this framework where applications of market research partly run parallel with theories of "active audience" developed within cultural audience studies.

For Finnish news organisations, the most influential of such tools is the international market research RISC Monitor (Research Institute for Social Change). RISC Monitor aims to detect changes in consumers' lifestyles, attitudes and values. One of its main components is the so-called RISC Quadrant, which organises immense amounts of survey data into a diagram building on two dimensions: Responsibility–Enjoyment, on the one hand, and Stability–Expansion, on the other (J. Hujanen, 2006). In the horizontal continuum, *responsibility* emphasises respondents' collective approach to community and public issues; *enjoyment* refers to individual empowerment linked with seeking pleasure, challenges, competition and risks. In the vertical continuum, *stability* denotes a need for security and reassurance through maintaining familiar ways of acting; *expansion* stands for pursuing active life, openness to new ideas and experimentation.

Unlike surveys measuring trust, RISC Monitor provides applicable ideas about how added value can be translated into news policies, routines and modes of storytelling. In the light of her interviews in Finnish news organisations, Jaana Hujanen (2006, pp. 190–1) detected a number of measures derived from RISC Monitor. These include, for instance, a tendency to portray everyday life from a positive (not negative or sensationalist) perspective, providing reader guidance, making use of emotions in coverage and rendering journalists' personalities more transparent.

A third, public connection between journalism and readership assumes a shared (political) culture wherein members of a polity may recognise issues affecting their lives and find opportunities to act upon them, when necessary (Couldry et al., 2007, p. 6; Taylor, 2004). In this framework, journalism is expected to be helpful for audiences (understood as products of the mass media) and to transform them into publics with regard to a given issue which is salient for them. It is not assumed that public connection always yields to public action but rather that such action opportunities are readily available. In order to build a public connection, journalism is supposed to mediate effectively between informal interactions within "communities" and formal procedures of a "society".

Public connection marks an important category with which social theory and contemporary social and media criticism have evaluated news (and modern society more in general). Most of these accounts tend to agree in that public connection would be essential for democracy and desperately called for but not likely to be achieved under the current circumstances. John Dewey, for one, wrote that:

> The ties which hold men together in action are numerous, tough and subtle. But they are invisible and intangible. [Despite the fact that] we have the physical tools of communication as never before, the thoughts and aspirations congruous with them [social relations] are not communicated, and hence are not common. Without such communication the public will remain shadowy and formless, seeking spasmodically for itself. (Dewey, 1954, 146 [1927])

Theoretical ideas about public connection have inspired academic audience research, but have been of relatively little use in news organisations. One notable exception is the work conducted by the Harwood Group that have been instrumental for the public journalism movement (Sirianni & Friedland, 2001). In one report the Harwood Group (1993) explored how the ways citizens make sense of public concerns differ from those of institutions (including journalism). The main difference, according to the report, lies in that whilst experts tend analytically to separate public concerns into manageable policy issues, citizens tend to draw connections between seemingly separate issues. These empirical findings have served as a basis for newsrooms in their attempt to find deliberation at unofficial "third places" such as barbershops, churches and playgrounds, and develop journalists' skills to listen and cover these deliberations (Harwood Group, 1996).

Recent academic audience research in this field suggests that public connection does exist, but that its forms are very diverse and also vulnerable (Couldry et al., 2007, p. 185; Eliasoph, 1998). The diversity stems from the fact that the ways people orient to public affairs are anchored to the habitual practices with which people discuss public affairs and, to choices on what they watch or read in the media. Vulnerability, on the other hand, owes to uncertainty over how patterns of news consumption and discussions are linked to wider social contexts, for instance, those of public action. All this, in turn, seems to depend on how *relevant* the public connection (and practices sustaining it) are for people. This question cannot be adequately addressed without paying specific attention to social contexts of everyday life. Any study aimed at understanding them, we argue, needs to draw inspiration from the sociology of communication.

"Public" in the "Social": Groundwork for Relevance

In a sense, both professional discussions about the "crisis of journalism" and recent research interest in the *public* connection, call for a better relationship between the complex and problematic terrain of the life-world of the readers and journalism as an institution.

Elaborating the idea of public connection needs to begin with clarifying what is meant by the *public*. The *public*, of course, is a notoriously complicated and contested term, and its several articulations with other concepts (space, sphere, opinion, etc.) complicate matters further. We argue here that a useful point of departure for elaboration would be a pragmatist understanding of the public as a *particular kind of social formation* (Dewey, 1954 [1927]; Blumer, 1946). In this sense, a *public* does not exist outside of or independent from other forms of interaction. Actual relationships of actual people are always shaped by a multiplicity of forces. Clearly, institutional logics (power) and market-driven logics of consumer cultures (money) play an important part in this. But just as clearly, "readership" cannot be completely reduced to merely these forces and dimensions. The public in this respect often plays the role of a residue of democratic hope in the language of journalism.

Whatever the "public" meaning and value of journalism may be, it is *anchored into the social*. Thus, the adjective public does not refer merely to an abstraction where people direct their attention to generally important issues or where they assume an institutionally defined role as citizens. In its full meaning, the public also refers to a sense of relevance of issues, viewpoints, and styles of mediated communication. In this sense, *relevance* has to be anchored into the everyday social interaction of the members of any given public. Thus, understanding the public connection directs attention to the ways in which the use of the media becomes a part of this fabric of the life-world.

As a preliminary conceptual shape for an empirical investigation, we begin to construct the public value dimension of journalism by focusing on three overlapping concepts that help to capture essential features in social interaction. Our point of departure is the notion of *networks*. In order to grasp the relationships of networked everyday life, we want to point to *habits* (more or less unreflective routines) and *interests* (more conscious or rationalised calculations) as analytic features of the networked relationships of everyday life. Below, we offer a sketch of how these concepts can be useful in analysing the public connection. In order to activate some of the existing wisdom of the field, we illustrate our points by incorporating earlier findings of audience research to our design of empirical study.

Networks

Given that publics consist of relationships between people, public meanings and their relevance, are thus embedded in the *social networks* in which people live and interact with each other. One of the most well-known studies in communication of interpersonal networks is Katz's and Lazarsfeld's (1956) *Personal Influence*. As is well known, this analysis was driven by concerns about the institutional and market value of the media. Yet, the research team was perceptive to a broader sociological phenomenon at hand.

Ideally, we should have liked to trace out all of the interpersonal networks in the community to see how they link up with each other; instead, we have had to content ourselves with a cross section of influential-influence relationships. (Katz & Lazarsfeld, 1956, p. 309)

Through its very basic design and results, the work offers solid information about the readership and sociological dynamics of journalism. Its still useful core idea is that the readership is, ultimately, a crucial part of the distribution system of mass media.[2] This is not only so in technical terms of transmitting the news and views further but also in terms of shaping the messages and embedding them into a social network structure. The degree in which distribution translates into *influence* depends on people's personal relationships and their networks of trust.

If social networks of people are indeed a part of media's distribution system, we should not only focus on information and influence, but also pay attention to other uses and structures of relevance *shaped in social networks*. Thus, questions of what the news *means* or how journalism *connects* with people should be studied in the context of everyday networks. This is particularly urgent today, as ICTs facilitate new modes of sharing the news and peer production. The most tangible and impressive example of social media networks at the moment is, of course, Facebook. We should not, however, ignore the fact that networks have always been there and that all these may be important in how meanings and relevance are created.

Habits

Network as a concept is useful in situating the public in conjunction with interpersonal and horizontal interaction among people. The notion of *habits* (or routines), in turn, helps to identify how part of the interaction among people is directed beyond the given network. While orientating to each other, members of a public are also oriented towards other social formations or imaginaries. This is the potential dual nature of all media rituals. Berelson's (1954 [1949]) classic study during a newspaper delivery strike in New York illustrates how broad and *socially* defined the meanings of newspaper reading were. In addition to the informational and rational uses, the study found several meanings that spring from social relations, for instance, "respite" as a way of escaping relations and "social prestige" as a way of earning rank. These observations give additional evidence of how the dynamics of the public is operated in networks. More to the point about public habits and routines, though, is the finding that during the strike, New Yorkers felt an intense sense of being "lost" without the newspaper. Berelson explained it like this:

> Apparently, the newspaper represented something like a safeguard and gave the respondents an assurance with which to counter the feelings of insecurity and anomie pervasive in a modern society. (1954 [1949], p. 125)

Phatic functions of journalism have been recognised by a number of other studies ever since. Silverstone (1993), for one, theorises them related to television and the production of "ontological security" for its viewers. A recent contribution to the analysis of media rituals by Couldry (2003) argues that the media have sustained the "myth of centre" of society and that this myth has been elemental for media professionals in reassuring that they are connected to their readership. It may very well be that the myth of the centre is withering away, as mediated communication is no longer simply or even mainly mass communication (Livingstone, 2004). Despite this argument, it seems plausible to argue that some sort of imaginaries (or myths) are needed for sustaining or creating the public connection to increasingly abstract social processes. Indeed, it seems plausible to argue that in order for interpersonal habits to function, there has to be a certain shared, but perhaps vaguely articulated, ontological ritualistic dimension. The "we" created in interpersonal habits and rituals is always situated in a sense of reality partly constructed and reproduced in the same rituals.

Interests

Habits seem important in how people imagine communities while drawing their attention to the public world. The notion of *interests*, on the other hand, refers to a more intentional, strategic, or even calculated aspect of this orientation. In broad terms, interest denotes that a person finds her/himself a stakeholder in a given social issue and evaluates facts and arguments related to the topic against his or her values or beliefs. Thus, the public relevance of journalism grows from the moment when a public (readers embedded in social networks) sees its interests represented in journalism (fairly or unfairly).

In the great part of the history of journalism, interests have been organised through collective identities based on, for instance, social class or political party. It has been clear for some that the interplay between interests and collective identities has become much more complicated, albeit this does not necessarily show in how interests are represented in news. In his classic study of the *Nationwide* audience, Morley (1983) noted that the ways in which the readership decodes messages does not immediately correlate with their social status. From this viewpoint, he called for a nuanced design for audience research that aims to:

> understand the potential meanings of a given message, we need a "cultural map" of the audience to whom that message is addressed—a map showing the various cultural repertoires and symbolic resources available to differently placed sub-groups with the audience. The "meaning" of a text or message must be understood as being produced through the interaction of the codes embedded in the text with the codes inhabited by the different sections of the audience. (Morley, 1992, p. 118)

Ever since Morley, cultural studies have effectively deconstructed the notion of class-based interest as a frame of interpretation.[3] Another important qualification is made by Couldry et al. (2007), who reiterate a classic pragmatist thought that publics are called into being when problems are recognised at the level of everyday life. Thus, the interests related to a problem originate from the seemingly private sphere, for instance, social networks. Where, when and why interests arise and what is the role of journalism in "pre-political" negotiations in social networks is very much an open question that needs to be addressed by empirical audience research.

Towards Engaging Journalism: An Outline of a Project

A: My eldest daughter very actively follows what's going on [in the news] and she often draws circles around news stories or clips something out of the newspaper . . . Last spring she took her final exam in high school and first I thought that this habit was about preparing for that. But it didn't stop there, and I think that is good . . . The stories she marks with a pen are usually about the life of people, not politics . . . It can be a cartoon, a photo of a person with a funny expression, or about an unusual event in a foreign country.

Q: Yeah, does she want to draw other people's attention to the stories, or is it just her personal habit?

A: Well, I think she wants to draw attention, even if it is for herself, really. She wants to show them to me, and then sometimes we discuss them. But part of this is about consumption too, I mean, if we are considering buying something. Or they can be stories about recycling.

The quotation is from a research interview in which a mother describes her daughter's personal habit of reading the newspaper at home. In the excerpt it becomes apparent that family constitutes a *network* (for many of us, perhaps the most everyday and elementary one) in which news and public affairs are discussed. In a miniature form, it shows how the daughter plays her part in the distribution system of news within the family, and perhaps even beyond that.

The aspect of everyday *habits* becomes clear in the mother's account. The daughter's way of reading the newspaper in some ways affects the whole family. Stories, adverts, cartoons and photographs become means to communicate and negotiate among the family members. In addition, it becomes apparent from the quotation that newspaper reading carries instrumental value, at least in the eyes of the mother. At first, she assumed that reading the newspaper would help her daughter to pass a forthcoming exam, but obviously its value is carried further. The *interests* surface at the end of the quotation, when the mother explains that newspapers may provide consumer information. Some of it informs rational choice, but some of it may develop into political action at the micro-level (recycling).

This brief moment in an interview and the peek inside the life of news which it provides, intend to demonstrate how the ideas presented in this paper begin to relate to empirical data. Given that the excerpt describes everyday life very narrowly, the observations drawn from it are still rather thin and obvious. Our ongoing research project "Towards Engaging Journalism" aims to go further from this through analysing the relevance of journalism from the perspective of social networks. The study attempts to shed light on what these social networks are like, how and where people discuss public affairs, and the role of newspapers in their discussions. The participants in the project represent nine groups of people. In each of them participants are linked to each other either through work, interests, or leisure. For instance, one group is composed of high school teachers, the second from members of the union for unemployed people and the third of choir members. The groups are not only regarded as representatives of their particular network, but each participant in the groups contributes to a broader understanding by informing discussions about his or her other social networks: families, neighbours, colleagues and friends.

The research was launched by interviewing all 78 participants individually. These interviews enable us to identify varying patterns of networking and uses of news media. Followed by interviews, each group will gather approximately once a month across a year to discuss how public affairs and their life-worlds intersect and whether or not news proves to be useful in their networks. In addition to understanding networks, this study has a particular interest in the future of journalism. The groups evaluate news stories, express criticism or suggest improvements for news organisations. The project co-operates with five newspapers, which are asked to respond to the input of the groups. The researchers will also organise joint meetings for readers and journalists in order to encourage interaction between news professionals and readers.

Conclusion

For a long time, the value of journalism was mostly measured against its institutional dimension: Does it help citizens make informed choices in elections and do citizens trust public institutions? On the other hand, journalism's value was measured against its commercial success. Are people willing to pay for news? Until recently, news organisations faced fairly low levels of competition in their area of business, and thus, the institutional role of journalism and its market value were kept separated from each other. Journalism was considered to be business with a social purpose.

We are now witnessing an increasingly intensified struggle over the value of journalism. This debate is played out at various levels. In newsrooms and professional discourses within them, the institutional and the market value are being converged into a quest for "added value". What it actually comprises, and how is it pursued, has become a key point for strategic decisions in media organisations.

This paper sketches out a third option for added value: How does journalism foster a public connection between the readership and the public world? Following our argument in this paper, such an approach has two objectives. Firstly, it needs to *detach* the notion of public from its earlier, dominantly institutional frameworks, in which being a member of a public is an abstraction that rests upon institutionally defined practices of citizens and voters. Secondly, it needs to *resist*, or at least balance out, the market-driven discourse that understands audiences as individual consumers.

In order to pursue this we argue that it is important to situate audience research at the level of the social fabric of everyday life and focus systematically on how the relevance of journalism is negotiated in social networks, in habitual aspects of media use, and against interests that occasionally stem from informal discussions in varying networks. Understanding the relevance of journalism in this context is arguably useful in expanding professional imagination for future journalists.

NOTES

1. The total circulation of newspapers in Finland peaked in 1990 (2.8 million copies). By 1999 it had dropped by 16 per cent (E. Hujanen, 2005, p. 34). The total loss of circulation (450,000 copies) is almost equal in size with the population of Helsinki.

2. Lazarsfeld et al. (1944) questioned the earlier belief in strong effects of mass media in a way that resembles sociological disputes in the nineteenth century. In France, for writers like Tarde the "public" functioned via sociability and complex communication and conversation networks (Mattelart, 1996, p. 251ff). Darnton (1999) illustrates how this may have functioned: "In short, the communication process took place by several modes in many settings. It always involved discussion and sociability, so it was not simply a matter of messages transmitted down a line of diffusion to passive recipients but rather a process of assimilating and reworking information in groups, that is, the creation of collective consciousness or public opinion".

3. Curran (1990) once termed this development in cultural studies "New Revisionism". He implied that the development cultural studies' active audience argument was a revival of the weak effects thesis.

REFERENCES

BERELSON BERNHARD (1954 [1949]) "What Missing a Newspaper Means?", in: Paul Lazarsfeld and Frank Stanton (Eds), *Communications Research 1948–49*, New York: Harper & Brothers, pp. 111–29.

BLUMER, HERBERT (1946) "The Crowd, the Mass and the Public", in: Alfred Lee (Ed.), *New Outline of the Principles of Sociology*, New York: Barnes & Noble.

COULDRY, NICK (2003) *Media Rituals. A critical approach*, London: Routledge.

COULDRY, NICK, LIVINGSTONE, SONIA and MARKHAM, TIM (2007) *Media Consumption and Public Engagement: beyond the presumption of attention*, New York: Palgrave Macmillan.

CURRAN, JAMES (1990) "The New Revisionism in Mass Communication Research: a reappraisal", *European Journal of Communication* 5(2), pp. 135–64.

DARNTON, ROBERT (1999) "An Early Information Society: news and the media in eighteen-century Paris", *American Historical Review* 105(1), http://historians.org/info/AHA_history/rdarnton. htm, accessed 15 August 2009.

DEWEY, JOHN (1954 [1927]) *The Public and Its Problems*, Athens, OH: Swallow Press/Ohio University Press.

ELIASOPH, NINA (1998) *Avoiding Politics: how Americans produce apathy in everyday life*, Cambridge: Cambridge University Press.

HARWOOD GROUP (1993) *Meaningful Chaos: how do people form relationships with public concerns*, Dayton, OH: Kettering Foundation.

HARWOOD GROUP (1996) *Tapping Civic Life: how to report first, and best, what's happening in your community*, Washington, DC: Pew Center for Civic Journalism.

HUJANEN, ERKKI (2005) *Lukijakunnan rajamailla. Sanomalehden muuttuvat merkitykset arjessa [On the Fringes of Readership. The changing meanings of newspaper in everyday life]*, Jyväskylä: Jyväskylä Studies in Humanities.

HUJANEN, JAANA (2006) "RISC Monitor Audience Rating and Its Implications for Journalistic Practice", *Journalism* 9(2), pp. 182–99.

KATZ, ELIHU and LAZARSFELD, PAUL (1956) *Personal Influence: the part played by people in the flow of mass communications*, Glencoe, IL: Free Press.

LAZARSFELD, PAUL, BERELSON, BERNARD and GAUDET, HAZEL (1944) *People's Choice*, New York: Columbia University Press.

LIVINGSTONE, SONIA (2004) "The Challenge of Changing Audiences. Or, what is the audience researcher to do in the age of the internet?", *European Journal of Communication* 19(1), pp. 75–86.

MATTELART, ARMAND (1996) *The Invention of Communication*, Minneapolis: University of Minnesota Press.

MORLEY, DAVID (1983) *The Nationwide Audience*, London: British Film Institute.

MORLEY, DAVID (1992) *Television, Audiences & Cultural Studies*, London: Routledge.

PICARD, ROBERT (2009) "Why Journalists Deserve Low Pay", presentation at Reuters Institute for the Study of Journalism, University of Oxford, 6 May.

SILVERSTONE, ROGER (1993) "Television, Ontological Security and the Transitional Object", *Media, Culture & Society* 15(4), pp. 573–98.

SIRIANNI, CARMEN and FRIEDLAND, LEWIS A. (2001) *Civic Innovation in America: community empowerment, public policy and the movement for civic renewal*, Berkeley and Los Angeles: University of California Press.

TAYLOR, CHARLES (2004) *Modern Social Imaginaries*, Durham, NC: Duke University Press.

YLE (2009) "YLE's Year 2008", http://www.yle.fi/fbc/pdf/2008Annualreport.pdf, accessed 23 November 2009.

EXPLORING THE POLITICAL-ECONOMIC FACTORS OF PARTICIPATORY JOURNALISM
Views of online journalists in 10 countries

Marina Vujnovic, Jane B. Singer, Steve Paulussen, Ari Heinonen, Zvi Reich, Thorsten Quandt, Alfred Hermida, and **David Domingo**

This comparative study of user-generated content (UGC) in 10 Western democracies examines the political economic aspects of citizen participation in online media, as assessed by journalists who work with this content. Drawing on interviews with more than 60 journalists, we explore their perceived economic motivations for an ongoing redefinition of traditional journalistic roles, as UGC becomes an increasingly dominant feature of news websites.

Introduction

It is an obvious statement that the media, including newspapers, are an intrinsic part of the economics of knowledge. Recent changes in media industries, heightened by technological evolution, underscore the need to monetize evanescent information and information exchange, both of which have economic significance (Babe, 1995).

This article explores journalists' reactions to the ongoing migration of readers to Web-based news sites and online newspapers, focusing on their perceived economic motivations for engaging with the participatory journalism phenomenon. Interviews for this study were conducted with journalists, including key editors, at the market-leading online newspapers in seven European countries, along with Israel, Canada and the United States. The analysis is tied to the neoclassical–neoliberal understanding of economics, markets and technology, as well as to globalization processes. We seek to contribute to an understanding of the economic motives behind participatory journalism practices and their effects on the self-perceptions of journalists in a rapidly changing media environment.

Political Economy of the Media

Economics, markets and technology are what Babe (1995) labels hegemonic doctrines. Journalism is a particularly relevant enterprise in this context, as its core premises include a desire to democratize communication, widen information exchange and narrow the gap in civic participation. Journalism by this idealistic definition has true democratic value only if it is seen as serving the public's need to be informed promptly and accurately (Curran, 1997).

Media industries have been consolidating since at least the early 1980s (Bagdikian, 2004). In the context of neoliberal capitalism, this ownership convergence means the industry currently functions much as any other profit-making sector. But as digital networks have grown, media organizations have found it difficult to find an economic model to sustain their own growth. The main difficulty is in the inadequacy of the old economic model, based on traditional factors of labor, capital and production (Babe, 1995). Once unlimited information joins the mix, production processes are transformed and outcomes inevitably become unpredictable.

In the logic of late capitalism, in which everyone in everyday life is potentially engaged with creating and distributing information (Jameson, 1991), the concept of citizen as informational laborer (Castells, 2001) seems to have considerable appeal for media industries. They might have been expected to dive into the opportunity to benefit from what is in essence a democratic notion of participation in a globalized, networked society (Castells, 2001). But recent trends suggest it would be premature to declare any profit-making expedition in online journalism a success. Faced with the ubiquitous nature of information technology but largely failing to capitalize on its transformational power, the media industries are instead discovering the weakness of the traditional economic model with which they remain most comfortable (Baker and Hart, 2008). For the most part, media owners have largely demonstrated the bandwagon mentality characteristic of disorganized capitalism (Lash and Urry, 1988).

Before we engage with a deeper understanding of participatory journalism in political economic terms, we would like to emphasize that user-generated content appears to be part of the commodification of work under the capitalist system. Lash and Urry (1994) argue that in the new capitalism guided by information economies, time has been divided between work and leisure, and hence between production and consumption. Yet UGC blurs the distinction between work and leisure—the work that users do in creating content is largely seen as a leisure activity. Moreover, users both produce and consume information almost simultaneously.

The political economy of participation in online news production and consumption thus merits further exploration and continuous reconceptualization. In the next section, we outline the theoretical premises on which our interview data analysis is based.

Participatory Journalism: Concepts and Practice

A number of scholars have attempted to define and explore contributions to online news media from people who are not professional journalists. Deuze (2001) refers to the phenomena as open-source journalism; others connect it to public journalism (Black, 1997; Paulussen et al., 2007). The term "user-generated content" (UGC) has become widely accepted. However, Bowman and Willis's (2003) term "participatory journalism" seems more apt to us because the phrase places the phenomenon in the larger context of participatory culture, or what Jenkins (2006) calls "convergence culture." In this context, media industry efforts to distribute their products across multiple platforms end up empowering the users to appropriate, reshape and redistribute those products.

Jenkins reminds us that two mid-1980s phenomena—the growth of digital technologies and the spread of cross-media ownership—enable the current convergence of digital media: for Jenkins, convergence culture is a result of the industry's economic desire to distribute content across multiple platforms. "Digitization set the conditions for convergence [while] corporate conglomerates created its imperative," he argues (2006, p. 11).

As the journalists in our study suggest, participatory media channels created in online newsrooms do not stem solely from democratic goals related to fostering participatory culture and empowering the public. Rather, as Jenkins argues, "convergence culture is a paradigm shift—a move from the medium-specific content toward content that flows across multiple media channels . . . driven by the economic calculations" of the media industries. The industries, he says, embraced convergence to create a platform for shaping consumer behavior and devising "multiple ways of selling content to consumers"; media executives also hoped to cement consumer loyalty at a time when market fragmentation and the rise of file sharing threatened old ways of doing business (Jenkins, 2006, p. 254). Even though market logic is evident behind participatory or convergence culture, the process itself is rather new; it leaves gaps through which the public can assert its bottom-up power to change the rules of participation and exert its own rules and needs.

Dean's notion of communicative capitalism, defined as "a form of late capitalism in which values heralded as central to democracy take material form in networked communication technologies" (2008, p. 104), is also useful here. Participation in this sense is no longer a simple expression of democratic actions by citizens but rather the result of the market value of participation, as well as the expression of commodity culture and information consumption.

Journalism is a result of historical and social development; informed by new media technology, it is taking a new form to meet current social circumstances. Some communication functions previously institutionalized by the news media can now be performed by individuals and non-journalistic organizations, as we previously argued in proposing a model to explore how participatory journalism works at various stages of news production (Domingo et al., 2008).

This paradigmatic shift involves both technological development and economic logic. As our data will show, it works in large part by building consumer loyalty or brand sustainability. It also can be driven by a management desire to cut the cost of information gathering by engaging audiences to perform a journalistic function previously performed by paid professionals.

Method and Data Gathering

This study builds on our preliminary study of participatory features on the websites of 16 leading quality newspapers in eight European countries (Belgium, Croatia, Finland, France, Germany, Slovenia, Spain and the United Kingdom) and the United States (Domingo et al., 2008). We have added four newspapers from two new countries, Canada and Israel. Slovenia has been dropped from the list, but we added another newspaper from Croatia, which provides insights from the only European nation outside the dominant European Union (see Table 1). Following our preliminary study in 2007, we interviewed journalists at each online newspaper in 2008, particularly seeking insights from an executive in charge of newsroom strategies, an editor overseeing the news production

TABLE 1
Countries, online newspapers and number of interviewees included in this study

Country	Newspaper online	Web address	Interviewees
Belgium	*De Standaard*	standaard.be	3
	Gazet van Antwerpen	gva.be	3
Canada	*The Globe and Mail*	theglobeandmail.com	3
	National Post	nationalpost.com	3
Croatia	*24 Sata*	24sata.hr	3
	Vecerbji list	vecernji.hr	3
Finland	*Iltalehti*	iltalehti.fi	3
	Helsingin Sanomat	Hs.fi	3
France	*Le Monde*	lemonde.fr	3
	Le Figaro	lefigaro.fr	3
Germany	*Spiegel*	spiegel.de	3
	Frankfurter Allgemeine	Faz.net	3
Spain	*20 Minutos*	20minutos.es	3
	El País	elpais.com	4
Israel	*Ynet*	ynet.co.il	3
	NRG	nrg.co.il	3
	Ha'aretz	haaretz.com	3
United Kingdom	*Guardian*	guardian.co.uk	2
	Telegraph	telegraph.co.uk	5
United States	*Washington Post*	washingtonpost.com	3
	USA Today	usatoday.com	3

process, and a journalist directly dealing with audience participation. A total of 65 journalists and news executives were interviewed in all. We developed a code sheet for qualitative coding based on the preliminary results of the 2007 study. Most researchers used qualitative data analysis software such as Atlas TI or Max QDA; otherwise, interviews were coded manually. Because qualitative coding is polysemic in nature, an "other" option also was available in each coding category to accommodate statements that did not fit one of the pre-determined options.

This paper draws on data from our "Motives for Participatory Journalism" coding category to identify rationales behind the pursuit of participatory journalism initiatives. Options included journalistic, technological, economic and political/ideological motives, along with a view that the phenomenon was "inevitable" and unstoppable, necessitating media involvement. Although our focus in this article is on economic motives, interviewees often referenced overlapping motives within an economic context, as described below.

Because of the large amount of data, we have chosen to identify themes across different countries and newspapers. Although media cultures and traditions vary, we found that the similarities greatly surpassed the differences, and a thematic analysis best served our purposes. Questions that guided our thematic analysis were:

- What economic discourses and motivations for participatory journalism are identified by journalists at the websites of leading national newspapers?
- How do these journalists talk about economic motivations behind participatory journalism?

Results and Discussion

Our analysis identified three primary themes:

1. Branding, particularly as a means of generating newspaper consumer loyalty.
2. Building traffic, involving strategies to boost the usage numbers that "still scream profit," as one journalist said.
3. Keeping up with or beating the competition, a bandwagon effect.

Journalists in smaller markets also discussed cost-cutting rationales, as described below.

Branding: Building Consumer Loyalty

This was the most dominant theme across the interviews analyzed in this study, appearing in every country. The fragmentation of both media and audiences seems to be prompting a move away from traditional mass media marketing strategies and toward journalism as strategic communication, both to address needs of newspaper consumers and to shape their behaviors. Editors and news managers are of course more likely than others in the newsroom to take a marketing perspective on participatory journalism, while those lower in the management hierarchy can be expected to emphasize journalistic motives. Even so, strategic communication methods seem to be gaining visibility for journalists at all levels: in a fragmented market, newspapers are seen as brands through which community is built and consumer loyalty created. "You must never ignore the community that you've got at the moment because you do that at your peril," as the chief information officer of Telegraph Media Group (UK) put it.

Moreover, this loyalty helps build an economically sustainable brand, creating a competitive edge and spurring further technological development. For example, the community manager at *Het Belan van Limburg* and *Gazet van Antwerpen* in Belgium felt that open communication between the newsroom and the marketing department is key to a successful newspaper industry. Hence marketing and strategic communication become prerequisites for creating communities, interest groups or even stakeholders:

> We want to create a platform where local football clubs can have their own page. We are trying to implement a lot of social network features in this platform, so that we got a lot of interaction between clubs and their fans. The idea is that such a platform should not focus on news only, but it must rather stimulate the whole social network around and between these football clubs ... So for instance if [the marketing department] wants to set up something for a certain target group, I will try to think of possible ways to do that.

Brand recognition also seems to be driving the perceived need to integrate social networking features and traditionally non-journalistic forms such as blogging—or an excuse for engaging in non-journalistic forms at the potential expense of reporting and news production. User blogs, for example, can encourage user loyalty by, among other things, providing a value to users that other sites cannot deliver. The communities' editor of telegraph.co.uk said:

We're not giving people a blog. We are giving people an audience ... You can go and start a blog on Blogger today, but nobody is going to read it apart from your mum ... and it would take you months to build an audience. You can start a blog with the *Telegraph* today, and I can deliver tens of thousands of people straight to your blog from Day One.

In Israel, where economic motives were commonly coupled with motives of inevitability, the *NRG* editor commented, "We are a part of the global market, and we have to keep up with it by adding new features ... and constantly checking needs and demands." Maintaining and increasing audiences was seen as important, and wooing potential customers was a primary strategic goal. If used well, editors of Israeli newspapers believed, participatory journalism can strengthen the website "product." One *Ha'aretz* editor remarked:

People's attention threshold today is a lot lower, and they want more and more ... The Web surfer moves rapidly from sites, to the radio, to the TV ... I want to make him stay here as long as possible. How do I achieve this goal? I engage him and motivate him to stay with me. He can add his own contents, see them and arrange the Web page to his preference.

In the United States, managing editors combined journalistic and economic motivation, but participatory journalism was seen as a necessary tool to boost brand loyalty by drawing and retaining audiences. The need to attract more audience members as stakeholders also was reflected in a move to create niche communities, for instance around topics such as cruises. An editor at *USA Today* said:

As Web content becomes increasingly distributed, as it becomes more and more difficult to maintain that walled-garden destination, you have to pose the question, "How do I maintain my brand?"

Similarly in Canada, *National Post* editors discussed both journalistic and economic motivations but pointed out that newspaper readers are not attracted solely by information delivery. They recognized that marketing builds brands and strengthens relationships between readers and newspapers. One editor said:

I think the role of a newspaper, the role of any media organization, is to inform the public. At the same time, you want to feel that connection with your reader ... Without readers, there's no need for newspapers. Your job is to attract as many people as you can ... [but] to be very cynical, from an advertising perspective, that is what you're delivering—the readers. So, yes you have to keep them occupied, keep them interested.

Journalistic motivations were especially prominent for British, Finnish, French, Israeli and Spanish interviewees, who highlighted a national tradition of journalism based on public service. Some journalists rejected economic discourses or repeatedly provided connections between journalistic and economic motivations. Some saw economic or marketing motives as negative and as something that "others" do, while journalists protect the function of media in the public sphere. The editor-in-chief of the Spanish *20 Minutos* explained:

I think that the mere fact that they thought it [UGC] a good marketing action is a victory and a recognition that other types of journalism are possible. Because they are implicitly acknowledging that the official classical discourse that we were taught in college is no longer valid ... Today the receiver is a producer as well, and they may be much wiser than us all [the journalists] ... That is wonderful, and in any case the changes are happening, and we just can be attentive to adapt to them and foster them.

Boosting Traffic: "Numbers Still Scream Profit"

Increasing website traffic was another commonly identified strategic goal. In Croatia, for example, it was clear that the pressure for more usage was applied top-down, from management to the newsroom. Journalists said their role was to develop participation channels that would attract new visitors and make existing users stay longer on the site. Growth in usage was often coupled with a desire to strengthen brand loyalty, especially in regards to experimentation with social networking and community building.

In Croatian as well as in Spanish and US organizations, this trend was seen as a strategy for the industry to survive rather than a way to promote public debate, fulfill a democratic role or endeavor to close the participatory gap. In Britain, the *Guardian*'s network editor remarked that the point is not so much to grab new consumers as to offer a variety of features to encourage them to stay longer on the site. The head of editorial development at the same newspaper talked about "a crude kind of metric," where only numbers matter: "In cold commercial terms, it's [about] page impressions." However, he immediately added, "it does improve journalism. You can see why that kind of debate and discussion is an interesting proposition."

The *Telegraph*'s communities' editor expressed strong links between branding and increasing traffic. The "My Telegraph" section of the newspaper website, which provides a space for users to create their own blogs and post other content, was designed specifically to attract consumers and encourage them to stay, building a community that will generate traffic:

I really think once we get My Telegraph to a significant size, once we can make My Telegraph the central arena for all the community stuff we do, we're suddenly going to see UGC representing a huge chunk of traffic.

Because it is easily quantified and resonates with managers and investors, website traffic is a popular way to demonstrate market value. Unlike print, the number of online "hits" any item receives can be tracked, an appealing way of arguing for the relevance of online news. The online news manager of the Belgium *Het Belang van Limburg* and *Gazet van Antwerpen* illustrates this point well:

A nice example concerned a caravan fire on a camping site in Dilsen-Stokkem, a small town in Flanders. For the paper edition of our newspaper, the story wasn't relevant enough, because there was nobody injured and almost no damage. But for the community there, the people living on or nearby the camp site, it was of course the talk of the town. Coincidentally we had one of our citizen journalists who made a piece about the fire, and we placed that story on the website. Well, the story generated quite a lot of website traffic. I won't say that the number of visitors was tremendous, but the good thing about it is that all these people read the story on our website and not somewhere else on the Internet.

The marketing director for the website of France's *Le Figaro* said participatory journalism is an extremely valuable tool for drawing traffic, in part because user content boosts visibility on search engine indices. In Croatia and Israel, editors and journalists were sometimes unable to articulate why or how they decided to develop participatory journalism offerings, but user participation was often described as a method to entice readers to stay longer on the site, as well as to attract new visitors who might become loyal customers.

The high traffic volume on US media websites was highlighted by journalists in other countries, notably the United Kingdom, Germany, and Croatia. At the *Washington Post* and *USA Today*, managing editors identified traffic as crucial to defining the success of the online news site. They saw increasing traffic as contributing to the larger goal of building loyalty, not only among the public in general but also among smaller groups with whom they can engage on a deeper level. The desire, they suggested, is to lure readers who will keep coming back. One US editor said:

> The extent to which we can involve them and let them involve themselves in our news reports, our journalism, is the way that we will become more a part of their lives and ultimately will help guarantee our success in the future.

Canadian interviewees also stressed the twin needs to maintain and increase page views. Online news sites were seen as a way to show the bright future of journalism. For example, the idea of building communities was expressed in strategic terms rather than as a desire to facilitate the exchange of information and news. "You build a community because you are a business and you don't want to lose readers," explained a *Globe and Mail* editor. "The more people you can persuade to look at your pages, the more money you can make." At the Canadian *National Post*, many of the UGC strategies were seen as ways of getting people to the site and persuading them to stay there. As one editor said:

> The bottom line is to improve the traffic ... Why don't newspapers just use YouTube? I'll tell you the answer right now. It is because from a business perspective, we need to keep people on our site.

Another *National Post* editor expressed the true value of numbers:

> There is a real business case to be made here. You know what, people are spending five, six, seven minutes on our website, engaging with the material ... That becomes a business thing. It becomes a very tangible number that you can go back to the core business of the Web and go to advertisers and say, "You can actually capitalize on that."

The Bandwagon Effect: Meeting and Beating the Competition

The *National Post* editor's quote also highlights the importance of media competition, the third theme that recurred throughout our interviews. Journalists described competition both with other strong newspapers and with sites that aggregate news rather than producing it. The second kind of competitiveness seemed especially to irk interviewees, who expressed concern about which type of business would win the war for consumers. The impact of news aggregation sites that "tap into our market," as one Croatian editor put it, was a concern expressed across the countries we studied. Journalists saw the future of online newspapers as depending on the success of the news aggregation sites as well as search engines such as Google or Yahoo!, which use indexing to draw attention to some websites and away from others.

The bandwagon effect often seemed to have been part of the rationale for initiating participatory journalism options. The head of editorial development of guardian.co.uk described it this way:

> Speaking generally about the newspaper industry in Britain, there's been a big thing with "Me Too." There's been no [thought] in this country about why are we doing it ... Some of our efforts, and many of our competition's efforts have been about "Me-Tooism." What are we doing? Why are we doing this? Why do we have that? ... Why should it exist? ... There's been a great deal of fear about missing out. There's a scramble to get this stuff up and running.

The desire to build communities among users as "principal stakeholders" was connected to competition across media outlets. In Belgium, for example, a dominant theme was that of "experimenting" with participatory journalism because it is a general trend everywhere. But facilitating UGC also was seen as enabling newspapers to compete with social networking sites such as Facebook. An editor of the Finnish newspaper *Kaleva* said:

> Newspapers are searching [for a] means to be part of their readers' everyday life and doings. They see that people use social media anyway, and in a worst case, we just stay put and observe. Often these materials would work also with us. Is the newspaper able to offer this, in a way, "social media platform"? Is it in our brand, can we renew like this?

In Germany, the issue of competition was addressed in conjunction with the need to find a business model for online newspapers and the need to maintain quality journalism—in order to compete with media that have little or nothing to do with traditional journalism. One journalist said:

> These are completely new media, communities that have nothing to do with news journalism ... There is no business model of news journalism. The business model is to obtain a certain reach or circulation, to play out some banners, to reach some type of community. There is no reason why we should be the only ones that profit here and not some other aggregators of reach. I think that this is the ongoing, non-trivial transformation.

"Inevitability," one of our motivation options, was also stressed in connection with competition. Israeli interviewees, for example, emphasized competition with other in-country media outlets; they saw fostering user participation as a way of remaining competitive and improving quality. In Croatia and Belgium, editors said the small size of the market made competition for readers especially important. In Croatia, *24 Sata* and *Vecernji list* compete with two other daily newspapers for a market of little more than four million; UGC and other participation strategies were seen as offering competitive advantages by making the websites more attractive.

One other theme emerged in interviews in two smaller countries, Croatia and Belgium, but not elsewhere: UGC as a cost-saving strategy, at least in management's eyes. Although some journalists said media executives saw participatory journalism as a cost-saving strategy for the industry, they expressed scepticism about that approach. In Belgium, the general editor-in-chief of *De Standaard* and *Net Hieuwasblad* remarked:

In the eyes of our management committee, UGC is considered something fantastic. They hope that they will be able to provide more content with less journalists ... I still try to convince the management to invest in UGC gathering and get rid of the idea that UGC is cost-saving. We need to invest in it.

Similarly, in Croatia, editors of both newspapers said that personally they saw UGC in terms of saving time rather than money. But, they said, management saw it as a money-saving opportunity—one that already had resulted in layoffs in traditional newsrooms, as well as workforce outsourcing from traditional to online newsrooms.

The fact that this cost-saving theme was not widely articulated by journalists in larger countries may indicate particular pressures in the smaller national markets, but it does not necessarily mean this strategy is not employed by media managers elsewhere. Other themes, such as increasing traffic or creating competitive advantages—in other words, the role of participatory journalism in saving the newspaper industry—simply may have been more dominant at the time the interviews were conducted. With eight researchers involved in this project, it also is possible that different interviewers focused on different issues.

Conclusion

Although this study left many unanswered questions about the economic motivations behind UGC, the results were intriguing. Similarities in how journalists in different countries understood and talked about UGC were striking. Economic discourses were often coupled with other motivations, such as technological, political and ideological ones, as well as the idea that the phenomenon was inevitable. However, we have sought here to highlight the economic discourses in order to probe those concepts more deeply. We identified three universal themes: branding strategies designed to build loyalty, strategies for increasing website traffic as a route to profitability and a bandwagon effect driven by a desire to remain competitive. Journalists in smaller countries, notably Belgium and Croatia, also said their managers viewed UGC as a cost-saving strategy—a view our interviewees tended not to share.

However, they did view participation at least partly in terms of its market value, part of the commodity culture to which the media contribute (Dean, 2008). Our findings also tap into what Jenkins (2006) identified as convergence culture. We identified considerable support for his proposition that convergence is driven by a need to develop consumer loyalty amid market fragmentation that threatens old ways of doing business. In fact, one German editor stressed exactly that incapability of the classic business model to function successfully in the new media environment.

Journalists in Europe, Israel, Canada and the United States all seem to be grappling with a vision for the future of the media that employ them. They see participatory journalism as valuable, but at the same time most admit a lack of clear vision about why and how to adopt it, either for democratic or economic purposes. As one *Guardian* editor remarked, "Every month, it is another fight to see how far we can push our traffic and see how far we can go beyond our competitors." This quote and others provided above suggest a strong market logic behind participatory journalism. But it is also true that few journalists were willing to submit completely to an economic discourse. "Our audiences and our customers and our users who enjoyed consuming our content also wanted a place to be heard," the *Telegraph* communities editor said. The editor of *USA Today* argued for the centrality of fostering democratic rights to debate and discuss: "Beginning to create that social network around the news was a very *USA Today* thing to do—the nation's newspaper with the nation's conversation." Such statements suggest that journalists have not given up on the contributions of traditional journalism to democratic discourse despite pressures created by technological and economic change.

Finally, the participation discourses analyzed here suggest the inevitability of constant compromise with the industry's existing economic models. In Dean's (2008) understanding of communicative capitalism, it is possible in a networked society to provide a sense of participation—a sense of engagement, democratic activity and contribution—without real democratic action. Interviewee statements such as "people feel more involved" or "you can hit submit, see your comment there ... you feel you've engaged," support the premise that true participation may be an illusion. Even so, professional journalists seem eager to hold on to the traditional value of journalism by helping develop participation opportunities that move beyond counting hits to the creation of a more meaningful dialogic exchange.

REFERENCES

BABE, ROBERT E. (1995) *Communication and Transformation of Economics: essays in information, public policy, and political economy*, Boulder, CO: Westview Press.

BAGDIKIAN, BENH (2004) *The New Media Monopoly*, Boston: Beacon Press.

BAKER, MICHAEL and HART, SUSAN (2008) *The Marketing Book*, 6th edn, Oxford: Elsevier.

BLACK, JAY (Ed.) (1997) *Mixed News: the public/civic/communitarian journalism debate*, Hillsdale, NJ: Lawrence Erlbaum.

BOWMAN, SHAYNE and WILLIS, CHRIS (2003) "We Media: how audiences are shaping the future of news and information", Report for The Media Center at The American Press Institute, http://www.hypergene.net/wemedia/weblog.php, accessed 17 August 2009.

CASTELLS, MANUEL (2001) *The Internet Galaxy: reflections on the Internet, business, and society*, New York: Oxford University Press.

CURRAN, JAMES (1997) "Rethinking the Media as a Public Sphere", in: Peter Dahlgren and Colin Sparks (Eds), *Communication and Citizenship: journalism and the public sphere*, London: Routledge, pp. 27–58.

DEAN, JODI (2008) "Communicative Capitalism: circulation and the foreclosure of politics", in: Megan Boler (Ed.), *Digital Media and Democracy*, Cambridge, MA: MIT Press, pp. 101–23.

DEUZE, MARK (2001) "Understanding the Impact of the Internet: on new media professionalism, mindsets and buzzwords", *EJournalist* 1(1), http://www.ejournalism.au.com/ejournalist/deuze.pdf.

DOMINGO, DAVID, QUANDT, THORSTEN, HEINONEN, ARI, PAULUSSEN, STEVE, SINGER, JANE B. and VUJNOVIC, MARINA (2008) "Participatory Journalism Practices in the Media and Beyond", *Journalism Practice 2*(3), pp. 326–42.

JAMESON, FREDRIC (1991) *Postmodernism, or, the Cultural Logic of Late Capitalism*, London: Verso.

JENKINS, HENRY (2006) *Convergence Culture: where old and new media collide*, New York: New York University Press.

LASH, SCOTT M. and URRY, JOHN (1988) *The End of Organized Capitalism*, Gerrards Cross: Polity Press.

LASH, SCOTT M. and URRY, JOHN (1994) *Economics of Time and Space*, London: Sage.

PAULUSSEN, STEVE, HEINONEN, ARI, DOMINGO, DAVID and QUANDT, THORSTEN (2007) "Doing It Together: citizen participation in the professional news making process", *Observatorio (OBS) Journal* 3, pp. 131–54.

TWITTERING THE NEWS
The emergence of ambient journalism

Alfred Hermida

This paper examines new para-journalism forms such as micro-blogging as "awareness systems" that provide journalists with more complex ways of understanding and reporting on the subtleties of public communication. Traditional journalism defines fact as information and quotes from official sources, which have been identified as forming the vast majority of news and information content. This model of news is in flux, however, as new social media technologies such as Twitter facilitate the instant, online dissemination of short fragments of information from a variety of official and unofficial sources. This paper draws from computer science literature to suggest that these broad, asynchronous, lightweight and always-on systems are enabling citizens to maintain a mental model of news and events around them, giving rise to awareness systems that the paper describes as ambient journalism. The emergence of ambient journalism brought about by the use of these new digital delivery systems and evolving communications protocols raises significant research questions for journalism scholars and professionals. This research offers an initial exploration of the impact of awareness systems on journalism norms and practices. It suggests that one of the future directions for journalism may be to develop approaches and systems that help the public negotiate and regulate the flow of awareness information, facilitating the collection and transmission of news.

Introduction

Twitter is one of a range of new social media technologies that allow for the online and instant dissemination of short fragments of data from a variety of official and unofficial sources. The micro-blogging service emerged as a platform to help organize and disseminate information during major events like the 2008 California wildfires, the 2008 US presidential elections, the Mumbai attacks and the Iranian election protests of 2009 (Lenhard and Fox, 2009). Twitter's emergence as a significant form of communication was reflected in the request by the US State Department asking Twitter to delay routine maintenance during the Iranian poll as the service was an important tool used by Iranians to coordinate protests (Shiels, 2009). Media restrictions led websites of *The New York Times*, the *Guardian* and others to publish a mix of unverified accounts from social media as "amateur videos and eyewitness accounts became the de facto source for information" (Stelter, 2009).

The micro-blogging service illustrates what Hayek described years before the invention of the Internet as "the knowledge of particular circumstances of time and place" (1945, p. 519). He proposed that ignorance could be conquered, "not by the acquisition of more knowledge, but by the utilisation of knowledge which is and remains widely dispersed among individuals" (Hayek, 1979, p. 15). At that time, he could not have predicted the development of a system that has created new modes of organising knowledge that rely on large, loosely organized groups of people working together electronically. A variety of terms have been used to describe this: crowd-sourcing, wisdom of crowds, peer production, wikinomics (Benkler, 2006; Howe, 2008; Surowiecki, 2004; Tapscott and Williams, 2006). Malone et al. (2009) suggest that the phrase "collective intelligence" is the most useful to describe this phenomenon, which they broadly define as groups of individuals doing things collectively that seem intelligent. I suggest that micro-blogging systems that enable millions of people to communicate instantly, share and discuss events are an expression of collective intelligence.

This paper examines micro-blogging as a new media technology that enables citizens to "obtain immediate access to information held by all or at least most, and in which each person can instantly add to that knowledge" (Sunstein, 2006, p. 219). It argues that new para-journalism forms such as micro-blogging are "awareness systems", providing journalists with more complex ways of understanding and reporting on the subtleties of public communication. Traditional journalism defines fact as information and quotes from official sources, which in turn has been identified as forming the vast majority of news and information content. This news model is in a period of transition, however, as social media technologies like Twitter facilitate the immediate dissemination of digital fragments of news and information from official and unofficial sources over a variety of systems and devices. This paper draws from literature on new communications technologies in computer science to suggest that these broad, asynchronous, lightweight and always-on communication systems are creating new kinds of interactions around the news, and are enabling citizens to maintain a mental model of news and events around them, giving rise to what this paper describes as ambient journalism.[1]

Definition of Micro-blogging

Micro-blogging has been defined as a new media technology that enables and extends our ability to communicate, sharing some similarities with broadcast. It allows "users to share brief blasts of information (usually in less than 200 characters) to friends and followers from multiple sources including websites, third-party applications, or mobile devices" (DeVoe, 2009). Several services including Twitter, Jaiku and Tumblr provide tools that enable this form of communication, although status updates embedded within websites such as Facebook, MySpace, and LinkedIn offer similar functionality.

One of the most popular micro-blogging platforms is Twitter. Between April 2008 and April 2009, the number of Twitter accounts rose from 1.6 million to 32.1 million (Vascellaro, 2009). This growth was partially fuelled by increased media attention to Twitter as celebrities such as Oprah Winfrey adopted the service (Cheng et al., 2009). Despite the rapid uptake, Twitter is still only used by a select number of people. In the United States, 11 percent of American adults use Twitter or similar tools (Lenhard and Fox, 2009) and research suggests that 10 percent of prolific Twitter users account for more than 90 percent of messages (Heil and Piskorski, 2009). However, Twitter users tend to be the people who are interested in and engaged with the news. Studies show that the largest single group of tweeters, making up 42 percent, are between the ages of 35 and 49, and that the average Twitter user is two to three times more likely to visit a news website than the average person (Farhi, 2009).

Twitter is a flexible system that routes messages sent from a variety of devices to people who have chosen to receive them in the medium they prefer. It asks users the question: "What are you doing?" Messages are limited to 140 characters as the system was designed for SMS messages, but there are no limits on user updates. The "tweets" can be shared publicly or within a social network of followers. Users have extended their use of Twitter to more than just answering the initial question. The service has been described as an example of end-user innovation (Johnson, 2009) as users have embraced the technology and its affordances to develop conventions such as the use of hashtags and the @ reply.

Twitter and Journalism

Twitter has been rapidly adopted in newsrooms as an essential mechanism to distribute breaking news quickly and concisely, or as a tool to solicit story ideas, sources and facts (Farhi, 2009; Posetti, 2009). UK national newspapers had 121 official Twitter accounts by July 2009, with more than one million followers (Coles, 2009). In a sign of how far Twitter has come, the UK-based Sky News appointed a Twitter correspondent in March 2009 who would be "scouring Twitter for stories and feeding back, giving Sky News a presence in the Twittersphere" (Butcher, 2009).

The relative newness of micro-blogging means there is limited academic literature on the impact on journalism. Studies such as the one by Java et al. (2007) have looked at the motivation of users, concluding that micro-blogging fulfils a need for a fast mode of communication that "lowers users' requirement of time and thought investment for content generation" (Java et al., 2007, p. 2). In their analysis of user intentions, they found that people use Twitter for four reasons: daily chatter, conversation, sharing information and reporting news. At least two of these—sharing information and reporting news—can be considered as relevant to journalism, though arguably so could daily chatter and conversation around current events. Two of the three main categories of users on Twitter defined by Java et al.—information source and information seeker—are also directly relevant to journalism.

When Twitter is discussed in the mainstream media, it is framed within the context of established journalism norms and values. There has been a degree of bewilderment, scepticism and even derision from seasoned journalists. New York Times columnist Maureen Dowd (2009) described it as "a toy for bored celebrities and high-school girls". There has also been discussion on whether the breadth and depth of news reporting would suffer as more reporters sign up to Twitter (Wasserman, 2009). Of particular concern has been how journalists should adopt social media within existing ethical norms and values (Posetti, 2009), leading news organisations such as the New York Times (Koblin, 2009), Wall Street Journal (Strupp, 2009), and Bloomberg (Carlson, 2009) to institute Twitter policies to bring its use in line with established practices.

Micro-blogging has been considered in the context of citizen journalism, where individuals perform some of the institutionalized communication functions of the professional journalist, often providing the first accounts, images or video of a news event (Ingram, 2008). The value of user-generated content is assessed by professional norms and values that are presumed to guarantee the quality of the information (Hermida and Thurman, 2009). The issue commonly discussed in media commentaries on Twitter and journalism is the veracity and validity of messages. Concerns by journalists that many of the messages on Twitter amount to unsubstantiated rumours and wild inaccuracies are raised when there is a major breaking news event, from the Mumbai bombings to the

Iranian protests to Michael Jackson's death (Arrington, 2008; Sutter, 2009). The unverified nature of the information on Twitter has led journalists to comment that "it's like searching for medical advice in an online world of quacks and cures" (Goodman, 2009) and "Twitter? I won't touch it. It's all garbage" (Stelter, 2009).

The professional and cultural attitudes surrounding Twitter have their roots in the working routines and entrenched traditional values of a journalistic culture which defines the role of the journalist as providing a critical account of daily events, gathered, selected, edited and disseminated by a professional organization (Schudson, 2003; Tuchman, 2002). It reflects the unease in adopting a platform which appears to be at odds with journalism as a "professional discipline for verifying information" (Project for Excellence in Journalism, nd).

However, there are indications that journalism norms are bending as professional practices adapt to social media tools such as micro-blogging. During the Iranian election protests of June 2009, news organisations published "minute-by-minute blogs with a mix of unverified videos, anonymous Twitter messages and traditional accounts from Tehran" (Stelter, 2009). Six months earlier, the BBC included unverified tweets filtered by journalists alongside material from correspondents in its breaking news coverage of the Mumbai bombings (BBC, 2008). The BBC justified its decision on the grounds that there was a case "for simply monitoring, selecting and passing on the information we are getting as quickly as we can, on the basis that many people will want to know what we know and what we are still finding out" (Herrmann, 2009). This approach means journalists adopt an interpretive standpoint concerning the utility of a tweet around a news event or topic, making a choice as to what to exclude or include. By filtering and selecting what tweets to publish, the gatekeeper role is maintained and enforced. Journalists apply normative news values to determine if a specific tweet is newsworthy, dismissing content that might be considered as "snark and trivia" (Farhi, 2009).

Social media technologies like Twitter are part of a range of Internet technologies enabling the disintermediation of news and undermining the gatekeeping function of journalists. Micro-blogging can be seen as a form of participatory or citizen journalism, where citizens report without recourse to institutional journalism. It forms part of a trend in journalism that Deuze has described as a shift from "individualistic, 'top-down' mono-media journalism to team-based, 'participatory' multimedia journalism" (Deuze, 2005). However, while micro-blogging services such as Twitter can be situated within the trend in citizen journalism, it should also be considered a system of communication with its own media logic, shapes and structures. While Twitter can be used to crowdsource the news, where a large group of users come together to report on a news event (Niles, 2007), this paper argues that the institutionally structured features of micro-blogging are creating new forms of journalism, representing one of the ways in which the Internet is influencing journalism practices and, furthermore, changing how journalism itself is defined.

Micro-blogging presents a multi-faceted and fragmented news experience, marking a shift away from the classical paradigm of journalism as a framework to provide reports and analyses of events through narratives, producing an accurate and objective rendering of reality (Dahlgren, 1996). Services like Twitter are a challenge to a news culture based on individual expert systems and group think over team work and knowledge-sharing (Singer, 2004). As Malone et al. (2009, p. 2) suggest, "to unlock the potential of collective intelligence, managers instead need a deeper understanding of how these systems work". This paper seeks to contribute an understanding of Twitter by introducing the concept of ambient journalism. I see new media forms of micro-blogging as "awareness systems", providing journalists with more complex ways of understanding and reporting on the subtleties of public communication. Established journalism is based on a content-oriented communication, whereas Twitter adds an additional layer that can be considered as what has been referred to as connectedness-oriented communication (Kuwabara et al., 2002). In an awareness system, value is defined less by each individual fragment of information that may be insignificant on its own or of limited validity, but rather by the combined effect of the communication.

Micro-blogging as Ambient Journalism

Drawing on the literature in the field of human–computer interaction, this paper suggests that broad, asynchronous, lightweight and always-on communication systems such as Twitter are enabling citizens to maintain a mental model of news and events around them. In this context, Twitter can be considered as an awareness system. Awareness systems are computer-mediated communication systems "intended to help people construct and maintain awareness of each others' activities, context or status, even when the participants are not co-located" (Markopoulos et al., 2009).

Awareness systems have largely been discussed in the context of Computer-Supported Cooperative Work, with a focus on the notion of connecting remote co-workers by audio/video links (Bly et al., 1993). But there have also been critiques of the benefits of awareness (Gross et al., 2005) and even criticism of the term awareness as vague and problematic, often used in contradictory ways in the literature (Schmidt, 2002). The emergence of the Web, coupled with increasingly affordable and ubiquitous information communication technologies, have helped foster a renewed research interest in awareness systems. One focus of research is awareness systems for use in personal settings, where lightweight, informal communication systems help people maintain awareness of each other (Hindus et al., 2001; Markopoulos et al., 2003). These systems are always-on and move from the background to the foreground as and when a user feels the need to communicate. Scholars suggest that awareness systems represent the next step in the evolution of communication technologies that have increased the frequency and amount of information transfer, offering "tremendous potential for innovation, with a wide range of forms and contexts for transforming the space around us" (Markopoulos et al., 2009, p. vii).

This paper adopts the definition of awareness proposed by Chalmers as "the ongoing interpretation of representations i.e. of human activity and of artefacts" (2002, p. 389). I suggest that this definition can be applied to social media networks such as Twitter, with messages considered as both the representations of human activity and as artefacts. Twitter becomes a system where news is reported, disseminated and shared online in short, fast and frequent messages. It creates an ambient media system that displays abstracted information in a space occupied by the user. In this system, a user receives information in the periphery of their awareness. An individual tweet does not require the cognitive attention of, for example, an e-mail. The value does not lie in each individual fragment of news and information, but rather in the mental portrait created by a number of messages over a period of time. I describe this as ambient journalism—an awareness system that offers diverse means to collect, communicate, share and display news and information, serving diverse purposes. The system is always-on but also works on different levels of engagement, creating an ecosystem where "a single user may have multiple intentions or may even serve different roles in different communities" (Java et al., 2007, p. 8). The question for journalism professionals and researchers is how individuals assign meaning to information from others, how they selectively attend to this information and how intentions are assigned to the information (Markopoulos et al., 2009).

In the literature on ambient media, scholars talk about improving people's quality of life by creating the desired atmosphere and functionality through intelligent, personalized, interconnected digital systems and services, with intelligent devices embedded in everyday objects (Aarts, 2005; Ducatel et al., 2001). In his discussion of ambient media, Lugmayr (2006) argues that today's technology is too complex, dominated by an individual's struggle to command the technology to do what they want. Instead, he suggests, we should aim to create media systems that can know what an individual desires and act autonomously on their behalf. If we consider Twitter as a form of ambient journalism, then the issue becomes the development of systems that can identify, contextualize and communicate news and information from a continuous stream of 140-character messages to meet the needs of an individual. In their concept of calm technology, Weiser and Brown (1996) talk about the need for systems that allow for information to attract attention at different levels of awareness, be it at the centre or periphery of our attention. With Twitter, such an approach would enable users to be aware of the ambient information in the periphery, but would also bring from the periphery of our attention into the centre of our attention as required.

Suggested Approaches in Ambient Journalism

As an initial exploration into the impact of awareness systems on journalism norms and practices, this section examines the implications of Twitter as ambient journalism. This paper has considered how the first reports of a news event are now coming from people at the scene in the form of a 140-character message. But as an awareness system, Twitter goes beyond being just a network for the rapid dissemination of breaking news from individuals. Rather, it can be seen as a system that alerts journalists to trends or issues hovering under the news radar. As Gillmor (quoted in Farhi, 2009) argues, journalists should view Twitter as a collective intelligence system that provides early warnings about trends, people and news. The immediacy and velocity of these micro-bursts of data, as well as potentially the high signal to noise ratio, presents challenges for the established practice of relying on the journalist as the filter for this information. During the Iranian election protests, the volume of tweets mentioning Iran peaked at 221,774 in one hour, from a flow of between 10,000 and 50,000 an hour (Parr, 2009). The need to reduce, select and filter increases as the volume of information grows, suggesting a need for information systems to aid in the representation, selection and interpretation of shared information.

The growing volume of content on micro-blogging networks suggests that one of the future directions for journalism may be to develop approaches and systems that help the public negotiate and regulate this flow of awareness information, facilitating the collection and transmission of news. The purpose of these systems would be to identify the collective sum of knowledge contained in the micro-fragments and bring meaning to the data. Bradshaw (2008) discusses some of the systems used to aggregate tweets at the time of the Chinese earthquake in 2008, with the development of Web applications that aim to detect and highlight news trends in real-time. These applications rely on a journalistic interpretative standpoint as to the utility or interest in a topic, based on choices on what to include and exclude, suggesting there is a filtering mechanism at work, albeit on a systems design level.

Considering Twitter as an awareness system also represents a shift in the consumption of news and information. In such systems, completeness of awareness is not the goal, as it would be if an individual were actively pursuing an interest in a specific news event in print, broadcast or online. Instead of overwhelming an individual with an endless stream of tweets, Twitter as an always-on, asynchronous awareness system informs but does not overburden. This notion draws on ideas advanced by Weiser and Brown (Weiser, 1991; Weiser and Brown, 1996) in which technology advances to the stage where it becomes embedded and invisible in people's lives. The extent to which such systems of ambient journalism allow citizens to maintain an awareness of the news events would be a fertile area for future study.

The trend to share links on Twitter provides a mechanism for what Johnson (2009) describes as a customized newspaper, "compiled from all the articles being read that morning by your social network". In this context, tweets provide a diverse and eclectic mix of news and information, as well as an awareness of what others in a user's network are reading and consider important. The information transmitted is content-oriented but also provides a context for the news-seeking activities of others on the network, which may make "visible the structure of implied communities" (Sarno, 2009). There are concerns that this may lead to a "private echo chamber" (Johnson, 2009) but, as Sunstein (2006) argues, such a position may be too simplistic. This is an area that merits further exploration as part of the discussion about whether Internet technologies are creating a "Daily Me" or a "Daily Us". Basing further research on an approach to networks such as Twitter as awareness systems, can, I suggest, help to contextualize the processes of the production, content, reception and circulation of news.

The link-based nature of many tweets, and the trend to re-send the links as a "retweet", can be analysed as both a form of data sharing and as a system for creating a shared conversation. This conversation can be considered as a form of ambient journalism. Since the retweets are not restricted by physical space, time or a delineated group, this creates what Boyd et al. (2010) argue is a distributed conversation that allows others to be aware of the content, without being actively part of it. They suggest that Twitter messages allow individuals to be peripherally aware of discussions without being contributors. This is significant in the context of engaging with audiences through the notion of journalism as a conversation (Gillmor, 2004). Awareness systems can be conceived as networks that engender information interactions and the development of a shared culture, which is particularly important for groups distributed across geography (Dourish and Bly, 1992; Kraut et al., 1990). Research is needed to determine how far Twitter, as an awareness system for news, is contributing to the creation or strengthening of social bonds. For example, the mass outpouring of tweets following the death of Michael Jackson in July 2009 has been described as an immediate and public "collective expression of loss" (Cashmore, 2009).

Conclusion

As with most media technologies, there is a degree of hyperbole about the potential of Twitter, with proclamations that "every major channel of information will be Twitterfied" (Johnson, 2009). Furthermore, social media services are vulnerable to shifting and ever-changing social and cultural habits of audiences. While this paper has discussed micro-blogging in the context of Twitter, it is possible that a new service may replace it in the future. However, it is important to explore in greater depth the qualities of micro-blogging—real-time, immediate communication, searching, link-sharing and the follower structure—and their impact on the way news and information is communicated.

The emergence of ambient journalism through new digital delivery systems and evolving communications protocols, in this case Twitter, raises significant research questions for journalism scholars and professionals. This paper offers an initial exploration of the relationship between awareness systems and shifting journalism norms and practices. Twitter is, due to the speed and volume of tweets, a "noisy" environment, where messages arrive in the order received by the system. A future direction for journalism may be to develop approaches and systems that help the public negotiate and regulate the flow of awareness information, providing tools that take account of this new mode for the circulation of news. Journalists would be seen as sense-makers, rather than just reporting the news. This broadens the journalist's role as proposed by Bardoel and Deuze of a professional "who serves as a node in a complex environment between technology and society, between news and analysis, between annotation and selection, between orientation and investigation" (2001, p. 101). In the case of ambient journalism, the role may be designing the tools that can analyse, interpret and contextualise a system of collection intelligence, rather than in the established practice of selection and editing of content.

Micro-blogging, and Twitter specifically, are in the early stages of development. The significance of Twitter as a news and information platform will be largely influenced by its adoption, both in journalism and other spheres. As Harrison and Dourish (1996) suggest, the richness and utility of a place increases as people build up a past that involves it and a record of experiences. The challenge for researchers is to understand how this place becomes, in the words of Harrison and Dourish, "the understood reality" through a conversational and collaborative user experience. Examining Twitter as an awareness system, creating ambient journalism, provides a framework to analyse the emergent patterns of human behaviour and data interaction that offer an understanding of this place. It shifts the journalistic discourse on micro-blogging away from a debate about raw data to a discussion of contextualized, significant information based on the networked nature of asynchronous, lightweight and always-on communication systems.

NOTE

1. Ian Hargreaves used the term "ambient news" to describe a media environment that is saturated with news in *Journalism: truth or dare?* (2003), referring to the ubiquitous presence of news in contemporary society.

REFERENCES

AARTS, EMILE (2005) "Ambient Intelligence: a multimedia perspective", *Multimedia, IEEE* 11, pp. 12–19.
ARRINGTON, MICHAEL (2008) "I Can't Believe Some People Are Still Saying Twitter Isn't a News Source", TechCrunch, http://www.techcrunch.com/2008/11/27/i-cant-believe-some-people-are-still-saying-twitter-isnt-a-news-source/, accessed 24 June 2009.

BARDOEL, JO and DEUZE, MARK (2001) "Network Journalism: converging competences of media professionals and professionalism", *Australian Journalism Review* 23, pp. 91–103.

BBC (2008) "As It Happened: Mumbai attacks 27 Nov", http://news.bbc.co.uk/2/hi/south_asia/7752003.stm, accessed 27 November 2009.

BENKLER, YOCHAI (2006) *The Wealth of Networks: how social production transforms markets and freedom*, New Haven, CT: Yale University Press.

BLY, SARA, HARRISON, STEVE R. and IRWIN, SUSAN (1993) "Media Spaces: bringing people together in a video, audio, and computing environment", *Communications of the ACM* 36, pp. 28–47.

BOYD, DANAH, GOLDER, SCOTT and LOTAN, GILAD (2010) "Tweet, Tweet, Retweet: conversational aspects of retweeting on Twitter", in: *Proceedings of HICSS-43, January 6*, Kauai, HI: IEEE Computer Society.

BRADSHAW, PAUL (2008) "The Chinese Earthquake and Twitter—Crowdsourcing Without Managers", Online Journalism Blog, http://onlinejournalismblog.com/2008/05/12/twitter-and-the-chinese-earthquake/, accessed 3 June 2009.

BUTCHER, MIKE (2009) "Sky News Realises News Breaks First on Twitter, Not TV—creates a Twitter correspondent", TechCrunch, http://uk.techcrunch.com/2009/03/05/sky-news-realises-news-breaks-first-on-twitter-not-tv-creates-a-twitter-correspondent/, accessed 1 July 2009.

CARLSON, NICHOLAS (2009) "Bloomberg's Insane Twitter Rules for Employees", Bloomberg, http://www.businessinsider.com/bloomberg-lps-insane-twitter-rules-for-employees-2009-5, accessed 17 June 2009.

CASHMORE, PETE (2009) "Michael Jackson Dies: Twitter tributes now 30% of tweets", Mashable, http://mashable.com/2009/06/25/michael-jackson-twitter/, accessed 25 June 2009.

CHALMERS, MATTHEW (2002) "Awareness, Representation and Interpretation", *Computer Supported Cooperative Work* 11, pp. 389–409.

CHENG, ALEX, EVANS, MARK and SINGH, HARSHDEEP (2009) *Inside Twitter: an in-depth look inside the Twitter world*. Sysomos, http://www.sysomos.com/insidetwitter, accessed 17 June 2009.

COLES, MALCOLM (2009) "Newspapers on Twitter: how the Guardian, FT and Times are winning", http://www.malcolmcoles.co.uk/blog/newspapers-on-twitter/, accessed 6 July 2009.

DAHLGREN, PETER (1996) "Media Logic in Cyberspace: repositioning journalism and its publics", *Javnost/The Public* 3, pp. 59–72.

DEUZE, MARK (2005) "What Is Journalism? Professional identity and ideology of journalists reconsidered", *Journalism* 6, pp. 442–64.

DEVOE, KRISTINA M. (2009) "Burst of Information: microblogging", *The Reference Librarian* 50, pp. 212–4.

DOURISH, PAUL and BLY, SARA (1992) "Portholes: supporting awareness in a distributed work group", in: Penny Bauersfeld, John Bennett and Gene Lynch (Eds), *Proceedings of the SIGCHI conference on human factors in computing system (CHI '92)*, New York: ACM Press, pp. 541–47.

DOWD, MAUREEN (2009) "To Tweet or Not to Tweet", *New York Times*, http://www.nytimes.com/2009/04/22/opinion/22dowd.html?_r=3&ref=opinion, accessed 3 June 2009.

DUCATEL, K., BOGDANOWICZ, M., SCAPOLO, F., LEIJTEN, J. and BURGELMAN, J.-C. (2001) "Scenarios for Ambient Intelligence in 2010", Technical report, IST Advisory Group, ftp://ftp.cordis.europa.eu/pub/ist/docs/istagscenarios2010.pdf, accessed 18 June 2009.

FARHI, PAUL (2009) "The Twitter Explosion", *American Journalism Review*, http://www.ajr.org/Article.asp?id=4756, accessed 24 June 2009.

GILLMOR, DAN (2004) *We the Media*, Sebastopol, CA: O'Reilly.

GOODMAN, ELLEN (2009) "Journalism Needed in Twitter Era", *Columbia Daily Tribune*, http://www.columbiatribune.com/news/2009/jul/05/journalism-needed-in-twitter-era/, accessed 5 July 2009.

GROSS, TOM, STARY, CHRIS and TOTTER, ALEX (2005) "User-centered Awareness in Computer-supported Cooperative Work Systems: structured embedding of findings from social sciences", *International Journal of Human–Computer Interaction* 18, pp. 323–60.

HARGREAVES, IAN (2003) *Journalism: truth or dare?*, Oxford: Oxford University Press.

HARRISON, STEVE and DOURISH, PAUL (1996) "Re-Place-ing Space: the roles of place and space in collaborative systems", in: Mary S. Ackerman (Ed.), *Proceedings of the 1996 ACM conference on computer supported cooperative work (CSCW '96)*, New York: ACM Press, pp. 67–76.

HAYEK, FRIEDRICH A. VON (1945) "The Use of Knowledge in Society", *American Economic Review* XXXV, pp. 519–30.

HAYEK, FRIEDRICH A. VON (1979) *Law, Legislation and Liberty: a new statement of the liberal principles of justice and political economy, Vol. 3. The political order of a free people*, London: Routledge and Kegan Paul.

HEIL, BILL and PISKORSKI, MIKOLJAI (2009) "New Twitter Research: men follow men and nobody tweets", Harvard Business Publishing, http://blogs.harvardbusiness.org/cs/2009/06/new_twitter_research_men_follo.html, accessed 2 June 2009.

HERMIDA, ALFRED and THURMAN, NEIL (2009) "A Clash of Cultures: the integration of user-generated content within professional journalistic frameworks at British newspaper websites", *Journalism Practice* 2, pp. 343–56.

HERRMANN, STEVE (2009) "Mumbai, Twitter and Live Updates", BBC The Editors, http://www.bbc.co.uk/blogs/theeditors/2008/12/theres_been_discussion_see_eg.html, accessed 4 December 2008.

HINDUS, DEBBY, MAINWARING, SCOTT D., LEDUC, NICOLE, HAGSTROM, ANNA E. and BAYLEY, OLIVER (2001) "Casablanca: designing social communication devices for the home", in: *Proceedings of the SIGCHI conference on human factors in computing systems (CHI '01)*, New York: ACM Press, pp. 325–32.

HOWE, JEFF (2008) *Crowdsourcing: why the power of the crowd is driving the future of business*, New York: Crown Business.

INGRAM, MATHEW (2008) "Yes, Twitter Is a Source of Journalism", MathewIngram.com, http://www.mathewingram.com/work/2008/11/26/yes-twitter-is-a-source-of-journalism/, accessed 4 June 2009.

JAVA, AKSHAY, SONG, XIAODAN, FININ, TIM and TSENG, BELLE (2007) "Why We Twitter: understanding microblogging usage and communities", in: *Proceedings of the 9th WebKDD and 1st SNA-KDD 2007 workshop on Web mining and social network analysis (WebKDD/SNA-KDD '07)*, New York: ACM Press, pp. 56–65.

JOHNSON, STEVEN (2009) "How Twitter Will Change the Way We Live", *Time*, http://www.time.com/time/printout/0,8816,1902604,00.html, accessed 5 June 2009.

KOBLIN, JOHN (2009) "Twitter Culture Wars at The Times: 'We need a zone of trust', Bill Keller tells staff", *The New York Observer*, http://www.observer.com/2009/media/twitter-culture-wars-itimesi, accessed 17 June 2009.

KRAUT, ROBERT E., CARMEN EGIDO and GALEGHER, JOLENE (1990) "Patterns of Contact and Communication in Scientific Research Collaboration", in: R.E. Kraut, Carmen Egido and Jolene Galegher (Eds), *Intellectual Teamwork: social and technological foundations of cooperative work*, Hillsdale, NJ: Lawrence Erlbaum, pp. 149–71.

KUWABARA, KAZUHIRO, WATANABE, TAKUMI, OHGURO, TAKESHI, ITOH, YOHIHIRO and MAEDA, YUJI (2002) "Connectedness Oriented Communication: fostering a sense of connectedness to augment social relationships", in: *Proceedings of the 2002 Symposium on Applications and the Internet (SAINT '02)*, Washington, DC: IEEE Computer Society, pp. 186–193.

LENHARD, AMANDA and FOX, SUSANNAH (2009) "Twitter and Status Updating", Pew Internet and American Life Project, http://www.pewinternet.org/Reports/2009/Twitter-and-status-updating.aspx, accessed 21 June 2009.

LUGMAYR, ARTUR (2006) "The Future Is 'Ambient'", in: R. Creutzburg, J.H. Takala and C.W. Chen (Eds), *Proceedings of SPIE, 607403 Multimedia on Mobile Devices II*, Vol. 6074, San Jose: SPIE.

MALONE, THOMAS W., LAUBACHER, ROBERT and DELLAROCAS, CHRYSANTHOS (2009) "Harnessing Crowds: mapping the genome of collective intelligence", MIT Sloan Research Paper No. 4732-09, http://ssrn.com/abstract=1381502, accessed 21 June 2009.

MARKOPOULOS, PANOS, DE RUYTER, BORIS and MACKAY, WENDY (2009) *Awareness Systems: advances in theory, methodology and design*, Dordrecht: Springer.

MARKOPOULOS, PANOS, IJSSELSTEIJN, WIJNAND, HUIJEN, CLAIRE, ROMIJN, ONNO and PHILOPOULOS, ALEXANDROS (2003) "Supporting Social Presence Through Asynchronous Awareness Systems", in: Giuseppe Riva, Fabrizio Davide and Wijnand Ijsselsteijn (Eds), *Being There: concepts, effects and measurements of user presence in synthetic environments*, Amsterdam: IOS Press, pp. 261–78.

NILES, ROBERT (2007) "A Journalist's Guide to Crowdsourcing", http://www.ojr.org/ojr/stories/070731niles/, accessed 24 May 2009.

PARR, BEN (2009) "Mindblowing #IranElection Stats: 221,744 tweets per hour at peak", Mashable, http://mashable.com/2009/06/17/iranelection-crisis-numbers/, accessed 17 June 2009.

POSETTI, JULIE (2009) "Twitter's Difficult Gift to Journalism", NewMatilda.com, http://newmatilda.com/2009/06/16/twitters-difficult-gift-journalism, accessed 17 June 2009.

PROJECT FOR EXCELLENCE IN JOURNALISM (nd) "Principles of Journalism", Pew Research Center, http://www.journalism.org/resources/principles, accessed 20 June 2009.

SARNO, DAVID (2009) "On Twitter, Mindcasting Is the New Lifecasting", *Los Angeles Times*, 11 March.

SCHMIDT, KJELD (2002) "The Problem with 'Awareness'", *Computer Supported Cooperative Work* 11, pp. 285–98.

SCHUDSON, MICHAEL (2003) *The Sociology of News*, New York: Norton.

SHIELS, MAGGIE (2009) "Twitter Responds on Iranian Role", BBC, http://news.bbc.co.uk/2/hi/technology/8104318.stm, accessed 17 June 2009.

SINGER, JANE (2004) "Strange Bedfellows: the diffusion of convergence in four news organisations", *Journalism Studies* 5, pp. 3–18.

STELTER, BRIAN (2009) "Journalism Rules Are Bent in News Coverage from Iran", *New York Times*, 28 June.

STRUPP, JOE (2009) "New 'WSJ' Conduct Rules Target Twitter, Facebook", http://www.editorandpublisher.com/eandp/news/article_display.jsp?vnu_content_id=1003972544, accessed 17 June 2009.

SUNSTEIN, CASS R. (2006) *Infotopia*, New York: Oxford University Press.

SUROWIECKI, JAMES (2004) *The Wisdom of Crowds*, London: Little, Brown.

SUTTER, JOHN D. (2009) "Celebrity Death Rumors Spread Online", CNN.com, http://www.cnn.com/2009/TECH/07/01/celebrity.death.pranks/, accessed 2 July, 2009.

TAPSCOTT, DON and WILLIAMS, ANTHONY D. (2006) *Wikinomics*, New York: Portfolio.

TUCHMAN, GAYE (2002) "The Production of News", in: Klaus Jensen (Ed.), *A Handbook of Media and Communication Research*, London and New York: Routledge, pp. 78–90.

VASCELLARO, JESSICA E. (2009) "Twitter Trips on Its Rapid Growth", *Wall Street Journal*, 26 May.

WASSERMAN, EDWARD (2009) "How Twitter Poses a Threat to Newspapers", *Miami Herald*, 28 May.

WEISER, MARK (1991) "The Computer for the 21st Century", *SIGMOBILE Mobile Computing and Communications Review* 3(3), pp. 3–11.

WEISER, MARK and BROWN, JOHN SEELY (1996) "Designing Calm Technology", *PowerGrid Journal* 1, pp. 94–100.

"WE'RE GOING TO CRACK THE WORLD OPEN"
Wikileaks and the future of investigative reporting

Lisa Lynch

This paper considers the current and future role played by the document-leaking site Wikileaks in the process of investigative journalism, by analyzing the way in which Wikileaks has articulated its own relationship with the press and then detailing how reporters have actually discovered and used the site. My research shows that Wikileaks is used both as a regular destination and as a one-time source for leaked material; additionally, it is increasingly used as a repository for leaked documents that are removed from print and online media outlets through legal action. I argue Wikileaks represents perhaps the most extreme of a number of new Web-based interventions into the troubled climate for investigative reporting, and might usefully be seen less as an "outlier" than as on the far end of continuum.

Introduction

On March 19, 2009, Australian citizens learned that their government was considering a mandatory national filtering system that would prevent them from accessing websites ostensibly identified as having connections to child pornography. This revelation, which engendered substantial political fallout, was remarkable to some observers because of the way the story emerged. The plan was made public neither through a leak to a print journalist nor through a whistle-blower's televised press conference, but instead via a copy of the filter list posted anonymously on Wikileaks, a Swedish-hosted website run by an international collective dedicated to untraceable document-leaking.

For regular followers of Wikileaks, the fact that the blacklist appeared first on the Wikileaks site was hardly surprising. Since its launch in early 2007, Wikileaks has published scores of documents never intended for public view, and its professed ability to safeguard the security of those who wish to publicize such documents has meant that the site has become an important destination both for leakers and interested citizens. It has also become a destination for journalists, who have covered newsworthy leaks and chronicled the drama of Wikileaks' tenacious survival in the face of legal and logistical challenges.

As a site whose mandate is to publish any leak they deem significant, without regard for political impact, violation of privacy or breach of copyright law, Wikileaks has been a controversial project since its inception. It is currently banned in China and can only be accessed via proxy names; over the past two years it has been issued with legal challenges by the Scientologists, the Mormons, and several banks; and it is blocked in the offices of the British Ministry of Defence. Even those who champion freedom of information and principled whistle-blowing have sometimes found Wikileaks' mandate noble but its practices irresponsible—pointing out, for example, that the site lacks "accountable editorial oversight" (Aftergood, 2007), and that it "encourages people living under oppressive regimes to do something they could be imprisoned, tortured, or even murdered for" (Kleeman, 2007).

Overall, however Wikileaks has managed to garner more praise than criticism. Advocates have described the site "as important a journalistic tool as the [US] Freedom of Information Act" (Schmidt, 2007) and an example of "the brave new world of investigative journalism" (Gonsalves, 2008) in which new information technologies chip away at corrosive government secrecy. In the wake of a court challenge in February 2008—a California judge issued and then reversed a takedown order in response to Wikileaks' refusal to remove documents connected to Swiss bank Julius Baer—the site won the *Economist* magazine's Index on Censorship Freedom of Expression Award. In 2009, Wikileaks received the New Media Award from Amnesty International for leaking documents that extrajudicial assassinations in Kenya.

Though the vast majority of the material on the site has yet to appear in the mainstream press, Wikileaks continues to publish leaks that attract media attention, including government documents from East Timor; the supporter database of ex-US Senator Norman Coleman; a list of military equipment in Iraq; information on US IED jamming technology; the final draft of a US Army Intel brief on Afghani insurgent groups; a selection of Scientology's "Operating Thetan" missives; the membership list of the British National Party; over 6000 US Congressional Research Service reports; briefs on UN activity around the world; and leaks suggesting improprieties at banks including Northern Rock, Barclays, Julius Baer, and Iceland's Kaupthing. Over the past two years, articles about these documents have appeared in print publications including *The New York Times*, and *The Guardian*, *The Telegraph*, *The Christian Science Monitor*, Dubai's *Khlaleej Times*, Australia's *The Age*, Canada's *Ottawa Citizen* and *The Globe and Mail*; on the Associated Press and Reuters wire services; and in the political blogs *Huffington Post* and *Talking Points Memo*.

If Wikileaks is thus increasingly being taken seriously as a means to collect and distribute sensitive information, can we say that it might play a more central role in the future of investigative journalism? Arguably, the site does suggest answers to some of the issues faced by diminishing newsrooms interested in investigative work. Wikileaks' encryption practices, while primarily intended to ensure safe leaking for whistle-blowers, also allow journalists to report on sensitive information without fear of being jailed for protecting sources. And the international scope of Wikileaks (documents relevant to over 100 countries are already included on the site) allows for the circulation of politically sensitive material from countries without a free media, and also provides a central repository for documents of international interest to compensate for the lack of on-the-ground reporters overseas.

Despite these seeming attractions, at present Wikileaks comes up only infrequently in conversations about innovative efforts to reinvigorate journalism. Though one can make the claim that Wikileaks' pushing of legal and ethical norms makes it marginal to such conversations, it is equally true to say that Wikileaks is unsettling to journalists because it represents a radical shift in the way information is collected and distributed in the media landscape. The site is one of the best existing examples of a phenomenon described by Yoachi Benkler in *The Wealth of Networks* (2006)—the emergence of a critical information media that is indebted neither to states nor markets. As Benkler notes, these emergent media enterprises are taking on some of the Fourth Estate function typically associated with older media forms:

> We are seeing the emergence of new, decentralized approaches to fulfilling the watchdog function and engaging in political debate and organization. These are being undertaken in a distinctly nonmarket form, in ways that would have been much more difficult to pursue ... before the networked information environment. (Benkler, 2006, p. 11)

Wikileaks is thus radical not only because of its content, practices and form—it is radical because its form, content and practices are inextricably woven together in a new kind of delivery platform only made possible through the emergence of technologies that many journalists are still negotiating with a fair amount of caution. Audaciously positioning itself as a new institution that will "crack the world open" (Wikileaks, 2007a) by serving as global watchdog, Wikileaks poses a challenge to traditional journalistic practice, in particular to the ways in which investigative journalists have cultivated source relationships and the ways in which media outlets have established themselves as the arbiters of fact. And the friction rubs both ways: the collective that runs Wikileaks has expressed frustration in their dealings with traditional media, in particular with the press's seeming indifference to some of their leaked material.

This paper explores this evolving dynamic between Wikileaks and the media in two ways. It begins with a discussion of how members of the Wikileaks collective have articulated the relationship between their project and the press. Then, it presents the results of a survey regarding the way in which reporters are discovering and using Wikileaks. Email queries were sent to 53 English-language journalists from both print media and online-only publications with traditional methods of newsgathering and large audiences that had written stories about Wikileaks. The answers of the 23 reporters who responded to the survey—though they represent only a fraction of the global engagement with Wikileaks in old and newer media outlets—suggest that while Wikileaks is not yet a first port of call for reporters looking for stories, an increasing number are using the site. And those who do visit Wikileaks often comment that the site is changing the confidential information economy in a variety of ways, some positive and some less so.

"A Romance with Journalists' Hearts:" Wikileaks as Journalists' Antagonist and Ally

Though its name might suggest otherwise, Wikileaks is not an affiliate of Wikipedia or the Wikimedia Foundation. Rather, it is one of a number of websites, including Paul Young's *Cryptome* (www.cryptome.org) and Russ Kick's *The Memory Hole* (www.memoryhole.org), dedicated to providing an outlet for information that might otherwise remain secret. Three primary differences set Wikileaks apart from these sites. First, Wikileaks foregrounds their ability to protect their sources, by using modified PGP and Tor encryption technologies to allow leakers to upload anonymously to the site and providing other encryption methods for those who wish to anonymously deliver physical documents. Second, the operation and staffing of the site is largely clandestine; though the most prominent spokesman and co-founder of Wikileaks is Australian activist Julian Assange, the site's "About" section (Wikileaks, 2007b) states Wikileaks is run by a mainly anonymous team that includes Chinese dissidents, journalists, mathematicians, and "startup company technologists" from the United States, Taiwan, Europe and South Africa. Third, Wikileaks is aggressively proactive in its attempts to bring their leaks to the attention of journalists, via RSS, Twitter, and direct contact with reporters.

Though such media outreach has been a core part of the Wikileaks mission since the beginning, the Wikileaks collective has persistently expressed ambivalence about their relationship with the press. This ambivalence is sometimes voiced during public presentations; for example, in a November 2009 talk at the New Media Days festival in Copehagen, Julian Assange described a leak he felt was particularly significant—a document outlining US policy on unconventional warfare—that had received no main-stream media coverage because it was "just not easy enough" for reporters to understand. But it is also apparent on the site's own website, which is critical of the media even as promises to serve as a tool for and ally of reporters. The "About" section of the Wikileaks site asserts that the Wikileaks authentication process, which combines forensic analysis of leaked documents with the public assessment allowed by a wiki interface, is more reliable than the authentication methods of conventional media outlets: "Peddlars of misinforma-tion will find themselves undone by Wikileaks, equipped as it is to scrutinize leaked documents in a way that no mainstream media outlet is capable of" (Wikileaks, 2007b). But the "About" section also suggests Wikileaks is a tool for journalists, characterizing the leaks they provided as "an enabling jump-off point for media," and asserting that "it's hard for a journalist to be an expert in all areas they cover [so] the comments attached to the documents online will provide the journalist with an instant source" (Wikileaks, 2007b). The site also suggests in several places that Wikileaks is a grassroots organization seeking direct communication with the public and thus not in need of any form of mediation; for example, the "About" section describes Wikileaks as "a social movement emblazoning the virtues of ethical leaking" (Wikileaks, 2007b), and the "the first intelligence agency of the people" (Wikileaks, 2007b). However, the "About" section also points out that some members of the collective are "working investigative journalists," suggesting that investigative journalists are skilled professionals necessary to the work of the organization (Wikileaks, 2007b).

Perhaps even more revealing of Wikileaks' conflicted sentiments regarding the press is a series of emails from the collective's internal mailing list about efforts to attract and then manage media coverage.[1] Among other things, the list chronicles how, in the months leading up to the launch of Wikileaks, members of the collective unsuccessfully solicited media attention for the site's first major leak—a 2005 memo on civil war policy by the Somali Islamic court system. After a Wikileaks-authored article describing the Somali leak was shopped around to various publications including *CounterPunch*, *Zmag*, and the *Christian Science Monitor*, collective members expressed frustration that their analysis was granted little authority by the press, with one member acknowledging that until the site was certified by someone with "a gold plated reputation," it might be hard for them to gain media credibility. Another member, however, argued that credibility would come not from the media, but rather directly from the public, via the wiki design of the site: "When Wikileaks is deployed, feedback will be, like Wikipedia, an act of creation and correction; the [document] will eventually face one hundred thousand enraged Somali refugees, blade and keyboard in hand, cutting apart its pages until all is dancing confetti and the truth" (Wikileaks, 2007a).

Wikileaks' frustration with the lack of press response to the leaked Somali document was heightened after the sites' unofficial launch, when collective members realized that the site itself, rather than particular leaks, might emerge as the focus of media attention. Concerned about the possibility of attracting bad press for their fledgling site's lack of polish, members discussed the best way to deflect any negative press attention.

One member opted to refer reporters to the site's "About" section in order to pre-empt certain questions, arguing that reporters might otherwise attack Wikileaks because they would consider it their competition: "Reporters—and keep in mind that they are competitors with Wikileaks as much as any keepers of secrets and peddlers of inside information, will most likely dig for unfriendly aspects of Wikileaks" (Wikileaks, 2007a). Another member, however, insisted the best way to defend the site was to be directly available for press interviews: "We are in a romance with journalists hearts; if our voices sweet are not easily reachable on the phone when their desire and deadlines peek, others' voices, less honeyed but always, always available will replace them" (Wikileaks, 2007a).

Despite the level of anxiety their initial press contact provoked, the first round of media articles about Wikileaks were, if sometimes skeptical, not as critical as the collective feared. Still, it was true that the site itself, at least in the beginning, was of greater interest to journalists than the leaks that Wikileaks had begun to evaluate and publish. It took almost a year for a leak on the site—namely copies of the 2003 and 2004 *Guantanamo Bay Officers' Handbook*—to attract attention from *Reuters* and *The New York Times*. Over time, however, a fairly steady stream of high-profile stories began to refer to material on Wikileaks, and the site developed a regular following among some journalists.

"It Can Be a Useful Resource:" Reporters Encounter Wikileaks

When queried about their encounters with Wikileaks, reporters varied widely in their responses. Some attested to longtime familiarity with the site and sympathy with the project's mandate, while others claimed to have given the site only brief consideration in the course of reporting a story. About half of the reporters responded that they had been familiar with the site for a number of years: for the most part, these reporters covered technology, politics, or both. For example, Ryan Singel of *Wired.com* and Noah Shactman, who writes for *Wired.com* and *Wired*, said they had visited Wikileaks regularly since its launch in late 2006. *Ottawa Citizen* technology writer Vito Pilieci also followed Wikileaks since its launch; as a result of his regular visits to the site, he was the first to write about a leaked draft of the Anti-Counterfeiting Trade Agreement in March of 2008. Ben Arnoldy, South Asia Bureau Chief for the *Christian Science Monitor*, learned about the site from blogs and forums around the time of its launch, and immediately signed on to the press release list. New Zealand *Dominion Post* correspondent Michael Field, a reporter specializing in both politics and technology, also said he had "known and read Wikileaks since it began and found it useful" (email exchange, June 22, 2009).

In some cases, reporters' long-term involvement with Wikileaks included contact with the site's founder, Julian Assange. After *Sydney Morning Herald* technology writer Asher Moses profiled the site in early 2007, he kept in touch with Assange via email: when Wikileaks published the Australian filter list in April 2009, Assange contacted Moses in advance and Moses went on to write four stories about the leak. Similarly, *Washington Post* reporter Brian Krebs heard about the leak of Congressional reports in February of 2009 from Assange, who had kept in touch with him after Krebs interviewed him for a piece in *Popular Mechanics*, and knew the documents would be of interest.

For these reporters, their continued use of the site and the positive note sounded in many of the stories they wrote about Wikileaks suggested a degree of approval for the project and an acknowledgment that it was useful to journalists. This does not mean that their approval was always wholehearted. Arnoldy, for example, noted that he had ethical concerns about Wikileaks even though basically trusted the information he found:

Society does set limits on information disclosure in many ways, even in the journalism community there are rules. Wikileaks is radical in that it recognizes very few such rules. As for journalism ethics of quoting anonymous people you can't meet or verify—I felt pretty confident with Wikileaks: the press contact is centralized, they have a press release list, the responses to my queries were obviously carefully considered and intelligently answered. (Arnoldy, email exchange, June 22, 2009)

Even though Arnoldy and other regular users might approach the site with ambivalence, they also demonstrated a willingness to engage with Wikileaks on its own terms, either because they understood the way in which the site might be changing the rules of investigative practice, or out of a sense that the newsworthiness of the leak in question outweighed whatever issues they might have with Wikileaks' methods.

The response by these reporters suggests that Wikileaks might be developing a media following, a core group of reporters who follow the site in the hopes that something interesting might emerge that would be useful to their own reporting. But an equal number of reporters asserted they had no familiarity with Wikileaks prior to encountering the site while working on a particular story. For these journalists, information about Wikileaks came via a wide variety of channels. In some cases, reporters found out about Wikileaks through a colleague who followed the site regularly and informed them about a newsworthy leak. Reuters correspondent Jane Sutton, who wrote in November 2007 about the leak of the Guantanamo Bay handbook, was told of the leak by a colleague aware that Sutton had been writing regularly about Guantanamo. Similarly, Associated Press reporter Bradley Klapper was told about leaked documents by a colleague aware that Klapper, who covers the United Nations, would be interested in documents alleging sex abuse claims against UN Congo "Blue Helmets."

Sometimes reporters discovered Wikileaks simply by reading an account of an intriguing leak in another media source. Reuters political correspondent Andrew Gray, who wrote in March 2009 about a leaked RAND study detailing poor civilians treatment during the conflicts in Iraq and Afghanistan, said that he had not heard of either Wikileaks or the study before reading an article in "a media source—most likely British." After obtaining the RAND study from the Wikileaks site, Gray went on to confirm the leak independently by consulting a spokesman for US forces in Afghanistan. He also spoke to one of Wikileaks' investigative editors directly. Gray found the RAND leak to be both authentic and newsworthy, but a longer perusal of the site left him unconvinced of the newsworthiness of some other leaks:

My impression of the site, and having talked to their investigations editor as part of my work on that Afghanistan story, is that it can be a valuable resource. But I think they may hype some of the information they have sometimes. I seem to remember they made a big deal of some Afghanistan statistics they had obtained which were not classified and possibly already in the public domain. (email exchange, June 23, 2009)

Gray's caution about the site was not unusual among reporters who found themselves confronted with Wikileaks for the first time while working to a deadline for a story: other journalists reported being frustrated with how the unconventional nature of the site thwarted their usual reporting practices. Though Gray was able to talk to a Wikileaks editor, in other cases reporters found the Wikileaks staff elusive or missing when they needed questions answered. *Globe and Mail* technology writer Ivor Tossell recalled a failed attempt to contact someone at Wikileaks that resulted in an apologetic email claiming the site had had a "hell of a week," while *New York Times* reporter Stephanie Strom said she had needed to enlist the efforts of a "well connected friend" to track down a Wikileaks spokesman through Twitter.

If Wikileaks itself often posed a challenge to traditional journalist–source relationships, it also at times indirectly benefited from such relationships, as journalists were sometimes told about leaks on the site that pertained to their "beat" by sources they had developed while pursuing investigative work. *Guardian* East Africa correspondent Xan Rice was physically handed a report by a contact in Nairobi about financial fraud perpetrated by former Kenyan leader Daniel Arap Moi; the report had been obtained by the source via Wikileaks. Lindsay Murdoch from *The Age*, who had previously covered political unrest in East Timor, was told by a regular source from Dili that someone from the government was sending leaks to Wikileaks, and subsequently wrote about an autopsy report that challenged official accounts of a 2008 assassination attempt on the East Timorese leader. Murdoch, who still returns to the site regularly, noted that though he would ideally prefer to remain the primary recipient of leaked documents, the fact that Wikileaks is still underutilized by reporters makes it a good source for material: "I would rather have [sources] leak to me, but few journalists seem to check the site so it's good for the occasional exclusive" (Murdoch, email exchange, June 15, 2009). In both of these cases, the sources in question passed along the information in order to better circulate documents that aligned with their political sympathies. However, sources hostile to Wikileaks have also drawn attention to the site: *New York Times* reporter Eric Schmitt, who co-authored a piece with Michael Gordon about a leak concerning cross-border chases in Iraq, said he first learned of the site after Gordon was contacted by someone in the military who was upset that Wikileaks was posting sensitive information.

Overall, journalists who said they learned about Wikileaks in the context of reporting a story were less likely to also report that they had continued to visit the site and draw on it as a resource. With some exceptions (Murdoch among them), these journalists saw Wikileaks more as a one-time story source than as a tool for investigative reporting. A few even asserted that they "barely remembered" Wikileaks, and turned to their notes to reconstruct their memories of the reporting process. For these journalists, Wikileaks was not something that changed their methods, but rather a source that was useful in one instance.

"Upload it to Wikileaks or Something:" Wikileaks as an Investigator's Archive

How useful Wikileaks eventually becomes to investigative reporters as a source of leaks depends both on the ability of the site to seem credible and the ability of its editors to collect newsworthy information. Thus far, it is fair to say that Wikileaks has been only partly successful at appearing credible and newsworthy in journalists' eyes: though the site has earned the confidence and respect of some journalists, it has left others wary, and the percentage of leaks which are covered by major media outlets is, if increasing, still low. However, the utility of Wikileaks to the process of investigative work is not limited to the ability of the site to catalyze new reporting through the publication of anonymous leaks. Several reporters queried about their encounters with Wikileaks also described an emerging use of Wikileaks that perhaps even its founders had not imagined—not as a place to discover fresh information that had been leaked directly to Wikileaks, but rather as a repository or 'safe house' for documents that had been leaked elsewhere—including those leaked to journalists themselves.

New York Times reporter Noam Cohen, a regular user of Wikileaks, first learned about the site in the context of this practice. In November 2008, Cohen came across Wikileaks while writing about a leaked address list for Britain's far-right British National Party (BNP), a document that had been cautiously discussed in the British press due to libel fears. Though the BNP list had not originated on Wikileaks, media accounts noted that the site had archived it. In a story about the list, Cohen described Wikileaks as a "home for orphaned material" (Cohen, 2008) and noted that interest in the BNP had overwhelmed Wikileaks' servers.

In March of 2009, Wikileaks became the host for another series of legally volatile documents; leaks suggesting that British bank Barclays was engaged in tax avoidance schemes. This time as well, Wikileaks was not the first to publish the documents; in this case, however, the documents were obtained by *Guardian* investigative journalists David Leigh and Felicity Lawrence in the course of reporting a story (Lawrence, email exchange, June 15, 2009). On March 17, however, Barclays obtained a high court injunction barring *The Guardian* from either hosting the documents on its own site or mentioning where else they might be found. Later that day, the documents were available on Wikileaks, along with an explanation of what had occurred at *The Guardian*. The gag order on *The Guardian* was short lived; about 10 days after the initial injunction, a Liberal MP mentioned Wikileaks in the House of Lords, and thus *The Guardian* could once again refer to the site.[2] But during that interval, the clash between old media constraints and the liberties claimed by Wikileaks became painfully clear. *The Guardian* was forced merely to allude to documents procured by their own reporters, while Wikileaks—a site *The Guardian* was enjoined from even mentioning—became the primary destination for members of the public who wished to see the documents.

This dynamic between Wikileaks, *The Guardian*, and the court repeated itself in November of 2009, when *The Guardian* obtained a leaked copy of a confidential report criticizing waste dumping by the oil company Trafigura off the shores of the Ivory Coast. When Trafigura learned that *The Guardian* was in possession of the report, they obtained a publication injunction. By this point, however, Wikileaks had obtained a copy of the report; following an energetic Twitter campaign publicizing the injunction and linking to the Wikileaks website, Trafigura gave up trying to suppress publication of the document. According to the company's official statement, the discharge of the injunction was directly tied to "widespread publication of the document overseas (particularly on websites)."[3]

Ian Douglas, technology blogger for *Telegraph.com.uk* and a close follower of the Wikileaks site, speculated that journalists and the public might increasingly consider Wikileaks as the repository of choice for sensitive documents, something that might have sweeping implications for traditional pathways of leaked material. According to Douglas, as he worked on a story about the MP expense scandal in June of 2009, he found that journalists around him were wondering aloud what should be done with the leaked documents connected to the story, and their suggestion reflected a fundamental change in attitude:

> Without exception, those who think that anyone finding such politically charged information in their hands should give it away said the phrase "upload it to Wikileaks or something". In the past, that would have been "hand it to the BBC." (Douglas, email exchange, June 22, 2009)

Douglas' remark suggests that something unexpected might be happening in the interaction between Wikileaks and the media; rather than Wikileaks simply influencing journalists' reporting practices, it might also be the case that journalists have begun to influence the direction of the site, changing it from a place where they might come across unfamiliar material to a place where they might store documents they have obtained in their own reporting without fear of legal reprisal. Though there is no hard evidence that journalists are uploading documents themselves, Assange recently remarked in a public appearance that it is becoming a common practice.

Conclusion

Since it first launched in 2007, Wikileaks may not have "cracked the world open" in the way the Wikileaks collective may had hoped, but it has definitely had an impact on the field of investigative journalism. Some reporters from mainstream media outlets are following the site regularly, while others have at least found their leaks newsworthy on specific occasions. Finally, the site is becoming a secure location for leaked documents that might be difficult for more conventional media outlets to place or keep before the public eye. In a moment when investigative journalism is recognizably in crisis, Wikileaks has emerged as something of a strange bedfellow to a beleaguered industry, one that holds itself up as a champion of principles many journalists hold dear—freedom of information and the sanctity of the source—yet embeds these principles in a framework of cyberlibertarianism that is frequently at odds with the institutional ethics of journalists and editors.

It is this framework, and the occasional glaring gaps in epistemology that it produces between Wikileaks and those who are trying to reinvent the profession of journalism, that leaves the future relationship between the two camps uncertain. The recent past has seen the launch of a series of new online ventures to aid the investigative enterprise, including the *Huffington Post Investigative Fund*, *Propublica*, *Spot.us*, and a Knight-funded multimedia project at the Center for Investigative Reporting. Though these ventures seek, like Wikileaks, to use new technologies to transform the way in which investigative work is produced and distributed, they are firmly committed to traditional journalistic values and see themselves as preserving an industry at least as much as reshaping it. How Wikileaks fits in along this spectrum of new online ventures—and whether the investigative journalism and the industry as a whole will be reshaped or revolutionized in the process—is yet to be determined.[4]

NOTES

1. These emails were not initially intended to be public—in an action that was perhaps as ironic as inevitable, the internal mailing list for Wikileaks were leaked by one of the defecting members and published on cryptome.org. Most emails had their names redacted by John Young of *Cryptome*; Assange's name remained attached to several emails.

2. For more on the *Guardian* injunction and its removal, see http://www.guardian.co.uk/business/2009/mar/26/barclays-tax-avoidance-gag-order.

3. See official statement on Trafigura website, http://www.trafigura.com/our_news/probo_koala_updates.aspx#NZSA1L4np8K0.

4. As this article went to press, Wikileaks remained partially offline pending a relaunch with a new user interface. The site has been trying to raise funds to accommodate increasing

budgetary expenses, including increased bandwidth needs. At the same time, Wikileaks has extended their concerns about journalism into the policy arena in Iceland, helping to shape the Icelandic Modern Media Initiative, legislation moving ahead in Iceland's parliament that would transform the country into a leader in freedom of expression and freedom of information.

REFERENCES

AFTERGOOD, STEPHEN (2007) "Wikileaks and Untraceable Document Disclosure", *FAS Blog*, http://www.fas.org/blog/secrecy/2007/01/wikileaks_and_untraceable_docu.html, accessed 9 July 2009.

BENKLER, YOACHI (2006) *The Wealth of Networks: How social production transforms markets and freedom*, New Haven, CT: Yale University Press.

COHEN, NOAM (2008) "In Britain, Outwitting Strict Laws Against Libel", *The New York Times*, http://www.nytimes.com/2008/11/24/technology/internet/24link.html, accessed 16 June 2009.

GONSALVES, SEAN (2008) "Will Wikileaks Revolutionize Journalism?", *Alternet*, http://www.alternet.org/media/90641?page=2, accessed 6 July 2009.

KLEEMAN, JENNY (2007) "Wikileaks—whistleblowing made easy", *The Guardian*, http://www.guardian.co.uk/media/2007/sep/17/digitalmedia.humanrights, accessed 16 June 2009.

SCHMIDT, TRACY (2007) "A Wiki for Whistle-Blowers", *Time*, http://www.time.com/time/nation/article/0,8599,1581189,00.html, accessed 16 June 2009.

WIKILEAKS (2007a) "Internal Development Mailing List", http://cryptome.info/wikileaks/wikileaks-leak.htm (Part 1) and http://cryptome.info/wikileaks/wikileaks-leak2.htm (Part 2), accessed 11 July 2009.

WIKILEAKS (2007b) "About", http://wikileaks.org/wiki/Wikileaks:About, accessed 11 July 2009.

COMPETITION, COMPLEMENTARITY OR INTEGRATION?
The relationship between professional and participatory media

Christoph Neuberger and **Christian Nuernbergk**

This article discusses how the relationship between professional and participatory media could be described in a changing media environment. It presents key findings of a two-year research project which explored online journalism in Germany. The findings draw a multilayered picture of the latest developments concerning professional online newsrooms and their counterparts in participatory media. The data consist primarily of standardised interviews with editors-in-chief of online newsrooms. In most newsrooms, they produce a supra-regional and comprehensive news offer on their websites each day. In total 183 newsrooms participated in the survey, which was conducted in 2007 (response rate: 44 per cent). At first glance, three different relations can be identified between professional and participatory media: competition, complementarity and integration. We found little evidence that weblogs or other forms of participatory media are replacing traditional forms of journalism. It seems to be more likely that they complement one another. Besides this, we observed that the integration of audience participation platforms into news websites is expansive. Therefore, the study also reflects on the following questions: How do newsrooms manage user contributions on their sites? What kinds of rules and features have already been implemented?

Introduction

What kinds of changes are journalism and current public spheres subject to, reflecting the arrival of new media? The research project "Journalism on the Internet" (2006–8) investigated the effects of this broad shift. Consequently, the emerging relationship between professional and participatory media was interrogated on an empirical basis. In addition, it was also assumed that there might be an increasing amount of technical intermediation due to specialised "search-engine journalism" (Hartley, 2008).

But will common social Web applications like weblogs and collaborative edited platforms really lead to a transformation of news journalism? And afterwards, are they going to replace traditional media? Despite the simplified communicative access to the public sphere, there still seems to be a need for professional middlemen. Yet, journalists' tasks and roles may currently start to exceed traditional routines.

Besides the traditional mass media model consisting of professional communicators, two additional types of communication are apparent on the Internet. On the one hand, practical capacities in general, and thus communications, tend to be more participatory, interactive, and networked. Yochai Benkler is speaking of "enhanced autonomy", when he describes the practical freedom of individuals in a networked public sphere (2006, pp. 8–10). This major change fosters the capabilities of news production; citizen journalism emerges.

On the other hand, as already indicated, a sort of "technisation" is evident—meaning that news reporting on the Web becomes more technical. Automated news selection is already processed by search engines like Google news.

Principally, three different relations between newly emerged news production models (participatory, technical) and the professional model are conceivable (see Figure 1). Firstly, if their outcome shares a comparable *identity*, they will probably *compete* in the same market. Secondly, some online newsrooms also try to integrate social media or special news techniques on their websites; we call this action *"integration"*. Thirdly, the relationship can be described as *complementary*. The different communication types may supplement each other by reporting about different issues or by targeting distinctive audiences. Moreover, participatory formats might serve as sources for traditional journalism (and vice versa), or as a space for follow-up communication of the media public. In the subsequent sections, which type of relationship might be the most appropriate will be discussed on the basis of empirical findings.

Literature Overview

Generally, "information on the people who provide us with news on the net is surprisingly scarce" (Quandt et al., 2006). It is certainly no exaggeration to say that this is still the case, especially with regard to broader empirical findings about the newly emerging forms and their relations with traditional media. A considerable body of work

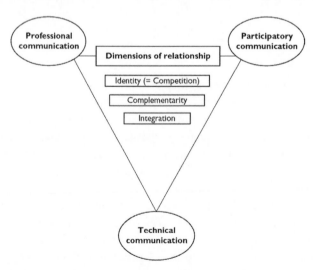

FIGURE 1
News-related types of communication on the Internet and their potential relations

discussing the connection between professional and citizen media has been conducted. For example, different models of audience participation have been sketched out in a typology (Nip, 2006). Bruns (2005) provided a distinguished overview on the possibilities of user participation in the news process. He differentiated between "gatekeeping" and "gatewatching" to demonstrate that journalistic roles are fundamentally transforming. Interesting typologies and broader concepts related to citizen journalism and user-generated content (UGC) have also been put forward by Bowman and Willis (2003), Gillmor (2004) or, in the form of an overview, by Outing (2005). Bowman and Willis analytically shaped the variety of relationships between professional journalists and citizen media in an "emerging media ecosystem".

There has also been a rapid growth in the amount of mainly empirical research concerning participatory media, but relations are mostly only partially investigated. Few studies have been undertaken to explore the role of blogs as sources for traditional media and their impact in terms of inter-media agenda setting (e.g. Messner and DiStaso, 2008, Reese et al., 2007). Reich (2008) analyses the limitations of citizen reporters by comparing their source contacts to mainstream journalists.

Audience participation within a professional journalistic framework was empirically investigated by Hermida and Thurman (2008). Their findings show that opportunities for reader participation on British newspaper websites have dramatically increased. Even so, they also had to admit finally that journalists are still trying (and successfully) to retain gate-keeping roles.

Research Design and Methodology

Our research aimed to draw a more comprehensive picture of different patterns of online journalism. Hence, it was necessary to interview not only traditional news organisations with their Internet branches but also representatives of those recently emerged offerings arising from Web. To specify "journalism on the Web" and the German websites which do regularly offer "journalistic" content we conducted a content analysis as a first (methodological) step. Thus, the number of journalistic websites in Germany was identified.

Until today, it has been rather untypical in empirical studies to identify relevant journalistic units by specifically considering their identities and content qualities. Researchers in Germany, for instance, have preferred to define journalism primarily by structural parameters (e.g. Quandt et al., 2006; Weischenberg et al., 2006). But new media technologies raised the question whether a journalistic function might also be fulfilled in deviating structures. Are organisational forms like editorial staffs or trained journalists, who regularly pursue a journalistic profession, still needed in order to gather information and select and disseminate news?

It must be assumed that there might be "functional equivalents" on the Internet, which have the ability to provide news like traditional media do. These equivalents, which commonly have no organisational affiliation with established media, tend to be based on different structures: bloggers can perform like journalists although they often work alone or are linked to a network (blogosphere), without the background of a newsroom and without professional training. We investigated this by extending our empirical research to conceivable formats (weblogs and other forms of participatory media, news search-engines), which may be considered as potential equivalents.

Content Analysis to Identify the Population of Journalistic Websites

One of the main challenges of the described research design was to develop criteria for very different types of news offerings. In order to decide whether the content of a website is mainly "journalistic" or not, five defining criteria were systematically checked: actuality, universality, periodicity, accessibility and autonomy.

In advance of the content analysis, relevant media types, which regularly offer news also on their Web branches, were selected. The list of websites related to traditional media contained the following types: daily and weekly newspapers, general-interest magazines, supra-regional TV/radio, and news agencies. A number of national media listings were deemed appropriate to identify relevant websites attached to the selected types for the content analysis. It was even more difficult to discover Internet-only news sites and especially different kinds of participatory media like weblogs for instance. It must be noted that a lack of scientifically proven, consistent directories was found in this Internet-only section. Reflecting this, a differentiated sample selection strategy was developed (for details see Neuberger et al., 2009, pp. 202–9).

As shown in Table 1, a total of 1242 websites were analysed. The unit of analysis was the full website. The content was not completely coded when, within 10 mouse clicks, it remained unclear whether relevant information was offered. The coding manual was pilot-tested and revised in advance of the analysis. Five trained coders analysed the material between September 2006 and May 2007.[1] The criteria mentioned above guaranteed that only the *core area* of journalism on the Web was part of the selected population.

TABLE 1

Population of German websites identified as "journalistic" (content analysis, 2006–7)

Media type/Internet format	Number of located and analysed websites (as of May 2007)	Therefrom as "journalistic" identified websites		Proportion of general population as % (N = 503)
		N	%	
Daily newspapers	300	265	88.3	52.7
TV/radio	408	89	21.8	17.7
Weekly newspapers/ Sunday newspapers	10	2	20.0	0.4
News agencies	13	2	15.4	0.4
Magazines	241	30	12.4	6.0
In affiliation with traditional media	*972*	*388*	*39.9*	*77.1*
Professional-edited news sites	59	40	67.8	8.0
Portals	53	39	73.6	7.8
Weblogs	97	18	18.6	3.6
Community-edited news sites	5	5	100.0	1.0
News search engines	16	13	81.3	2.6
Others	40	0	0.0	0.0
Internet-only websites	*270*	*115*	*42.6*	*22.9*
Total	1242	503	40.5	100.0

The following overview merely summarises the most important steps of the protocol. Firstly, the investigated websites had to be generally accessible (accessibility). Paid content and user registrations were not regarded as access limitations. Secondly, the editors had to be independent and the content should not contain advertising or promotions (autonomy). Thirdly, the websites had to offer full news content and not just headlines or teasers (completeness). Fourthly, they had to provide articles or postings which coders could identify as up to date and relevant (actuality). Fifthly, the news content had to be updated at least twice within the last seven days before coding (periodicity). Sixthly, it was necessary that the content was not limited to single specific subjects or target groups (universality).

The results of this pre-study indicate that the *core area* of journalism on the Internet is still occupied by news websites affiliated with traditional media (77 per cent, $N = 503$). A mere 23 per cent of the identified news websites belong to the Internet-only division. All in all, just two-fifths of the investigated units can be considered as "journalistic" (41 per cent); i.e. they match all given criteria. Especially websites related to newspapers have been successfully coded. Up to May 2007, only a small number of print magazines have kept substantial news websites. They have often supplied incomplete articles or have only occasionally been updated. The small number of identified weblogs might lead to the conclusion that most German bloggers do not compete with traditional news journalism.

Online Newsroom Survey

A comprehensive survey of members of editorial departments subsequent to the content analysis was also central to the empirical research. The selected respondents were either editors-in-chief of traditional news branches in the Internet, or they were responsible for the sampled Web-only media, in case they had no editorial staff. The population of respondents did not match exactly the number of identified websites because of organisational reasons. Some of the newsrooms supervised different news sites. Follow-up research was conducted to identify such organisational links.

The survey of online newsrooms took place between June and October 2007. A mail questionnaire was preferred for handling reasons. Thus, respondents particularly had the opportunity to undertake background research. The extended survey consisted of various dimensions, which themselves contained several complex questions.

Two major research directions were investigated: on the one hand, the relationship between old and new media, and on the other hand, the relations between professional, participatory and technical news formats. In the course of a pre-study, in-depth interviews with 12 senior news executives helped to design the questionnaire.

Table 2 provides an overview of the response rate and the population of identified organisational units which supervise news sites on the Web. In total 183 editors-in-chief participated in our 2007 online newsroom survey (44 per cent).

Comparable data were also generated through a second survey conducted in 2006. In this survey, 218 newsrooms of old-media divisions (newspapers, radio, television, news agencies) were investigated; 93 editorial board members participated (43 per cent).

TABLE 2
General population of German online newsrooms and response rate by type (survey, 2007)

	General population	Proportion of response	Response rate as%
Traditional media websites			
Daily newspapers	216	98	45.4
Weekly newspapers	2	2	100.0
Magazines	28	12	42.9
TV/radio	61	32	52.5
News agencies	2	0	0
Internet-only websites			
Professional-edited news sites	36	17	47.2
Portals	35	6	17.1
News search engines	12	5	41.7
Community-edited news sites	5	3	60.0
Weblogs	16	8	50.0
Total	413	183	44.3

Research Dimensions

This paper focuses on three selected research dimensions. Findings from each item listed below will be reviewed in the subsequent discussion. Due to limitations of space, the particular relations between new- and old-media divisions within traditional news organisations will not be outlined here.

1. *Competition*: Do professional and participatory news formats compete with each other? How does this competition affect professional journalism?
2. *Complementarity*: What kind of complementary relations exist between professional and participatory Web news? Furthermore, what kind of affection does their mutual presentation have? What power do the recently emerged formats have in terms of journalistic investigation?
3. *Integration*: In what ways do professional news organisations adopt participatory elements? What impact does increasing reader participation have?

Findings

Competition

As a first step, different aspects of competition between professional and participatory media will be presented. Respondents do not perceive a major threat to the reader market of traditional journalism. The statement "Journalistic intermediation is less important on the Internet because anyone can publish without much effort" is widely seen as "not at all true" (62 per cent, $N = 172$, four-point scale). But the survey results also indicate that current changes in advertising markets are noticed as a pending risk for professional news organisations.

Can blogs do journalism? Answers generally remain ambiguous about this matter (see Table 3).

TABLE 3

Statements about competition among journalism, blogs, and community-edited sites (only answers stated as "appropriate to a high degree", as %, online newsroom survey, 2007)

Statements	Daily newspapers (N =74–92)	Magazines/weeklies (N =8–14)	TV/radio (N =21–32)	Internet-only (N =25–34)	Total (N =128–172)
Competitive relations between journalism and blogs					
Weblogs have nothing to do with journalism (Cramer-V =0.148)	33.0	7.7	17.2	18.2	25.2
Weblogs are a new type of journalism (Cramer-V =0.146)	11.5	8.3	16.1	12.1	12.3
Bloggers perceive themselves as journalists (Cramer-V =0.160)	22.7	0	26.1	10.3	19.3
Bloggers believe that journalists are reporting negatively about bloggers because they perceive them as competitors (Cramer-V =0.153)	18.9	37.5	14.3	24.0	20.3
Information in the blogosphere is regularly accurate because of mutual control among bloggers (Cramer-V =0.181)	10.8	33.3	12.5	32.1	17.4
In the blogosphere bias is avoided due to mutual control among bloggers (Cramer-V =0.197)	6.8	15.4	3.8	24.1	10.6
Competitive relations between journalism and community-edited sites					
Community-edited sites are a new type of journalism (Cramer-V =0.243)**	9.0	14.3	29.0	39.3	18.5
Information is regularly accurate [in community-edited sites] because of mutual control among users (Cramer-V =0.156)	30.7	23.1	32.3	25.8	29.4
In community-edited sites bias is avoided due to mutual control among users (Cramer-V =0.139)	27.1	15.4	33.3	32.3	28.3
Community-edited sites need to be professionally moderated (Cramer-V =0.243)**	70.5	53.8	66.7	48.4	64.2

*p <0.05, **p <0.01, ***p <0.001. Three-point scale. Expressions not shown are "somewhat appropriate" and "not appropriate". The expression "I cannot say" was not considered in the analysis.

On the one hand, some editors assume that bloggers perceive themselves as journalists ("appropriate to a high degree": 19 per cent, "somewhat appropriate": 62 per cent, $N = 135$). In addition, one-fifth support the statement that bloggers think that journalists recognise them as an upcoming competitor to a great extent ("appropriate to a high degree": 20 per cent, "somewhat appropriate": 57 per cent, $N = 128$).

On the other hand, the editorial leaders seem to be sceptical about the influence of bloggers in assuring quality through mutual control. Respondents favour community-edited platforms like Wikipedia in that case. Additionally, the interviewees were asked to identify three blogs with a journalistic performance. Only a small number of "journalistic" blogs was revealed: *Bildblog*, a watchblog to the German tabloid newspaper *Bild*, is mentioned most often.

Additionally, the study compares the characteristics and profiles of blogs and journalism (for details see Neuberger et al., 2009, p. 278). What it comes down to is, traditional characteristics related to journalism are more often attributed to this format by the editors than to blogs (neutrality, accuracy, credibility, continuity, relevancy, in-depth reporting). Characteristics which apply to each format to a great extent are actuality, comments on daily events, the entertaining style of writing, and the selection of exciting issues. Respondents identify the following qualities as mainly appropriate for weblogs: personal perspective, direct contact to authors, diversity of opinions, intensive discussions, and hyperlinks to external sources. The editors' perception of bloggers and journalists seems to be dissimilar. Preliminary surveys of bloggers and of journalists have shown as well that both self-perception, as well as third-person-perception, is clearly different. Hence, it must be concluded that direct competition between blogs and journalism is rather unlikely.

Complementarity

In this section we offer answers to the question: To what extent and in which ways do citizen media formats complement journalism? The interviewed online editors-in-chief, as illustrated above, do not perceive the relationship between blogs and journalism to be a competitive one; substitution tendencies are mostly rejected. Furthermore, different citizen media formats like community-edited news sites are similarly not seen as a competitor.

In what ways then do blogs supplement traditional media? Principally, news coverage could be initiated by weblogs. Journalists may also write about the blogging phenomenon. Weblogs and mainstream media could use each other as sources. Blogs have become agenda-setters for traditional media in certain situations. In the specific German environment, this has been the case to a smaller extent, but weblogs have often been reported as sources during natural disasters, terrorist attacks, wars etc. (Messner and DiStaso, 2008). In addition, the possibility of reciprocal critic offers another form of complementarity.

As can be seen in Table 4, respondents' answers are pointing towards a more harmonious liaison. The given statement "weblogs and journalism complement each other and do not compete" is widely accepted ("appropriate to a high degree": 45 per cent, "somewhat appropriate": 50 per cent, $N = 161$). That media criticism within weblogs fosters the quality of journalism is regarded by a majority (55 per cent, $N = 148$) as "somewhat appropriate".

TABLE 4

Statements about complementarity among journalism, blogs, and community-edited sites (only answers stated as "appropriate to a high degree", as %, online newsroom survey, 2007)

Statements	Daily newspapers (N=73–93)	Magazines/weeklies (N=11–13)	TV/radio (N=24–31)	Internet-only (N=21–34)	Total (N=136–171)
Complementary relations between journalism and blogs					
Weblogs and journalism complement each other and do not compete (Cramer-V =0.124)	39.3	50.0	51.6	50.0	44.7
Within weblogs the audience communicates about mass media coverage (Cramer-V =0.168)	28.6	23.1	25.0	40.0	29.7
The balance of power between journalism and the audience is changing towards the audience because of the advent of weblogs (Cramer-V =0.173)	7.8	16.7	22.2	24.1	14.5
Weblogs foster the quality of journalism through their media criticism (Cramer-V =0.178)	8.5	27.3	10.7	18.5	12.2
Blogging is spreading fast because of the press and broadcasting coverage (Cramer-V =0.089)	16.0	23.1	21.4	9.7	16.3
Journalism is orientating about the blogosphere and criticises it (Cramer-V =0.066)	7.9	8.3	7.4	9.5	8.1
Complementary relations between journalism and community-edited sites					
Community-edited sites and journalism complement each other and do not compete (Cramer-V =0.131)	50.5	69.2	56.7	61.3	55.2

*p <0.05, **p <0.01, ***p <0.001. Three-point scale. Expressions not shown are "somewhat appropriate" and "not appropriate". The expression "I cannot say" was not considered in the analysis.

TABLE 5

Motifs for the use of weblogs (in terms of work) by editorial staff members in traditional newsrooms and online newsrooms (as %, newsroom surveys, 2006–7)

What are staff members searching for on weblogs?	In traditional newsrooms (2006)			In online newsrooms (2007)		
	Often	Seldom	Never	Often	Seldom	Never
Topic ideas (N =33/N =87)	42.4	48.5	9.1	34.5	47.1	18.4
Facts concerning a current occasion (N =29/N =81) (Cramer-V =0.293)**	31.0	24.1	44.8	14.8	56.8	28.4
Watching weblogs as a phenomenon (N =32/N =85)	28.1	46.9	25.0	45.9	37.6	16.5
Eyewitness reports, which may be cited (N =33/N =83) (Cramer-V =0.228)*	18.2	66.7	15.2	14.5	47.0	38.6
Thematic background information (N =34/N =84)	17.6	47.1	35.3	23.8	52.4	23.8
Criticism on companies, political parties etc. which may be taken up (N =32/N =86)	15.6	43.8	40.6	19.8	50.0	30.2
Pros and cons of a controversial issue (N =35/N =87) (Cramer-V =0.241)*	14.3	54.3	31.4	32.2	54.0	13.8
Response to own reporting (N =29/N =81)	13.8	44.8	41.4	32.1	40.7	27.2
Insider reports which may be cited (N =31/N =84)	12.9	51.6	35.5	15.5	50.0	34.5
Range of opinion with regard to a controversial issue (N =31/N =87) (Cramer-V =0.292)**	12.9	32.3	54.8	37.9	35.6	26.4

*$p < 0.05$, **$p < 0.01$, ***$p < 0.001$. Only newsrooms which use weblogs were asked here. The expression "I cannot say" was not considered in the analysis.

What impact do weblogs have in terms of journalistic investigation? The potential use of citizen media as a source describes another sort of complementary relation. Therefore, we asked the online editors-in-chief to provide information on the investigation practices in their newsrooms. These data are most widely comparable to the newsroom survey we conducted in 2006. In this earlier survey, traditional, non-Internet divisions had been subject to research. Forty-one per cent (N =90) of the interviewed non-Internet newsrooms use weblogs in terms of work. By comparison, about three-quarters (76 per cent, N = 131) of the online editors-in-chief stated that their staff are using blogs.

Table 5 illustrates, *inter alia*, the trend that weblogs could serve as a source of inspiration. They are particularly employed to identify topic ideas. Another common aim of using weblogs is their observation as a phenomenon. While traditional newsrooms rather prefer to search for facts concerning current events, online newsrooms more often search for pros and cons of a controversial issue. Online staff members also rather watch responses to their own reporting.

Additionally, in the 2006 newsroom survey, the editors-in-chief were asked in an open question to identify those blogs which they acknowledge to be most important in terms of journalistic activities. Again, *Bildblog* is favourite here (50 per cent, $N = 22$). Other blogs are only mentioned in individual cases.

Integration

The last section of our findings is devoted to the integration of participatory formats within professional journalistic frameworks. To what extent do German newsrooms offer user-generated features on their websites? What consequences are observed?

Fifty-five per cent ($N = 148$) of the surveyed newsrooms have implemented the "Web 2.0" applications blog, video blog and/or podcast already. At least, blogs and podcasts are mostly limited to editors. However, these editors may now address their audience in an easier and more comfortable way, and users may comment on their blogs. By now, online divisions from magazines, weeklies and broadcasting operators have mainly adopted blogs and podcasts. Indeed, only a few news websites offer user-edited blogs.

Concerning the opportunities of audience participation, our study revealed that readers are limited to comment on stories in most cases. In addition to that, readers often are encouraged to submit photos. But more extensive citizen contributions within the news process are less common (see Table 6). This means that users may not complement editor's work in the form of a "pro-am-journalism" like Bruns (2008) sketched. Only a small number of newsrooms offer the opportunity to assist editors in writing or investigation tasks. Thus, up to now, the audience has mainly been limited to a role they already had in traditional media. User participation is at the very beginning; it still seems to be a field where online journalism is at an experimental stage.

Why may users not be allowed to take on more active roles? We asked the newsrooms which provide UGC opportunities to provide some information about the potential effects. Though it is often supposed that reader photos might offer cost reductions, only 1 per cent of online editors state this as "appropriate to a high degree" ($N = 96$, three-point scale). Another 85 per cent ($N = 106$) believe that user contributions do not ease journalistic investigation in general. The opposite might be a more likely scenario: findings indicate that more personal effort is needed due to more participation initiatives ("somewhat appropriate": 56 per cent, $N = 108$). Nevertheless, the range of opinions may also increase ("appropriate to a high degree": 45 per cent, $N = 104$) and the websites' general reach might rise ("appropriate to a high degree": 24 per cent, $N = 101$).

Evaluating the subject of user participation as a whole, many editors do not believe that the journalist's role perceptions have changed very much. A majority of respondents concede that journalists have difficulties in accepting users as co-editors ("mainly appropriate": 53 per cent, $N = 165$, four-point scale). An extended level of audience participation still remains to be achieved.

TABLE 6

Proportion of online newsrooms which offer elements of user participation on their websites (as %, online newsroom survey, 2007)

Present opportunities for reader participation. Readers are allowed to …	Daily newspapers (N=92–94)	Magazines/weeklies (N=14)	TV/radio (N=29–30)	Internet-only (N=22–33)	Total (N=160–171)
Send in photos for publication (Cramer-V =0.191)	53.2	35.7	53.3	40.0	49.7
Comment on news stories written by editors (below the article) (Cramer-V =0.256)**	41.5	64.3	13.3	56.5	40.4
Create a personal profile (Cramer-V =0.196)	24.5	42.9	24.1	32.0	27.2
Self-select the topics of their own stories (Cramer-V =0.267)**	27.2	28.6	3.3	44.0	25.5
Publish their own contributions without previous vetting (Cramer-V =0.185)	21.3	42.9	6.7	24.2	21.1
Create an own weblog (Cramer-V =0.140)	16.0	7.1	13.3	16.7	14.8
Support editors in writing and investigation (Cramer-V =0.211)*	12.8	7.1	0	26.1	11.8
Rate contributions from other users on a grade scale (Cramer-V =0.207)*	2.1	21.4	6.7	12.0	6.1
Participate as moderators (Cramer-V =0.202)*	2.1	14.3	6.7	16.0	6.1
Rate contributions from editors on a grade scale (Cramer-V =0.213)*	3.2	21.4	0	13.6	5.6
Vet contributions of other users before publication (Cramer-V =0.203)*	1.1	0	0	12.0	2.5

*$p < 0.05$, **$p < 0.01$, ***$p < 0.001$. The group of Internet-only websites is limited to professional-edited sites, portals and community-edited sites. Expressions not shown are "planned within the next 12 months" and "later or not planned".

Conclusion

The empirical findings of our research project generally reveal that participatory media tend to complement rather than to replace professional journalism. The foregoing website analysis already signified that only a few blogs and other social media routinely perform in a traditional journalistic manner. Verified by both surveys, weblogs in particular show deviating characteristics compared to traditional news and usually fulfil alternative needs. Just a small number of bloggers prefer general news reporting, as examined here, while many others—like media watchbloggers, tech bloggers etc.—try to shine in very particular areas.

That is also why social Web applications have become important sources in terms of journalistic investigation. In their flourishing environment, journalists may find topic ideas as well as eyewitness reports. But weblogs and collaborative edited platforms also allow the audience to have a place for follow-up conversation; a "closed-off annex where readers can talk and discuss" (Bowman and Willis, 2003). As demonstrated above, the diversity of relations also includes the mutual influence which traditional and participatory media are beginning to exert on each other, especially via reciprocal comments. Interesting research is conducted in this area; especially the work of Messner and DiStaso (2008) on a potential "source cycle" between blogs and mainstream media.

Journalism is confronted with new challenges: the integration of user contributions within professional websites still lacks innovative and comprehensive approaches. News sites in most cases are just experimenting, and editors are not really involved in this process. Moreover, competition sharpens on the advertising market as new enterprises like Google gain share. News organisations will have to reinvent journalism, when they get under pressure reflecting declining audiences and financial losses. Thus, the concepts of "gatewatching" and "produsage", which mark structural shifts within modern public spheres of networked societies, should be considered as a supplementary initiative—besides fostering the quality of journalistic cores.

NOTE

1. The data reflect an intercoder reliability of 87 per cent on the basis of Holsti's formula.

REFERENCES

BENKLER, YOCHAI (2006) *The Wealth of Networks*, New Haven, CT: Yale University Press.

BOWMAN, SHANE and WILLIS, CHRIS (2003) *We Media: how audiences are shaping the future of news and information*, Reston, VA: The Media Center at the American Press Institute, http://www.hypergene.net/wemedia/download/we_media.pdf, accessed 17 May 2005.

BRUNS, AXEL (2005) *Gatewatching: collaborative online news production*, New York: Peter Lang.

BRUNS, AXEL (2008) *Blogs, Wikipedia, Second Life, and Beyond. From production to produsage*, New York: Peter Lang.

GILLMOR, DAN (2004) *We the Media. Grassroots journalism by the people, for the people*, Beijing and Cambridge: O'Reilly.

HARTLEY, JOHN (2008) "Journalism as a Human Right. The cultural approach to journalism", in: Martin Löffelholz and David H. Weaver (Eds), *Global Journalism Research. Theories, methods, findings, future*, Malden, MA: Blackwell, pp. 39–51.

HERMIDA, ALFRED and THURMAN, NEIL (2008) "A Clash of Cultures. The integration of user-generated content within professional journalistic frameworks at British newspaper websites", *Journalism Practice* 2(3), pp. 343–56.

MESSNER, MARCUS and DISTASO, MARCIA WATSON (2008) "The Source Cycle. How traditional media and weblogs use each other as sources", *Journalism Studies* 9(2), pp. 447–63.

NEUBERGER, CHRISTOPH, NUERNBERGK, CHRISTIAN and RISCHKE, MELANIE (Eds) (2009) *Journalismus im Internet. Profession, Partizipation, Technisierung [Journalism on the Internet. Professionalization, participation, technization]*, Wiesbaden: VS-Verlag.

NIP, JOYCE Y. M. (2006) "Exploring the Second Phase of Public Journalism", *Journalism Studies* 7(2), pp. 212–36.

OUTING, STEVE (2005) "The 11 Layers of Citizen Journalism. A resource guide to help you figure out how to put this industry trend to work for you and your newsroom", 13 June, http://www.poynter.org/content/content_view.asp?id_83126, accessed 7 December 2006.

QUANDT, THORSTEN, LÖFFELHOLZ, MARTIN, WEAVER, DAVID H., HANITZSCH, THOMAS and ALTMEPPEN, KLAUS-DIETER (2006) "American and German Online Journalists at the Beginning of the 21st Century", *Journalism Studies* 7(2), pp. 172–86.

REESE, STEPHEN D., ROUTIGLIANO, LOU, HYUN, KIDEUK and JEONG, JAEKWAN (2007) "Mapping the Blogosphere Professional and Citizen-based Media in the Global News Arena", *Journalism* 8(3), pp. 235–61.

REICH, ZVI (2008) "How Citizens Create News Stories. The 'news access' problem reversed", *Journalism Studies* 9(5), pp. 739–58.

WEISCHENBERG, SIEGFRIED, MALIK, MAJA and SCHOLL, ARMIN (2006) *Die Souffleure der Mediengesellschaft. Report über die deutschen Journalisten [Prompters of Media Society. Report about journalists in Germany]*, Konstanz: UVK.

THE IMPACT OF "CITIZEN JOURNALISM" ON CHINESE MEDIA AND SOCIETY

Xin Xin

This paper discusses the political and social implications of the rise of "citizen journalism" (CJ) in China, a country where mainstream media are still under tight control while social conflicts are intensifying and nationalistic sentiments are exacerbating. The impact of CJ on mainstream journalism (MJ) and public participation is mostly discussed in respect of Western democratic societies. We know little about CJ and its political and social impact in nondemocratic societies like China. This paper provides an analysis of four case studies of CJ practice in China, which show that the impact of CJ on Chinese mainstream media and society is multifaceted. There is evidence that CJ is used by MJ as a news source as well as an alternative channel for distributing politically sensitive information. Therefore, it can be argued that CJ can work effectively together with MJ to make it more difficult for the Party to control online information flows within the country, even though CJ alone is unlikely to be a driving force in promoting social change in China. Meanwhile, CJ is also establishing itself as a vehicle for the expression of nationalistic sentiments.

Introduction

This paper discusses the political and social implications of the rise of "citizen journalism" (CJ) in China, where mainstream media are still under tight control while social conflicts are intensifying and nationalistic sentiments are exacerbating. Web 2.0 has enabled grassroots-citizens to do the job which used to be conducted exclusively by professional journalists (Gillmor, 2004). Here "Web 2.0" is seen as a new range of Internet-based services, such as YouTube, Facebook, Flickr, MySpace, for social networking and sharing user-generated content (UGC) (O'Reilly, 2005). Meanwhile, with the emergence of mainstream journalist-bloggers, the divide between blogger-amateurs and journalist-professionals is blurring (Robinson, 2009).

In the Web 2.0 environment, scholars are concerned with the impact of CJ on mainstream journalism (MJ) and public participation in Western democracies. In democratic societies the weblog community is growing and now attracts a sizeable audience, exerting political influence by reporting disasters and controversies (Allan, 2007; Nguyen, 2006). The Asian tsunami, the London bombings, Hurricane Katrina and the Presidential elections in the United States, Australia and South Korea are good examples of CJ's activism and its media impact. Some scholars suggest that CJ is posing challenges as well as creating opportunities for MJ (Allan, 2007). According to Gillmor (2004), CJ has an advantage over MJ in that it greatly enhances public participation. Some scholars have also suggested that CJ has taught MJ how to communicate with the public, in and outside the newsroom (Chang, 2005; Nguyen, 2006). With self-generated content and self-managed distribution/reception, Web 2.0 applications in general and CJ in particular, as suggested, are transforming the traditional mode of communication (one to one and top-down) into "mass self-communication" (many to many and bottom-up) (Castells, 2007: 248, quoted in Allan, 2007: 2). Of course, whether such self-communication is really a mass phenomenon remains questionable, as Pippa Norris's (2001) research on the "digital divide" reminds us. Even in affluent and technologically-advanced democracies like Britain, in 2008 only 13 percent of the population used the Internet for "citizen participation", engaging in such activities as "giving views, getting in touch with elected representatives, joining organisations and taking part in surveys and consultations" (Ofcom, 2009). Moreover, some studies have shown that the adoption of UGC by the newsrooms of mainstream media is likely to be hindered by a combination of professional, organizational, socio-cultural and economic factors (Paulussen and Ugille, 2008; Paulussen et al., 2007).

As we can see, the impact of CJ on MJ and politics is mostly discussed in respect of Western democratic societies. We know little about CJ practice and its political and social impact in authoritarian societies like China. What role does CJ play in a society where the Internet, media and public participation remain subject to tight ideological control? What are the likely consequences of the fact that China is embracing Web 2.0 technology and digitalization, on the one hand, while being reluctant to relinquish its control over content distributed by traditional media and the Internet on the other? What impact does CJ have on traditional media and on the level of public participation in debates on social injustices in China? To explore these questions, this paper provides four case studies of CJ practice in China in order to analyze the multifaceted role that CJ plays in China's fast-changing media and social environment.

The country's economy is growing fast, reflecting the processes of rapid urbaniza-tion, industrialization, marketization and integration into the world capitalist economy: so is the gap between rich and poor (Blue Book of China's Society, 2007). Over 60 per cent of Chinese residents surveyed in 2007 were concerned about inequality and injustice in the distribution of income, welfare and job opportunities among different social groups and between urban and rural areas of China. Most cases of social injustice in China are related, directly or indirectly, to corruption, governmental misadministration, merchant misbehavior, property and labor rights violations, and environmental problems (Blue Book of China's Society, 2005). According to China's official statistics, the number of substantial protests increased six times in 10 years, growing from 10,000 cases in 1993 to 60,000 cases in 2003 (Blue Book of China's Society, 2005). The population which took part in the protests jumped from 730,000 to 3 million in 10 years (Blue Book of China's Society, 2005). Although official figures have not been updated since 2003, there is strong circumstantial evidence that social conflict is intensifying (Zhu, 2009). These problems are compounded by the lack of the rule of law and information transparency, and the failure of the media to act as a "watchdog" checking on corruptions and wrongdoings (Blue Book of China's Society, 2005).

As part of the country's modernization package, the Internet is developing fast. China has the largest online population in the world: at the end of June 2009 there were over 330 million Chinese Internet users (China Internet Network Information Center, 2009). The vast majority of these Internet users live in urban areas. Only one in every 100 rural residents had access to the Internet in 2005 (Zhao et al., 2006). As a key component of the Chinese media and ideological system, content distributed over the Internet is still under tight control. A "Great Firewall" is used to filter out all sorts of sensitive information which might challenge the rule of the Communist Party or undermine national unity and social stability (Zhang, 2006). Still, the Internet provides Chinese Internet users with a freer space than any traditional media outlets (Zhang, 2006).

According to Min Dahong, a Chinese communication scholar, "critical online realism" and "online nationalism" are the two dominant frames adopted by the Chinese online community to engage with discussions of domestic and foreign affairs, respectively (Youth Journalist, 2004). A critical attitude towards China's social reality is widespread within the Chinese online community. Meanwhile, Chinese neo-nationalism—a combination of national pride, nationalistic/patriotic sentiments, xenophobia and public anxiety about a perceived crisis in Chinese national identity—is emerging in the context of globalization. With weblogs broadening the social geography of journalism activities, it is essential not to ignore their impact on national identity, particularly on the way in which "we" and "others" (i.e., those from outside the nation) are divided. The Internet has become a popular place where Chinese young people identify themselves and judge those "others" in China.

Min sees moderate expressions of nationalistic sentiment online in a positive light (Youth Journalist, 2004). However, Chinese nationalism seems threatening to others while the Internet is transformed into a vessel for nurturing a new generation of "angry youth" (fengqing) (Osnos, 2008). Li Datong, an outspoken journalist, points out that there is a difference between the new generation of "angry youth" and the rebelling generation demonstrating in 1989. The latter turned up against corruptions and social injustice, while the current young generation tends to blame the West while turning a blind eye to the Chinese reality (Osnos, 2008). As Chinese official statistics suggest, two in three Chinese Internet users are young people aged 30 and under (China Internet Network Information Center, 2008). There is a sizeable pool of potential "fengqing" to grow up online.

Against this background, I argue that the progressive role that Web 2.0 technologies can play in China in empowering grassroots journalists to fight against the political, economic and ideological establishment, should not be overstated. What we need is a realistic assessment of the role of CJ in relation to MJ bearing in mind China's complex socio-political context. This does not mean that the impact of the weblog phenomenon on the country's political and media system is any less dramatic than in Western democracies. The impact of CJ in China is multifaceted and serves as a useful example to understand the complexity of the relationship between CJ, MJ and social change.

This paper explores CJ's multifaceted role in China from three main perspectives. It begins with an examination of the ways in which CJ influences the journalistic practices adopted by Chinese mainstream media. It then uses two case studies to show that CJ serves as a complementary news source for mainstream media as well as an alternative channel for releasing "politically sensitive" news. The third case discusses how in some circumstances both CJ and MJ might fail to break through China's Internet and media censorship. Finally, this paper discusses how CJ and the online community nurture Chinese neo-nationalism. Drawing on a contextual analysis of these four case studies, I suggest that the weblog phenomenon and CJ in China are still far away from becoming an engine of radical political change. CJ, just like MJ, is facing challenges posed by a combination of forces, including tightened ideological control, severe market competition and the rise of extreme forms of Chinese nationalism.

Citizen Journalism is More Than a Source of Information: The Case of the "Nail House"

It is quite common nowadays for Chinese mainstream journalists, particularly investigative journalists, to use CJ or weblogs as a source of news and information (Zheng and Hao, 2008). In the case of the "nail house" in Chongqing, CJ not only served as a source of information for MJ, but also conducted field reporting traditionally associated with MJ. The interaction between CJ and MJ was the key factor to explain the effectiveness of the investigation into the "nail house".

"Nail house" is a term which was used to describe a household which disobeyed the official command to move out from a state-owned property 20–30 years ago. Here it refers to a modest two-story brick building, which stood in the centre of a 10-meter-deep pit as the only house left in the construction site in Chongqing, Southwest China (Xinhua News Agency, 2007). The origin of the Chongqing nail house can be traced back to 2004 before the existence of China's Property Law, which came into effect three years later. It was associated with one of the disputes which are likely to occur in today's China between ordinary citizens and real estate developers—symbols of capitalism. The story about the Chongqing house began with its owners' refusal of the offer of compensation from a local real estate company, who planned to demolish their home for a business purpose. The house's owners were then sued by the company. Later, the local court ruled that the house owners must move out from their own house within three days.

The first image of the "nail house" appeared online in February 2007. A photo taken by a local resident was posted to an online forum under the title "The Coolest "nail house" in History". This photo was soon spread among online forum participants and bloggers. The issue did not attract attention from the Chinese mainstream media until 8 March 2007, when the *Southern Metropolitan Daily* for the first time published the photo attached to a small story about online discussions of the house disputes. More coverage appeared after 19 March. On 2 April the house owners ultimately reached agreement with the real estate company through the mediation of the local government. On the same day, the building was demolished.

Zola Zhou, a young Chinese blogger, took a self-financed trip to Chongqing and reported the dispute over the "nail house" on site (Zhou, 2007). Zhou interviewed the house owners and chatted with other homeowners, who were likewise threatened with losing their own homes because of the urban development plan of Shanghai, Guangzhou and other cities. Zhou won the trust of interviewees and Internet users because of his independent stance and his role as a grassroots-blogger. Hundreds of Internet users left favorable comments on Zhou's blog, which became an open platform for Internet users to comment on both sides of the house dispute: something that mainstream media failed to provide.

Still, it is too early to conclude that bloggers, like Zhou, are able to replace professional journalists and undertake the whole investigation and fully inform the public. Having no journalistic training, Zhou did not know how to handle the field investigation and asked professional journalists and supporters for advice, as he admitted in his blog-diary (Zhou, 2007; Zheng and Hao, 2008). Moreover, as an individual blogger, Zhou was in considerable need of support from mainstream media and relied heavily on the latter's coverage of his own story to justify the reliability of his reporting. Zhou posted a blog entry to the article published by *The Southern Metropolitan Daily* about him. In order to draw weblog hits, Zhou added an entry to the investigative report completed by

The Southern Metropolitan Daily about the "nail house". As an individual blogger, Zhou suffered from financial constraints. Zhou's trip to Chongqing was sponsored by a small family fund and some support from Internet users. Without adequate financial support, it is difficult for independent bloggers, like Zhou, to carry out field reporting. Although mainstream media may face the same problem, CJ practitioners are likely to suffer much more. Last but not least, Zhou seemed to lose interest in the house dispute immediately after the two sides of the conflict had reached an agreement, while professional journalists continued to report.

To sum up, the case suggests that CJ is an important news source for MJ and that the slow response of Chinese mainstream media to social conflicts enhances CJ's investigative role. CJ played a watchdog role in unveiling violations of property rights (Zheng and Hao, 2008). Even though CJ had a positive impact on the exposure of social injustice and facilitated public discussion of the house dispute, CJ is unable to function alone. In the case of the "nail house", CJ with support from MJ carried out the investigation and made the public aware of the dispute.

Citizen Journalism as an Alternative News Distribution Channel for Journalists-Bloggers: The Case of the "Loufan Landslide"

The case of the "Loufan landslide" indicates how a journalist-blogger used his weblog to expose the cover-up of an accident in Northwest China. Work-related accidents due to poor safety measures are another important aspect of social injustice in today's China. The landslide took place at a local iron mine in Loufan County in the suburbs of the Shanxi provincial capital Taiyuan on 1 August 2008. Initially, the local authorities attempted to cover up the causes of the disaster by blaming the "bad weather" and deliberately concealed the real number of casualties.

Sun Chunlong, a reporter of the news journal *Oriental Outlook* (a commercial affiliation of Xinhua News Agency), was not convinced by the information about the accident provided by the Loufan local authorities (Sun, 2008). After Sun traced the record of the discussions in "Loufan online forum" run by the Chinese search engine Baidu and consulted his local friends about the accident, he decided to undertake further investigation. The outcome of Sun's filed research is a co-authored article "Loufan: the Delayed Truth", published in the *Oriental Outlook* in late August. The article explains the real cause of the disaster and reveals the real number of casualties. However, the article failed to attract attention from high-level officials in China. Sun decided to write an open letter to a Chinese officer, who was in charge of workplace-related safety issues. He posted an entry of his letter in his personal weblog on 14 September 2008. The letter quickly travelled among bloggers and online forums' participants. However, the blog entry to Sun's letter was soon blocked by some Chinese Internet portals, including Sina.com and 163.com.

To Sun's surprise, his blog, though it had been blocked, drew attention from the top leaders, who issued an order on 17 September demanding Shangxi local authorities verify the figure of casualties and reinvestigate the cause of the disaster. Three weeks later, the State Council announced the results of the investigation into the Loufan case on the website of the State Administration of Work Safety (2008). The investigation concluded that the disaster was a major liability accident, for which the managers of the iron mine and related local officers should take full responsibility.

The major implications of this case for CJ and MJ in China are at least threefold. Firstly, the case of Loufan suggests that the boundaries between MJ and CJ are blurring. Sun Chunlong, a professional journalist, used both mainstream media (the news magazine) and CJ channels (his individual blog) to present the outcomes of his investigations. The fact that the news journal in which Sun's investigative report was first published failed to draw public attention, while Sun's blog succeeded in this, suggests the increasing attention towards CJ by Chinese decision-makers.

Secondly, the case shows that the fundamental approach to dealing with social injustice in today's China has not fundamentally changed in the Internet age. It is true that Sun's investigatioins into the disaster and his letter to the Chinese safety officer are evidence of his efforts to play a watchdog role. It is also true that Sun and his colleagues' efforts were partly aimed at informing the public about the Loufan accident and increasing public awareness about a social problem. However, Sun's main purpose was not to expose failures of the system but to draw the attention of the Chinese central government to ensure that the "bad guys" would be punished. Blaming the "bad guys" at lower levels of public administration with support from the "good guys" at higher levels is a strategy that has been widely used by mainstream journalists as a pragmatic approach to handle social injustice at local levels. Clearly, there were and still are conflicting interests between the central government, local authorities and grassroots. Instead of relying on the rule of law, Chinese journalists and the victims of the accident had to depend on the officials at higher administrative level for a solution. From this perspective, CJ and MJ share the same approach to handling social injustice in China. Apart from the fact that Sun used a weblog to report the accident to the top officials, there is not very much difference with the past in the way in which social injustice is currently handled.

Finally, in comparison with an amateur-blogger like Zhou, Sun was equipped with better journalistic training and was backed by a mainstream media outlet. However, this does not mean that Sun won the trust of grassroots-interviewees any more easily. In fact, as Sun claimed, at the beginning many victims of the "Loufan landslide" did not trust him (Xinhuanet.com, 2008). Surely, though, as a journalist-blogger, he used mainstream media resources and his individual blog for good advantage.

Citizen Journalism and Mainstream Journalism's Failure to Empower Grassroots-Citizens to Fight for Social Justice: The Case of the "Milk Scandal"

This scandal concerned Sanlu and another 21 dairy brands, which were found to contain melamine, an industrial chemical used to produce plastics (Wang et al., 2009). Melamine was added by some suppliers to make the infant milk appear to be higher in protein than it actually was. These companies were judged to be in good standing and were exempt from inspections by the food safety watchdog in China (Wang et al., 2009). The tainted milk resulted in at least six deaths and made almost 300,000 infants ill by the end of November 2008 according to Chinese statistics (Wang et al., 2009). More than 50,000 infants were hospitalized (World Health Organization, 2008).

The disastrous impact of the tainted milk on children was "aggravated by delays in reporting at a number of sources", which were explained by "a combination of ignorance and a deliberate failure to report" (Spears and Lawrence, 2008). The contamination was first detected in Sanlu's dairy products in December 2007. Sanlu received complaints about its infant formula in March 2008, when kidney stones were found in 10 babies in a hospital based in Nanjing, capital of Jiangsu province. All affected infants consumed Sanlu's milk. In July, more cases were diagnosed in Gansu province. Melamine was confirmed in Sanlu tests on 1 August 2008. The company reported the results only to the local authority of Shijiazhuang, capital city of Hebei province, where Sanlu was based. The decision made by the local authority and Sanlu in early August was to withhold the information about the contamination until the end of the Beijing Olympics. In order to cover up the scandal, Sanlu tried to buy off the media, parents and even the Internet search engine Baidu (Wang et al., 2009). The company did not order a full recall for its tainted milk until mid-September when the scandal was exposed by media and the State Council began its investigation.

Both CJ and MJ failed to inform the public promptly about the food safety crisis in China. The first media coverage about the "milk scandal", which pointed directly to Sanlu, appeared in the *Oriental Morning Post*, a Shanghai-based newspaper, on 11 September 2008. It was written by Jian Guangzhou, a reporter of the newspaper. Before Jian's story was published, a Gansu-based newspaper *Lanzhou Moring Post* published an article about 14 babies in Gansu who were found ill after consuming the same brand of tainted milk. However, the author did not identify the brand name of the milk. This story was available online. Worried parents, readers and Internet users started demanding that the brand name of the tainted milk should be disclosed. In response to the "overwhelming" reaction from the general public, Jian decided to reveal the name of Sanlu, as he recounts (Jian, 2008), believing that any journalist in his position would behave similarly in the same circumstances. As early as August, a media outlet based in Hubei province released a story about three babies suffering from kidney stones after consuming the tainted milk (Jian, 2008). However, this report failed to alarm Chinese audiences (Jian, 2008). In addition to the fact that Sanlu and local authorities were trying to cover up the milk scandal, information delays were also due to the banning order from the Party's Propaganda Department, which considered the food safety issue to be a sensitive topic during the Beijing Olympics (Fu, 2008). As Fu Jianfeng (or He Feng), a reporter of the newsweekly *Southern Weekend* pointed out in an editorial note, he spotted the contaminated milk in late July. However, because of the banning order, Fu's investigative report was not allowed to appear on the website of *Southern Weekend* and *Southern Metropolitan Daily* until mid-September 2008 (Fu, 2008). CJ and Internet users started taking part in reporting and discussing the milk crisis after the mainstream media's coverage appeared on 9 September (Lianhe Zaobao, 2008).

This case shows that both CJ and MJ failed to inform the public adequately about the tainted milk both before and during the Olympics. This also means that both failed to empower grassroots-citizens to fight for social justice. The banning order from the Propaganda Department, the lack of information transparency at the local level, Sanlu's attempts to cover up the scandal, the food safety watchdog's exemption, and the local protection granted to a popular home dairy brand—all these factors point to major flaws in China's communication and administration system. However, neither CJ nor MJ managed or dared to pinpoint the essence of the problem when the milk crisis broke out at the moment of national celebration of economic achievements and openness before and during the Beijing Olympics. In this respect, it is too optimistic to talk about the revolutionary role of CJ in the Internet age. It is true that in theory the Web 2.0 environment provides journalists and bloggers with a technologically advanced channel to inform the public. However, this channel can still be blocked by political and economic forces in an authoritarian society, where the rule of law is not guaranteed. This is particularly the case when political and economic interests combine together under the banner of the national interests and pride.

Citizen Journalism as a Vessel for Chinese Nationalism: The Case of the New Generation of "Angry Youth" (*Fengqing*)

The following three episodes outline what we mean by the "angry youth" and how the extreme form of nationalistic sentiments is expressed in the virtual world by Chinese Internet users.

Episode I

"Imperialism will never abandon its intention to destroy us."

"Obviously, there is a scheme behind the scenes to encircle China. A new Cold War!"

"We [Chinese] will stand up and hold together always as one family in harmony!"

These quotes come from a short video entitled "2008 China Stand Up!" (quoted by Osnos, 2008). The video was made by Tang Jie, a young Chinese graduate based in Shanghai. This video clip appeared on Sina.com, a popular Chinese portal, on 15 April 2008. According to the *New Yorker*, it "captured the mood of nationalism that surged through China after the Tibetan uprising, in March, [and] sparked foreign criticism of China's hosting of the 2008 Summer Olympics" (Osnos, 2008). The video was then posted on YouTube, which by then had been blocked in mainland China. It drew more than a million hits in the first 10 days and very favorable comments (Osnos, 2008).

Episode II

Grace Wang, a Chinese student at Duke University, tried to take a different approach to Chinese patriots by mediating between pro-Tibet and pro-China protesters on campus in April 2008. Her photo and a video clip with her speech in front of two groups of people were posted on Chinese websites, labeled "traitor" and "the most ugly student" (Chen, 2008). Wang's parents' address, workplaces and IDs were publicized on the Internet. Her parents were called "traitors" too (Chen, 2008). After that their home was vandalized, Wang's parents had to leave and hide (Osnos, 2008). However, as a journalist-blogger noted, a few Chinese Internet users really paid attention to what she actually said in her speech made available online (Chen, 2008).

Episode III

Jin Jing, a disabled torchbearer, was praised at home for her courage and heroic behavior in fending off pro-Tibet protesters, who were trying to extinguish the Olympic torch during the relay in Paris in April 2008 (Times Online, 2008). Later, after that Jin expressed her disagreement with the action of boycotting Carrefour, a French super-market chain, in China, she began to be called "traitor" on the Internet (Zhang and Chen, 2008).

These three episodes are representative of the "online nationalism" in today's China, which is as widespread as its offline version; if not more. The group of active citizen-bloggers is likely to be provoked by extreme nationalistic sentiments and turn up not only against Westerners who are critical of Chinese reality, but also people belonging to the same race with them but called "traitors". Under the name of national interests or patriotism, the Internet is in danger of becoming a space not for rational public discussion, but for xenophobia or hate speech. The slight difference between the first episode and the other two lies in the discourse to which respectively they are connected. The first episode mainly reflects the old "Cold War" discourse, which divides the West and the East by ideology. The latter two mostly address the discourse of national identity—anxiety about the crisis in national identity in the process of globalization. Both discourses seem relevant to the rise of blogging and online forums in relation to China's social changes in the Web 2.0 environment. Few studies draw attention to them. However, the three episodes vividly demonstrate the complex nature of blogging or online public participation in China. They also suggest that active online participation by a youth-dominated community in China does not necessarily lead to rational activism for a global civil society or social justice at home. Rather, it excites nationalistic sentiments or even xenophobia in the online world, which quite often has a negative influence on offline activism (Finlay and Xin, forthcoming).

Concluding Remarks

This paper has examined the political and social context within which CJ is currently practiced and has tried to make sense of its complex relationship with MJ. In China, the Internet and Web 2.0 are growing fast. In parallel, the gap between rich and poor is also growing fast. Traditional media as well as content distributed over the Internet continue to be tightly controlled and censored. Meanwhile, Chinese nationalistic sentiments are accumulating online, exerting an influence on offline activism. There are therefore competing factors: technological advances versus information censorship; journalism and blogging for social justice versus online activism for Chinese neo-nationalism; political control versus economic interests. These factors are shaping the emergence of CJ and the role it plays in promoting or hindering social change in China. These factors sometimes neutralize each other, sometimes reinforce each other. Understanding their interactions is a challenging task for researchers.

The four case studies presented in this paper contribute to the debate on the implications of the rise of CJ for the relationship between journalism and democracy. The analysis demonstrates the complexity of CJ practice in China. It illustrates how in certain circumstances CJ is used by MJ as a news source as well as an alternative channel for distributing information. From this perspective, CJ appears to be performing a valuable function in aiding MJ to perform the sort of Fourth Estate role that liberal theories expect from the media. At the same time, however, CJ is establishing itself as a vehicle for the expression of nationalistic sentiments or hatred speech. Moreover, CJ remains subject to the Party's control, similarly to MJ, and therefore often fails to provide the public with information it needs badly (this was apparent in the case of the "milk scandal"). In short, political, economic, social and journalistic factors *can* and *do* constrain the technological potentials of the Web 2.0 environment. Consequently, CJ alone is unlikely to be the driving force behind social progress in China, even though in collaboration with MJ it makes it markedly more difficult for the Party to control online information flows within the country. In the long term, if CJ along with MJ as well as other social forces continue to denounce social injustice, it is possible that a more democratic, but not necessarily a less nationalistic, country will eventually emerge. Undoubtedly, the relationship between democracy and nationalism, which lies outside the scope of this study, is a key but under-researched area, deserving serious investigation in future.

REFERENCES

ALLAN, STUART (2007) "Citizen Journalism and the Rise of 'Mass Self-communication': reporting the London bombings", *Global Media Journal* (Australian Edition) 1(1), pp. 1–20.

BLUE BOOK OF CHINA'S SOCIETY (2005) *Analysis and Forecast on China's Social Development in 2005*, Beijing: Social Science Academic Press.

BLUE BOOK OF CHINA'S SOCIETY (2007) *Analysis and Forecast on China's Social Development in 2007*, Beijing: Social Science Academic Press.

CASTELLS, MANUEL (2007) "Communication, Power and Counter-power in the Network Society", *International Journal of Communication* 1(1), pp. 238–66.

CHANG, WOO-YOUNG (2005) "Online Civic Participation, and Political Empowerment: online media and public opinion formation in Korea", *Media, Culture & Society* 27(6), pp. 925–35.

CHEN, YAOWEN (2008) "Chen Yaowen's Weblog", http://chenyaowen.blshe.com/post/943/191280, accessed 1 April 2009.

CHINA INTERNET NETWORK INFORMATION CENTER (2008) "Statistical Survey Report on the Internet Development in China", http://www.cnnic.net.cn/uploadfiles/pdf/2008/8/15/145744.pdf, accessed 10 January 2009.

CHINA INTERNET NETWORK INFORMATION CENTER (2009) "Statistical Survey Report on the Internet Development in China", http://www.cnnic.net.cn/uploadfiles/doc/2009/7/16/125040.doc, accessed 1 October 2009.

FINLAY, CHRISTOPHER and XIN, XIN (forthcoming) "Public Diplomacy Games: a comparative study of American and Japanese responses to the interplay of nationalism, ideology and Chinese soft power strategies around the 2008 Beijing Olympics", *Sport in Society*.

FU, JIANFENG (2008) "An Editorial Note About the Investigation into the Sanlu Poisoning Milk", http://www.minzhuzhongguo.org/Article/wl/sj/200809/20080922120933.shtml, accessed 11 April 2009.

GILLMOR, DAN (2004) *We the Media: grassroots journalism by the people*, Sebastopol, CA: O'Reilly.

JIAN, GUANGZHOU (2008) "The Story Behind the Report about 14 Gansu Babies Caught Kidney Diseases Because of Consuming Sanlu Milk", http://blog.hsw.cn/139297/viewspace-345305.html, accessed 5 January 2009.

LIANHE, ZAOBAO (2008) "A National Shock Caused by Babies with Kidney Stones", http://www.zaobao.com/special/china/milk/pages/milk080912e.shtml, accessed 10 April 2009.

NGUYEN, AN (2006) "Journalism in the Wake of Participatory Publishing", *Australian Journalism Review* 28(1), pp. 143–55.

NORRIS, PIPPA (2001) *Digital Divide: civic engagement, information poverty, and the internet worldwide*, Cambridge: Cambridge University Press.

OFCOM (OFFICE OF COMMUNICATION) (2009) "Citizens' Digital Participation", http://www.ofcom.org.uk/advice/media_literacy/medlitpub/medlitpubrss/cdp/main.pdf, accessed 1 July 2009.

O'REILLY, TIM (2005) "What is Web 2.0: design patterns and business models for the next generation of software", http://www.oreillynet.com/pub/a/oreilly/tim/news/2005/09/30/what-is-web-20.html, accessed 1 April 2009.

OSNOS, EVAN (2008) "Angry Youth: the new generation's Neocon nationalists", http://www.newyorker.com/reporting/2008/07/28/080728fa_fact_osnos, accessed 1 August 2008.

PAULUSSEN, STEVE and UGILLE, PIETER (2008) "User Generated Content in the Newsroom: Professional and Organizational Constraints on Participatory Journalism", *Westminster Papers in Communication and Culture* 5(2) pp. 24–41, http://www.wmin.ac.uk/mad/pdf/WPCC-Vol5-No2-Paulussen_Ugille.pdf, accessed 1 April 2009.

PAULUSSEN, STEVE, HEINONEN, ARI, DOMINGO, DAVID and QUANDT, THORSTEN (2007) "Doing It Together: citizen participation in the professional news making process", *Observatorio (OBS*)* *Journal* 1(3), pp. 131–54.

ROBINSON, SUSAN (2009) "The Mission of the J-blog: recapturing journalistic authority online", *Journalism* 7(1), pp. 65–83.

SPEARS, LEE and LAWRENCE, DUNE (2008) "China Delays in Milk Scandal 'Deliberate,' WHO Says (Update1)", http://www.bloomberg.com/apps/news?pid=washingtonstory&sid=aNGZNTdtW5a8, accessed 1 March 2009.

STATE ADMINISTRATION OF WORK SAFETY (2008) "The State Council Began to Investigate the Landslide Accident in Lofan on 1 August", http://www.chinasafety.gov.cn/gongzuodongtai/2008-10/06/content_288791.htm, accessed 11 October 2008.

SUN, CHUNLONG (2008) "A Letter to a Chinese Safety Officer", http://blog.ifeng.com/article/1727838.html, accessed 1 April 2009.

TIMES ONLINE (2008) "Sarkozy Apologises to Disabled Torchbearer Jin Jing Over Torch Melee", http://www.timesonline.co.uk/tol/news/world/asia/article3788922.ece, accessed 25 March 2009.

WANG, HEYAN , ZHU, TAO and YE, DOUDOU (2009) "The 'Poisoning Milk' Trial Opens in China", http://magazine.caijing.com.cn/2009-01-02/110057114.html, accessed 6 January 2009.

WORLD HEALTH ORGANIZATION (2008) "Expert Meeting to Review Toxicological Aspects of Melamine and Cyanuric Acid", http://www.who.int/foodsafety/fs_management/Exec_Summary_melamine.pdf, accessed 2 April 2009.

XINHUA NEWS AGENCY (2007) "'Nail House' in Chongqing Demolished", http://www.chinadaily.com.cn/china/2007-04/03/content_842221.htm, accessed 5 January 2008.

XINHUANET.COM (2008) "The Journalist-Blogger Exposed the Covered Truth in Lofan Landslide", http://news.xinhuanet.com/video/2008-10/18/content_10213544.htm, accessed 1 April 2009.

YOUTH JOURNALIST (2004) "Dialogues with Prof Ming Dahong: online opinion and public expression", http://news.xinhuanet.com/newmedia/2004-10/22/content_2115745.htm, accessed 26 March 2009.

ZHANG, LENA (2006) "Behind the 'Great Firewall': decoding China's internet media policies from the inside", *Convergence: The International Journal of Research into New Media Technologies* 12(3), pp. 271–91.

ZHANG, XIONG and CHEN, XUAN (2008) "Chinese Anger: inconceivable boycotts", http://news.sina.com.cn/c/2008-04-28/140615443763.shtml, accessed 29 April 2009.

ZHAO, JINQIU, HAO, XIAOMING and INDRAJIT, BANERJEE (2006) "The Diffusion of the Internet and Rural Development", *Convergence: The International Journal of Research into New Media Technologies* 12(3), pp. 293–305.

ZHENG, JIAWEN and HAO, XIAOMING (2008) "The Internet and Citizen Journalism in China: a case study of Zola Zhou's Blog", in: Michael Bromley (Ed.), *AMIC Conference Proceedings Convergence, Citizen Journalism & Social Change: building capacity*, Brisbane: The University of Queensland, http://www.uq.edu.au/sjc/docs/AMIC/Zheng_Jiawen_and_Hao_Xiaoming.pdf, accessed 10 April 2008.

ZHOU, ZUOLA SHUGUANG (2007) "Zou Shuguang's Weblog", March–April, http://www.zuola.com/weblog, accessed 10 November 2007.

ZHU, LI (2009) "An Analysis of Chinese Social Risks: the nature of the mass incidents in China", http://www.minzhuzhongguo.org/Article/wl/sx/200904/20090409125730.shtml, accessed 10 April 2009.

CHANGES IN AUSTRALIAN NEWSPAPERS 1956–2006

Rodney Tiffen

In the 50 years between 1956 (when television began) and 2006, Australian newspapers grew and changed in fundamental ways. A content analysis of six of Australia's leading papers, taken at decade intervals, showed, most obviously, that their size increased very substantially. The increase in editorial space was even greater, as the proportion of space taken by advertising declined. While in absolute terms, advertising volume grew steadily in the early decades, in the last two decades classified advertising declined both absolutely and proportionally, while the volume of feature advertising held up better. Newspapers in 2006 were very different visually from 1956. Several of these changes were introduced slowly, with only relatively modest changes between 1956 and 1976, but then change occurred at an accelerating rate, especially with the introduction of colour throughout the newspaper from the 1990s. The other significant trend in newspapers has been their increasing segmentation, with more specialised sections, many of them with distinctive advertising appeals.

Introduction: Australian Media and Newspapers

Australian newspapers in 2006 looked very different from their predecessors in 1956, and they offered their readership a very different type of product. Their role had also changed. In 1956, newspapers were the primary vehicle through which the public learned about news. Long before 2006 that was no longer true.

Three broad drivers of change can be distinguished—changes in the media environment, other social changes affecting the environment in which newspapers operate, and internal forces for innovation. There is not a one to one, automatic response by newspapers to changes in their environment, since change has been mediated by business strategy and editorial vision.

Television began in Australia in 1956, in time for the Melbourne Olympics which were held in December that year. When probing the impact of broadcasting news on the role of the press, it must be remembered that the capacities of broadcasting journalism developed only gradually. Television in those early days, although immediately popular with the public, was not the technologically and professionally sophisticated industry it became. In particular, television news was initially quite primitive, essentially being read by a presenter at a desk with limited logistics for gathering news film. Indeed it was only in 1964 that the laying of the coaxial cable between Melbourne and Sydney meant that news film no longer had to be transported by plane (Lloyd, 1988). Colour television began in 1975, the same year that daily Visnews satellite feeds from London to Sydney began, increasing greatly the amount of international news on television (Alysen, 2005, p. 34). From around 1980, tape began to replace film as the principal means of gathering news film and ENG (Electronic News Gathering) made the logistics of television reporting and editing much easier (Tiffen, 1989). Similarly the introduction of digital technology in the 1990s carried this even further.

By 2006 TV networks had easy and immediate access to global news, and the logistics to gather news from anywhere around the country and transmit it to their home studios instantaneously, while editing was much easier and much more elaborate than it used to be. Moreover, while news was at first limited to an early evening and late night broadcast, now there are several news programmes a day, and often headline services between programmes. But all these only developed over decades.

While radio is a more venerable medium than television, dating back in Australia to the late 1920s, its impact as an important medium for news also developed over a protracted period. Regular radio news services existed from the 1930s, but again it was only from the 1960s that radio news began to acquire all the characteristics we take for granted today. It was only then that telephone interviews were permitted to be broadcast, which eventually enabled the large enterprise of talk radio. It also made gathering news from anyone with a telephone much faster and more immediate. This was part of the increasing use of actuality in radio news where reporters' and sources' voices increasingly became part of the product. Also from the late 1960s, the ABC began public affairs radio programming, which immediately became a central source for the most politically interested (Inglis, 1982).

So the press has been displaced in terms of speed and immediacy. However, while it is true that broadcasting increasingly became the public's initial source of news about events, this took a considerable time to become true. But by the end of the period, newspapers were the public's initial source of important news only on stories which the broadcast media had not covered because of lack of access or priority.

Moreover, by the end of the half century, newspapers faced a challenge perhaps even more basic to their operating assumptions. The Internet has drained advertising income from newspapers and has also increasingly been used by people as a substitute for reading the news.

Apart from changes in the mix of media, many factors in the social environment have impacted on the commercial viability of the press. Almost any factor which affects how people spend their time can be said also to impact on newspapers. Newspaper sales in Australia have declined quite sharply in relation to population, but have also begun to decline in absolute terms (Tiffen, 2009; Tiffen and Gittins, 2009). It is impossible to associate causally any such decline with any particular social trend with any degree of certainty. As the number of women employed in the labour force has increased radically, there have been changes in household and family habits affecting the times and places where newspapers are read. Similarly, the declining proportion of people travelling to work by public transport—one of the traditional periods when newspapers were read—could likely have impacted on sales.

Beyond these external changes stimulating adaptive responses, many other developments in newspapers have been internally driven. Some of these have been technological, in particular better printing and production capabilities. This was most obvious to readers with the widespread introduction of colour in all parts of the newspaper in the 1990s, and the increasing supplementation of the main news pages with magazines and other inserts. It was also true in a professional sense as newspaper journalists expanded their sense of their own prerogatives and sought to probe beyond the surface of public events, adding value to what audiences could already gather from

THE FUTURE OF JOURNALISM

broadcasting news. Apart from technological and professional internal drivers of change, the last is commercial. Making themselves more attractive vehicles for advertising as well as a more attractive product for consumers has been a continuing force for change inside newspapers.

Research Design and Sample

The data reported in this paper are based upon analyses of the pages and total issues of six newspapers, each sampled for one constructed week, at 10-year intervals between 1956 and 2006. This research design has led to the construction of two files. In the first, the unit of analysis is the page and data on 15,502 pages are included. In the second, the unit of analysis is the individual paper for a given day and there are data for 210 days. This comprises 36 days each for five papers plus 30 days for the *Australian*, which only began publication in 1964.

Choice of Newspapers

There can be no perfect sample of Australian daily newspapers, but the current study has the virtue of including the most important general daily newspapers in Australia. Only surviving newspapers were included, so that all the afternoon newspapers—which went out of business in the period between 1987 and 1992—were excluded. Apart from the *Australian*—the national newspaper founded by Rupert Murdoch, and included because of its political and professional importance—all the sample newspapers existed across the whole period.

Australia has a city-state press structure rather than a national one (Mayer, 1964). With the exception of two national daily newspapers—the *Australian* and the *Australian Financial Review*, both founded in the 1960s—the most important newspapers are those published in the state capital cities. Only in Melbourne and Sydney are there competing locally published daily newspapers—a broadsheet quality paper and a tabloid popular paper. Elsewhere local monopoly reigns.

In terms of professional leadership, size and political impact, the Melbourne, Sydney and national newspapers are the most important. The special priorities of the business-oriented *Financial Review* make it different from all others, so it has been excluded from this more general examination.

The three largest regional dailies—in Perth, Brisbane and Adelaide—are all around the same size, and have much in common. South Australia has shown less growth than the other two, and the circulation of the *Advertiser* is somewhat less than the *Courier-Mail* and *West Australian*, and so for that reason they have been preferred. Although in other aspects of this total project, the *Courier-Mail* is included, in this first part lack of affordable access to print editions ruled it out. A problem that was not anticipated before research began was just how difficult it has become to access physical copies of old newspapers. Storing them poses great space problems for libraries, which have understandably decided that the growth first of microfilm and then the availability of electronic versions of newspapers (major Australian newspapers are available on Factiva from 1996 on) will satisfy most of the demand. However, for present purposes access to hard copies of newspapers was necessary to examine space and layout. Inability to include the *Courier-Mail* from this stage does have the unfortunate consequence that there is not a direct comparator for the regional monopoly paper, the *West Australian*. If we had been able to code the *Courier-Mail* as well, we could be more confident about generalising about trends in these papers.

Australian media ownership, and in particular Australian press ownership, is probably more concentrated than in any other democratic country. In 1956, the Herald and Weekly Times owned two of the five papers being sampled (the *Herald-Sun* and the *West Australian*) and accounted for roughly half the metropolitan daily circulation. In 1956, the Fairfax Company owned the *Sydney Morning Herald* and had a minority share holding in *The Age*, although its share in *The Age* was still a minority holding with the local Melbourne David Syme and Company being the major shareholder (Souter, 1982). The *Daily Telegraph* was then owned by Frank Packer.

Press ownership has become even more concentrated in the decades since, mainly reflecting the inexorable rise of Rupert Murdoch. He launched the *Australian* in 1964 (the sixth paper in all subsequent years of our sample), purchased the afternoon *Daily Mirror* in Sydney in 1960 and the *Daily Telegraph* in 1972. Most importantly and spectacularly he took over the Herald and Weekly Times in 1987, which had many follow-on effects (Bowman, 1988; Chadwick, 1989). His company now accounts for more than two-thirds of metropolitan daily circulation. As a result of the Herald and Weekly Times takeover by Murdoch, the *West Australian* reverted to local ownership, the only metropolitan newspaper not owned by the Murdoch or Fairfax companies. (When Murdoch decided afternoon newspapers were no longer a profitable proposition, the company launched in Melbourne and Sydney what they called 24-hour newspapers, meaning that many features and all advertisements remained the same all day, but some of the news content was renewed. This only lasted a couple of years, but at the time both newspapers changed their names. The *Daily Telegraph* reverted to its original name, but the Melbourne paper kept its new amalgamated name, the *Herald-Sun*, its current title.)

The other major proprietor in 2006 was the Fairfax Company. It always owned Australia's oldest surviving newspaper, the *Sydney Morning Herald*, and from the 1960s started to take over the second oldest surviving newspaper, *The Age*, by buying stock in David Syme and Company, taking it over completely in the early 1980s. After some very damaging internal upheavals, following a family split and attempted self-privatisation, the Fairfax family lost control and its ownership register became more open (Souter, 1991). A few years ago, an agreement with Rural Press, ironically owned by John B. Fairfax, who made his exit in 1988, has centralised control to a greater extent. The Fairfax Company accounts for around a quarter of metropolitan daily circulation.

So the selection of newspapers has the virtue of including six of the eight largest, representing the major types—competing metropolitan broadsheets and tabloids, a national broadsheet paper and regional monopoly tabloid—and also the major ownership groups in each of the periods.

Choice of Years

Newspapers were sampled every decade, giving six years of data—1956, 1966, 1976, 1986, 1996 and 2006. It was felt that anything less than this would leave gaps that were too long to trace the processes and timing of change, and that more frequent years would devour too many resources while not adding sufficient extra information to justify them.

Sampling Within Years

The familiar stratified sampling method of one constructed week was used, so that six days were chosen for each year, one each of Monday through to Saturday, with one day each from every second month from February through to December. The result is a stratified random sample. Constructed weeks constitutes a widely used sampling method in journalism research (Holsti, 1969) in order to guard against skews in data that might arise from day of the week, time of year, or the immediate influences of whatever events are dominating the news at any one time.

Sundays are not included. Sunday titles tend to be separate from the other days in Australia, separately staffed and with some papers not publishing a Sunday edition. For well into the time frame explored in this study, there were restrictions on Sunday trading in many states, which inhibited the growth of Sunday newspapers. Especially for the present purposes of charting the changing structure of newspapers, this is broadly sufficient. For tracing some of the more intricate aspects of news content, more days per year would be preferable.

Although this sample is more extensive than any other study of Australian newspapers—and indeed to gather this much data was a very expensive and labour-intensive project—it should also be remembered that six days per year is a limited basis from which to generalise. Some "blips" and gaps in the data would no doubt have been rectified by taking a larger number of days, as just one or two special or extraordinary days falling within the six sampled can affect the results.

Coding Procedures and Reliability

The coding was completed by research assistants, who were mainly honours and post-graduate students. They were trained for two days, and then their initial coding was checked and any problems in the coding resolved. Although there was considerable variation in length, on average, each newspaper took around 12 hours to complete. Later two senior coders checked the analysis once again. Further checks were conducted after initial statistical analysis, with outliers and internal inconsistencies being further examined. There are some remaining issues of reliability, but as a percentage of cases they are very small, and certainly do not affect the findings reported below.

Newspaper Change in Australia 1956–2006: Findings

Size

The first and most basic change is the great increase in newspapers' size. On average, in 2006 each paper had five times as many pages as in 1956, and about three times as great an area.

The number of pages (Table 1) increased steadily over each decade in nearly all papers. On average, they have four times as many pages at the end of the period as at the beginning. With only a couple of exceptions, all newspapers increased their number of pages in every decade. The biggest proportional jump was between 1976 and 1986. It is pertinent to note that even though (as we shall see) some advertising volumes fell in the final decade, and newspapers managements were already gloomy about their financial prospects, the size of the newspapers continued to increase.

TABLE 1

Size of newspaper (mean number of pages in each day's paper)

Year	Total	SMH	DT	Age	Sun	WA	Aust
1956	31.7	26.7	28.0	29.3	38.0	36.7	–
1966	42.1	41.7	44.7	38.0	60.0	50.7	17.7
1976	53.7	41.0	42.7	56.3	76.7	82.7	23.0
1986	76.7	67.3	71.3	77.3	91.3	124.7	38.0
1996	96.7	102.3	97.2	87.0	97.3	146.0	50.3
2006	128.9	159.5	118.7	142.3	138.7	170.0	67.3

SMH, Sydney Morning Herald; DT, Daily Telegraph; Age, The Age; Sun, Herald-Sun; WA, West Australian; Aust, Australian.

The area of newspapers (Table 2) has similarly increased in a parallel, although not quite as dramatic, fashion. The growth in area is not as substantial as the increase in the number of pages because the broadsheet papers in particular have added many segments with smaller-sized pages. In this table, the difference in size between the broadsheets (*Sydney Morning Herald, The Age, Australian*) and the tabloids (*Daily Telegraph, Herald-Sun, West Australian*) is clearer.

Another strong trend is that the gap between Saturdays and weekdays has grown. Saturday newspapers have increased their number of pages much more dramatically (Table 3). The number of pages in Saturday editions increased on average around six-fold; in weekdays around three and a half-fold. At the same time, the gap between weekday and Saturday circulations has grown, especially for the broadsheet papers.

Advertising

Analysts have shown how newspapers' share of advertising has declined (Meech, 2008). In parallel, the percentage of space taken by advertising has decreased in all the established papers (Table 4). So, when this trend is combined with the increase in the size of newspapers, it has meant a very substantial increase in editorial space.

The *Australian* has always had a distinctive profile, both a smaller newspaper overall, especially in its early years, and with a smaller proportion of advertising. If that newspaper is omitted, advertising has declined as a percentage of all space in all the others. This is most marked in the *Sydney Morning Herald* and *The Age*, but is true to a lesser extent in the three tabloid newspapers. The regional monopoly newspaper, the *West Australian*, is the only one where more than 50 per cent of all space is taken by advertising in 2006.

TABLE 2

Area of papers (mean thousand square centimetres in each day's paper)

Year	Total	Metropolitan broadsheet	Metropolitan tabloid	WA	Aust
1956	48.1	63.7	34.4	44.1	–
1966	63.5	89.7	52.4	61.4	35.5
1976	79.8	106.7	60.5	95.1	49.2
1986	118.5	163.1	82.4	141.9	78.1
1996	134.9	174.3	98.9	160.5	102.4
2006	161.3	200.4	127.5	191.6	120.2

WA, West Australian; Aust, Australian.

TABLE 3

Size of Saturday papers (pages per paper)

Year	Total	SMH	DT	Age	Sun	WA	Aust
1956	48.0	52	32	64	40	52	–
1966	63.7	88	60	76	60	76	22
1976	91.3	108	60	136	96	112	36
1986	127.0	144	120	196	88	192	80
1996	185.5	200	136	180	104	336	88
2006	283.8	404	188	376	204	404	194

See Table 1 for newspaper abbreviations.

Since 1966 it has been the newspaper with the highest proportion of advertising and much of the time by a clear margin. The two metropolitan broadsheets have always carried a higher proportion of advertising than their tabloid competitors. This gap was always narrower among the Melbourne papers than the Sydney papers, and has narrowed in both over time.

The other notable trend in advertising, apparent in Table 5 which gives the area of feature and classified advertising per day, is that while feature advertising has continued to increase in total space, classified advertising has declined. Between 1956 and 1986 classified advertising increased in all the papers, but in all of them except the *West Australian* its total space in 2006 was less than in 1986. This is particularly important for the metropolitan broadsheets. Rupert Murdoch famously described the classified advertising in these Fairfax papers as rivers of gold, although more recently he observed that rivers sometimes dry up (Plunkett, 2005). *The Age*'s total space devoted to classified advertising was less in 2006 than it had been in 1956, when the paper was only roughly one-third of its 2006 size. Its 2006 area was half its 1986 figure. The *Herald*'s decline has not been so dramatic, but it was still only at around two-thirds of its 1986 area. In contrast, in all papers except the *Australian* the space devoted to feature advertising is higher in 2006 than in 1986 and also than in 1996.

Visual Presentation

By 2006, the appearance of these newspapers had changed greatly from 1956. Tables 6–9 illustrate the ways in which the various visual aids and accompaniments to the news increased in use. In each of the four visual aspects on which we have data—(1)

TABLE 4

Advertising (% of overall newspaper space featuring advertising)

Year	Total	SMH	DT	Age	Sun	WA	Aust
1956	51.3	62.5	37.2	54.5	42.5	61.5	–
1966	50.9	61.5	49.5	55.7	54.7	63.5	20.7
1976	53.0	58.0	42.7	56.7	61.3	71.2	28.3
1986	52.8	58.3	44.3	59.7	54.2	66.5	34.0
1996	41.2	49.5	38.7	46.0	35.0	53.8	24.0
2006	37.5	46.0	33.2	37.0	33.5	54.0	21.3

See Table 1 for newspaper abbreviations.

TABLE 5
Areas of feature and classified advertising (mean thousand square centimetres per day)

Year	Total	SMH	DT	Age	Sun	WA	Aust
Feature							
1956	11.5	9.5	8.2	9.4	14.4	15.9	–
1966	18.6	18.8	17.8	20.7	· 25.4	22.5	6.0
1976	22.6	12.9	11.7	30.4	32.2	40.9	7.7
1986	36.9	41.9	15.9	52.7	35.1	61.2	14.3
1996	38.5	53.8	28.9	51.8	21.9	55.1	19.6
2006	49.8	74.3	31.5	58.8	38.0	76.3	20.0
Classified							
1956	15.4	29.7	5.6	31.9	2.6	10.5	–
1966	17.8	42.2	4.3	33.5	8.3	16.9	1.7
1976	26.2	44.8	6.5	54.8	16.3	27.1	7.7
1986	34.4	55.5	17.4	66.2	15.7	34.3	17.4
1996	26.8	48.9	12.0	35.3	12.7	43.7	8.4
2006	23.4	35.3	10.9	31.7	9.1	43.0	10.9

See Table 1 for newspaper abbreviations.

editorial cartoons; (2) maps, diagrams and illustrations; (3) tables and graphs; and (4) photographs—there was limited change between 1956 and 1976. From 1986 onwards changes are more apparent and in some cases at an accelerating pace, although in some newspapers reduction in their use is evident between 1996 and 2006. It should be remembered that 1996 was the first of the sample years when all sample newspapers had routine colour production throughout the paper. Interestingly in most of these visual innovations, the broadsheet papers introduced the innovations before the tabloids.

Editorial cartoons (Table 6) flourished, especially in the broadsheet papers. They increased particularly between 1976 and 1986, although their use contracted somewhat between 1996 and 2006. But they are still roughly double their 1976 number and area.

Similarly the use of maps, diagrams and illustrations divides the period into two (Table 7). Their use in the papers between 1986 and 2006 was around three times as great as in the period 1956–1976, and they occupied almost four times as much area. Again the decade between 1976 and 1986 was the turning point, and again their adoption in the broadsheets was greater than in the tabloids, a difference that was even more marked when measured in terms of area.

Table 8 on the use of tables and graphs shows a consistent, but slightly different pattern. Again there is a decisive growth between 1976 and 1986, but then an even

TABLE 6
Cartoons (number per day and area in square centimetres)

Year	Total	Broadsheet	Tabloid	Total area
1956	1.5	1.1	2.0	178
1966	2.6	2.0	3.2	310
1976	2.2	1.5	2.0	354
1986	6.1	6.8	5.3	624
1996	6.1	7.6	4.6	807
2006	4.4	5.4	3.4	676

TABLE 7

Maps, diagrams and illustrations (number per day and area in square centimetres)

Year	Total	Broadsheet	Tabloid	Total area
1956	1.9	1.7	2.1	127
1966	2.0	2.0	1.9	184
1976	1.6	1.7	1.4	112
1986	5.0	5.7	4.2	432
1996	6.8	7.5	6.1	536
2006	7.0	8.3	5.7	615

greater growth between 1986 and 1996. In 2006 they occupied more than five times the space than they did in the period before 1976. The tabloid papers were slower to use such visual aids, but by 2006 the gap had narrowed.

The growth in the use of photographs is even more dramatic. Yet again, the period between 1956 and 1976 shows little change, but from then on change becomes more substantial (Table 9). In this case, the growth is even greater from 1986 on, in many papers doubling in number between 1986 and 1996, and showing a similar growth between 1996 and 2006, although not as great on a proportional basis. Nevertheless, on average the papers had almost five times as many photographs in 2006 as in 1976.

Overall, as Table 10 shows, there has been little change overall in the percentage of space devoted to editorial text, the verbal content, because two contradictory trends tend to cancel each other out. On the one hand, the reduction in the percentage of space devoted to advertising has meant more space for editorial content, while on the other hand, the increasing use of visual aids and more dramatic presentations has meant that the proportion of editorial space devoted to text has declined. So the proportion of the papers given to editorial text is roughly the same in 2006 as in 1956. There are variations between papers, however. The metropolitan tabloids have declined, while the *Sydney Morning Herald* has substantially increased, and in the others the proportion has remained broadly the same.

Page One

When considering the appearance of a newspaper, a central question is how has the front page changed (Stepp, 1999)? The four tables (Tables 11–14) in aggregate offer a clear perspective on the extent of the change.

The proportion of page one devoted to headlines (Table 11) has remained broadly similar, but this masks contradictory trends in the tabloids and broadsheets. By 2006 the

TABLE 8

Tables and graphs (number per day and area in square centimetres)

Year	Total	Broadsheet	Tabloid	Total area
1956	0.5	0.6	0.4	29
1966	0.8	0.5	1.1	40
1976	0.9	0.8	1.1	87
1986	2.9	3.9	1.9	136
1996	8.5	10.3	6.7	444
2006	8.9	8.3	9.5	539

TABLE 9
Photographs (average number per day)

Year	Total	SMH	DT	Age	Sun	WA	Aust
1956	27.8	23.8	16.5	33.7	44.8	20.2	–
1966	29.4	31.0	22.0	30.8	47.3	19.5	25.8
1976	35.3	30.5	30.2	43.2	58.5	21.8	27.8
1986	59.4	55.0	64.3	53.5	78.5	64.2	41.0
1996	109.0	128.8	95.8	100.2	132.0	123.2	74.2
2006	170.4	169.5	187.2	178.2	229.3	137.5	120.8

See Table 1 for newspaper abbreviations.

proportion had substantially declined in the broadsheets, but increased in the metropolitan tabloids.

However, the most substantial change is the sharp reduction in the number of articles appearing on the front page (Table 12). This shows a steady decline, so that the 2006 figure is about 40 per cent of the 1956 figure. As would be expected the broadsheets have more stories than the tabloids, with the *Australian* having the most. By 2006, the metropolitan tabloids often had only a single story, dominating the whole front page.

This marked decline provides context for the broad stability of space which newspapers have devoted to headlines. While total headline space is similar, Table 13 shows the dramatic increase in size of each story's headline. Overall they are two and a half times the size in 2006 that they were in 1956. But the difference between the papers is just as great. Essentially the *Daily Telegraph* and the *Herald-Sun* have far bigger headlines than the others, and they have continued to grow, especially the *Herald-Sun*. By comparison, the other newspapers look quite sober.

Again while there are differences in the extent of change between the papers, the percentage of page one devoted to editorial text (Table 14) has declined from almost a half to just over a quarter. The change has been least in the *Australian* and *West Australian*, and the reduction greatest in the two metropolitan tabloids.

Segmentation and Sections of the Newspaper

While the previous section traced one major change in the appearance of newspapers, namely the increasing use of visual aids to supplement written text, another has been the increasing segmentation of the papers, especially the broadsheets.

TABLE 10
Editorial text (% total space devoted to editorial text)

Year	Total	SMH	DT	Age	Sun	WA	Aust
1956	23.3	16.3	33.0	21.3	24.3	21.5	–
1966	23.1	18.3	28.2	17.8	15.2	20.8	38.0
1976	19.8	16.7	18.2	16.8	13.2	16.0	38.2
1986	22.0	21.8	24.3	19.0	18.2	22.0	31.8
1996	24.6	24.5	23.3	19.5	18.8	18.8	39.3
2006	23.9	24.7	20.0	20.5	18.5	19.4	41.2

See Table 1 for newspaper abbreviations.

TABLE 11
Front page headlines (as % of front page)

Year	Total	SMH	DT	Age	Sun	WA	Aust
1956	18.1	13.1	13.3	20.2	31.0	13.2	–
1966	16.7	13.0	16.5	19.7	23.0	12.8	15.2
1976	19.0	13.1	23.7	16.5	27.5	15.0	18.2
1986	19.5	12.8	26.7	12.0	33.8	13.6	18.0
1996	18.5	8.7	18.8	11.5	43.2	18.0	11.0
2006	20.4	9.5	22.2	12.5	52.0	15.5	10.7

See Table 1 for newspaper abbreviations.

Table 15 gives the percentage of pages that have their own numbering system, in other words, the pages which are part of supplements and magazines and which consequently do not follow a simple sequence of numbering from the front page onwards. Until 1976 these were very marginal in the newspapers, comprising less than 4 per cent of pages, and in three of the six papers nothing at all. The examples in these early decades were such things as weekly TV schedules and racing guides.

From that year they increase considerably in number, but most especially in the metropolitan broadsheets. Between 1986 and 1996 they double, and then in the following decade double again. So by 2006, half the pages have their own distinctive numbering system, but in *The Age*, it is almost two-thirds and in the *Sydney Morning Herald* almost three-quarters. This demonstrates the extent to which the contemporary daily newspaper is in essence a coalition of magazines.

This is also manifest in the different size of pages in 2006. While the tabloid newspapers overwhelmingly have pages of tabloid size, the broadsheet newspapers have many inserts of different sizes. Indeed *The Age* and *Sydney Morning Herald* only had one-third of their pages of broadsheet size.

A sign that this is very much driven by a wish to have more advertising is shown in Table 16. In the early decades these supplements did not have a higher percentage of advertising than pages with normal numbering. It is only from 1996 that this is the case, but by 2006 the ratio is four to three, with a higher proportion of advertising now in special supplements. This is by far the most pronounced in the *Sydney Morning Herald*.

Another way of charting such changes is demonstrated in Table 17. It groups the types of pages in newspapers into seven broad types. Two of these are wholly advertising—pages devoted wholly to feature advertising and to classified advertising.

TABLE 12
Articles on front page (mean number)

Year	Total	SMH	DT	Age	Sun	WA	Aust
1956	8.2	12.8	4.2	12.0	4.8	7.3	–
1966	6.5	9.7	3.5	7.0	2.5	5.5	10.8
1976	5.5	8.2	2.2	6.3	3.5	5.3	7.5
1986	4.6	8.0	2.0	5.8	2.2	2.5	7.3
1996	3.8	6.3	1.7	5.5	2.2	2.2	4.7
2006	3.2	4.5	1.5	3.7	1.8	2.2	5.5

See Table 1 for newspaper abbreviations.

TABLE 13
Headline area per front page story (square centimetres)

Year	Total	SMH	DT	Age	Sun	WA	Aust
1956	40.0	23.1	33.7	39.0	82.6	21.6	–
1966	59.8	33.3	49.4	69.7	136.9	29.6	40.0
1976	66.4	35.8	144.3	64.3	82.2	31.9	52.7
1986	84.5	32.2	130.9	46.0	183.2	63.3	51.3
1996	91.6	30.0	126.8	46.4	205.8	90.4	50.0
2006	125.0	46.5	170.0	73.9	341.5	66.9	41.9

See Table 1 for newspaper abbreviations.

In 1956 almost one in two pages of a broadsheet newspaper consisted of classified advertising. This was down to one in eight by 2006. After an initial drop, the percentage remained stable between 1966 and 1986, but then drops precipitately in the last two decades. The trend for tabloid papers is somewhat different. They became better at securing classified advertising after beginning from a low base, but have joined in the general decline in recent decades. The two types of newspapers show contrasting trends in pages devoted wholly to feature advertising. The tabloids peaked in 1976, and show a declining proportion since, while the broadsheets show a recent surge.

Three of the five editorial categories end up being broadly stable, while two show clear trends. Each of the three "stable" categories shows some movement in the intervening decades, however. The percentage of pages devoted to sport reveals that tabloids began and finished the period with about double those of the broadsheets, with the tabloids, after an initial drop, showing an increasing proportion in recent decades. Similarly, the stable total in review and opinion pages masks opposite trends, a steady increase in the broadsheets and decline in the tabloids. After increasing the proportion of specialist news pages (principally international and business) in the decades after 1976, the broadsheets in the most recent decade again revealed a reduction.

The two categories which show strong and secular trends in all papers are general news and advertising-focused sections. The proportion of pages devoted to general news, consisting of miscellanies of stories, has steadily declined, from around one in four to one in 10, with an even sharper decline in the tabloids than the broadsheets. On the other hand, pages devoted to topics where the editorial content aligns with advertising content as a proportion of the total has multiplied by a factor of eight. It has grown from just under 3 per cent to just on one in four. These pages include some areas that have grown

TABLE 14
Editorial text on front page (% space devoted to editorial text)

Year	Total	SMH	DT	Age	Sun	WA	Aust
1956	49.8	57.5	52.3	48.5	39.2	51.4	–
1966	43.9	52.3	47.3	37.5	24.5	52.2	49.3
1976	37.8	52.0	23.7	29.8	27.7	45.7	48.2
1986	39.1	56.0	30.7	36.0	32.3	33.5	46.2
1996	31.8	44.3	25.7	35.7	18.7	32.5	34.0
2006	28.9	32.2	20.7	25.5	13.7	40.8	40.5

See Table 1 for newspaper abbreviations.

TABLE 15
Special supplements (% pages in special supplements with own numbering)

Year	Total	SMH	DT	Age	Sun	WA	Aust
1956	2.1	2.5	0	4.4	3.5	0	—
1966	2.9	4.1	0	2.6	5.6	0	7.5
1976	3.6	3.2	0	5.8	9.6	0	0
1986	11.8	12.9	0	25.3	25.2	1.6	7.0
1996	26.2	42.2	0	26.4	8.2	47.6	17.2
2006	50.0	74.2	26.7	65.8	32.7	49.6	39.6

See Table 1 for newspaper abbreviations.

substantially across the decades—IT did not exist at the beginning, while travel has increased markedly as an economic activity. Others such as lifestyle have also increased, while some papers, especially *The Age*, have sought to put more editorial content around traditional areas of classified advertising, such as property and motoring, perhaps in order to increase readership, and thus perhaps also to stop the drift to the Internet for such advertising.

Conclusions

Tracing changes in the overall size and structure of newspapers is an important task for two principal reasons. Newspapers exist and survive first and foremost as commodities which consumers purchase and which must be financially viable to continue. Charting changes in size and format provides insights into the product available to the consumer, and hence also into their experience of it. It also offers some information on how newspapers have sought commercial viability by the amount and nature of their advertising, and how this coexists with their value and appeal to readers.

Secondly, data on the size and structure of newspapers provides a context against which particular changes in news coverage can be better understood. If the amount of one type of news has doubled, for example, at the same time that the total amount of news has also doubled, then it shows that despite increased size, editorial priorities have not changed. Equally if the proportion has remained the same of a product that is twice the size, then readers are able to access double that type of news. It also allows us to chart changing conceptions inside journalism about ways to structure the news and appeal to the reader.

Change did not come all at once. Nor was it linear and regular. Perhaps the most obvious feature of the changes in Australian newspapers over these 50 years is that they

TABLE 16
Advertising in normal pages and in supplements (% of area devoted to advertising)

Year	Normal	Special supplements
1956	53.9	5.8
1966	58.0	48.9
1976	61.5	58.5
1986	60.4	50.0
1996	45.3	56.7
2006	39.3	53.2

TABLE 17
Page types (% pages of different types)

Year	1956	1966	1976	1986	1996	2006
Total						
Classified ads	26.2	25.2	29.3	26.0	17.9	13.8
Feature ads	3.6	8.5	10.0	10.6	5.1	9.0
General news	26.7	23.7	21.1	16.3	13.1	10.8
Sport	13.6	10.3	11.3	11.3	13.1	15.0
Focused news	16.8	18.3	13.8	15.9	19.9	16.7
Advertising focus	2.8	4.9	6.5	9.5	20.0	24.3
Reviews, opinion	10.2	9.3	8.1	10.3	10.8	10.4
Broadsheet papers						
Classified ads	47.6	36.6	37.9	31.9	16.8	13.1
Feature ads	0.9	3.0	1.5	4.9	3.3	11.1
General news	20.0	19.4	17.1	11.4	10.1	9.5
Sport	8.5	9.1	10.2	7.7	8.1	9.8
Focused news	15.0	20.1	16.8	22.9	23.2	17.9
Advertising focus	2.1	1.4	6.2	11.4	26.1	25.9
Reviews, opinion	5.9	10.4	10.2	9.9	12.3	12.7
Tabloid papers						
Classified ads	14.5	17.5	24.1	22.2	18.7	14.5
Feature ads	5.2	12.1	15.0	14.3	6.4	7.1
General news	30.3	26.5	23.5	19.5	15.2	11.9
Sport	16.5	11.1	11.9	13.7	16.6	19.3
Focused news	17.7	17.1	12.0	11.5	17.7	15.8
Advertising focus	3.2	7.2	6.7	8.3	15.8	22.9
Reviews, opinion	12.6	8.6	6.8	10.6	9.7	8.5

offer their readers much more than previously. They are much larger and the proportion of advertising has declined, so there is much more content on offer, although because of increased use of visual aids the proportion of editorial text is much less changed.

The newspapers of 2006 look very different from those of 1956. Interestingly on the measures used here, there was little change between 1956 and 1976, but from then on it was considerable. Most notable in the era of colour has been the sustained expansion of photographs, so that by 2006 there were almost five times as many as in 1976.

The data which most suggests the possible financial vulnerability of contemporary Australian newspapers is the decline in classified advertising, both proportionately and absolutely. This is most serious for the two metropolitan broadsheet papers, which traditionally relied heavily on this revenue stream. All newspapers, but especially the broadsheets, have been studiously trying to cultivate new formats attractive to advertisers.

That explains the final important trend. One of the most dramatic changes has been the growing segmentation of newspapers. As newspapers have become ever larger, specialist sections have grown and proliferated. In many ways, contemporary daily newspapers are now coalitions of magazines.

ACKNOWLEDGEMENTS

I would like to thank Erin Kelly, Ashley Townshend, Dennis Han Liao, and the other people who undertook the coding work for this paper.

REFERENCES

ALYSEN, BARBARA (2005) *Electronic Reporter: broadcast journalism in Australia*, 2nd edn, Sydney: UNSW Press.

BOWMAN, DAVID (1988) *The Captive Press*, Ringwood, Victoria: Penguin.

CHADWICK, PAUL (1989) *Media Mates: carving up Australia's media*, Melbourne: Sun Books.

HOLSTI, OLE (1969) *Content Analysis for the Social Sciences and Humanities*, Reading, MA: Addison-Wesley.

INGLIS, KEN (1982) *This is the ABC*, Melbourne: Melbourne University Press.

LLOYD, CLEM (1988) *Parliament and the Press: the federal parliamentary press gallery*, Melbourne: Melbourne University Press.

MAYER, HENRY (1964) *The Press in Australia*, Melbourne: Landsdowne Press.

MEECH, PETER (2008) "Advertising", in: Bob Franklin (Ed.), *Pulling Newspapers Apart: analysing print journalism*, London: Routledge, pp. 235–44.

PLUNKETT, JOHN (2005) "Murdoch Predicts Gloomy Future for Press", *Guardian*, 24 November, http://www.guardian.co.uk/media/2005/nov/24/pressandpublishing.business1/print.

SOUTER, GAVIN (1982) *Company of Heralds*, Melbourne: Melbourne University Press.

SOUTER, GAVIN (1991) *Heralds and Angels: the House of Fairfax 1841–1990*, Melbourne: Melbourne University Press.

STEPP, CARL SESSIONS (1999) "Then and Now: the state of the American newspaper", *American Journalism Review* 21(7), pp. 60–75.

TIFFEN, RODNEY (1989) *News and Power*, Sydney: Allen and Unwin.

TIFFEN, RODNEY (2009) "The Press", in: Stuart Cunningham and Graeme Turner (Eds), *The Media and Communications in Australia*, 3rd edn, Sydney: Allen and Unwin, pp. 97–112.

TIFFEN, RODNEY and GITTINS, ROSS (2009) *How Australia Compares*, 2nd edn, Melbourne: Cambridge University Press.

WHERE ELSE IS THE MONEY?
A study of innovation in online business models at newspapers in Britain's 66 cities

François Nel

Much like their counterparts in the United States and elsewhere, British newspaper publishers have seen a sharp decline in revenues from traditional sources—print advertising and copy sales—and many are intensifying efforts to generate new income by expanding their online offerings. A study of the largest circulation newspapers in the 66 cities in England, Scotland, Wales and Northern Ireland showed that while only a small minority did not have companion websites, many of the publishers who do have an online presence have transferred familiar revenue models. It has also been recognised that income from these sources is not enough to sustain current operations and innovative publishers have diversified into additional broad categories of Web business models. Significantly, this study did not only compare the approaches of various news publishers with each other, but it also considered how active newspaper publishers were in taking advantage of the variety of business models generally being employed on the Web—and which opportunities were ignored.

Introduction

The newspaper business has never been simple, but the business model has typically been straightforward: compile news and information for which readers pay in time and/or money, and then also sell their attention on to advertisers looking to connect with customers. Until recently, that approach proved pretty robust. No longer. The industry's health, under pressure since advertising share started slipping in 2005 (Kirwan, 2009), continued to worsen in 2008. Circulation, advertising revenues and profit margins all fell—in many instances taking staff numbers and even entire operations down with them. The prognosis is grim and the prescribed remedies are sometimes drastic. Speaking to a media convention earlier this year, then UK culture secretary Andy Burnham was blunt:

> The old media world has ended—and the sooner we say so the better. With it must go old thinking. But the difficulty we all have is this: it doesn't yet feel like an era of new possibility, and change we can all believe in, but one of threat and decline. My main message today is: we need to break out of this thinking and we can—but only if we look beyond our own backyards and see the bigger picture. (2009, p. 1)

That UK regional newspapers need to look beyond their "backyards" and consider new ways of thinking about their business models is clear. That they also intend to do so is suggested by the upbeat headline to the news release announcing the Newspaper Society's annual report for 2008–9: "Local Newspapers Evolving into Successful Multimedia Businesses" (Newspaper Society, 2009).

Just how they are going about that—and to what extent these activities could be considered indicators of a "new way of thinking"—is the subject of a longitudinal study that commenced in the summer of 2008. Findings from the first exploratory cycle of that investigation are reported here, preceded by a brief review of the context for the study, critical perspective and a note on methodology.

Critical Perspective in the Context of UK Regional Newspapers

Researchers have pointed out that while few concepts in business today are as widely discussed as the concept of business models, it is also a concept that is often misused (Picard, 2000), poorly understood, particularly in the context of the Web[1] 2 (Rappa, 2001), and seldom systematically studied (Weill et al., 2004). A major obstacle in classifying online business models is that many are still evolving, changing rapidly and dynamically (Wang and Chan, 2003). Evolving online business models may render the taxonomy of today obsolete tomorrow. Those wanting to understand the range of perspectives on businesses models are advised to step back from the business activity itself to look at the basis and the underlying characteristics that make commerce in the product or service possible (Chaharbaghi et al., 2003). The researchers argue that an essential first step is to acknowledge the models we employ are rooted in the underlying assumptions and context that govern their creation: "It is this relationship that determines the meaning, legitimacy and impact of models" (2003, p. 372). They observe business model waves which they liken to Kuhnian paradigmatic shifts, where "a series of peaceful interludes [is] punctuated by intellectually violent revolutions" (Kuhn, 1996). They note that in both science and business one conceptual worldview periodically replaces another and that, "as with all successful business model waves, what emerges is a view on how best to conduct business, an ideal, which promises a panacea to current business developments and pressing problems" (Chaharbarghi et al., 2003, p. 372).

Against that background, they propose a meta business model consisting of three interrelated strands: (1) the way of thinking; (2) the operational system; and (3) the capacity for value creation. The researchers caution that while the distinction of each is essential for explaining the concept of business, using each of these strands "will lead to a dead end" (Chaharbarghi et al., 2003, p. 375). With that in mind, an exploration of the changing business models of newspapers would need to consider not only the activities in which the companies are engaged but also the mindsets that inform them and the outcomes of those efforts.

In the context of the newspaper industry in the UK, the struggle between the "old way of thinking" which Burnham (2009) claimed underpinned the "old media world" and a new way of thinking that would bring about a "new media world" centres on assumptions about whether the Web is a revolutionary force, or an important, but merely evolutionary influence. These opposing perspectives also underpin what UK media analyst Peter Kirwan (2007) saw as divergent views on the fortunes of the UK regional press coming from the "Cyclists" and the "Structuralists". For both camps, a key question was the future of advertising, which had typically provided the lion's share of revenues for UK regional papers (Newspaper Society, 2006, 2007).

The Cyclists were said to have seen the downturn as a consequence of cyclical changes in the economy, while Structuralists considered it to be the result of structural changes in the business context brought on by the Web (Kirwan, 2007). The "new thinking" Structuralists believe that the Web's ability to facilitate interaction creates a markedly different relationship between users and traditional media, as well as amongst users. As a result, there is a need to re-imagine the value propositions that the newspaper companies offer and the operational systems that deliver them.

Change is, of course, a process. So too is the shift in paradigms from "old thinking" to "new thinking" about revenue models. In a "New Revenue Strategies" report (Stone, 2006) from the World Association of Newspapers' (WAN), Shaping the Future of the Newspaper project, the psychology of media companies about the Web is said to have reflected the "predictable two- to five-year [four-stage change] cycle" described by Scott and Gaffe—denial, resistance, exploration and commitment:

> First, publishers reject the new idea, in this case, the development of a new media business. Then, resisting *developing online advertising strategies*, but perhaps allow some dabbling in them. Then, convinced a revenue stream exists, publishers change gears and accept the new orientation, and finally become completely engaged in the new business when the medium proves itself as a moneymaker. (1990, p. 10, emphasis added)

Significantly, the introduction to that report seemed to imply publishers varied in their views about the extent to which "new revenue" would come from activities on new channels, i.e. the Web, but not necessarily that such revenues could come from new activities, i.e. revenue streams other than advertising. Studies into the online business models of UK regional publishers are limited. Herbert and Thurman's (2007) investigation of selected national and two large regional "online newspapers" showed that while heavily reliant on advertising, some publishers were starting to explore other online revenue streams. Industry reports suggest these practices have not been widely diffused across the regional press.

In order to contribute to the growing understanding of the Web activities of the UK's regional press in general and the extent to which they reflected the "new thinking" about mass communication and business models in particular, a longitudinal study of the companion websites of regional newspapers in Britain commenced in the summer of 2008. This paper draws on selected findings to address three research questions. First, what revenue streams are featured on the companion websites of regional newspapers? Second, which online business models are the regional publishers not engaging in? Third, to what extent could these activities be considered to reflect 'new thinking' about business models on the Web?

Method

To explore how regional newspapers[2] across the United Kingdom were engaging with the Web, it was decided to construct a purposive sample comprising the companion websites of the largest circulation newspaper in each of the country's 66 cities listed on UKCities.com. These range in size from London, population 7,172,091, to Ely, population 15,102 (Office for National Statistics 2001). Details of newspapers in England (50 cities), Scotland (six) and Wales (five) were taken from the Newspaper Society database (nsdatabase.co.uk), while the Audit Bureau of Circulation data were used to identify the newspapers in the five cities of Northern Ireland. We aimed to identify the paid newspapers with the highest circulation for each city. Where there was no paid newspaper, we used the highest circulating free paper and if there was neither, we used the highest circulating newspaper that covered the city (for example, *The Ulster Gazette* for Armagh) (see Appendix A). We defined "companion websites" as sites on which the print product enjoyed significant presence, i.e. beyond a simple listing on a corporate site or group news portal.

Since the research aimed to identify not only the online business models the news publishers were employing but also to note areas that remained unexplored, it was decided to reference the taxonomy of general online business models identified by Rappa (2001), who observed 41 distinct configurations of value streams, logistical streams and revenue streams that he grouped into nine categories: Advertising, Brokerage, Infomediary, Merchant, Manufacturing, Affiliate, Community, Subscription and Utility. Mindful of Rappa's (2001) point that the Internet continues to evolve and that "new and interesting" variation can be expected in the future, the researchers were guided, but not limited to, Rappa's models.

Data were collected between 28 July and 31 August 2008 by two coders using a 105-item audit instrument. The findings were compared and variances in findings by coders were investigated and resolved. The findings were analysed using simple descriptive statistics; as the number of sites studied was small and the sample was not random, more sophisticated statistical measurements were not viable here.

Findings

The newspapers in the 66 cities in the research sample were owned by 16 publishers. Of those, only Scottish Provincial Press, Alpha Newspaper Group and Edward Hodgett Ltd are outside the top 20 UK regional newspaper publishers. The top four publishers—Trinity Mirror, Johnston Press, Newsquest and Northcliffe—owned 51 (or 77.27 per cent) of the sites surveyed.

Though a newspaper's brand is thought to be a valuable commodity, there was no single approach to brand extensions online. Three approaches to the sites were noted: mirror websites, portals and online brochures. The print newspapers' titles were clearly mirrored on 59 (or 89.39 per cent) of the sites, such as www.liverpoolecho.co.uk, although some also chose a common abbreviation, such as www.lep.co.uk for the *Lancashire Evening Post*.

News portals, which aggregated news from several newspapers of a group (e.g. WalesOnline.co.uk that hosts the news of the Cardiff daily, the *South Wales Echo* and 11 of Trinity Mirror's other South Wales newspapers) accounted for six (9 per cent) of the sites. Where the newspaper had no significant presence on the larger site beyond being listed, the paper was deemed to simply have an electronic brochure and was discounted from the audit. Two papers fell into this category: *The Wells Journal*, part of the Mid Somerset Series hosted on www.thisissomerset.co.uk, and *The Ely Weekly News*, listed on www.cambridge-news.co.uk along with the *Cambridge Evening News*, which was also included in the audit. Only one newspaper did not have any website presence at the time of the audit, the *London Informer*.

Advertising and Sponsorship Models

While advertising has been the primary form of online revenue for regional publishers, their share of that market has been tiny. In 2007, online advertising revenues accounted for 4.9 per cent of total advertising revenues for regional publishers, but that income

(£137 million) was only about a third of 1 per cent (0.035 per cent) of the total spent on UK online advertising (£2,812.6 million) (Internet Advertising Bureau (IAB), 2008; Newspaper Society, 2007).

The extent to which publishers took advantage of the evolving variety of online advertising opportunities varied. Traditional forms of advertising featured prominently, but few publishers were exploiting new technologies that are fast becoming central to the Internet users' online experiences.

All but two of the sites (61 or 97 per cent) carried external display advertising and 57 (90.48 per cent) offered classified advertising on the site. Few publishers were taking advantage of the additional advertising inventory that multimedia provided. Video material was available on most of the sites (56 or 88.89 per cent), but only video from one of the sites carried internal commercial messages (called "pre-roll sponsorship", i.e. sponsorship message inserted at the start of the video before the news footage rolls). Links under the tag, "Sponsored Links", appeared on 30 (47.62 per cent) of the sites.

While display and classified formats dominate advertising revenues for print products and their companion websites, they account for much less than half of total online revenues. According to an annual study by PricewaterhouseCoopers and the IAB, display advertising made up 21 per cent of UK online advertising during 2007, while classified accounted for 20.8 per cent (IAB, 2008).

Search engine-generated advertising is by far the largest advertising format online. In 2007, search engine advertising accounted for 57.6 per cent of the market and revenues grew 39 per cent from the previous year to £1,619.1 million (IAB, 2007, 2008). For publishers, major search engines such as Google and Yahoo, which dominate search advertising, have been seen to represent a threat to newspapers' control of their content (Stone, 2006). However, more than half of the sites audited (33 or 52.38 per cent) had agreements with Google and Yahoo.

While just over a third of the sites (39 or 61.90 per cent) offered e-mail newsletters, few were drawing revenue directly from these activities: there was no charge for any of the e-mail newsletters and very few of those (five or 12.83 per cent) carried advertising or sponsorship. Still a relatively new area in the IAB study, this format, described as solus-email marketing, accounted for 0.6 per cent (£16.2 million) of total UK online advertising spend in 2007 (IAB, 2008). All the newsletters had internal links, suggesting the primary benefit would be to draw readers back to the main websites.

Driving traffic was also the likely strategy behind the use of RSS (Real Simple Syndication) feeds. Such feeds were available on more than three-quarters of the sites (76.19 per cent or 48) of the sites reviewed. While the feeds can be both a vehicle for content and advertising (Bellam, 2007), none of the feeds reviewed offered commercial messages. None of the sites sold subscriptions to their RSS feeds.

Subscription and Utility Model

Setting a price for online content has perplexed commercial news publishers since the early days of their involvement in the Internet, starting before the World Wide Web was widely introduced (Picard, 2000). Along the way, publishers have experimented by building paywalls around all or some of the content and varied charges by type, volume or time. Rappa (2001) distinguishes between two models, describing subscription models as those where fees are paid irrespective of actual usage rates, while utility models (also called "on-demand" or "pay-as-you-go" models) are based on metered usage.

None of the websites in the audit charged users a periodic—daily, monthly or annual—fee to access the general content on the site. However, 57 (90.48 per cent) required registration to access certain features and/or content such as receiving newsletters or posting comments on articles.

Paid-for subscriptions to digital facsimiles of the newspapers was available on 12 (19.05 per cent) of the sites, while seven (11.11 per cent) offered free access to digital facsimiles of branded supplements. One paper, the Newsquest-owned *St Albans Review*, offered a free version of a two-day-old edition of the paper, including supplements. Those pages did not carry any additional advertising.

Though companion websites have traditionally been seen as a way to drive sales of the print product (Herbert and Thurman, 2007), only 23 (36.51 per cent) of the sites audited allowed a subscription to the newspaper to be purchased online. The remainder directed the potential purchaser to call a subscription hotline number or forward an email—or did not offer any option at all to try to purchase a subscription.

Infomediary Model

Publishers have long recognised that data about their readers and their consumption habits are valuable, especially when that information is carefully analysed and used for target marketing campaigns. On the other hand, independently collected data about producers and their products are useful to consumers when considering a purchase. Rappa (2001) categorises those who function as information intermediaries, assisting buyers and/or sellers to understand a given market, as "infomediaries" and identifies the following types: advertising networks, incentive marketing and audience measurement services.

Advertising Networks, which feed ads to a network of member sites, thereby allowing advertisers to deploy marketing campaigns, were identified on 37 (58.73 per cent) of the sites in the audit. The most prominent of these was the Fish4 brand, established in 1999 as a joint effort of six regional press groups and nine independent publishers but which is now owned by only two of the original partners, Trinity Mirror and Newsquest. The strategies of the former Fish4 partners varied. For example, Johnston Press established the "Today" branded network (e.g. JobsToday), while the network featured on Newsquest's sites were not additionally branded. The extent to which independent publishers used "white label" networks was not immediately obvious.

Incentive Marketing activities, such as loyalty programmes that provided readers with discounts or vouchers for making purchases at associated retailers, was found on 17 (26.98 per cent) of the sites. The majority of the sites, 57 (90.48 per cent), also collected data from users that could potentially be sold on for other targeted advertising activities. Such activities earned the regional press £1.866 million in 2007 (Newspaper Society, 2008).

About 43 per cent of the sites (27) could be described as what Rappa (2001) calls a "Metamediary": one which facilitates transactions between buyers and sellers by providing comprehensive information and ancillary services, without being involved in the actual exchange. These sites use databases (credit cards, loans, utility bills etc.) that provide comparative information on credit card rates, loans, utility rates and the like and then also offer up-sell opportunities (such as company logos and links) to the companies featured. Metamediaries differ from catalogues in that companies are featured regardless of whether they choose to take advantage of the "up-sell" proposition or not. The extent to which publishers were reselling their online audience measurement data to other businesses was not discernible from the audit.

Merchant Model

Merchants are described by Rappa (2001) as wholesalers and retailers of goods or services with sales based on list prices or through auctions. Almost a third (19 or 30.16 per cent) of the sites audited co-operated with an "e-tailer" or virtual mall, such as shoppersworld.com.

Affiliate Model

Rappa (2001) distinguishes between the merchant model and the affiliate model, which rewards partners on a pay-per-performance basis. Just over 58.73 per cent (37) of the sites were seen to have active affiliate deals, including premium rate horoscope services and a will-writing service via an external local solicitors firm. The single most popular affiliate deals that were obvious at the time of the audit were in travel, with seven (11.11 per cent) sites offer branded reader holidays.

Broker Model

Brokers are market-makers: they bring buyers and sellers together and facilitate transactions. Usually a broker charges a fee or commission for each transaction it enables. While some publishers were affiliated with broker services, such as online mortgage brokers, from the audit it was not clear if these relationships extended beyond affiliate and advertising models to provide payment mechanisms for buyers and sellers to settle a transaction on which the broker would get a commission.

Manufacturing Model

While publishers typically acted as intermediaries, they were also taking advantage of the Web's power to allow a manufacturer to reach buyers directly, thereby compressing the distribution channel. Publishers were manufacturing additional online content beyond that available in paper—videos (56 or 88.89 per cent), podcasts (22 or 34.92 per cent), e-mail newsletters (39 or 61.90 per cent), and blogs (36 or 57.14 per cent had blogs written by reporters; 43 or 68.25 per cent had blogs written by members of the public or other external authors)—which potentially provided additional advertising and sponsorship inventory. However, very few were selling the new content directly: 11 (17.46 per cent) sold video content, allowing readers to download the content to their mobile phones, while two sites sold CDs, which they had produced. At the time of the audit, only the Scotsman.com site, which incorporated the *Edinburgh Evening News*, had a paid-for digital archive.

Almost half of the sites (29 or 46.03 per cent) sold brand-integrated content which, in contrast to sponsored-content (i.e. the advertising model), is created by the company itself for the purpose of product placement. However, inventory was very limited, with branded calendars being the most common items.

Community Model

The Internet is inherently suited to community business models since it affords newspapers the opportunity to develop new and different relationships with readers, but also opens up the possibility of fostering relationships amongst current and would-be readers, sources and commercial customers. The viability of the community model depends on user loyalty, and revenues streams can derive from a variety of sources. Rappa (2001) identified the key ones: sales of ancillary products and services; voluntary contributions; contextual advertising; and subscription to premium services.

A prerequisite of the community model is, of course, that participants need the tools with which to interact. With that in mind, the audit explored the extent to which the publishers enabled interaction both with and amongst users on their news sites, as well as off the sites. The research also considered the extent to which users were given opportunities to contribute their own original content.

Onsite interaction about news content through user comments posted directly below stories featured on 46 (or 73.02 per cent) of sites, and 37 (58.73 per cent) hosted discussion forums or notice and message boards. Also popular were reader polls, which were featured on 42 (66.67 per cent) of the sites and interactive games and/or quizzes, which were featured on 29 (46.03 per cent) of the sites. In addition to asynchronous communication, two sites (3.17 per cent) were facilitating synchronous communication through scheduled webchats, using instant messaging software.

The vast majority of sites, 53 (or 84.13 per cent) also helped readers to engage with the content offsite by providing email-forwarding functions and 41 (65.08 per cent) sites included social bookmarking applications, such as del.icio.us, Digg and Reddit.

Some newspapers were also engaging with users on other social networking sites: eight (12.70 per cent) had a presence on Bebo and the same number featured on MySpace, while 22 (34.92 per cent) had Facebook pages. Interestingly, only three sites carried both Bebo and Facebook (*Worcester News*, *Plymouth Herald* and *Wakefield Express*) and all three are owned by different publishers, Newsquest, Northcliffe and Johnston Press. None of the sites was seen to be active on Google Groups. YouTube was being used by 22 (34.92 per cent) sites and six (9.52 per cent) had a presence on the photo-sharing site, Flickr. Twitter was being used by a small number of the sites: eight (12.70 per cent) had a general news feed on Twitter, while five (7.94 per cent) had a specifically themed feed (i.e. entertainment or sport). Only three (4.76 per cent) feeds from individual journalists were found.

In addition to interactions around content produced by the news site, sites were also soliciting original content from users. Rappa (2001) identified this as an "Open Content" strategy (after open source programmes created through collaboration by software developers). The most popular platform for user-generated content was blogs which featured on 48 (76.19 per cent) sites. About half the sites (31 or 49.20 per cent) had both public and staff blogs, while five (7.94 per cent) had just staff blogs and 12 (19.04 per cent) had just public blogs; almost three-quarters of the sites, 46 (73.02 per cent), allowed comments on these blogs. Users were able to contribute video to 37 (58.73 per cent) sites and 36 (57.14 per cent) sites had user-generated photo galleries. Audio contributions by users were much less popular, featuring on only three (4.76 per cent) of the sites. Social Networking around specific interests was also facilitated. The most popular of these were affiliations with dating services, such as DatingDirect.com, which featured on 46 (73.02 per cent) sites; six (9.52 per cent) sites, all owned by Newsquest, had links to the parenting site, netmums.com. None of the sites solicited donations from users, which Rappa (2001) refers to as the public broadcasting approach after the model used by the US National Public Radio.

Discussion and Conclusion

In line with the findings of research into other markets (Chyi and Sylvie, 2001; Krueger and Swatman, 2004; Mensing and Rejfek, 2005), the audit of the revenue streams featured on the companion websites of the regional newspapers in this study found that advertising remained the most popular source of online revenue for newspapers' companion websites. However, contrary to the findings of a study into the online strategies of a selection of the top national and regional newspaper sites in the United Kingdom (Herbert and Thurman, 2007), regional publishers had erected few paywalls around content on their sites. Instead, many were looking beyond the business models traditionally considered by newspapers to the revenue streams Rappa (2001) had found employed by other online businesses.

The audit revealed that the newspapers in this study were expanding their offline roles as intermediaries on to the Web and building a variety of partnerships that drive revenue. However, from analysing the websites alone, the logistics chain remained opaque. For example, a site may offer a mobile application, but it is not clear whether that application is provided by the organisation itself or by a third party. Therefore, it was also not clear to what extent publishers were extracting revenues from the various steps in the value chain, as suggested by Sylvie (2008).

Such limitations notwithstanding, the findings did demonstrate that there were significant differences in the levels to which regional publishers were engaged in various business models. It also showed there were opportunities for growing their value propositions in three areas: Manufacturing, Intermediary and Networks.

Manufacturing

All the publishers had expanded their online content into areas not available in print (including video, audio, e-mail newsletters, RSS and Twitter feeds, blogs, comments and discussion boards) but, with the exception of digital facsimiles (available on 12 of the sites), there were no discernible revenue models to sustain these activities, beyond driving traffic to the host site where it could possibly contribute to increases in general advertising revenues.

There was also very limited evidence from the audit alone of the extent to which regional publishers in the sample were involved in new manufacturing activities directly related to the newspaper brands, such as archives which other researchers found to be widely used by other publishers (Herbert and Thurman, 2007; Ihlstrom and Palmer, 2002; Mensing and Rejfek, 2005).

At the time of the audit, the regional publishers in the study had almost no involvement on mobile platforms, which has also been considered an area with significant revenue potential for content makers (Joakar and Fish, 2006; Moore, 2007; Sylvie, 2008). Inventory of brand-integrated content was also very limited.

Intermediary

While publishers are expanding their activities as intermediaries into a range of partnerships (such as dating sites), one related area identified by Rappa (2001) seemed unexplored: the broker model. In the case of the *Liverpool Echo* site, for example, customers were steered to the company's buysell.co.uk site on which both private and trade advertisements for goods and services are sold and displayed but, unlike online brokers eBay and Amazon, the site did not facilitate the transactions. Elsewhere on the *Liverpool Echo* site, there were links to Echo Outdoor where the offer to advertise on "up to 45,000 [taxis] across our national network, or to advertise on digital advertising units" suggest the company is acting as brokers for other advertising inventory. Customers were invited to call or email an advertising representative, but not to complete the transaction online. No link to the Trinity Mirror-owned advertising broker, Amra, was found either. However, unlike Google Adsense, for example, the Amra site (amra.co.uk) did not facilitate online transactions either.

Networks

Networks, considered by some (Niewiarra, 2002, in Krueger and Swatman, 2004) to be keys to success in content distribution, are another area that may provide publishers with further revenue opportunities. Again, while site audits alone are not sufficient to discern the logistics chains behind the content, it was clear that some, but not all, publishers were engaged in a variety of advertising networks that leveraged resources within companies (e.g. Johnston Press' PropertiesToday), across publishing companies (e.g. Fish4) and with non-publishing companies (e.g. Echo Outdoor).

Most publishers were also building internal content networks that drew in traditional sources and formerly passive readers through activities such as blogs. Some were also building links with outside content networks (e.g. netmums.co.uk). There was, however, no evidence found that these networks were providing unique value propositions that could allow them to be sustained by revenue streams, other than advertising (i.e. through sales, subscriptions, membership or donations).

To what extent could these activities be considered to reflect "new thinking" about the Web? The findings indicate that while there is much room for growth (some newspapers were not online at all), the majority of UK regional publishers reported in this study reflected what could be considered "new thinking" about the Web and by offering so-called Web 2.0 tools that facilitate interactivity with and between users.

And while some were clearly missing out on the most obvious revenue opportunities (such as facilitating subscriptions to their printed papers), we also found that, in line with Krueger and Swatman's (2004) study of regional newspapers in Germany, France and Italy, the online revenue models used by some of the UK regional publishers were more sophisticated and more complex than those generally suggested in the literature or reflected in the major industry reports. However, the extent to which these activities reflect a shift in paradigm, or are simply the "puzzle-solving" that Kuhn (1996) notes is characteristic of "normal science" is less conclusive; further investigation is needed into the other elements of Chaharbaghi et al.'s (2003) meta business model—the operational system and the capacity for value creation—with particular attention to the logistics chains, value chains and enabling technologies that underpin the activities observable on the websites.

ACKNOWLEDGEMENTS

The author would like to acknowledge the support from the Centre for Research-informed Teaching at the University of Central Lancashire, Preston, which funded the Undergraduate Summer Internship Programme that enabled Mark Bentley, Sophie Scott and Louise Steggals to contribute to the study. For comments on earlier drafts of this paper the author would like to thank Jane Singer and Bob Franklin.

NOTES

1. Web is here broadly defined as the network of all connected devices and applications, not just the PC-based application formally known as the World Wide Web.
2. The Newspaper Society (UK) defines a regional/local newspaper as: "Any publication in written form, on newsprint or similar medium, published in the British Isles (excluding the Irish Republic) at regular intervals not exceeding seven days, and available regionally rather than nationally (i.e. not available throughout all or most of the British Isles). It should contain news and information of a general nature, updated regularly, rather than being devoted to a specific interest or topic" (Newspaper Society, 2007).

REFERENCES

BELLAM, MARTIN (2007) "Newspapers 2.0: how Web 2.0 are British newspaper web sites?", *Currybetdotnet*, http://www.currybet.net/cbet_blog/2007/05/newspapers_20_how_web_20_are_b.php, accessed 20 June 2009.

BURNHAM, ANDREW (2009) "Secretary of State's speech to the Oxford Media Convention", 22 January, http://www.culture.gov.uk/reference_library/minister_speeches/5763.aspx/, accessed 4 June 2009.

CHAHARBAGHI, KAZEM, FENDT, CHRISTIAN and WILLIS, ROBERT (2003) "Meaning, Legitimacy and Impact of Business Models in Fast-moving Environments", *Management Decision* 41(4), pp. 372–82.

CHYI, HISANG IRIS and SYLVIE, GEORGE (2001) "The Medium Is Global; the content is not: the role of geography in online newspaper markets", *Journal of Media Economics* 14(4), pp. 231–48.

HERBERT, JACK and THURMAN, NEIL (2007) "Paid Content Strategies for News Websites: an empirical study of British newspapers' online business models", *Journalism Practice* 1(2), pp. 208–26

IHLSTRÖM, CARINA and PALMER, JONATHAN (2002) "Revenues for Online Newspapers: owner and user perceptions", *Electronic Markets: The International Journal of Electronic Commerce & Business Media* 12(4), pp. 228–36.

INTERNET ADVERTISING BUREAU (IAB) (2007) "Fact Sheet: online adspend 2007", http://www.iabuk. net/media/images/iabonlineadspendfactsheeth220072_2720.pdf, accessed 20 June 2009.

INTERNET ADVERTISING BUREAU (IAB) (2008) "Fact Sheet: online adspend 2008", http://www.iabuk. net/media/images/OnlineadspendfactsheetH22008_4293.pdf, accessed 19 June 2009.

JAOKAR, A. and FISH, T. (2006) *Mobile web 2.0*, London: Futuretext.

KIRWAN, PETER (2007) "Hiding the Heartbreak Behind the Regional Revenue Decline", *Press Gazette*, 18 May, http://www.pressgazette.co.uk/story.asp?storyCode=37563&section code=1, accessed 29 May 2008.

KIRWAN, PETER (2009) "The Decline and Fall of Local Newspapers", *Press Gazette*, 23 June, http:// blogs.pressgazette.co.uk/mediamoney/2009/06/23/the-decline-fall-of-local-newspapers-part-1/, accessed 29 June 2009.

KRUEGER, CORNELIA C. and SWATMAN, PAULA M.C. (2004) "Developing eBusiness Models in Practice: the case of the regional online newspaper", *International Journal of Information Technology Management* 3(2–4), pp. 157–72.

KUHN, THOMAS (1996) *The Structure of Scientific Revolutions*, 3rd edn, Chicago: University of Chicago Press.

MENSING, DONICA and REJFEK, JACKIE (2005) "Prospects for Profit: the (un)evolving business model for online news", paper presented to the International Symposium on Online Journalism, Austin, TX, April.

MOORE, ALAN (2007) "Mobile as the 7th Mass Media: an evolving story", An SMLXL White Paper, June.

NEWSPAPER SOCIETY (2006) *Analysis of the Annual Regional Press Survey findings for 2005*, www.newspapersoc.org.uk/PDF/RP-Survey-2005.pdf, accessed 22 June 2009.

NEWSPAPER SOCIETY (2007) *Analysis of the Annual Regional Press Survey Findings for 2006*, http://www.newspapersoc.org.uk/PDF/RP-Survey-2006.pdf, accessed 22 June 2009.

NEWSPAPER SOCIETY (2008) *Analysis of the Annual Regional Press Survey Findings for 2007*, http://www.newspapersoc.org.uk/PDF/Industry-Survey-2007.pdf, accessed 22 June 2009.

NEWSPAPER SOCIETY (2009) "Local Newspapers Evolving into Successful Multimedia Businesses", News Release, 21 May, http://www.newspapersoc.org.uk/Default.aspx?page=4486, accessed 20 June 2009.

OFFICE FOR NATIONAL STATISTICS (2001) "Census 2001", conducted 29 April, http://www.statistics.gov.uk/census2001/census2001.asp, accessed 20 June 2008.

PICARD, ROBERT (2000) "Changing Business Models of Online Content Services: their implications for multimedia and other content producers", *International Journal of Media Management* 2(2), pp. 60–8.

RAPPA, MICHAEL (2001) "Managing the Digital Enterprise—business models on the Web", http://ecommerce.ncsu.edu/business_models.html, accessed 20 May 2008.

SCOTT, CYNTHIA D. and GAFFE, DENNIS T. (1990) *Managing Organisational Change: a guide for managers*, London: Kogan Page.

STONE, MARTHA (Ed.) (2006) *New Revenue Strategies: shaping of the future of the newspaper*, strategy report 5.1, June, Paris: World Association of Newspapers.

SYLVIE, GEORGE (2008) "Developing an Online Newspaper Business Model: long distance meets long tail", University of Texas at Austin, 24 March, http://online.journalism.utexas.edu/2008/papers/Sylvie.pdf, accessed 20 June 2009.

WANG, CHIOU-PIRNG and CHAN, KWAI-CHOW (2003) "Analyzing the Taxonomy of Internet Business Models Using Graphs", *First Monday*, http://firstmonday.org/htbin/cgiwrap/bin/ojs/index.php/fm/article/view/1058/978, accessed 20 April 2008.

WEILL, PETER, MALONE, THOMAS W., D'URSO, VICTORIA T., HERMAN, GEORGE and WOERNER, STEPHANIE (2004) "Do Some Business Models Perform Better Than Others? A study of the 1000 largest US firms", MIT Centre for Coordination Science Working Paper No. 226, 6 May, Massachusetts Institute of Technology, Cambridge.

Appendix A. The Newspapers in the Study

England

Bath Chronicle	*Manchester Evening News*
Birmingham Mail	*Newcastle Evening Chronicle*
Bradford Telegraph & Argus	*Norwich Evening News*
Brighton Argus	*Nottingham Evening Post*
Bristol Evening Post	*Oxford Mail*
Cambridge Evening News	*Peterborough Evening Telegraph*
Kentish Gazette	*The Herald (Plymouth)*
Carlisle News and Star	*Portsmouth News*
Chester Chronicle	*Lancashire Evening Post*
Chichester Observer	*Harrogate Advertiser*
Coventry Telegraph	*Salford Advertiser*
Derby Evening Telegraph	*Salisbury Journal*
Northern Echo	*The Star*
Ely Weekly News	*Southern Daily Echo*
Exeter Express and Echo	*St Albans and Harpenden Review*
The Citizen	*The Sentinel*
Hereford Times	*Sunderland Echo*
Hull Daily Mail	*West Briton*
Lancaster Guardian	*Wakefield Express*
Yorkshire Evening Post	*Wells Journal*
Leicester Mercury	*London Informer*
Lichfield Mercury	*Hampshire Chronicle*
Lincolnshire Echo	*West Midlands Express and Star*
Liverpool Echo	*Worcester News*
Evening Standard	*York Press*

Northern Ireland
Ulster Gazette and Armagh Standard
Belfast Telegraph
Ulster Star
Derry Journal
Newry Reporter

Scotland
Evening Express
Evening Telegraph
Evening News
Evening Times
Inverness Courier
Stirling Observer

Wales
Bangor Mail
South Wales Echo
South Wales Argus
Western Telegraph
South Wales Evening Post

TRANSPARENCY AND THE NEW ETHICS OF JOURNALISM

Angela Phillips

Professional journalists rate investigating, fact checking, and standards of accuracy high among the qualities that set them apart from amateur journalists and bloggers. This paper addresses the spread and the implications of news "cannibalisation" (taking material from other news organisations, without attribution). It asks how the loss of exclusivity is impacting on practices of reporting and on standards of "accuracy" and "sincerity" and suggests that establishing new standards of transparency could help protect professional reporting in the new, networked era, as well as improving ethical standards in journalism.

Introduction

Research into source relationships for the "Spaces of the News" project at Goldsmiths, University of London found that a high proportion of story ideas were taken, not from news agencies (which provide a legitimate paid service), but lifted, without attribution, from other news outlets. The number varied across the newspapers examined but in no case was the source of the original story actually credited. "Lifting" from cuttings is not new in journalism. What is new is the ability to lift exclusive material such as quotes and case histories, within minutes of its publication. This paper addresses the spread and the implications of this form of "cannibalisation".

Vanilla News

Organisations seeking publicity have always looked for ways to simplify the circulation of information to the public and news organisations are happy to share sources of routine news. Both sides have made use of the telegraph, news agencies, news conferences, press releases, news pools and, more recently, the Internet, in order to do so. Much of the material used by news organisations is pushed out to news desks by public relations professionals who are trained to catch the attention of journalists (Fenton, 2009a). Most information circulating is doing so precisely because those responsible for it want people to know about it. This serves the function of alerting the public to information that they need to know and it is part of the mix of all news (McNair, 2009).

Research by a team at Cardiff University suggested that 54 per cent of news is derived from, uses, or has some connection with PR sources (Davies, 2008, p. 84). Indeed this figure may be low. Virtually all news reports make some use of public relations sources because journalists are expected to follow up rumours and allegations by approaching the organisations concerned for comment. Most of that comment will be organised by PR professionals. This information is fed into news-rooms directly via press release and email, and indirectly, via news agencies. News agency copy was found by the Cardiff reporters to figure in 70 per cent of stories surveyed (Davies, 2008, p. 74) and in German research (Carsten, 2004) 90 per cent of political journalists said that news agencies were an important source of stories. This is not surprising: news agencies were established by newspapers in order to reduce the considerable cost of news-gathering (Silberstein-Loeb, 2009).

Original reporting should add value to "vanilla news". It questions, or follows up information provided by official sources, or is derived from unofficial sources that have been cross-checked and verified. This is the kind of reporting that holds power to account rather than merely reporting on the powerful. It is only via questioning and investigating that journalists challenge the information that is sliced, diced and packaged for their consumption. Investigation is often singled out as a special category of news but in a reasonably well-resourced news-room, original reporting is both a means of un-earthing new stories and also of questioning the information that is presented via the various news feeds. An experienced reporter, on a specialist beat, should have the knowledge to recognise inconsistencies and contradictions in information received via "vanilla" news-feeds and press releases.

The balance of investigative and "vanilla" news is as important to the future of news (and democracy) as are worms and soil to the future of agriculture. If routine reporting was abandoned and Public Relations professionals ignored, citizens would be deprived of a great deal of the information they need to stay informed about the operations of government and business. On the other hand, if information is not questioned, and politicians and officials are not held to account, information too easily becomes propaganda. The job of public relations is to present the story most favourable to the organisation it represents. The job of journalism is to dig behind the facade. If a lively, plural media is to survive, the diggers need to represent a variety of viewpoints, all of which will have different questions to ask and different secrets they want to uncover.

The question under examination here then is not whether routine news should be disseminated by journalists, but how it is used and interrogated. Is the routine pushing out the original, or making more space for it? Is the flow of information from one medium to another, via news aggregators and blogs, a straightforward benefit to democracy, or is it muddying the news pool and making it harder for citizens to verify and follow up information? Should there be a greater commitment to transparency so that citizens are more easily able to trace information to its source? Would greater transparency improve the quality of the news that is produced and the health of those organisations in the news production business? These last questions are important because original reporting may not only serve the immediate requirements of democracy and the audiences. It may also have an important role in maintaining the diversity of news outlets in the longer term.

Bourdieu (2005), discussing field theory in relation both to individual journalists and also to news organisations, describes the paradox at the centre of the journalism field:

> To exist in a field ... is to differentiate oneself. It can be said of an intellectual that he or she functions like a phoneme in a language: he or she exists by virtue of difference from other intellectuals. Falling into undifferentiatedness ... means losing existence. (Bourdieu, 2005, pp. 39–40)

In the news industry, Bourdieu suggests that the fierce competition for differentiation is: "usually judged by access to news, the 'scoop', exclusive information and also distinctive rarity, 'big names' and so on". However, he suggests, commercial competition functions, paradoxically, to undermine the very differentiation it seeks, as competitive pressures force organisations to copy one another in order to monopolise the greatest number of readers who are assumed to occupy the middle ground (2005, p. 44). The results can readily be seen: as new technologies lower the cost of entry into news production, far from an increase in the number of different news outlets, competition has led to greater consolidation (Bourdieu, 1996; Herman and McChesney, 1997; House of Lords, 2008, p. 41). There may be more outlets but they tend to be servicing the same people and largely with the same information.

This pressure intensifies as news organisations are forced, increasingly, to look to advertisers for funding rather than to the audience itself. Pressure has been particularly intense since the move to online news delivery. Roy Greenslade, writing in *The Guardian* (2009), listed 53 newspaper closures with a net loss of 42 in the United Kingdom since the start of 2008. In May 2009, the *Economist* suggested that 70 had closed in that time (*Economist, 2009*). As small to medium-sized news organisations continue to be squeezed out of the business, the news agencies, which depend on subscriptions for their own survival, are also coming under pressure. Associated Press (in the United States) and the Press Association (in the United Kingdom) are owned by the newspapers and as they contract, so do the subscriptions they pay to the agencies.

Journalists who remain are expected to work faster and to fill more space, as described by Nick Davies, in *Flat Earth News* (2008, p. 60). Davies dubbed this form of journalism "churnalism" and "churnalism" was also described by Deirdre O'Neill and Catherine O'Connor (in Ponsford, 2007) when they examined 2994 stories from four daily newspapers: the *Halifax Courier*, the *Huddersfield Examiner*, the *Yorkshire Evening Post* and the Bradford *Telegraph & Argus* and found that 76 per cent of stories relied on just one source. Relying on press releases without any follow-up calls may disseminate information but it cannot interrogate it.

News Cannibalisation and the Leverhulme Study

At least as worrying is the practice of taking material from other news outlets without follow up or attribution. Before convergence, newspapers were inhibited from simply taking copy from another paper by the strictures of the technology. They would have to wait for the early editions of rival newspapers before they were able to take any material, and then they would be limited by the sheer inconvenience of re-placing large swathes at the last minute. A big newspaper scoop would give that publication a day to pick up new readers who were unable to get the same news elsewhere. Today news can be immediately "scraped" off the site of a rival and re-organised a little. The intensity of competition on the Internet, coupled with the lack of technical or temporal barriers to making use of information lifted from elsewhere, means that it is difficult for any news organisation to retain exclusivity for more than a few minutes. In one interview, a journalist working at the *Daily Telegraph* remarked:

> I'd imagine people are really pissed off with me because I'm quite often told to take things. I put my by-line on there and it just looks as though I'm just stealing stuff all the time. (Research interview, 2008[1])

In the qualitative research undertaken to investigate changing relationships between journalists and their sources (Phillips, 2009), it was journalists on the *Daily Telegraph* who most often described using stories and material, unattributed, taken directly from other newspapers. Journalists interviewed in depth for this project were taken from national and local newspapers and the intention was not to compare practices across news organisations but to look for changes in the way in which journalists are currently using news sources. However the practices at the *Telegraph*, the only national newspaper with a "Web first" approach at that time (early 2008), were starkly different. Journalists were interviewed in detail about the original and follow-up sources of recent stories. A third of the *Daily Telegraph* stories discussed had been lifted directly from another news organisation. *Telegraph* reporters also made fewer follow-up calls when covering a story. One junior reporter explained the routine:

> They go: "Can you do 400 words on this", and it's something from the *Daily Mail* or something. I'd read it through, find out who the people are, try and move it forward a bit. So I was doing that one day . . . and the news editor came over and goes, "You haven't filed that thing . . .", and I was like, "I'm just speaking to the mother now to get some quotes", and he was like, "don't bother with that, it's been in the *Daily Mail* just rewrite it". (Research interview, 2008)

On another story:

> I got that [indicates story selected by interviewer] this morning when I came in. It's Page 5 in *The Sun* I think. That bit wasn't in it . . . I added that in yeah, but all the quotes are from *The Sun*. (Research interview, 2008)

A specialist reporter on *The Guardian*, remarked that her exclusive stories were routinely picked up by the *Daily Telegraph* within minutes of appearing on-line (Research interview, 2008). They were slightly re-organised but never attributed. The attitude in the United Kingdom seems to be that taking copy from other news organisations is normal and accepted behaviour, part and parcel of the rough and tumble of journalism as it is practised. However, the merging of platforms has speeded up the flow of news so radically that it is impossible (as the Media Standards Trust has pointed out) for any casual observer to know where a story originated, or how to verify the information. Editors can simply copy original stories at will without mentioning the journalist who put all the hard work into unearthing them. This practice means that the journalist no longer gets the credit for an exclusive and the newspaper can no longer count on the added value of a scoop. Why buy *The Guardian* for an exclusive story when you can just go online and read the same thing in *The Times*?

Maintaining the News Pool

It is hard to see why news organisations will continue to invest in original reporting if all they do is give it away. It is a great deal cheaper to take material from another source and then spend money on colouring it. The difficulty is that if news organisations do go further down this route, they will be contributing to a diminution of the news pool that will, in turn, impoverish all news organisations. This journalist was explaining why he had not attempted to follow up a story by going to the place where it happened and knocking on doors:

I mean it's all to do with money. The agencies don't do things because they can't afford it because we don't pay them enough and we don't go out because there's not enough of us to fill all the holes in the website and the paper so it just becomes a sort of vicious circle I think. The sources, become ever fewer sources and more and more outlets for them. (*Telegraph* reporter, research interview, 2008)

If there are no commercial reasons for pursuing exclusives, then there is little reason for a purely commercial media to maintain the considerable cost of pursuing investigations and scoops. However, without an investment in producing exclusive content, the main force for differentiation between news outlets will disappear. This would lead to increasing homogenisation of news delivery, and to a collapse of the major means by which journalists and news organisations derive the cultural capital that sets them apart from rivals within the journalism field. If the job of a journalist is simply to re-write material which has been generated by public relations professionals, it is hard to see how high-calibre entrants to journalism will find the means to "differentiate themselves" within the field (Bourdieu, 2005, pp. 39–40). They are likely to look elsewhere for rewarding work and news journalism will be even further impoverished.

Ironically perhaps, the best recent example of the power of a real "scoop" in the United Kingdom is the *Daily Telegraph*'s revelations of the MPs' expenses scandal. According to reports in *The Guardian* newspaper (Wilby, 2009), the exclusive led directly to an increase in sales of 50,000 or more per day which is a rise in paid-for print circulation of some 14 per cent. By buying a disc of material taken from the House of Commons fees office, the *Telegraph* invested in a source of data which it then went on to mine and exploit on a drip-feed basis. Initially six journalists were devoted to the task, 12 hours a day, increasing to a dozen journalists as the enormity of the task, and its commercial value, became clearer (Bell, 2009). The information proved to be so explosive that within two weeks it had forced the resignation of the Speaker of the House of Commons—the first time this had happened in 300 years—and over time a number of MPs also resigned or decided to stand down at the next elections.

For a 24 hours a day, Web first, newspaper, it is instructive to note that the revelations were first published, not online, but in print. This provided the paper with a 24-hour lead on the other print media and ensured that it would be difficult for other news media simply to scrape the information off their website and re-use it unattributed. The rival news media, led by the BBC, were scrupulous about attributing the *Telegraph* throughout the considerable length of the story's run. This generosity might have been due, at least partly, to initial fears that the *Telegraph* might be prosecuted for receiving stolen goods (*The Guardian*, 18 May 2009, p. 3) but the result was a massive publicity campaign for the *Telegraph* newspaper and its website.

This investigation (which relied heavily on the use of computers for data mining) is a good example of what could be lost if big, independent, news organisations are further undermined by the fragmentation occurring online. No single blogger, alone in a bedroom, would have had the means to buy the material in the first place, or the staff to spend time analysing it. It might have been possible to have just put the whole lot on line and allow "citizens" to do the analysis but would lone individuals have seen the necessary connections and, without the power of "big media", would it have had the impact? It is not likely either that a single, dominant or state-supported media organisation would have taken the risk of prosecution. The *Telegraph* took that risk for competitive, commercial reasons (Bell, 2009) as much as for any concern about "the public interest". Indeed this scoop demonstrates rather effectively why newspapers neglect, at their peril, the need to invest in research and investigation. Without any means of differentiating their product, the process of consolidation, homogenisation and monopoly building, noted by numerous researchers (Herman and McChesney, 1997; Witschge et al., 2009), will rapidly accelerate as smaller organisations fail to compete for advertising, and news sources merge both vertically and horizontally.

There is little sign yet that the reporting functions of either newspapers or agencies will be replaced by new—Web native—brands. Most of those currently gathering readers on-line have done so entirely through the practice of "cannibalising" information from existing news organisations (Kovach and Rosenstiel, 2001; Messner and Distaso, 2008, p. 458). True the *Huffington Post* has announced a small fund which will be made available to investigative journalists (Bauder, 2009) but this cannot replace a system in which trained professionals are paid to gather, interrogate and disseminate news which then circulates through local, to national and international hubs, and then back again.

Accuracy, Sincerity and Transparency in the Internet Age

If the news pool is to be retained (even in its current much reduced form) then news organisations need to have some incentive to interrogate and investigate at every level of society (not just when there is a big story to cover) and journalists need to feel some kind of investment in standards which set them apart from casual users of the Internet. Fact checking, following up sources, verifying information are the core skills which journalists believe set them apart from what they consider to be an inferior product produced online by bloggers (Fenton and Witschge, 2009).

If this professionalism is what divides "real" journalists from amateurs then the differences are in places paper thin and desperately in need of strengthening. If journalists are using material without checking it, or attributing its source, readers are in no position to know who wrote the original story, where the information originated, or how it could be checked. Attribution of sources is standard practice in academic circles and to re-use someone's work without doing so would be an act of plagiarism. A journalist on the *Daily Telegraph* explained that similar rules obtain when handling journalism from the United States: "You have to attribute American newspapers because they get annoyed", he explained. Yet a casual attitude towards attribution goes largely unquestioned in UK newsrooms.

The coverage of the Maureen Dowd plagiarism affair in May 2009 goes some way to show the difference in approach between the United Kingdom and the United States in relation to attribution but more pertinently between newspapers and "Web native" publications. Maureen Dowd was found to have lifted a line from a blog (*TalkingPoints-Memo*). The line was of no particular importance and, as plagiarism goes it was of minimal significance, but it was clear that she had used someone else's formulation in writing her sentence and bloggers were very quick to point it out.

> Now, I'm all for cutting & pasting. As a blogger I do it all the time, but I always give credit. (thejoshuablog, 2009)

Another blogger commented:

If I was e-mailed a 40-plus-word block of text for this blog, and I used it, I'd include some sort of attribution—whether "a reader writes in," "media insider points out" or whatever the case may be. (Calderone, 2009)

British newspapers were quick to jump on the discussion. *Daily Telegraph* US editor, Toby Harnden, even entered the fray. None of course pointed out that this sort of behaviour is utterly commonplace on their own pages and rarely, if ever, is a correction or apology offered, even when they are caught in the act. Brian Attwood (2008), editor of *The Stage*, wrote to the United Kingdom's *Press Gazette* complaining that the *Daily Telegraph* had lifted material without attribution and had not responded to a complaint.

According to cross-national research comparing major newspapers with a significant online presence it would appear that old media, as it has moved on-line, has not taken on the obligation of transparency, Indeed it seems to be moving in the opposite direction (Quandt, 2008, p. 729). As the Cardiff study underlines, the use of agency copy is commonplace and as the Leverhulme study indicates, use of copy from other news organisations is also common and yet Quandt found that (with the exception of *Le Monde*, in France, and *USA Today*) the standard approach, internationally, was to credit only one author for news items.

Research by Redden and Witschge (2009) found that mainstream British news websites rarely link to other outside sources either. Where there are links in news items they are almost always to other parts of their own website or previous stories they have generated themselves. (The BBC and the *Independent* were cited as exceptions to this rule. The BBC consistently provided links to outside source material. The *Independent* provided links to Wikipedia.) Quandt (2008, p. 732) found a similar reluctance to link to outside organisations in all but two of the news organisations examined. One exception was the BBC, the other was Russian site Lenta.ru.

Transparency: A New Ethic

Journalism, if it is to contribute anything beyond entertainment to the life of the community, must be rooted in truth telling. This does not mean an adherence to some non-negotiable essential version of events, it does mean that journalists, in telling their version of events, should be able to say, with sincerity, that they believe their version of events to be correct. "Accuracy is the disposition to take the necessary care to ensure so far as possible that what one says is not false, sincerity the disposition to make sure that what one says is what one actually believes" (Phillips et al., 2009).

On-line, where speed is considered to be more important than painstaking fact checking, accuracy and sincerity reside in transparency (Blood, 2002; Singer, 2007). Bloggers see truth as a work in progress. They will publish rumours and wait for readers to react to them, believing that the interactivity of the Web will provide its own corrective. That is the reason why attribution on the Web is one of the few ethical norms agreed by bloggers: "What truth is to journalists, transparency is to bloggers" (Singer, 2007, p. 86). If the "public" is to act as a corrective it needs to be aware of where the information originated.

This should not be difficult for main-stream news organisations to do. The Media Standards Trust is currently working to produce the metadata that would allow every piece of news to be tagged with information about where it originated as well as information about the news principles of the organisation that produced it. The data would not be intrusive; it is visible only to those who want to access it. The Associated Press (Smith, 2009) has shown an interest (for commercial reasons as it will allow them to keep tabs on their own material) but so far no other significant-sized news organisation has signed up.

Attribution is not only a means of allowing people to trace a story back and check it. It is also a means of giving credit to the originators of information. If professional journalism was to embrace the blogger's code fully and attribute story sources routinely it would help to produce a different form of competition for cultural capital and differentiation.

Clearly there must be some limits to this. The obligation not to reveal a confidential source should still trump the obligation to be transparent, if journalists are to be able to investigate behind the scenes. However, protection of confidentiality is not an issue with the vast majority of material routinely handled by journalists. And there is absolutely no reason (beyond a distorted concern for commercial and brand protection) why journalists should not credit fellow professionals from other news organisations when the occasion demands that a real scoop should be recognised. Routine use of attribution and linking would also make it rather more difficult for journalists to quote selectively and in so doing completely distort the facts.

There would be other benefits too. If journalists could no longer pretend that the material they have lifted from another source is written by them there would be little point in spending a great deal of time re-angling it. Press Association copy could be used and attributed and journalists could spend their time following up angles and investigating original stories. The expansion of the news pool would be of value to readers and clear attribution would help those searching for stories because search engines would not be clogged up with endless repetitions of exactly the same story with the lead paragraph re-written. The value of original investigation would start to rise again and, with it, the cultural capital of journalists who produce it. If every time an original story is produced it is properly credited and points traffic back to the source, then it will also, albeit at the margins, help to stimulate greater differentiation of content.

In a time-pressured world in which few people really have the time to source their own news, journalists and news organisations must continue to have a role. It seems unarguable that a well-resourced news-room is better able than an individual blogger to afford the cost of employing journalists who can spend time verifying information and following up sources. If the news base is to be broadened it has to be possible for a mixture of large and small organisations to co-exist because, without companies sufficiently well funded to put 12 journalists on to a single story in order to find out what really happened, all news organisations, and the public, will be the poorer.

Time and budgetary pressures are pushing news organisations in the wrong direction—towards an increasing reliance on re-purposing the same material and a decreasing amount of time spent on the kind of investigation which allows for differentiation. The inevitable result of this increasing homogenisation of news will be a decrease in the diversity of news organisations and a narrowing of the number of views available. While it is clear that there was no golden age in which every journalist did his or her own reporting without recourse to PR or agency copy, it is equally clear that good, solid, regular reporting, alongside the use of PR and agency copy, is necessary for a functioning democracy. PR people will tell journalists what they want them to know—not what they would rather cover up, and investigative journalism has never been the responsibility of the agencies. If governments and business are to be held to account, as more than ever they need to be, then democracy requires a functioning, independent news media. A move towards greater transparency in sourcing might be a step in that direction.

NOTE

1. Research interviews with Angela Phillips for the "Spaces of the News" project, Goldsmiths College, Leverhulme Trust, 2008.

REFERENCES

ATTWOOD, BRIAN (2008) "Letter", *Press Gazette*, August, p. 14.

BAUDER, DAVID (2009) "Huffington Post Launches Investigative Journalism Venture", *Huffington Post*, March, http://www.huffingtonpost.com/2009/03/29/huffington-post-launches-_0_ n_180498.html.

BELL, MATTHEW (2009) "One Disk, Six Reporters: the story behind the expenses story", *The Independent*, 12 June, http://www.independent.co.uk/news/media/press/one-disk-six-reporters-the-story-behind-the-expenses-story-1711261.html, accessed 26 June 2009.

BLOOD, REBECCA (2002) *The Weblog Handbook*, Cambridge: Perseus.

BOURDIEU, PIERRE (1998) *On Television*, Priscilla Parkhurst Ferguson (trans.), New York: The New Press.

BOURDIEU, PIERRE (2005) "The Political Field, the Social Science Field and the Journalistic Field", in: Rodney Benson and Eric Neveu (Eds), *Bourdieu and the Journalistic Field*, Cambridge: Polity.

CALDERONE, MICHAEL (2009) "NYT Defends Dowd in TPM Flap", 18 May, http://www.politico.com/ blogs/michaelcalderone/0509/NYT_defends_Dowd_in_TPM_flap.html.

CARSTEN, REINEMANN (2004) "'Everyone in Journalism Steals from Everyone Else'. Routine reliance on other media in different stages of news production", conference paper, International Communication Association, http://www.allacademic.com/meta/p112639_index.html, accessed 6 February 2009.

DAVIES, NICK (2008) *Flat Earth News*, London: Chatto and Windus.

ECONOMIST (2009) "Tossed by a Gale", 14 May, http://www.economist.com/displaystory. cfm?story_id=13642689 (accessed 20 July 2009).

FENTON, NATALIE (2009) "NGOs, New Media and the Mainstream News: news from everywhere", in: N. Fenton (Ed.), *New Media Old News*, London: Sage.

FENTON, NATALIE and WITSCHGE, TAMARA (2009) "Comment Is Free, Facts Are Sacred: journalistic ethics in a changing mediascape", in: Graham Miekle and Guy Redden (Eds), *OnLine News and Journalism*, London: Palgrave Macmillan.

GREENSLADE, ROY (2009) "Britain's Vanishing Newspapers", *The Guardian*, 19 February, http://www.guardian.co.uk/media/greenslade/2009/feb/19/local-newspapers-newspapers.

HERMAN, EDWARD and MCCHESNEY, ROBERT (1997) *The Global Media: the new missionaries of corporate capitalism*, London: Cassel.

HOUSE OF LORDS SELECT COMMITTEE ON COMMUNICATIONS (2008) *The Ownership of the News*, Vol. I, *Report*, Norwich: The Stationery Office, http://www.publications.parliament.uk/pa/ ld200708/ldselect/ldcomuni/122/122i.pdf.

KOVACH, BILL and ROSENSTIEL, TOM (2001) *The Elements of Journalism: what newspeople should know and the public should expect*, New York and London: Crown.

MCNAIR, BRIAN (2009) *News & Journalism in the UK*, 5th edn, London: Routledge.

MESSNER, MARCUS and DISTASO, MARCIA WATSON (2008) "The Source Cycle", *Journalism Studies* 9(3), pp. 447–63.

PHILLIPS, ANGELA (2009) "Old Sources: new bottles", in: N. Fenton (Ed.), *New Media Old News*, London: Sage.

PHILLIPS, ANGELA, COULDRY, NICK and FREEDMAN, DES (2009) "An Ethical Deficit: accountability, norms and the material conditions of contemporary journalism", in: N. Fenton (Ed.), *New Media Old News*, London: Sage.

PONSFORD, DOMINIC (2007) "Survey Criticises Dailies for Single-sourcing", *Press Gazette*, 20 September, http://www.pressgazette.co.uk/story.asp?storycode=38881.

QUANDT, THORSTEN (2008) "News on the World Wide Web", *Journalism Studies* 9(5), pp. 717–38.

REDDEN, JOANNA and WITSCHGE, TAMARA (2009) "A new news order? Online news content examined", in: N. Fenton (Ed.), *New Media, Old News: Journalism and Democracy in the Digital Age*, London: Sage.

SILBERSTEIN-LOEB, JONATHON (2009) "Free Trade in News, 1850–1945", paper presented at the Cambridge Economic History Seminar, Cambridge, 19 February.

SINGER, JANE B. (2007) "Contested Autonomy: professional and popular claims on journalistic norms", *Journalism Studies* 8(1), pp. 79–95.

SMITH, PATRICK (2009) "AP, Media Standards Trust Propose News Microformat", July, http://paidcontent.co.uk/article/419-ap-media-standards-trust-propose-news-microformat/.

THEJOSHUABLOG (2009) "Maureen Dowd Plagiarism", *TalkingPointsMemo*, May, ttp://tpmcafe.talkingpointsmemo.com/talk/blogs/thejoshuablog/2009/05/ny-times-maureen-dowd-plagiari.php.

WILBY, PETER (2009) "Return of the Old Fashioned Scoop", *Media Guardian*, 1 June, http://www.guardian.co.uk/media/2009/jun/01/daily-telegraph-mps-expenses.

WITSCHGE, TAMARA, FENTON, NATALIE and FREEDMAN, DES (2009) *Carnegie UK Inquiry into Civil Society and the Media UK and Ireland: media ownership*, London: Carnegie Foundation.

THE DEVELOPMENT OF PRIVACY ADJUDICATIONS BY THE UK PRESS COMPLAINTS COMMISSION AND THEIR EFFECTS ON THE FUTURE OF JOURNALISM

Chris Frost

Privacy is one of the key ethical restrictions for journalists. It is the ethical dilemma that most often, and certainly most contentiously, collides with the right to freedom of expression that is used as the rationale to underpin press freedom. The attempts by UK courts to determine this balance by developing the law of privacy through the law of confidence and the Human Rights Act, have attracted much attention and often condemnation by a UK media concerned that their freedom to publish popular, but intrusive, celebrity news might be more tightly controlled. Court cases won by celebrities have sparked outrage in the press as they have tightened the definition of confidence, so making intrusion in some cases more difficult. However, definitions of privacy are also being tightened by regulators, including the statutory broadcast regulators and the Press Complaints Commission (PCC; which covers press and many news Internet sites) following a number of important incidents requiring adjudication—many of which have received very little attention. Broadcasting has been more prominent with a couple of cases seizing the headlines, but the PCC has been working more quietly although just as importantly, defining new levels of privacy with a series of cases that will set the standard for photographs and reports concerning suicide, as well as privacy over health issues—all elements a good deal more central to standard reporting than their titles suggest. As the PCC is self-regulatory, the press it controls must either agree its rulings or risk making it unworkable; as doomed as its predecessor the Press Council. This study of its key judgements in this area over the past five years is therefore important since it is likely that these rulings will have far more effect on the future of reporting in the press and on the Internet than any of the much-criticised cases from the courts.

Introduction

Privacy as an ethical dilemma has a relatively short history in the United Kingdom. The Judicial Proceedings (regulation of reports) Act 1926, which limited what could be written about divorces, was one of the first pieces of UK legislation detailing what could be published about people's personal lives (Frost, 2007, p. 94). But it was not until 1970 that the Justice Committee made a serious attempt to introduce a privacy law in the United Kingdom (Frost, 2007, p. 94). This was closely followed by the Sexual Offences Act (1976) that introduced the concept of anonymity to court cases, making it an offence to name victims of rape. The Data Protection Acts of 1984 and 1989 introduced the concept of sensitive personal data which added to individual freedoms but it was the passing of the Human Rights Act (1998) that finally confirmed the legal right to privacy in the United Kingdom.

Several controversial invasions of privacy over the past few years, including stories about entertainer Zoe Ball, model Naomi Campbell, footballer Gary Flitcroft and Max Mosley, President of the Fédération Internationale de L'Automobile (FIA), have kept the issues of privacy and journalistic sensation seeking firmly in the public eye. The Culture, Media and Sport Select Committee of the House of Commons is due to publish its findings shortly following a lengthy examination of press intrusion and defamation.

Media Regulators and Privacy

The Press Complaints Commission

The Press Complaints Commission (PCC), Britain's press regulatory body, came into existence in January 1991 in the wake of growing concerns about the invasive nature of some of the media and the falling reputation of the Press Council, the previous self-regulatory press body.

The PCC received 4698 complaints in 2008. The annual number of complaints has increased steadily since 1991. Of those complaints, 12.2 per cent concern privacy. The majority of complaints concern accuracy. But the complaints that matter most to the public, as opposed to solely the complainant, concern intrusion, discrimination, children and privacy.

The PCC adjudicates only a tiny fraction of all the complaints made—2.18 per cent (an average of 51.8 per year) over its full 18 years of work, but this rate has reduced recently falling to only 0.8 per cent (an average of 30.6 per year) for the five years of the study. The PCC says that this reduction in adjudications is because there are more resolutions of cases and it argues this makes for a better service (PCC reports, 2004–2008) but 97.5 per cent of all resolved cases concerned accuracy, generally of a relatively trivial matter, although of course important to the complainant.

On average, 408 complaints about privacy are made to the PCC every year of which an average 48 are resolved and 12 adjudicated with fewer than three of those adjudications being upheld. Only 21.8 per cent of adjudicated privacy cases were upheld; a total of only 14 over the five years of this study. All the other complaints were rejected or resolved.

Ofcom

Ofcom was introduced by the government as the regulator for broadcasting and telecoms by the Communications Act 2003. It is a statutory regulator, and controls the use of broadcast frequencies and telecoms in the United kingdom as well as regulating content. Only its powers to control content and protect audiences—what Ofcom calls Tier One regulation—are of concern to this paper.

Ofcom receives and adjudicates complaints from the public about TV and radio programmes, but its powers to punish are much tougher than the PCC's since it can insist on publication of its adjudication, but also levy fines, impose conditions on licence holders or even revoke a licence to transmit for serious breaches. It also has a content code that outlines areas of ethical concern (this is a statutory obligation).

Since Ofcom started work in 2004, licence holders have been fined a total of £13.145 million for 52 breaches of Ofcom's code and one station has had its licence revoked (Table 1).

TABLE 1
Types of complaints requiring sanctions by Ofcom

	N
Poorly handled competitions	21
Explicit sex	9
Commercial promotion	7
Political impartiality	5
Advertising	4
Bad language	4
Privacy	2

Complaints about standards form the greater part of Ofcom's work and are dealt with by its Content and Standards Group. The typical number of complaints is around 5000 a year, but this can be hugely inflated by programmes such as *Jerry Springer the Opera* (BBC2) (8860 complaints; Ofcom, 2006/7, p. 86) and *Celebrity Big Brother* (Channel 4) (45,228 complaints; Ofcom, 2007/8, p. 42). Newspaper items which provoke the public more typically attract complaints in the hundreds, but these major events aside, the level of complaints to the PCC and to Ofcom are surprisingly similar— approximately 4500 per year for newspapers and 5000 per year for broadcasting. A comparison of privacy complaints is even more revealing (Table 2). The PCC receives an average of 408 privacy complaints a year according to its annual reports.[1] Ofcom receives an average of 189 fairness and privacy complaints a year over the same period, slightly less than half. The majority of these complaints to Ofcom concern fairness—not a concept on which the PCC regulates. Although the PCC therefore receives substantially more privacy complaints than Ofcom, the latter, through its Fairness Committee, adjudicates more than double the number of cases that the PCC handles and upholds an average 26 a year (14.5 per cent) compared with an average 12.8 (22.8 per cent) upheld by the PCC. It is clear that when consumers are really upset, the PCC receives complaints in the hundreds while Ofcom receives them in the tens of thousands. This suggests a higher background of concern about newspaper behaviour and intrusion and so a higher number of day-to-day complaints about newspapers than for broadcasting.

An examination of typical cases from both regulators will enable comparison and identify trends in privacy regulation.

TABLE 2
Privacy adjudications: number of cases upheld and not upheld

	Ofcom				PCC			
Year	Upheld	Not upheld	Total	% Upheld	Upheld	Not upheld	Total	% Upheld
2004	4	21	25	16.0	1	17	18	5.6
2005	3	21	24	12.5	1	6	7	14.3
2006	5	27	32	15.6	4	10	13	30.8
2007	13	21	34	38.2	5	8	13	38.5
2008	7	23	30	23.3	3	11	14	21.4
Average			29	21.1			13	22.1

Public Interest

Claiming an issue is in the public interest either in the filming or gathering of information for a story and/or in the broadcast or publication of such a story, is the only reasonable way of judging which Human Right should take precedence: article 8 (privacy) or 10 (freedom of expression). Many newspaper editors still resent the need for this balancing act, seeing any restraint on press freedom as a diminution of their right to publish. Of course for some editors, the debate about what is 'private' continues not just because exposure allows them to build circulation but because they claim it is a serious public duty to ensure acceptable standards of social behaviour and therefore in the public interest. *Daily Mail* editor Paul Dacre (chair of the PCC's code committee) told the Society of Editors in 2008:

> Since time immemorial public shaming has been a vital element in defending the parameters of what are considered acceptable standards of social behaviour, helping ensue that citizens—rich and poor—adhere to them for the good of the greater community ... the press ... has the freedom to identify those who have offended public standards of decency ... and hold the transgressors up to public condemnation.[2]

This spirited defence of intrusion helps explain the PCC's interpretation of public interest in its code:

The public interest includes, but is not confined to:

i.   Detecting or exposing crime or serious impropriety.
ii. Protecting public health and safety.
iii. Preventing the public from being misled by an action or statement of an individual or organisation.

2. There is a public interest in freedom of expression itself.[3]

Ofcom's interpretation of public interest is derived from its duty under the Communication Act 2003 and the Broadcasting Act 1996. Ofcom talks about intrusions being warranted and by this they mean that broadcasters should be able to:

> demonstrate why in the particular circumstances of the case, it is warranted. If the reason is that it is in the public interest, then the broadcaster should be able to demonstrate that the public interest outweighs the right to privacy. Examples of public interest would include revealing or detecting crime, protecting public health and safety, exposing misleading claims made by individuals or organisations or disclosing incompetence that affects the public.[4]

Ofcom's code goes on to specify that the location of a person's home or family should not be revealed unless it is warranted. There are clear differences here between the PCC and Ofcom over how they determine the public interest.

Trends

There are several identifiable trends in the privacy decisions of both the PCC and Ofcom. Nearly two-thirds, of the 2004–2008 privacy complaints upheld by Ofcom concerned mainly news or documentary items which identified people without their permission in places where, or at times when, they could reasonably expect privacy. Nearly all of the remainder involved surreptitious filming that was not justified by public interest. Complaints to Ofcom are generally clear and straightforward. People are shown doing things which they believe should not be in the public domain, often, but by no means always, because they are not shown in a good light. Often this intrusion is justified by public interest and in those cases Ofcom has dismissed the complaint. The PCC's adjudications are less clear. In no case of intrusion is agreement cited as an excuse; often the filming or interviewing is surreptitious. Usually the revelation, whether of celebrity or private person, is done without the consent or involvement of the subject of the story. Table 3 identifies different types of intrusion raised as complaints with the two bodies.

This is seriously problematic because newspapers are now using their websites to transmit video and audio, in much the same way as a terrestrial broadcaster, yet the regulatory bodies are taking very different lines in their regulatory decisions about essentially the same activities. Already broadcasters are complaining that newspapers have a much freer hand to broadcast material on their websites—and typically on seemingly identical websites—because broadcasters are regulated by Ofcom and must comply with impartiality rules.

Cases

A key element of developments in privacy cases, far more important than the argument taking place in the courts over confidentiality, are the rulings on identity, limitations on private life and public interest. The other element to be examined here is the technological developments that mean the distinction between websites run by broadcast media, websites run to support newspapers and freestanding websites is now entirely artificial. All are beginning to stand alone from their parent, providing a service and facilities that are unique. If parliament thinks it appropriate to limit broadcast websites, then surely print and free-standing websites should also have similar limits?

The Data Protection Act and the Human Rights Act are influencing the meaning of privacy in terms of home life and health and the extent of public interest justification for intrusions. Whilst the courts have also been concerned with these elements, they have focused on confidentiality as a measure of equity and the rights people may have to access the private information. Lord Justice Buxton said, when upholding Justice Eady's judgement on Canadian folk singer Loreena McKennitt's privacy suit, that Ms Ash (the appellant) had no right to tell her story because it was not her story she wanted to tell:

TABLE 3
Complainant issues referred to Ofcom and PCC (number of cases)

	Ofcom	PCC
People identifiable in pictures and videos, by name or e-mail, etc. without or with limited public interest	22	26
Surreptitious filming/reporting not justified by public interest	7	1
Pranks	2	
Photos broadcast without consent	1	
Celebrity intrusions		5
Revelation of health details		4
Innocent friend or relative		4

While Ms Ash had been involved in some of the matters revealed, and (which is rather different) a spectator of many others, the book, which is what this case is concerned with, is not in any real sense about her at all ... It is the central role of Ms McKennitt, and the revelations about her, which provide the main reason for people to acquire the book. It is, I have no doubt, why her name appears in the title.[5]

Exposure of identity is at the heart of many complaints. What limitations should there be on identifying people, their homes or relatives in stories about them or about those close to them? Celebrity is significant here (although not a feature of the Ofcom cases apart from the infamous Jonathan Ross/Russell Brand case) but it is significant for the PCC. Five of the cases in the five-year period concern celebrities ranging from author J. K. Rowling, known to be very protective of her privacy, to singer Charlotte Church who, while not necessarily seeking publicity, cannot be described as publicity shy. These have brought mixed results in terms of the judgements. However, celebrities' public identity places them in a different class of privacy (Kieran et al., 2000). However, with public figures becoming more protective, there is a risk that there will be more unacceptable revelation concerning private figures, and so judging where the line should be drawn is important.

Identity

Ofcom and the PCC seem to have similar approaches to identity: whether this is a name, phone number, address, or other personal details such as a photograph or video.

A case was upheld by the PCC after a couple complained that a story about their home being damaged by a building developer was used without consent and that a private telephone number had been published in the story. In the adjudication, the newspaper concerned, *The Loughborough Echo*, admitted making a serious error in publishing the phone number.[6]

Ofcom also upheld similar complaints. A Mr Anthony said his e-mail had been "read out live on air and that the programmes' presenter encouraged listeners to misuse his e-mail address". After he had sent in e-mails that the station—*Talksport*—described as insulting, unprovoked and littered with obscene language, the host, James Whale, read one out and also twice read out his e-mail address. Ofcom upheld the complaint, saying "the inclusion of Mr Anthony's e-mail address did infringe his privacy ... the disclosure of Mr Anthony's e-mail address was not warranted and noted that the broadcaster did not seek to argue that it was warranted".[7]

In a second case the Welsh programme *Y Byd ar Bedwar* on S4C in 2005 reported a landlord's decision to end a tenancy for a sheep farmer in a Welsh valley. The landlord, Mrs Holland, had said she did not wish to appear in the programme and did not want to be filmed but the programme filmed her anyway and Ofcom said, in upholding the complaint:

> there was no over riding public interest justification in recording the material, which persistently intruded on Mrs Holland's private life around her home and on her land despite her protestations ... The Committee therefore found that Mrs Holland's privacy was unwarrantably infringed in the making of the programme.[8]

These cases illustrate what seems to be a distinct change in expectation of privacy from the public although whether this is driven by new expectations of privacy developed by the Human Rights Act or other effects, such as the ubiquity of media, it is not possible to say but another case suggests the former. A *Wales This Week* programme which looked at a planning application from a Ms Elwen Rowlands led Ofcom to find that:

> The programme had not unfairly represented the circumstances surrounding Ms Rowlands' planning application. Ms Rowlands did not have a legitimate expectation of privacy in relation to her surname, age, occupation and details about her property as this information was already in the public domain and therefore her privacy was not infringed.[9]

There are a number of other examples of complaints of intrusion from people going about their ordinary business being incidentally filmed or photographed, and then complaining after broadcast or publication. There seems to be a growing expectation that permission will be sought for even the most fleeting glimpse on television, in stark contrast to the excitement that would have greeted such an appearance 20 or 30 years ago, suggesting a change in the public perception of the media and or a greater understanding of or desire for privacy and therefore a right of privacy.

E-mails

E-mails are another difficult area for intrusion into the privacy of identity. The PCC upheld a complaint from a Mr Brian McNicholl that the *News of the World (Scotland)* had carried a story saying he had been caught by his long-term partner engaging in "secret internet sexychat with a string of Kazakhstani beauties". The information and photographs had come from private e-mails which were held on his company's secure server in Kazakhstan.

The newspaper said the complainant's partner had obtained the e-mails—which were not intrinsically private as they had been sent from a work address—from a shared family computer to which the couple both had access. This is an interesting interpretation of private and family life. It suggests that if you conduct any part of your private or family life on your work premises, then this is not private. However, the PCC went on to say:

> it was not in dispute that she had obtained his emails without consent and supplied them to the newspaper. The paper had, in turn, published extracts from them ... This sort of intrusion would normally require a very strong public interest justification, something that was not a feature in this case.[10]

The newspaper told the PCC that as the woman had discovered that the complainant had been leading a "secret life of internet pornography, chatrooms, and escort agencies", her right to freedom of speech in exposing her partner's activities—in addition to the public interest element—outweighed his right to privacy.

This was not a man in the public eye but a businessman operating in East Europe. He held no public office, he had not sought celebrity, nor was he particularly notorious (or at least not until the newspaper article). Upholding the complaint the PCC said:

> While the woman had a right to discuss their relationship, and clearly had strong views about the complainant and his behaviour, this was not sufficient to warrant publishing information taken from private e-mails to which the woman was not a party.[11]

In another case a woman complained about a *Daily Mirror* report of her suspension from an army college after explicit photographs were discovered by her employers. The newspaper published a headshot of the complainant taken from one of the photographs. The pictures had been sent from a work e-mail address by the woman but, she said, they had to be seen as part of a relationship and were therefore part of her home and family life. The picture had not previously been in the public domain.

The newspaper said it had restricted publication of the image to the complainant's face and that the article related to her suspension from a military college, which it claimed was a valid subject for a newspaper article. But the complainant said her suspension was a direct consequence of the publication of the article; her professional life and private life were separate and the publication of the photograph intruded into her privacy. The PCC decided that publication was legitimate but that the newspaper, by choosing to crop the photograph and publish only a headshot, had made the correct decision to avoid gratuitously humiliating the complainant. There was no breach of the Code.

Mobile Privacy

Even mobile phones with their ubiquity, ease of transport and technical facility can intrude where previously invasion would have been difficult. A recent complaint to the PCC concerned a young woman and revealing mobile phone pictures of her published in *FHM magazine*. The magazine said it received 1200 such pictures from or on behalf of young women every week. They apologised for publication and said they had put in place new measures to ensure such a situation did not recur. The PCC upheld the complaint saying it represented a serious intrusion into her private life.

Video

Video triggers particular problems as the PCC enforces different rules for video on newspaper websites to those applying on broadcast websites or terrestrial or satellite broadcasts.

In two recent separate cases, newspapers followed the police on raids to recover stolen goods or search for drugs. They then put video of the raids on their websites. A complaint against the *Barking and Dagenham Recorder* involved a 17-year-old who was shown in his room, was upheld even though the picture was pixellated to hide his identity, on the ground that no public interest defence for such a serious intrusion had been illustrated. In another case involving the *Scarborough Evening News*, a drugs raid was filmed which showed the complainant's son's bedroom. This complaint was also upheld, with the PCC saying: "Showing a video and publishing a picture of the interior of the complainant's house, without her consent, was clearly highly intrusive". There were two strands to the public interest defence. The first was that the footage showed an important part of local policing in operation. The second was that it allegedly exposed a specific criminal offence. "The Commission considered that, while it may have been in the public interest to illustrate the police campaign against drugs, insufficient regard had been paid to the complainant's right to privacy in this case".[12]

Health

Health is a clearly defined area of private life specifically mentioned in the Human Rights Act. However, the extension of privacy in this area brought about first by the Data

Protection Act and more latterly by the Human Rights Act extends a long way beyond doctor/patient confidentiality. Not only is the condition of a road accident victim likely to be seen as private, but even pictures taken at the scene of a major road accident need to be handled with considerable care in order to protect privacy as much as possible. A woman was filmed for the BBC1 programme *Front Line* at the scene of a major road accident in which one of her children died. It was filmed in a public place, but Ofcom found she had a reasonable expectation of privacy. As there was other footage available of other accidents or material that did not identify her Ofcom felt there was no public interest defence for the broadcast of the film, although there was no infringement of her privacy in the making of the programme. The PCC has also dealt with similar complaints, although their adjudication is less clear as the paper took sufficient remedial action and so the PCC did not come to a decision. This case also involved a road accident in which a picture was published in the *Wiltshire Gazette and Herald* of a woman receiving medical treatment from emergency services by the roadside. The PCC said: "The code requires newspapers to handle publication sensitively and to respect the privacy and health of those involved".[13] There is some evidence that the PCC has slowly evolved its position on privacy claims over health. Complaints in 2001 about a school pupil contracting tuberculosis being named were rejected. In 2004, a similar complaint, but this time from a teacher contracting tuberculosis was also rejected, but on this occasion the fact the teacher was an adult was seen as significant as was the extent to which the information was in the public domain. By 2008 the PCC seemed more determined to protect privacy about health issues when a complaint from a man about a story in the *Dorset Echo* concerning his cystic fibrosis was deemed to be an intrusion into his privacy. His mother had been questioned in a vox pop on current affairs and mentioned her son's condition. The paper built it into a story with a picture of the man (the complainant). The PCC said that failing to get permission from the complainant himself was intrusive and a clear breach of the code of practice.[14]

Pranks

It is impossible to talk about privacy cases over the past five years in the United Kingdom without mentioning the pranks that have brought the most condemnation for broadcasters. The two key examples are based in non-journalistic broadcasting when people are phoned up or otherwise contacted and some kind of prank is played. These can easily become intrusive, as was the case with *The Russell Brand Show* when he and Jonathan Ross broadcast crude and offensive messages left on actor Andrew Sach's answer-phone. The heavy fines levied by Ofcom combined with the public outrage and penalties faced by Brand and Ross mean that most broadcaster will think twice before including such material in their programmes. It is clear from Ofcom's decisions that these are not in the public interest and would in future require the consent of the subject of the prank to be broadcast, ruling out live broadcast of such material.

Conclusion

Although the court cases looking at intrusions of privacy into the lives of celebrities by the print media have been attacked as meaning the end of press freedom (mainly in attacks by the press media itself, such as that of PCC code chair Paul Dacre), hardly any of the landmark cases do anything more than firm up the law of confidence (Mosley, McKennett, Flitcroft). Although the PCC's and Ofcom's approaches are cautious (especially the PCC), there do seem to be significant moves on developing privacy rights around identity, health and children.

To say that the PCC's approach to identity is idiosyncratic would be an understatement as the two identity examples concerning e-mailed pictures illustrate, but Ofcom is much clearer about the concept of identity in all its forms: pictures, names and identifiers such as address, phone number or e-mail. These are much more significant guides than any of the court cases, all of which concern the clear breach of someone's privacy with the only defence not being public interest, but the right of someone else to freedom of expression—the right to kiss and tell.

These developments in privacy seem to be led by a clear expectation from the public of greater privacy rights and a freedom from media intrusion, paradoxical at a time when intrusion into privacy by the state has never been greater. People now seem to expect to be asked for their permission before any story or pictures identifying them are used, regardless of whether these were gathered in a public space or not. Journalists may now need to consider very seriously if their desire to get names and other identifiers into newspapers is now an outdated professional requirement.

NOTES

1. See www.pcc.org.uk.
2. See www.pressgazette.co.ukstory.asp?sectioncode=1&storycode=42394&c=1, accessed 18 May 2009.
3. See www.pcc.org.uk/code, accessed 8 June 2009.
4. See www.ofcom.org.uk/tv/ifi/codes/bcode/privacy/, accessed 18 May 2009.
5. See http://portal.nasstar.com/75/files/McKennit%20v%20Ash%20QBD%2021%20Dec%20 2005.pdf.
6. PCC Report 78 Adjudication, issued 2 January 2009 (PCC, 2009).
7. See www.ofcom.org.uk/tv/obb/prog_cb/obb103/bb103.pdf, accessed 14 May 2009.
8. See www.ofcom.org.uk/tv/obb/prog_cb/obb75/issue75.pdf, accessed 14 May 2009.
9. See http://www.ofcom.org.uk/tv/obb/prog_cb/obb125/issue125.pdf, accessed 18 May 2009.
10. See http://www.pcc.org.uk/cases/adjudicated.html?article=NDczMQ==, accessed 2 June 2009.
11. See http://www.pcc.org.uk/cases/adjudicated.html?article=NDczMQ==, accessed 2 June 2009.
12. See http://www.pcc.org.uk/cases/adjudicated.html?article=NTE0OQ==, accessed 1 June 2009.
13. See http://www.pcc.org.uk/cases/adjudicated.html?article=NTA4Nw==, accessed 18 May 2009.
14. See http://www.pcc.org.uk/cases/adjudicated.html?article=NTeyOA==, accessed 18 May 2009.

REFERENCES

FROST, CHRIS (2007) *Journalism Ethics and Regulation*, London: Pearson.

KIERAN, MATTHEW, MORRISON DAVID, E. and SVENNEVIG, MICHAEL (2000) "Privacy the Public and Journalism", *Journalism* 1(2), pp. 145–69.

OFCOM (2006/7) *Annual Report*, London: Ofcom.

OFCOM (2007/8) *Annual Report*, London: Ofcom.

PRESS COMPLAINTS COMMISSION (PCC) (2004) *Annual Report*, London: PCC.

PRESS COMPLAINTS COMMISSION (PCC) (2005) *Annual Report*, London: PCC.

PRESS COMPLAINTS COMMISSION (PCC) (2006) *Annual Report*, London: PCC.

PRESS COMPLAINTS COMMISSION (PCC) (2007) *Annual Report*, London: PCC.

PRESS COMPLAINTS COMMISSION (PCC) (2008) *Annual Report*, London: PCC.

PRESS COMPLAINTS COMMISSION (PCC) (2009) *Quarterly Reports Nos 65–78*, London: PCC.

LETTERS *FROM* THE EDITORS
American journalists, multimedia, and the future of journalism

Wendy Weinhold

Trade magazines devoted to coverage of the changes and challenges facing the American journalism industry and the practitioners of its craft are vital resources for understanding journalism's terrain. However, scholars tend to prefer institutionalized qualitative and quantitative methods for the study of journalism, so these magazines—as windows into the field—have been underutilized as scholarly resources. Letters to editors of American Journalism Review, Columbia Journalism Review, *and* Editor & Publisher *feature unique, monologic conversations involving a wide range of American journalism's laborers, profiteers, and consumers. The introduction of online publication and other forms of multimedia as valid journalism has afforded a cacophony of voices access to publication methods traditionally reserved for members of the commercial press. The implications of this change are reflected across a broad spectrum of the media landscape, including the letters pages used as data here. Deuze's (2005) model of professional journalism's occupational ideology is deployed here to provide a model for critical analysis of letters published in the magazines from 1998 to 2008. Ultimately, the letters suggest journalists' ideological constraints have withstood many of the cultural and economic pressures of the past decade despite ample opportunities for growth and progressive change.*

Introduction

The publisher creates a communication which is intended for an audience which not only reacts to the communication but which, in one form or another, itself initiates communications back to the original communicator. (Morris Janowitz, 1952, p. 9)

Whether prompted by news articles, retirement announcements, market fluctuations, or desires to contribute to the ongoing conversation about their industry, letters to editors of American journalism trade magazines offer insight into a debate where scholarship rarely ventures. These periodicals are neither peer reviewed nor the exclusive territory of intellectuals, and they are often overlooked as subjects of scholarly research. In order to gain an insider's perspective on media professionals' impressions about the future of journalism, I turned to a turf dominated by people dedicated to professional journalism— letters to the editor pages of three leading American journalism trade magazines: *American Journalism Review, Columbia Journalism Review,* and *Editor & Publisher.* While the magazines' websites are teeming with spaces where people contribute ideas and opinions, the letters selected for publication in the magazines' increasingly scant and expensive printed versions represent a select population of those viewpoints. However, letters to editors published in these journals' printed versions are neither uniformly nor consistently transferred into the digital research databases that often serve as resources for academic studies. Thus, my study highlights a unique kind of media production and hones in on a key topic of conversation in a contemporary Janowitzian community long overdue for study.

My analysis of the letters is inspired by the work of Deuze (2005, 2007a, 2007b, 2009), particularly his articulation of the occupational ideology of journalists as professionals. His research over the past decade has contributed to the growing field of applied and theoretical studies of multimedia and journalism. Deuze (2007a) emphasizes the need to probe whether and how journalism responds to "the fragile fences of modernity" staged in the contemporary media milieu. In order to gain perspective on the forces shaping contemporary American journalists' professional identities, I begin by considering Deuze's (2005, 2007b) model of journalists' occupational ideology. I then analyze the letters within the context of Deuze's ideological framework, and conclude by drawing implications about the future of professional journalism in an ever-unstable marketplace of ideas.

There is little agreement about the best pedagogic and research approaches to study journalism practice in a multimedia environment. Scholars identify the economic and cultural antagonists that could constrain the future of quality journalism future (e.g. Haas, 2005; Harrington, 2008; Mosco, 2009; O'Sullivan & Heinonen, 2008; Peters, 2009; Reese, 2001; Singer, 2004). Peters concludes that "new media need to be understood not as emerging digital communication technologies, so much as media with uncertain terms and uses" (2009, p. 13). Deuze (2007b) offers a slightly different articulation of multimedia's relationship to journalism practice. He explains, "journalism continuously reinvents itself— regularly revisiting similar debates (for example on commercialization, bureaucratization, 'new' media technologies, seeking audiences, concentration ownership) where ideological values can be deployed to sustain operational closure, keeping outside forces at bay" (2007b, p. 164). In other words, journalism is constantly reinventing the wheel in order to justify its social utility. Multimedia is just one spoke in the ever-evolving re-invention of journalism.

Journalism's Ideology Defined and Deployed

Regardless of the approach used to study journalists, Deuze (2005, 2007b) argues the five key concepts that form journalists' ideology remain unchanged. He explains:

> An occupational ideology develops over time, as it is part of a process through which the sum of ideas and views of a particular group about itself is shaped, but also as a process by which other ideas and views are excluded or marginalized. (2007b, p. 163)

Understood this way, journalists' ideology helps to reinforce the boundaries of who counts under the definition of the journalist. Deuze explains: "Conceptualizing journalism as an ideology . . . primarily means understanding journalism in terms of how journalists give meaning to their newswork" (2005, p. 444). Given the contemporary media climate of unlimited, unrestricted publication, a model that explains the ideological forces shaping how journalists decide "who's in" and "who's out" is a tremendous resource.

Deuze (2005, 2007b) draws his ideological model of journalism from studies that employ a wide range of quantitative, qualitative, and critical methods of analysis. Ultimately, Deuze contends that existing literature outlines five "ideal-typical traits or values that are generally shared among (or expected of) all journalists" (2007b, p. 163). The five concepts are: public service, objectivity, autonomy, immediacy, and ethics (Deuze, 2005, p. 447). In the following paragraphs, I examine each tenet to develop a full framework from which to conduct my analysis.

Public service is the first key concept in the ideological framework. Deuze (2005, 2007b) explains that journalists are tasked with the responsibility of being society's watchdogs and thus are responsible for tracking down and publicizing information of public import. As Gant (2007) explains, journalists reference the public service they perform while pursuing avenues generally closed to the public. Whether gaining access to the White House Press Room, press boxes in sports arenas, backstage interviews with performers at Madison Square Garden, or, as was the case during my professional career in print journalism, free admission to a county fair, journalists rely on the tremendous symbolic weight of their public service mandate to justify their labor and practices.

Objectivity is the second value that shapes journalists' occupational ideology. Deuze (2005, 2007b) explains that impartiality, distance, neutrality, and fairness guide journalists to be credible, objective arbiters of facts. Critiques of journalistic notions of objectivity abound in literature. Tuchman's (1972) study of objectivity as a "strategic ritual" suggests that journalists employ objectivity as a defense against accusations of bias. Reese identifies objectivity's connection to positivism and explains that the "ideal of objectivity" holds that facts can and should be separated from values (1997, p. 424). He contends that "journalists rely more heavily than scientists on routines as a basis and justification for descriptions of reality" (1997, p. 423). Ultimately, as Deuze makes clear, whether embracing, rejecting or re-evaluating objectivity, such efforts reinforce objectivity's foundational role in journalism ideology (2005, p. 448). Rename it, reframe it—objectivity retains its hold on journalists' professional identity.

Autonomy is the third component of Deuze's (2005, 2007b) ideological model. Editorial support, training and continuing education, and a supportive work environment play key roles in journalists' sense of autonomy. Furthermore, journalists' notions of autonomy reassure them that it is possible for them to work free of market influences and protected from censors. Deuze (2007b) explains that media employers have clear profit motives for keeping the line drawn between producers and consumers of news. Altschull furthers this observation and suggests that autonomy is used to reinforce a key part of journalism mythology: "Among the most remarkable aspects of the folklore of the press is the absence of references to money" (1997, p. 260). Faced with the pressures of their market-driven industry, journalists rely on the guise of autonomy to insulate themselves from the realities of the news business.

Immediacy is the fourth concept that is central to professional journalism's ideology (Deuze, 2005, 2007b). Given the contemporary climate of media saturation, it is not surprising that the ability to deliver information quickly and completely is key to defining journalism professionals. Bauman points to the influence of rapid information transfer in shaping journalism when he calls it "a profession running after itself, it is never as good as its last moment. It constantly reinvents and reproduces, as always exclusively focused on the new" (quoted in Deuze, 2007a, p. 677). Rapid delivery of news is not a new goal for journalists; in contrast, it is as enduring a concept as the other four.

Ethics are the final component that shapes the occupational ideology of journalists. Deuze (2005, 2007b) explains that this concept instructs journalists to have a sense of right and wrong, or ethical, practice. Journalists aspire to do socially valid, truthful, objective work. The watchdog role adds legitimacy to journalists' work, and its value to society reinforces the importance of journalists' ethical practice. For example, when its members gathered over a span of four years to evaluate the condition of the American press, the Commission on Freedom of the Press assigned ethics a paramount role in the professional ideology of journalists. The commission concluded that media have a responsibility to provide the public with "an accurate, truthful account of the day's events" (1947, p. 67). By adopting a code of ethics as part of its professional ideology, professional journalism avoids excessive external regulation while loosening the likelihood of restraints on its profit-oriented activities.

After he describes the key values of his framework, Deuze (2005) theorizes how multimedia and multiculturalism could serve as forces to reshape and expand journalism ideology. Harrington represents the lone scholar who has examined Deuze's (2005, 2007b) ideological model. However, she does so only cursorily and within the context of a brief review and critique of literature dedicated to contemporary journalism research. My analysis builds on and expands Deuze's theoretical efforts to understand multimedia's relationship to journalism ideology by testing the ideological model in the field of journalism. My analysis focuses on letters that discuss the real-world implications of multimedia on journalism practice.

Before I describe the magazines that are the subject of my study, it is important that I point out the interrelated nature of the five concepts. Deuze (2007b) emphasizes how the concepts sometimes blend and bleed. He explains, "these values can be attributed to other professions or social systems in society as well, and that these values are sometimes inevitably inconsistent or contradictory. To journalists this generally does not seem to be a problem" (2007b, p. 163). Although they are used as tactics to exclude some communities from consideration for membership in journalism's cadre, the key values' boundaries themselves are insecure. The definitions and characteristics of the model's five steps often overlap, and journalists alone claim the rights to indulge in such slippage. With this description in mind, I turn my attention to an explanation of the methods I use to analyze the letters.

Methods

1998–2008: A Monumental Decade for Media

I gathered and analyzed letters to editors published between the years 1998 and 2008 in three leading American journalism trade journals: *American Journalism Review*, *Columbia Journalism Review*, and *Editor & Publisher*. I chose to begin my study in 1998 because it is the year journalism, particularly work stemming from online publication, helped propel bloggers into the forefront of traditional, professional journalists' awareness. Two of 1998's major journalism events—blogger Matt Drudge's online revelation of former US President Bill Clinton's infidelity with White House intern Monica Lewinsky and *Forbes.com*'s breaking story of Stephen Glass's fraudulent reporting in *The New Republic*—were hailed as breakthroughs for online journalism in America. Internet publishers such as these demonstrated that quality journalism and this *new-ish* form of journalism were not mutually exclusive. The implications of this change are reflected across a broad spectrum of the media landscape, including the letters that serve as my data.

Cataloging Journalism's Contested Terrain

Whenever possible, I examined the letters in the context of the printed journals in which they appeared. I devoted eight weeks of summer 2009 to the examination of the journals in bound collections at Southern Illinois University Carbondale's Morris Library. The 10 years of data constitute a total of 2061 letters and 461 journal issues: 917 letters published in 313 issues of *Editor & Publisher*, 643 letters published in 88 issues of *American Journalism Review*, and 500 letters published in 60 issues of *Columbia Journalism Review*. By reviewing the letters in their printed versions (versus online publication on the journals' websites or via a searchable research database) whenever possible, I was able to consider the letters within the context of their historical specificity: the cover stories of the journals in which they were printed, the letters and articles to which they referred, and the monthly or weekly corpus of letters to which they belonged.

I began by establishing basic, descriptive categories. These categories helped me to analyze the letters within the context of their content, their writers' self-described profession, and the geographic location from which they hailed. Throughout the process I avoided attempts to quantify the letters in any way beyond compiling a basic count of the population; instead, I looked for letters related to issues of journalism practice and multimedia to assist in the emergence of themes. My aim was to assemble a catalog of information that would help me understand the letters within the individual ideological framework of the community of people who volunteer their opinions for publication in these journals.

After compiling the corpus, I conducted a critical analysis to understand how discourses in the letters reflect or reshape Deuze's (2005, 2007b) five criteria—public service, objectivity, autonomy, immediacy, and ethics—that form journalism's occupational ideology. As my analysis proceeded, I began to recognize layers of meaning within the letters. Ultimately, Deuze's model helped me to understand the ideological layers that tend to be obscured by complaints about the industry and forecasts about its future.

Trade Magazines as Cultural Texts

As trade periodicals, *American Journalism Review*, *Columbia Journalism Review*, and *Editor & Publisher* are designed to serve anyone with an interest in the journalism industry. The magazines' readers include journalism practitioners, consultants, business partners, scholars, fans, and enemies. Each hones in on a specific segment of the journalism industry; accordingly, their letters to editors' pages reflect distinct characteristics. I describe each publication in its specificity and then cast a wide net to describe the writers who contribute letters to the editors.

American Journalism Review is a national magazine dedicated to coverage of the media landscape—print, television, radio and multimedia publication. The magazine has published six issues a year since June 2003; prior to that, the magazine had published 10 times a year since its foundation in 1981. The magazine is housed and published by the Philip Merrill College of Journalism at the University of Maryland. *Columbia Journalism Review* covers the press in its many forms, including print, broadcast, cable and multimedia. The magazine has printed six issues annually since 1961. Columbia University Graduate School of Journalism publishes the magazine, and *American Journalism Review* is its main competitor. *Editor & Publisher* is the most industry-oriented magazine of the triad, and its focus is limited to the business of newspapering. Based in New York City, the magazine was

FIGURE 1

Bound copies of *Editor & Publisher* illustrate how the magazine shrank over the 10 years of publication studied here. The volumes at the bottom of the photograph are the oldest in my study; the ones toward the top of the pile are the most recent years. The magazine was founded in 1901 and published weekly until 2004 when it became a monthly. Photo by Edyta Blaszczyk

first *The Journalist*, a weekly publication that was founded in 1884 and then became *Editor & Publisher* in 1901. When it moved to monthly publication in 2004, the magazine cited financial problems and declining advertising revenues common to the industry it covers (Figure 1).

Analysis of Letters from the Editors

The letters to editors' pages in the magazines represent a wide community of people who voluntarily participate in the pages' conversations about journalism. Letters represent a broad spectrum of public and private interest in debates on journalism—press managers, reporters, editors, publishers, advertising executives, paper suppliers, software technicians, bloggers, media activists, and media consumers all contribute letters. As a result, the letters provide a window into the world of professional and amateur journalists' conversations with one another. In the following section, I analyze letters that discuss the issues of multimedia and journalism practice as they relate to the five key concepts—public service, objectivity, autonomy, immediacy, and ethics—of Deuze's (2005, 2007b) model.

Public Service

Letters that discuss the value of the first layer of journalism's ideology, public service, represent the bulk of my data. The earliest letters discuss the role of blogger Matt Drudge in shaping what counts as news. For example, Bendix writes to *Columbia Journalism Review*:

Can you picture a reporter saying to her editor, "I don't care what Matt Drudge is reporting! Marvin Kalb says we shouldn't run it until we have independent confirmation from two sources, so let's wait"? Neither can I . . . while the press will always indulge in half-truths, rumors, and misinformation, with enough competing voices, something approaching the truth will eventually emerge. (1998, p. 9)

Bendix employs multiple values to arrive at his argument that a diversity of opinions will triumph in a society enriched by multimedia and multicultural perspectives. As Deuze (2005) explains, the move from dishing the news out to engaging in a multi-level conversation has the potential to shift the balance of power and redefine the public service mandate to be more inclusive.

While letters previous to 2007 touch on all five of the ideological concepts, two issues—market forces and public service—are almost exclusively the focus of letters relating to multimedia and journalistic practice afterward. For example, Young et al. remark on the value of local media in their letter to *Editor & Publisher*: "articles written by real local reporters, compared to AP [Associated Press] articles, usually are more insightful and personal, not unlike a local family-owned restaurant is compared to McDonald's" (2007, p. 4). Additionally, Stevens writes about the enduring importance of journalism as a public record: "When people want to keep a record of history, young or old, they turn to newspapers" (2008, p. 4). In sum, longevity plays an important role in the letter writers' concept of public service in journalism.

A similar focus on the value of the community press as public service is reflected in multiple letters to *Columbia Journalism Review*. Effron writes that the discussion about the future of journalism needs to turn "toward a broader discussion about how, in the digital age when information 'wants to be free,' citizens don't merely end up getting exactly what they pay for" (2008, p. 5). Brigham chimes in to lament the changes in journalism that he fears "will lead to even more careless representations of our complex world" (2009, p. 7). The message seems clear: multimedia may come at little expense, but it can also mean low quality.

Objectivity

Writers of letters to the editors of the three magazines are generally concerned with objectivity, its changing shape, and the various terminology used to call it up across the 10-year period I analyze. For example, Smith points to bloggers leading the charge to investigate fraud in the 2000 US Presidential election. Smith vents to *Columbia Journalism Review* that "Too often now we are seeing citizen activists who are ahead of the pundits and the reporters, who simply burp up superficial stories provided by the spinners" (2001, pp. 4–5). In other words, citizens are doing real, objective reporting by looking for the truth and questioning the status quo.

However, it does not take long before multimedia is understood to be a threat to objectivity's hallowed ground. In his letter to *Editor & Publisher*, Kimmel voices his concern about multimedia:

> it is going a bit overboard in trying to integrate basically unfiltered content adjacent to a Web story in order to conjure up more community involvement. Perhaps my five decades of association with the news business has left me a trifle skeptical and resistant to change, but I believe a professional eye is necessary to determine what is fact and what is fiction. (2008, p. 5)

Such a preference for the "professional eye" reflects Deuze's (2005, 2007b) explanation that journalists close ranks when their ideological territory is threatened. Ultimately, whether calling for greater transparency or a return to journalism's unbiased, professional core, the writers are talking shop about objectivity.

Autonomy

Autonomy, the third value Deuze (2005, 2007b) identifies in the professional ideology of journalism, is referenced in letters that are published in the early years of my study. Unlike the other tenets that shape the ideological boundaries of professional journalism, autonomy gets a bad name that is never recovered. To illustrate, after an *American Journalism Review* article depicts bloggers as renegades, several people write to complain. Maizell offers a clear perspective in the first published letter that addresses the question of multimedia: "The concerns expressed regarding online 'pamphleteers' (Without a Rulebook, Jan/Feb) not having to undergo the checks of an editor seem as much a matter of jealousy as concern for accuracy. This country was, in large part, founded by pamphleteers" (1998, p. 5). A similar opinion is expressed in a letter published in *Editor & Publisher*. Hagan issues this warning to professional journalists: "The real reason that many of us have left the mainstream media is that we simply don't trust you anymore, and, in addition, we don't like you very much" (2000, p. 18). Ultimately, autonomy is the only value to go unchecked and released from the ideological fold within the context of the letters.

Public dissatisfaction dominates discussions of autonomy that are provided by the letters, and it is no wonder. Ideology guides many of journalism's routines, but there is no ideological principle to rescue the realities of journalism's inherent ties to the demands of the market. And when its publics become aware of journalism's ties to industry, journalists have nowhere to retreat. As in the case of this community of letter writers, they just fall silent.

Immediacy

Immediacy, the fourth concept Deuze (2005, 2007b) outlines in his model of the professional ideology of journalism, summons complex and conflicting responses in the magazines' letters to editors. Early in my study, the rush to publish news is targeted as a source of journalism's eroding quality. Take Jacobs' letter to *Editor & Publisher*, where he writes that "this 'damn the torpedoes, all speed ahead attitude' will cost newspapers their audiences' trust and attention in the long run" (1999, p. 33). Similarly, Tierney writes in to *Columbia Journalism Review* with a lament: "'Give me the news, but give it to me quickly,' the audience seems to be saying" (2001, p. 5). Media consumers' demand for immediate news leaves some journalism professionals questioning whether speed is good for their work and for their audiences.

But by the end of my period of study, the tune has changed in most of the letters. For example, Brown reports to *Editor & Publisher*, "The electronic media have the edge in immediacy. The print media ought to figure out why their readers are going for the immediacy first. Perhaps journalism courses need a rewrite" (2008, p. 4). This attitude is also expressed in the other magazines. Brody writes to *American Journalism Review* to explain what Brown leaves unanswered: "Give the information quick and dense. Leave Sunday for the long features when people spend an entire morning consuming the newspaper" (2006, p. 8). The value is restored because it is in journalism's best interest for the ideological principle to persist: the quicker the news is delivered, the more information journalists can add to the newsfeed, regardless of the quality. The overlapping quality of the key traits reassures journalists they will not only be able to do their job fast, but well.

Ethics

Ethics are the final concept that Deuze (2005, 2007b) contends defines journalism's occupational ideology. Deuze (2005) claims that ethics are the most researched of the concepts that form journalism's ideology, yet ethics are rarely the topic of letters to editors of the trade magazines studied here. One clear example of an articulation of journalistic ethics comes from Carpenter, who writes to *American Journalism Review*, "If anything will rebuild my faith in journalists, it is their willingness to accept being unpopular, unread and even uneulogized, but never untruthful" (2000, p. 4). By highlighting journalists' search for popularity in trade for legitimacy, the letter points to a thread that otherwise is not immediately obvious as an ethical issue.

Additionally, ethics surface as the subject of Wettenstein's letter to *Editor & Publisher*. She writes that her work as a journalist leaves her especially concerned: "Media outlets are competing to win ratings (read revenues) by seeing just how far they can lower the bar—without getting hurt—particularly when covering celebrities" (1999, p. 21). Wettenstein separates individual guardianship of journalism's ideology from the broader media system. Thus, her letter suggests how ethics can be summoned to defend against the profit imperative that is an inherent contradiction for the practice of ethical journalism.

Conclusion

With my analysis of the letters as they relate to Deuze's ideological framework (2005, 2007b) complete, I conclude with implications of an analysis focused on journalism's ideological framework. First, journalism's occupational ideology functions to limit cultural access to spaces that require participation in the market. A dominant strain of letters that my analysis has not yet noted is the need to calculate readers in order to set advertising rates. As Sturm, who was at the time of his writing the president and chief executive officer of the Newspaper Association of America, tells *Editor & Publisher*, "Competition for audiences in a time of massive attention deficit means that we have to get full credit for all the people we reach and how we reach them" (2006, p. 4). Professional journalism is not just about *serving* publics; it is about *selling* them.

Furthermore, just as multimedia is thought to be a potential source of liberation for some groups, it is important not to overlook the ways multimedia can be used to constrain them as well. Any view of technological development should be wary of assumptions that do not account for history. As Schiller warns, "This utopian vision—Internet as salvation—expresses ancient yearnings. Historical detoxification through scientific knowledge: the truth—information?—will make us free" (2000, p. xiii). As Deuze (2007a) suggests, journalism is a perfect fit for the contemporary lifestyle that values redefinition and improvisation while cruising the waves of permanent change. The letters uphold Deuze's view that the future of journalism will not be shaped by multimedia alone: "Ultimately, journalism is not going to end because of cultural or technological convergence" (2007b, p. 142). Nearly every letter celebrating multimedia's liberating potential was reigned back into the framework of established journalism practice and its guiding professional ideology. The letters offer a reminder—everything old can be new again.

Whether the potential for publication rests in the hands of few or many, it is worth arguing that the existence of journalists is key to the future not just of quality journalism, but of quality social life. As Deuze states: "for all its faults and problems, a profession of journalism without journalists cannot bode well for the necessary checks and balances on a future global capitalist democracy" (2009, p. 317). In other words, there is a lot at stake and a multitude of forces shaping journalism's future.

Finally, while it is important not to lean too heavily on perspectives that over-emphasize the potential of multimedia to reshape journalism's landscape, it is equally important to see journalists' ideology for what it is—a process of naturalization that becomes sedimented over a period of time. As Mattelart suggests, "nothing takes us farther from the future than history caught in the obsessions of the present" (1996 [1994], p. x).

Furthermore, drawing on Williams' study of television's deep historical roots, it must be remembered that "Technologies may constrain, but they do not determine" (2003 [1974], p. xi). If people can use media to reign in social and economic deviants, it is equally possible that we will be able to use media as a method to bring about productive social and economic rupture. Judging by the strength of ideology's hold on journalists' occupational mindsets, it is probably best not to put money on the professionals quite yet.

REFERENCES

ALTSCHULL, J. HERBERT (1997) "Boundaries of Journalistic Autonomy", in: D. Berkowitz (Ed.), *Social Meanings of News*, London: Sage, pp. 259–68.

BENDIX, JEFFREY (1998) "Letters", *Columbia Journalism Review*, May/June, p. 9.

BRIGHAM, WILLIAM (2009) "Letters", *Columbia Journalism Review*, 48(1), May/June, p. 7.

BRODY, MEGAN (2006) "Letters", *American Journalism Review*, August/September, p. 8.

BROWN, DAVID (2008) "Letters", *Editor & Publisher* 141(8), August, p. 4.

CARPENTER, RON (2000) "Letters", *American Journalism Review*, January/February, p. 4.

COMMISSION ON FREEDOM OF THE PRESS (1947) *A Free and Responsible Press*, Chicago: The University of Chicago Press.

DEUZE, MARK (2005) "What Is Journalism?", *Journalism* 6(4), pp. 442–64.

DEUZE, MARK (2007a) "Journalism in Liquid Modern Times", *Journalism Studies* 8(4), pp. 671–9.

DEUZE, MARK (2007b) *Media Work*, Cambridge: Polity Press.

DEUZE, MARK (2009) "The People Formerly Known as the Employers", *Journalism* 10(3), pp. 315–8.

EFFRON, ERIC (2008) "Letters", *Columbia Journalism Review*, 47(2), July/August, p. 5.

GANT, SCOTT (2007) *We're All Journalists Now: the transformation of the press and reshaping of the law in the Internet Age*, New York: Free Press.

HAAS, TANNI (2005) "From 'Public Journalism' to the 'Public's Journalism'? Rhetoric and reality in the discourse on weblogs", *Journalism Studies* 6(3), pp. 387–96.

HAGAN, P. JOHN (2000) "Letters", *Editor & Publisher*, 12 June, p. 18.

HARRINGTON, STEPHEN (2008) "Popular News in the 21st Century", *Journalism* 9(3), pp. 266–84.

JACOBS, WILLIAM (1999) "Letters", *Editor & Publisher*, 17 April, p. 33.

JANOWITZ, MORRIS (1952) *The Community Press in an Urban Setting*, Chicago: The University of Chicago Press.

KIMMEL, BOB (2008) "Letters", *Editor & Publisher*, 141(9), September, p. 5.

MAIZELL, JERRY (1998) "Letters", *American Journalism Review*, March, p. 5.

MATTELART, ARMAND (1996 [1994]) *The Invention of Communication*, S. Emanuel (Trans.), Minneapolis: University of Minnesota Press.

MOSCO, VINCENT (2009) "The Future of Journalism", *Journalism* 10(3), pp. 350–2.

O'SULLIVAN, JOHN and HEINONEN, ARI (2008) "Old Values, New Media", *Journalism Practice* 2(3), pp. 357–71.

PETERS, BENJAMIN (2009) "And Lead Us Not into Thinking the New Is New: a bibliographic case for new media history", *New Media & Society* 11(1), pp. 13–30.

REESE, STEPHEN (1997) "The News Paradigm and the Ideology of Objectivity", in: D. Berkowitz (Ed.), *Social Meanings of News*, London: Sage, pp. 420–40.

REESE, STEPHEN (2001) "Understanding the Global Journalist: a hierarchy-of-influences approach", *Journalism Studies* 2(2), pp. 173–87.

SCHILLER, DAN (2000) *Digital Capitalism: networking the global market system*, Cambridge, MA: The MIT Press.

SINGER, JANE B. (2004) "Strange Bedfellows? The diffusion of convergence in four news organizations", *Journalism Studies* 5(1), pp. 3–18.

SMITH, EILEEN (2001) "Letters", *Columbia Journalism Review*, March/April, pp. 4–5.

STEVENS, PAUL (2008) "Letters", *Editor & Publisher*, 141(12), December, p. 4.

STURM, JOHN (2006) "Letters", *Editor & Publisher*, 139(11), November, p. 4.

TIERNEY, ELAINE (2001) "Letters", *Columbia Journalism Review*, July/August, p. 5.

TUCHMAN, GAYE (1972) "Objectivity as Strategic Ritual: an examination of newsmen's notions of objectivity", *The American Journal of Sociology* 77(4), pp. 660–79.

WETTENSTEIN, BEVERLY (1999) "Letters", *Editor & Publisher*, 21 August, p. 21.

WILLIAMS, RAYMOND (2003 [1974]) *Television: technology and cultural form*, E. Williams (Ed.), London and New York: Routledge.

YOUNG, DAVE, LEWIS, JERRY and SHERWOOD, ANNE (2007) "Letters", *Editor & Publisher* 140(7), p. 4.

NOT REALLY ENOUGH
Foreign donors and journalism training in Ghana, Nigeria and Uganda

Anya Schiffrin

The media in much of sub-Saharan Africa is severely constrained by several factors: lack of resources, government pressure, the influence of media ownership and the declining quality of secondary education and professional journalism education. In many countries, newspapers are unable to perform the role of watchdog or effectively educate the public in part because of the difficulties faced by the journalists in their employ. Into the breach has stepped a plethora of foreign organizations which provide journalism training. Some of these are non-governmental organizations with a development agenda that seek to promote education about their causes. Others are the training arms of professional media groups (Thomson Reuters, BBC Trust) or are organizations that work on journalism education (the Berlin-based International Institute for Journalism and the International Center for Journalism in Washington, DC). This study—which includes content analysis and interviews with journalists who have received journalism training— considers these training efforts to see how effective they have been. The paper argues that given the challenges faced by the African media, donor-driven training programs will have only a limited effect on the larger media climate.

Introduction: The Scope of Journalism Training in Africa

Journalism training is a growing concern in the developing world. A part of public diplomacy since the Cold War, it has expanded as the media have grown, as organizations have sought to offer journalism training as part of their public relations and outreach efforts and in some cases in response to frustration with low quality journalism. Figures for total spending on journalism training are not available but an estimated $1 billion is spent on media assistance each year by non-US organizations (Becker and Tudor, 2005)

Today there are hundreds of organizations around the world that are involved in journalism training (Hume, 2004). These include well-respected trusts that are part of news organizations such as the BBC and Thomson Reuters, The International Center for Journalism in Washington, DC which receives funding from US AID and the Knight Foundation, and the International Institute for Journalism in Berlin which is part of the German government aid agency, InWent. These groups offer training in topics such as business reporting, environmental reporting, investigative reporting, covering elections as well as courses in digital media, community radio and even publishing and the business side of running a media company. The business/economic journalism training offered is usually not focused on advocacy or development but on topics that typify European and US agendas such as stock markets, covering company earnings and economic indicators. There is a long-standing debate about journalism education in Africa and whether it should be more informed by African values and traditions (Murphy and Scotton, 1987). More recent critiques have argued that the model of democratic governance underlying much of the current media assistance is based on establishing and maintaining a "political climate conducive to private economic enterprise" (Kareithi, 2005, p. 7).

Certainly the type of training offered by Thomson Reuters Foundation and International Institute for Journalism is based on US and European reporting traditions and standards (McCurdy and Power, 2007) although there are generally some topics added in to the curriculum that are relevant to the African context. These could include discussion of local topics such as covering corruption, poverty alleviation, the international financial institutions which lend to Africa (such as the World Bank) or a budget reporting course aimed at promoting transparency.

The World Bank Institute also runs journalism training programs and during the 1990s benefited from Tim Carrington, who in his eight years managing their business and economic journalism training program was instrumental in the foundation of press associations around Africa. As well, there are a numerous small groups founded by journalists (Independent Journalism Foundation, Indochina Media Memorial Fund, Institute of Financial and Economic Journalists) in Ghana, that may receive foundation funding or partner with universities or hire journalists who are no longer working in the profession. In general, media assistance and journalism training efforts are often uncoordinated (Center for Media Assistance, 2007). A 2007 report published by the African Media Development Initiative (AMDI) noted that much of the media assistance programmes in Africa are "ad hoc," and noted the existence of "non-sustainable and short-term approaches to projects; disconnected programmes; unnecessary competition amongst donors; and, consequent wasted investment of donor funds" (AMDI, 2006, p. 11).

Other organizations that offer journalism training are non-governmental organizations (NGOs) that hope to encourage journalists to write about the causes that interest them such as HIV AIDS, the trafficking of women, the environment, water, the need for transparency in the extractive sector, the importance of social entrepreneurship, and public health initiatives. They may run the training themselves or hire/fund an organization such as the Thomson Reuters Foundation to do it.

A number of government agencies (including the Central Banks of Barbados, Kenya, Nigeria, Turkey and Mexico) do their own training because they are frustrated with the modest level of economic coverage and want to make sure that journalists understand the economic topics they write about and to familiarize journalists with economic concepts and the workings of the central bank.[1]

Most of the training that is undertaken by these two groups (NGOs and central banks) is short term and does not include extensive, if any, follow up (Ogundimu et al., 2007). Typically they offer two- or three-day seminars which involve little writing. This is partly because these groups are not as much interested in media development as a whole as they are in promoting coverage of the subjects that their organizations are interested in. And even if they did want to expand their activities into media development, they usually lack the funding and knowledge to carry out long-term trainings.

A fourth category of groups that offer journalism training are newspapers and news outlets that hire and train their own reporters. This is common practice at the US news organization, Bloomberg, and at the *Times of India* and is starting to take place in Nigeria as well. The advantage for these organizations is that they can train their reporters to meet their needs (Berger and Matras, 2007). It is common for business editors to say that they want to hire good writers because they will learn about business and economics on the job. Typically editors describe hiring someone with a business or economics background and finding it impossible to teach them to write.

The first category of training organizations is the one that we studied this past year at Columbia University. A team of six students from Columbia University's School of International and Public Affairs traveled to Ghana, Nigeria and Uganda to research the effectiveness of journalism training programs in business and economic reporting. We surveyed reporters and editors who had training and spoke with a number of professors and others in the field. We employed standard qualitative research techniques using an online survey which we supplemented with interviews, research and a content analysis of coverage. Our study was commissioned by Revenue Watch Institute, an NGO based in New York which promotes good governance in resource-rich countries. Revenue Watch Institute is considering funding journalism training programs as part of their work-building capacity in civil society. Before embarking on such programs they wanted to get a sense of past journalism training efforts. Given the paucity of training on covering the extractive sector we surveyed business and economic journalism training to see what impact it has had. We looked at Ghana, Nigeria and Uganda because all have revenues from extractive industries (oil and mining). They also seemed like suitable choices for a comparative study as their points in common include the fact that they were all British colonies, have reputable journalism programs at local universities, are Anglophone and emerged from authoritarian regimes to become stable democracies with a relatively free press. Despite these factors, we found that the media faces a number of constraints and our (unsurprising) conclusion was that journalism training does help develop skills and knowledge but on its own will not solve the difficult problems faced by journalists in many of these countries.

The State of the Media in Africa Today

Space constraints prevent us from delving into the history of the African media in the twentieth century but it is worth noting that there were 179 newspapers in Africa in 1969 (Hachten, 1971, p. 24) with the media climate declining under the authoritarian regimes of the 1970s and 1980s (Bourgault, 2005, p. 34). Today there are thousands of outlets including radio stations (with very broad reach), private and public print and television outlets, and a burgeoning online community.[2] There are a growing number of journalism schools and departments throughout the continent (Diedong, 2008) including Ghana, Nigeria, South Africa and Uganda, a number of which were identified as potential centres of excellence in a 2007 UNESCO report (Berger and Matras, 2007).

In general, the media have become freer in much of Africa as many countries have transitioned to democracy and this is certainly true of Ghana, Nigeria and Uganda.

However, there is still a long way to go in much of Africa and even in Ghana, Uganda and Nigeria journalists still face pressure from government and suffer from a lack of resources (Adeyanju and Zakari, 2006; Kafewo, 2006; Wotsuna Khamalwa, 2006). The Freedom of Information bill has still not been passed in Nigeria despite a decade of attempts. The Freedom of Information Act bill in Ghana has been delayed in Parliament since 2003. The Ugandan constitution protects freedom of expression and freedom of the media but the government sometimes prosecutes journalists and is now considering a new bill which would further curtail freedom of expression.[3] Most dangerous of all is the oil-producing area of the Niger Delta where journalists often face harassment, arrest and the threat of violence.

Badly paid, poorly trained and working under both political and commercial pressures, many African journalists suffer from the devaluing of their profession which has left them vulnerable and isolated. Typifying these conditions, in countries such as Ghana and Nigeria, some journalists are not given a salary but simply left to rely on payments from sources.

The Need for Training and its Benefits

The need for training in African journalism has been discussed for decades (Ainslie, 1966, pp. 228–30; Hachten, 1971, pp. 138–40) and many of the problems mentioned in the 1960s are still noted today (Steyn and De Beer, 2004). Writing in 1966, Rosalynde Ainslie hoped that training would lessen the dependence of African media on imported "tape, film and features". Andrew Hachten, whose book was published in 1971, noted that a 1962 UNESCO meeting in Paris called for more training throughout the Third World. In Africa, editors hoped that training would prepare Africans to replace the Europeans who were running many of the local newspapers. Numerous foreign organizations—including some with Cold War-era public diplomacy agendas—supported training (Hachten, 1971, p. 133).

For many years it was hoped that training would help ameliorate the many problems that journalism faced. These problems have been characterized as everything from superficial coverage lacking in context or follow up (Ainslie) extreme partisanship, lack of professionalism (Diedong) and laziness on the part of reporters who print gossip and scandal (Nyamnjoh, 2005, p. 59) to low pay which breeds poor ethics and makes the profession unattractive. In the 1960s, Ainslie noted that the Nigerian press published personal attacks and scandal that would not have been found in the East African newspapers or in the British press. Even today, journalists have been accused of practicing vendetta journalism (Nyamanjoh, 2005, p. 60) and making personal attacks which "do not augur well for sustainable democratic tolerance" (Tettey, 2001, p. 22).

Even as journalism training was discussed decades ago, it was understood that training could not solve all the media's problems such as those related to the lack of resources or a viable business model for African newspapers. Clearly, journalism training could not prevent government pressure on journalists or threats to freedom of the press. Nor could training provide an in-depth education in writing or social science techniques, but it was hoped that even short courses would help develop basic skills (Hachten, 1971, p. 138).

Findings

We talked to almost 100 people for our research, including some 40 journalists who had received training in business reporting. The interviews were mostly conducted in person. Of the 100 interviews about 40 respondents had also completed a written survey. Some respondents completed the survey via email while others answered the survey questions with our researchers when they were on-site for interviews. In a few cases, we conducted interviews by email and over the phone. Most of these journalists worked for urban, daily newspapers although a few were employed in broadcast journalism. Sixty-five percent of respondents claimed their most recent employer was in the private sector and 15 percent said they worked for a government-owned outlet. On average, our respondents had 11 years of work experience in journalism. About one-third had been to multiple journalism trainings. Of those who had received training, 18 had attended International Institute for Journalism trainings, 11 had been trained by Thomson Reuters, nine by the World Bank Institute, two by the BBC, five had studied at overseas universities and three were in the "other" category.

The lack of training and lack of skills were obvious in the business and economic stories we read from Ghana, Nigeria and Uganda. Many of the journalists are not well educated and write extremely poorly. Nor do they have in-depth understanding of the topics they write about. The result is often confusing stories which skate over complex issues or which appear to be regurgitating press releases issued by companies and government. The journalists are themselves aware of the problem. In our survey asking journalists what they viewed as the challenges to reporting on economics and business 79.1 percent said that lack of knowledge and skills were "very important" while 18.6 percent said that lack of knowledge and skills was "important" (see Appendix A).

Overwhelmingly the journalists said that training helped them in a number of areas and many described the experience as transformational (Colmery et al., 2009). Courses such as those offered by Thomson Reuters Foundation, the World Bank Institute and the International Institute for Journalism helped in two areas: the first was promoting their overall understanding of government budgets, international trade, development and macro-economics, such as macroeconomic indicators and inflation. They also said training helped them to report companies and institutions such as the stock market, and international financial institutions like the World Bank and International Monetary Fund.

The training also helped the journalists surveyed to learn how to locate information and which sources to use, how to present information including how to keep a story focused and how to make their writing clear enough for a general audience, along with the importance of balance. Some of the journalists interviewed also said journalism training gave them the confidence to write on topics they would have previously been reluctant to cover.

Editors also told us that training has a beneficial effect and that they encourage their journalists to enroll in short courses. The business editor of a government-owned paper told us that he tries to send all of his reporters on training courses, especially those run by Thomson Reuters, because the effect is so noticeable. (A major limitation of our survey was that we were unable to see many examples of the work they had produced because in many cases newspaper libraries were non-existent or inadequate and much of the work was not available online.)

The brain drain seemed to be less of a problem than we expected. We had observed that journalists who enrolled in longer programs which give a certificate at the end, such as the Knight-Bagehot Fellowship which sends journalists to Columbia Business School for a year and the World Bank Institute program which provided more in-depth training in developmental economics, tended to leave journalism often to go into better-paid public relations jobs. But of the journalists we surveyed, only 22 percent left their employer and of these only 30 percent left journalism. However, it is likely that our sample was disposed towards people still working in journalism because they were easier to contact. Some Nigerian journalists told us that during the period of banking consolidation, around 2005, there was a need for public relations personnel and that a number of journalists left the profession at that time but that, in recent years, several have come back to journalism.

But although African reporters and their editors say that training has helped them a good deal, they note that they face other challenges which are not addressed by training.

Our study uncovered three other critical problems. (1) Lack of funding means that they are often unable to go on reporting trips and rely on corporate sponsorship to cover travel costs. They often feel compelled to accept payment from their sources, with the obvious risk of slanting of stories. (2) Lack of access to information hampers the work of journalists in Africa (and elsewhere). The lack of adequate access to what in advanced industrial countries is viewed as information that should be publicly available is not the only way that the legal environment affects coverage. (3) Libel laws and physical intimidation may discourage press coverage of key stories, such as those relating to corruption and environmental disasters. Our research suggests that unless these problems are addressed, the effects of journalism training will continue to be piecemeal.

Lack of Information

One of the problems facing journalists is lack of information. The absence of freedom of information laws means that all kinds of data are unavailable—including some of the most important sources for economic and business reporting. This includes oil contracts, data on government spending, bidding processes and details on infrastructure construction. In countries with mining and gas, activists and journalists say that it is very difficult to report on corruption because of the paucity of data. While such contracts between private parties are seldom available, for a country whose major source of revenue is oil, and where there is suspicion of corruption in the leasing of oil lands, access to the contracts and bidding process is obviously essential for adequate coverage.

In our survey, 71.4 percent said that "lack of a Freedom of Information Act and/or poor information" was a "very important" challenge to reporting on business/economics and 19.0 percent called it "important" (see Appendix A). Many reporters blamed the government for making it impossible to get hold of information and cited the fact that Ghana and Nigeria have still not passed a Freedom of Information Act.

Other observers, however, said that journalists are wrong to blame the government because it is often the journalists themselves who are simply unaware of how to find information and/or unwilling to spend the time looking. Indeed, a reading of the print media in many African countries reveals the preponderance of stories with three or fewer cited sources. One of the important functions of journalism training is to make journalists aware of the sources available, and to make them aware of the biases that may be latent in the sources to which they have to turn in the absence of publicly available information (e.g. the corporations themselves or the international economic institutions).

Political Constraints

As in many African countries, Nigeria and Uganda still have a number of laws including those relating to libel and sedition as well as licensing requirements. These contribute to a climate in which the fear of prosecution (or even) violence is always lurking in the background. One reporter apologized for his late reply to our email query: he explained he had been in hospital after a beating by local police!

Threats to safety and government pressure are also a problem in some countries. The Niger Delta is notoriously dangerous with local security forces frequently arresting and harassing journalists. The journalists we spoke to in Uganda also faced attacks (Colmery et al., 2009). In listing the challenges to business and economic reporting, the threat of violence against journalists was considered by 41.5 percent of journalists as "very important" and by 39.0 percent as "important" (see Appendix A).

Lack of Resources

But lack of funding is probably the single most significant impediment to improvements in journalism. One Ghanaian editor put it simply: "our main problem is lack of resources". We should note here that there is a vast range of outlets, with different economic circumstances and business models. While the diversity is part of the strength of African journalism, it is also part of the problem. A small market is splintered, non-economic motives drive many of the publications, and there is often "unfair" competition between government and non-governmental publications—with government publications having an advantage both economically and in terms of access to sources.

Government-run publications and broadcast channels tend to be well financed, have the best equipment and pay competitive salaries. They also receive preferential access to government sources, press conferences and information given by the government (Hasty, 2005, pp. 35, 84). They may also receive most of the government advertising.

At the other end of the spectrum are tiny vanity newspapers which are run by one person with a political or personal agenda; they have a tiny circulation and pay little or no salary to reporters. These sorts of papers are quite common in Ghana, which is estimated to have 100 print publications, appearing during and after Ghana's transition to democracy (Gadzekpo, 1997). They have no sustainable business model and are not profitable but do not want to merge or consolidate.[4]

Circulation, subscription and advertising figures are generally not released by media houses in Ghana, Nigeria[5] and Uganda,[6] but it is clear that the lack of a sustainable business model is a serious obstacle in several ways. First, it makes the job of journalism less attractive for older, experienced journalists who need to earn substantial salaries. Second, there is a lack of equipment—it was common to visit newsrooms and find there were not enough computers to go around. Journalists lack laptops, digital tape recorders and are unable to make long-distance phone calls. Third, journalists often rely on sponsorship in order to make reporting trips with the concomitant problem that their coverage may be influenced/limited. Fourth, newspapers are very vulnerable to pressure from advertisers. In a market where there are only a couple of major advertisers or where government advertisements (for tenders and the like) make up the bulk of advertising, newspapers are afraid of losing advertising. If one advertiser pulls out, then losing a second advertiser is disastrous. In our interviews with journalists, we heard numerous accounts of advertisers who suspended advertising because they were displeased with a story that appeared. Fifth, salaries are low and journalists resort to taking payments from the people they report. Some journalists even extort money from government officials/businessmen by inventing stories and threatening to publish them if they are not paid off. According to our research, journalists at the smaller publications are paid as little as zero or $100 a month and more or less left to fend for themselves. This often means taking money from individual sources or companies/government bodies. Better-paid journalists working for official media or in television may be paid several hundred dollars a month. Staffers at New Vision newspaper in Uganda are paid between $500 and $1000 a month. A job in public relations in these same countries pays several times this sum.[7] Finally, government officials may contribute to this sort of behavior by paying journalists to write about them or place their stories in prominent positions in the newspaper. A senior Nigerian official told us that his office routinely pays journalists so as to make sure that stories emanating from his government agency are placed prominently on the front page of the paper "otherwise they pop it in a little corner somewhere" (Schiffrin, 2009)

Conclusion

Journalism training can make an important contribution to the quality of professional day-to-day journalism and the ability of journalism to fulfill its basic missions. This study focused on the impact of training on business and economics reporting, an area where few journalists have adequate training, and where on-the-job training is unlikely to suffice. But even in this technical area, journalism training can have general benefits. It can enhance a sense of professionalism, and at least an awareness of professional ethics. It can expose reporters to ideas, concepts and people that they otherwise would not have access too. Such contacts can be particularly important in ensuring adequate coverage of complex topics. It can help them build contacts more broadly in the journalism community and promote networking which could lead to working jointly on stories. If properly reinforced by editors and colleagues upon returning to their publication/media outlet, training can lead to more sophisticated coverage which touches on subjects they might not have felt competent to write about previously.

But such training will have only a piecemeal effect. Most of the problems facing African journalism cannot be addressed by journalism training alone. Journalists may know that they should not receive money from sources, but with limited pay, they may see no alternative. The quality of journalism rests, of course, on the quality of the labor force and that means there needs to be more investment in secondary education. But more than an educated and trained labor force is required: for African media to improve rapidly, more funding—entailing new business models—and a better legal climate are necessary.

ACKNOWLEDGEMENTS

This paper is based on research funded by Revenue Watch Institute in New York City (www.revenuewatch.org). Thanks to the students of Columbia University's School of International and Public Affairs who carried out the survey in spring 2009: Ben Colmery, Adriana Diaz, Emily Gann, Rebekah Heacock, Jonathan Hulland and Eamon Kircher-Allen. We are very grateful for the assistance of Kendra Bischoff, Paul Busharizi, Tim Carrington, Manoah Espisu, Lloyd Evans, Dr. Audrey Gazdzekpo, Vanessa Herringshaw, Astrid Kohl, Karen Lissakers, Jed Miller, Peter Prufert, Eugenia McGill, Ndidi O. Nwuneli, Professor Onuora Nwuneli, Jose Antonio Ocampo, Rosie Parkyn, Joseph E. Stiglitz and Jo Weir.

NOTES

1. See http://mail.google.com/mail/?ui=2&view=js&name=js&ver=rUPyrM6 PosQ.en.&am=f3EopdTXcGGZBf_s0fQ2RjalhXafHw#_edn1.
2. Internet penetration in Africa is 5.3 percent and Nigeria is the biggest user (http://www.internetworldstats.com/stats1.htm).

3. Section on freedom of expression in the Uganda section of the *Amnesty International Report 2009* (Amnesty International, 2009).
4. Author interview with Dr. Audrey Gadzekpo, April 2009.
5. Data on circulation is hard to come by and Punch declines to release the numbers. For more information, see http://www.rap21.org/article18257.html which says that in 2004, circulation was 80,000—larger than any other newspaper in Nigeria (accessed 2009).
6. The *New Vision* newspaper in Uganda told me that their circulation is 35,000.
7. Author correspondence, June 2009.

REFERENCES

ADEYANJU, AKEEM M. and ZAKARI, OKWORI (2006) "Nigeria AMDI Research Report", http://www.bbc.co.uk/worldservice/trust/researchlearning/story/2006/12/061206_amdi_nigeria.shtml.

AINSLIE, ROSALYNDE (1966) *The Press in Africa: communications, past and present*, New York: Walker and Company.

AFRICAN MEDIA DEVELOPMENT INITIATIVE (AMDI) (2006) London: BBC World Service Trust, http://downloads.bbc.co.uk/worldservice/trust/pdf/AMDI/AMDI_summary_Report.pdf, accessed 11 March 2009.

AMNESTY INTERNATIONAL (2009) *Amnesty International Report 2009*, http://thereport.amnesty.org/en/regions/africa/uganda#freedom-of-expression.

BECKER, LEE B. and TUDOR, VLAD (2005) *Non-U.S. Funders of Media Assistance Projects*, Athens, GA: James M. Cox Center for International Mass Communication Training and Research, University of Georgia, http://www.grady.uga.edu/coxcenter/knight.htm, accessed 15 May 2009.

BERGER, GUY and MATRAS, CORINNE (2007) *Criteria and Indicators for Quality Journalism Training Institutions & Identifying Potential Centres of Excellence in Journalism Training in Africa*, Paris: UNESCO.

BOURGAULT, LOUISE (2005) *Mass Media in Sub-Saharan Africa*, Bloomington and Indianapolis: Indiana University Press.

CENTER FOR MEDIA ASSISTANCE (2007) *Media Assistance: challenges and opportunities for the professional development of journalists*, Working Group Report, Washington, DC: National Endowment for Democracy

COLMERY, BEN, DIAZ, ADRIANA, GANN, EMILY, HEACOCK, REBEKAH, HULLAND, JONATHAN and KIRCHER-ALLEN, EAMONN (2009) *There Will be Ink: a study of journalism training and the extractive industries in Ghana, Nigeria and Uganda*, New York: Revenue Watch Institute and Columbia University's School of International and Public Affairs, www.journalismtraining.net.

DIEDONG, AFRICANUS LEWIL (2008) "Informing the Public: how Ghana's newsrooms are learning to change", paper presented to the International Association for Media and Communication Research conference, Stockholm, http://www.iamcr.org/content/blogcategory/0/308/, accessed 1 June 2009.

GADZEKPO, AUDREY (1997) "Communication Policies in Civilian and Military Regimes: the case of Ghana", *Africa Media Review* 11(2), pp. 31–50, http://digital.lib.msu.edu/projects/african-journals/html/itemdetail.cfm?recordID=1120, accessed 15 June 2009.

HACHTEN, WILLIAM (1971) *Muffled Drums: the news media in Africa*, Ames: The Iowa State University Press, pp. 24, 133, 138–40.

HASTY, JENNIFER (2005) *The Press and Political Culture in Ghana*, Bloomington and Indianapolis: Indiana University Press.

HUME, ELLEN (2004) *The Media Missionaries: American support of journalism excellence and press freedom around the globe*, Miami: The John S. and James L. Knight Foundation.

KAFEWO, SAMUEL (2006) "Ghana AMDI Research Report", http://www.bbc.co.uk/worldservice/trust/researchlearning/story/2006/12/061206_amdi_ghana.shtml.

KAREITHI, PETER (2005) "Rethinking the African Press: journalism and the democratic process", in: Peter Kareithi and Nixon Kariithi (Eds), *Untold Stories: economics and business journalism in African media*, Johannesburg: Wits University Press, pp. 2–16.

MCCURDY, PATRICK and POWER, GERRY (2007) "Journalism Education as a Vehicle for Media Development in Africa: the AMDI Project", *Ecquid Novi: African Journalism Studies* 28(1/2), pp. 127–46.

MURPHY, SHARON M. and SCOTTON, JAMES F. (1987) "Dependency and Journalism Education in Africa. Are there Alternative Models?", *Africa Media Review* 1(3), pp. 11–35.

NYAMNJOH, FRANCIS B. (2005) *Africa's Media, Democracy and the Politics of Belonging*, London: Zed Books, pp. 59–60.

OGUNDIMU, FOLU F. OYEWO, YINKA, OLUSOLA and ADEGOKE, LAWRENCE (2007) "West African Journalism Education and the Quest for Professional Standards", *Ecquid Novi: African Journalism Studies* 28(1/2), pp. 191–7.

SCHIFFRIN, ANYA (2009) "Power and Pressure: African media and the extractive sector", *Journal of International Affairs* 62(2), pp. 127–41.

STEYN, ELAINE and DE BEER, ARNOLD (2004) "The Level of Journalism Skills in South African Media: a reason for concern within a developing democracy?", *Journalism Studies* 5(3), pp. 387–97.

TETTEY, WISDOM (2001) "The Media and Democratization in Africa: contributions, constraints and concerns of the private press", *Media, Culture & Society* 23, pp. 5–31.

WOTSUNA KHAMALWA, JOHN (2006) "Uganda AMDI Research Report", http://www.bbc.co.uk/worldservice/trust/researchlearning/story/2006/12/061204_amdi_uganda.shtml.

Appendix A: Responses to 2009 Survey

TABLE A1
How important are each of the following challenges journalists face when reporting on economic and business issues?

	Very important	Important	Not important	Response count
Lack of Freedom of Information Act and/or poor freedom of information	71.4% (30)	19.0% (8)	9.5% (4)	42
Libel laws	29.3% (12)	51.2% (21)	19.5% (8)	41
Political and business pressure not to publish	67.4% (29)	23.3% (10)	9.3% (4)	43
Threat of violence against journalists	41.5% (17)	39.0% (16)	19.5% (8)	41
Lack of adequate knowledge and skills	79.1% (34)	18.6% (8)	2.3% (1)	43
Pay for journalists	84.1% (37)	13.6% (6)	2.3% (1)	44
Inadequate Internet access	44.2% (19)	34.9% (15)	20.9% (9)	43
Lack of new media and Internet skills	58.1% (25)	27.9% (12)	14.0% (6)	43
Answered question				45
Skipped question				1

TABLE A2

What topics were covered in the economic journalism trainings you had? Please rate them in terms of their impact on your ability to report on economic issues. If a topic was not covered, please mark the "Not covered" box and rate it according to how helpful you believe it would be

	Very helpful	Somewhat helpful	Neutral	Somewhat unhelpful	Very unhelpful	Not covered	Response count
Government budgets and fiscal spending	70.0% (28)	15.0% (6)	10.0% (4)	0.0% (0)	0.0% (0)	7.5% (3)	40
International trade	66.7% (28)	14.3% (6)	11.9% (5)	0.0% (0)	0.0% (0)	23.8% (10)	42
Accounting	41.0% (16)	28.2% (11)	12.8% (5)	2.6% (1)	0.0% (0)	43.6% (17)	39
Economics of extractive industries (oil, mining, gas, etc.)	50.0% (20)	20.0% (8)	7.5% (3)	2.5% (1)	2.5% (1)	37.5% (15)	40
Investigative reporting	61.9% (26)	19.0% (8)	7.1% (3)	4.8% (2)	0.0% (0)	23.8% (10)	42
Corporate finance	42.5% (17)	25.0% (10)	7.5% (3)	2.5% (1)	0.0% (0)	35.0% (14)	40
Economic development	70.7% (29)	14.6% (6)	4.9% (2)	0.0% (0)	0.0% (0)	19.5% (8)	41
Business reporting	90.2% (37)	7.3% (3)	0.0% (0)	0.0% (0)	0.0% (0)	12.2% (5)	41
Stock markets	67.5% (27)	7.5% (3)	5.0% (2)	2.5% (1)	0.0% (0)	25.0% (10)	40
Corporate reporting/financial results	68.4% (26)	13.2% (5)	0.0% (0)	0.0% (0)	0.0% (0)	28.9% (11)	38
Retail companies	46.2% (18)	12.8% (5)	7.7% (3)	2.6% (1)	0.0% (0)	51.3% (20)	39
Macroeconomic indicators	68.3% (28)	19.5% (8)	0.0% (0)	0.0% (0)	0.0% (0)	26.8% (11)	41
New media/new technology	45.9% (17)	18.9% (7)	5.4% (2)	0.0% (0)	0.0% (0)	51.4% (19)	37
Online resources of economic information	75.0% (30)	17.5% (7)	0.0% (0)	0.0% (0)	0.0% (0)	22.5% (9)	40
Answered question							43
Skipped question							3

Index

Page numbers in *Italics* represent tables.
Page numbers in **Bold** represent figures.

INDEX

INDEX